An Introduction
To Exercise and Sport for
People Who Have Autism

Amanda Durrant

An Introduction To Exercise and Sport for People Who Have Autism

Copyright © Amanda Durrant 2009

Published in 2009 by Amanda Durrant
Unit 9, Mimosa Close, Chelmsford, Essex, CM1 6NW

Amanda Durrant has asserted her right under the copyright, Designs and Patents Act, 1988, to be identified as the author of this work.

Amandadurrant2004@blueyonder.co.uk

ISBN 978-0-9562729-0-4

A CIP record for this book is available from the British Library.

The author would like to thank all teachers, coaches, parents and children involved with this book, especially those from 'Springfield Gym Club' Chelmsford, 'Colchester School of Gymnastics' and 'Parc' Braintree.

CONTENTS

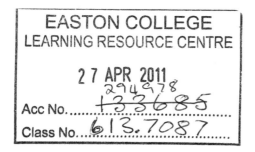

Disability friendly Agility Sports Award Scheme
Available for Schools
Please enquire
amandadurrant2004@blueyonder.co.uk

Introduction

Individuals with autism, (wherever on the spectrum) and sports games, sometimes share a difficult partnership, if one at all. Some adults have expressed that as children, the very concept of rules and team play seemed ridiculous and pointless. We know sport is good for our health; it strengthens our heart, muscles and bones, it can give us flexibility, speed and stamina, and improve our agility too. Sport can also induce feel- good hormones, aid relaxation and reduce anxiety. Importantly, participation in sport can give people access to community resources that might be of individual interest. All of these benefits are too good to be ignored.

'**An Introduction To Exercise and Sport for People Who Have Autism**' came about to support sports and recreation providers with the means of offering a method of exercise to individuals who found it extremely difficult to interact in an organised sport setting. Ribbon Time, Jog and Stop, Roll Ball, and Kick Football give the benefits of sport but within an environment that has been adapted to suit the player.

It is helpful to be aware of how we might change the environment further, where possible, to accommodate the needs of an individual who has autism. Try to find out what the individual's main stressors are and where possible reduce them. Look at the room you are using, does the light stream in? Are there fluorescent lights? Is it noisy? Is the room the right size for your needs? Could some distractions be put away out of sight? The equipment you use and the very nature of the game or sport is also of great importance- is it accessible? Is the equipment relatively easy to control?

What you do personally can also make a difference. Are your expectations too low or high or just right? Do you explore different methods of communication?

Do you praise your participants enough? Are your instructions concise and unambiguous? Does where you stand and how you move complement the activity? Are you wearing calm neutral colours rather than bright colours and logos?

Most of us have a calming inner voice, one that reassures us and helps us to self regulate even when times are very difficult. It can spur us on and motivate the expectations of our very self, and give us a sense of understanding and order of our past, present and future. An individual with autism might find it difficult at times to self regulate their emotional state, so you may need to reassure and be a calm external influence in times of stress or apprehension.

Always look for an individual's strengths, but also be aware of any unevenness in ability which could be a barrier to enjoying sport; an individual might have lots of information internally but not always be able to express it verbally or be able to motor plan their physical actions in a proficient way. Look out for an individual's likes and dislikes and what motivates them as a player. Be aware of an individual's path of learning; for some it might be made up of small increments built up day by day, week by week or yearly; for others they may copy or learn part or the whole move straight away. Some individuals also have great difficulty with understanding cultural rules and a limited sense of real time. It is not surprising that at times, individuals can be highly stressed, inflexible and easily fragmented.

So what advantages can Ribbon Time, Jog and Stop, Roll Ball, and Kick Football bring to an individual? With practice, some benefits could be improved shoulder control, pelvic control, visual skills, hand to eye co-ordination, the ability to cross the midline, directional awareness, spatial awareness, symmetrical awareness, bilateral integration, memory, motor planning, fine and gross motor skills. Skills can take many repetitions to master, and do remember that small milestones, in reality, can be huge! Good luck... and don't forget to have fun!

Individual potential

Each individual is unique. The following case study is factual and demonstrates how important it is to see potential at all times.

Case Study – Angela aged six years

Angela enters the village hall for the first time. She runs in all directions, she is highly excitable but not distressed. She seeks the highest point in the room, climbs it and perches looking down until coaxed back down. Mum asks the coach if it is likely her daughter will learn any childhood agility skills.

Each week the gymnastics class would start with the register, followed by 'Jog and Stop', and followed on by a body stretch, then a stage of a physical skill, and finally a cool down.

Angela is now eight years old, and participates for the duration of the gymnastics class. She has learned many physical skills such as hopping, jumping, throwing, catching, and has taken her first gymnastics award. Angela enjoys riding her bike in an open space with her family; she enjoys trampolining and now attends school. At times Angela has great difficulty organising her body to do what she would like it to do, and at other times shows great agility. Angela responds best to the coach using concise language and demonstration.

General preparation

Try to find something out about the individuals that are going to play. You could ask a parent or carer about the sort of interests and the type of personality they have. Are there any communication difficulties? And if so what is the best way to interact?

Always make a risk assessment and prepare all that you can before players arrive. Let staff know your intentions. Each person should be appropriately dressed for playing sport.

Warming up

Warming up before each activity is very important. We should aim to prepare not only our physical body for exercise but mentally too.

Start with walking around the room. You may need to encourage participants to follow a buddy to encourage movement in the same direction. Next, try some stretching exercises such as:

- Move the head from side to side
- Make slow arm circles
- Rotate the hips
- Sit and stretch with legs apart

If an individual finds these difficult, you might like to try the following specific actions instead:

- Hands up high
- Place hands on the floor
- Hands out wide
- Hands to your sides
- Wave your hands
- Hands on your head
- Hands on shoulders
- Hands on knees
- Hands on toes
- Hands on your stomach
- Hands behind your back
- Stand up and sit down

Cooling down

After exercising, it is advisable to calm everyone down to a more restful state both mentally and physically.

When you have finished your main activity, walk slowly around the room then come to rest by standing still.

Either repeat the warm up stretch exercises or use the alternative specific actions, but this time, do so more slowly. Each person could then rub their own arms, legs, face, feet and stomach.

Give praise to your players during and at the end of the game. Discuss with staff how you can improve the game next time to meet the needs of the players.

Ribbon Time

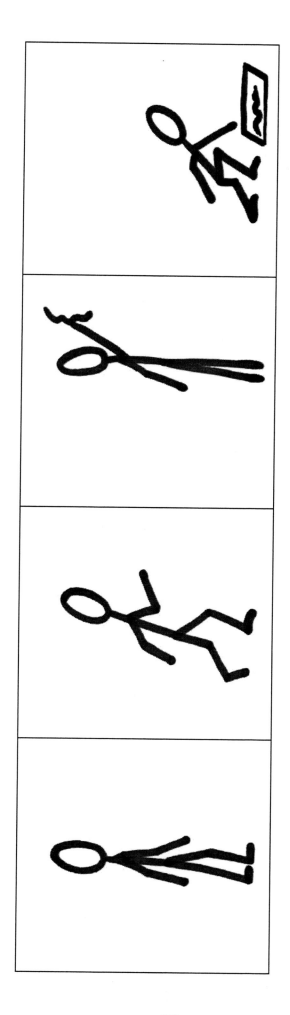

Ribbon Time (*Visual Aid*)

Ribbon Time Introduction

For Ribbon Time you will need a space with a boundary, some ribbons and a mat. An ideal playing space could be a room, or an outdoor play area which is fenced in.

The game consists of one or more players, there are no teams or ends.

There are no set game rules, only safety guidelines, which the organiser gives to the players and helpers depending on the variation of Ribbon Time played.

Initially, the ribbons could be placed around the room prior to the game starting. When the game starts, the players collect the ribbons. When all the ribbons have been collected and placed at the collection point the game has finished.

To ensure you have a good supply of ribbon you could use a roll that is 1cm wide, and cut it into 45 cm lengths.

Points to consider

- A risk assessment should be made before starting, and safety should be ensured at all times
- It might be beneficial to include siblings
- How many children that can play at any one time will depend on their size, and the size of your play area

- Not all children are comfortable with strong or bright colours
- Some children might find it beneficial to see a picture sequence of the game first
- If some children prefer visual cues, use red, orange and green cards which can be shown alongside the words, 'stop', 'ready' and 'go'. You could also show a picture of what is to be collected
- The ribbons should come away easily from where they are located
- If some children are very quick at collecting the ribbons, you may need to put plenty out to keep the game going, or more of a different colour
- Place ribbons at all levels to encourage bending, stretching and jumping
- Keep the collection point clear of all obstructions

Game One- Stages

Ribbon Time can be introduced in stages as follows:

Stage one - Show by demonstration

Begin the game with an individual player, or small group of players. Reduce as many distractions in the play area as possible (such as electrical equipment unplugged and play items out of sight). Place a single yellow ribbon approx 45cm in length in full view on a wall somewhere in a room, or on the inside of the metal fencing of an outside play area.

Say your own name then call out, "Ready, steady, go!" Go and get the ribbon yourself, and place it on a mat approximately 1m x 1m which is placed on the floor. To finish, sit in a designated area such as on a bench.

Stage two – Playing the game

Now place three ribbons around the room. Choose a player, say their name and then call out "Ready, steady, go!" Encourage the player to retrieve the ribbons (you might need to buddy the player). When all of the ribbons have been collected, encourage the player to put them on the mat and then sit on the bench. When giving praise, say the player's name first. Give praise freely throughout the game for finding the ribbons, for the quantity collected, when the ribbons have been placed on the mat and when seated on the bench.

Stage three – Introduce more players

Next, place six ribbons around the room. Pick two players to retrieve the ribbons. Say their names and then call out "Ready, steady, go"! When all ribbons have been collected, call for the ribbons to be put onto the mat and the players to sit on the bench. Gradually introduce more players and more ribbons to the game. For players who have difficulty focusing, raise your emotional state when speaking, such as, "Look up there Tommy! There is a ribbon! Pull the ribbon down Tommy!"

Game Two – Sets of items

Place a set of items (which could be similar items but of a different colour such as bean bags) or a set of items that go together such as paper plates and paper cups around the room. Other objects you could use are:

- Small items of clothing such as socks
- Textured strips
- Pictures of children in the class
- Small model cars
- TV characters
- Signs around the school
- Wiggly snakes
- Topic work items
- Gloves
- Cut outs of hand or footprints
- Flowers

The collection point could be in the same theme as the sets of items. Clothing items could be placed on dolls, flowers placed in an unbreakable vase and plastic bugs on a piece of wood.

Or, when all items have been placed on the collection point, try matching up a pair of items (such as two blue coloured cars) that have been found in the set.

Game Three - Pictures

Pick different pictures from a general theme to place around the room. Hold the pictures in your hand and call out what they are as you show them to the class. If the class are not focused on you and what you are saying and doing, call out where you are putting the pictures as well. Different themes could be:

- The seaside
- Food
- Travel
- Personal hygiene
- People
- Sport
- Animals
- Temperature or weather
- Geography
- Clothing

Game Four - The discrimination of similar objects

Place ribbons in or on similar objects in a room such as different types of seat. Explain to the class that the ribbons are placed on items which you can sit on, such as chairs, benches, stools, and a bean bag chair. You can also choose a selection of items that have the same use but look different, such as:

- Different types of mat
- Musical instruments
- In various open containers

You might also like to try reversing the game, and ask the players to place the ribbons on selected items.

Game Five – Spatial Awareness

Choose various places to put the ribbons around a room that will challenge the class to explore its dimensions, such as:

- The corners of the room
- Placing ribbons at different heights to encourage stretching and standing on tiptoes
- Place some ribbons along the edge of the floor close up to the wall
- Inside a hoop which is placed on the floor in the centre of the room
- Hook an agility pole over two large trestles and drape the ribbons over the pole. Encourage the players to stretch up to retrieve them
- Hook one end of a bench up onto an agility table to create an incline. Now place a ribbon on the top of the table. One person walks up the bench at a time, collects the ribbon, then turns and walks back down the bench onto the floor

Game Six – Parts of the body

Playing Ribbon Time with pictures of body parts (instead of ribbons) can help give a person an understanding of the human body.

You could either (a) draw a picture of a segment of the body or (b) draw the whole or part of the body and circle the part you want to highlight.

- This time make the pictures of the body parts actual size. When the class have finished collecting them all, put them together to make a whole picture on the floor
- Try making some pictures of items that go with that body part, such as scarf, gloves, jumper, jeans, socks and shoes. When all the pictures of the body parts and items have been collected from around the room, assemble the body parts first and then place the picture such as the gloves, on the body part such as the hand

Game Seven – Body Awareness and directionality

- Everyone sits down on the ground (including you). Take a ribbon and place it somewhere on your body. Call out, "Ribbon on my knee" and place the ribbon on your knee. Then call out "Ribbon off my knee" and take the ribbon off your knee
- Now place the ribbon on some one else in the group. For example, call out "Ribbon on Tom's shoulder" then take the ribbon off, and call out "Ribbon off Tom's shoulder"
- This time give out ribbons to everyone. When you place the ribbon on an area of your body, encourage the group to copy you with theirs
- Call out to different people, "Where shall we place the ribbon Robert? On our knee? Or on our

shoulder?" If there is no response, make a choice and express it clearly

- Place the ribbon somewhere on or around your body such as your foot. Position the ribbon in different places about the foot and use the words to describe its location

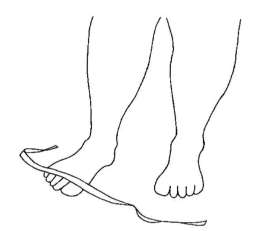

Some ideas could be on, under, beside, behind, and in front. Then give out the ribbons to the whole group and encourage them to copy your actions of placing the ribbons around different parts of the body.

Game Eight – Taking Turns

- Ask the players to sit in a circle. For each player, call out the same part of the body but a different position for the ribbon to be placed. Each time a player has a turn, the rest of the group then copies the action
- Again, sitting in a circle, place a ribbon about your whole self, such as to the side, behind you, in front, on top of your head, under your seat. Now, when you place the ribbon about you, say if it is close to you or far away. Ask the group to copy you.

Game Nine – Visual Processing

- Play Ribbon Time in the home or school. Place the ribbons in one or more rooms. Red ribbons could be placed in one room and green ribbons in another. Other colours could be put in other rooms to find
- You could also make a model of a room that is familiar to a player, with small ribbons positioned inside. Then put full size ribbons in the same places in the full size room
- Put out six circles and six squares (or more or less) for the class members to find. Then place all squares up high and all circles down low
- Place some floor spots around the room. Partially hide some squares under them. Call for them to be collected. In turn use different shapes such as circles, stars, and squares
- Eventually you could place a number of ribbons along a simple obstacle course. Remember that whoever collects the ribbons will not have their hands free to climb, so keep the obstacles at floor level. You can also use different pictures to collect such as flowers, fruit, bugs, or people

Game Ten – Items that match with a room

Place pictures of objects to collect around a room or on an item that you would normally find there. Some ideas could be:

- Pictures of sports items placed around a sports hall
- Pictures of classroom items found in a classroom

- Pictures on a table of items you would find there
- If at home, pictures of bedroom items found in a person's bedroom
- Pictures of items found in a hallway
- Take some items from around a room and place them on a table. Each player then takes an item and puts it back where it came from

 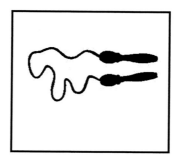 

Game Eleven – Colours

Place four primary coloured mats down on the floor that can be easily seen but not in the way of play to use as collection points. Put out ribbons for class members to collect which match the colours of the mats. Each time a ribbon is collected, encourage class members to place them on the corresponding coloured collection mat. Continue until all the ribbons have been collected. If a player is attracted to a particular colour which stops engagement of play you may need to remove it for a while.

- Instead of collecting ribbons, you could use soft objects. Make sure the colour of the objects closely match the colour of the collection mats
- Put pictures around the room of the same colour, but of different shades to collect

- Cut out squares of different textured material of the same colour and stick it to some card. Place the cards around the room and ask players to collect them. At the end, place them down and encourage the players to feel the textures
- You could put out long ribbons around a room that are the colours of a rainbow. When all have been collected, place them on the mat in a curved shape in order to resemble a rainbow
- Try using pictures of different objects that are of the same colour such as a green bean, green pepper, green cucumber, green cabbage and green lettuce

Game Twelve - Differentiation of colours

Put out ten red ribbons, ten green ribbons and ten yellow ribbons. Call for the players to collect all of the red ribbons first. When all of the red ribbons have been collected, call for the other colours to be collected in turn

- Instead of putting out ribbons, place a number of identical pictures around the room such as ten red apples, ten yellow bananas, and ten bunches of green grapes. Call for all the red apple pictures to be collected first, then move on to the other pictures in turn
- Display all the pictures of the fruit, but only ask for two types out of the three to be collected. This could be red apples and yellow bananas

Game Thirteen – Letters

Either cut out around the boundary of a letter, or write a letter in the centre of a square piece of plain card.

Before you start play, put the letters on the ground, point to each one and call out what they are. Then place the letters around the room.

- Ask the players to collect all of the letters of the alphabet from around the room. When the letters have been collected and placed at the collection point, spread out the letters and select the letters that the players' names begin with. Describe the connection for each player. For example, T for Tim, P for Penny, and J for John. Initially, do not mix upper case letters with lower case

- This time, put out all the letters of a player's name. When the letters have been collected, arrange the letters in order to spell out that name. Next, play the game with two players' names. They can collect any letters but encourage them to sort between them at the collection mat whose letters are whose

- Make up some letters and pictures that go together, like snake and s, dog and d. When all have been collected, match the letters with the pictures

- Draw some letters to collect that are the same, but are of different sizes and styles

Game Fourteen - Numbers

Either cut out the whole shape of the number, or write the number in the centre of a square piece of plain card. Before you start the game, hold the numbers up and call out what they are called. Call out what the numbers are as you place them around the room.

- Use the same number for all the players to collect
- Try the same numbers but different sizes
- Use two, three or four different numbers and when all have been collected place them into piles
- Number sequences, not collected in order, but when finished, sorted in order
- Pairs of numbers that can be matched at the end
- All the same numbers but of different styles

Game Fifteen – Number Challenges

Numbers are around us everywhere. It can take some time to understand what relevance they have in our world. Games with numbers may help us understand their role in our daily life.

- Numbers and a picture showing the corresponding number of objects. Collect and sort into pairs
- Make a number of cards with number bonds on them such as 2 + 2 and 3 + 3. Make another set of cards with the answers such as = 4 and = 6. Collect all the cards and place them on the floor. Finally, put the cards together that belong with each other. You could also use pictures instead of numbers

- Place square cards around the room that have a different number of dots on them just like the face of a die. When all have been collected, match them in pairs
- Roll some small balls onto the floor. Encourage the players to pick them up and put them in an upright tube. Count out loud how many it takes to fill it
- Put out a number of floor spots all over the floor. When the players have collected them, place them down in a line close to each other. Walk along the path of spots counting out loud as you go. Encourage the players to follow you

Different ways to begin the game

As the player becomes used to playing Ribbon Time try to make the game more challenging. You can do this by starting the game in a particular way.

- Players can sit inside a marked out area or on a line while waiting to start
- The players can wait sitting on a bench
- The players can wait standing on a bench
- Each player places a hand on the wall until the game starts
- Each player places a hand on a stable object until the game starts

The intention for exploring different ways to start the game is to encourage independence and confidence of players. Ways to do this could be:

- Encourage the players to say how they would like to start the game, or give them a choice from two suggestions
- Give a player the opportunity to start the game
- Give a player the opportunity to choose what they would like to play Ribbon Time with, such as which item and what colour
- Ask for assistance from players to prepare or sort what small items will be used
- A player can place the objects around the room

Ending the game and collection point ideas

Once the players are comfortable with collecting items and placing them at a collection point such as a mat (with or without a buddy), explore other collection point ideas that could be enjoyable for the players. Some ideas to try are:

- Use different objects to collect the ribbons or items in. These could be part of a theme, such as placing seaside pictures, shells or postcards into a seaside bucket. Shopping items could be put into a large shopping bag or trolley, and plastic eggs could be put into an egg carton
- Place velcro onto each object, and place velcro onto a board which is fixed to the wall. Place items on the board when all or each are collected
- Players can end the game sitting on the floor, standing in a marked area, sitting on a bench, or standing behind a line

Praise the players throughout the game, either verbally (well done), with gesture (thumbs up), action (high five), or visually (a card with a smiley face) for their efforts shown throughout the game. It may be necessary to use more than one method.

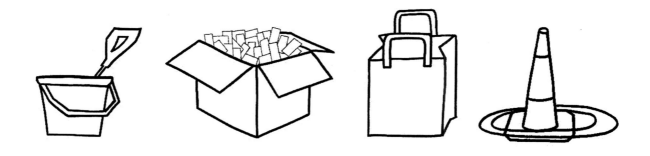

Ending the game with music

You might like to end the game with a song that corresponds to your game or theme used. Some ideas that could be used are:

- Seaside – Oh I Do Like To Be Beside The Seaside
- Parts of the body – Head shoulders Knees And Toes
- Numbers – 12345 Once I Caught A Fish Alive
- Letters – The Alphabet Song
- Colours – I Can Sing A Rainbow
- Food – One Potato, Two Potato
- Music – I Am The Music Maker
- Toys – The Teddy Bear's Picnic
- Travel – The Runaway Train Ran Down The Track And She Blew
- Animals – Old Macdonald Had A Farm
- Dressing – The Mulberry Bush

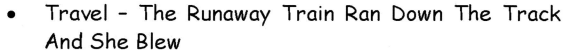

Older players may enjoy listening to music of different styles and types, such as relaxing, party or pop.

Ask the players what music they like so you know for next time you play.

Jog

and

Stop

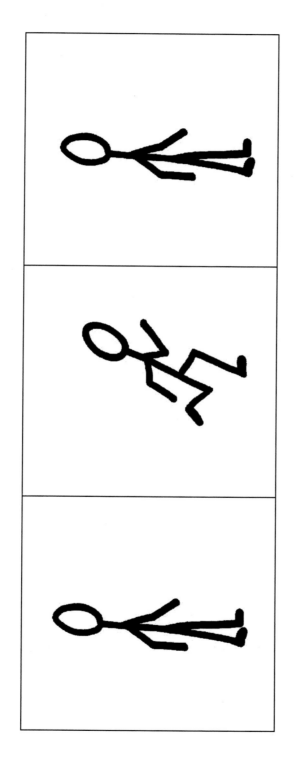

Jog and Stop *(Visual Aid)*

Introduction

Jog and Stop is a running game. Everyone is encouraged to run around in the same direction. When the leader (who has been running with the group) calls "stop", every one stops. The leader then calls out an action such as "star". When the star has been made the leader calls "run" and the game continues. Before ending the game, everyone should slow down to a walk and end with stretching exercises.

The duration of the game should be relevant to the age of the participants, their fitness level, and temperature of the room. Ask someone to watch the class, as not all children know their limitations or feel pain and an individual might need to be stopped.

The room or designated area should not be too large and should be clear of any objects and distractions.

Points to consider with Jog and Stop

- Learn each stage slowly, this could mean days, weeks, months or longer
- Give participants time to process what has been asked and do not repeat what you have said more than is necessary
- You may wish to ask a buddy to partner a child
- How many children that can play at any one time will depend on their size, and the size of your play area

- Some children might find it beneficial to see a picture sequence of the game first
- If some children prefer visual clues, have a red and a green card that can be shown alongside the words, 'stop' and 'run'
- If participants find it difficult to run in the same direction, place a long bench in the middle of the room and use it as a marker to travel around
- Once a bench is successful, use flat markers each end of the room to run around
- Initially, it might be helpful to the players if the leader stops in the same place each time they call "stop"

Warming up

Encourage everyone to walk around the room in any direction. Now call for everyone to walk in the same direction. You may need to use something visual such as a bench to walk around.

Stop and move your head side to side and then nod gently. Now wave your hands and shake your arms. Next sway your arms side to side then rotate them round and round. Place hands around the waist and move your hips to the left and right. Sit down and stretch your arms forward towards the knees while keeping the back flat. Once the warm up becomes routine and players are comfortable doing it, gradually add more exercises.

Game One – Start and Stop

Stop when the leader calls out "stop". When the leader calls "run", the whole group runs. This is Jog and Stop in its simplest form. You might need to keep this format until the participants are comfortable with the game.

Game Two – Standing shapes

This time, when the leader calls "stop", make a standing static shape (non locomotive) such as a star shape. The leader may also need to say how, such as "arms out wide and legs out wide". Other static standing shapes to try are:

- Arms stretched up, out or down
- Hands on head or shoulders
- Hands around waist
- Hands on knees or feet
- Crossed arms
- Hands together
- Fingers interlocked

Game Three – Sitting shapes

When shapes are made other than in a standing position, the leader should be aware that participants may need more time to enter into, and out of a shape. The leader should also call for everyone to stand up before continuing the game.

Now try a static ground shape on the ground such as sitting (pike) with legs straight and together, hands could be placed on legs. Other shapes you can try are:

- Tuck
- Straddle (legs astride)
- One leg straight, the other bent
- Legs long and crossed (do not hold position for long due to danger of compromising circulation)
- Sitting, legs out straight with hands on thighs, knees, shins or ankles
- Sitting with soles of feet touching
- Legs out straight, feet turned out

Game Four – Lying on back shapes

Next, make a static shape on the back, such as a lying down star or:

- Knees tucked up
- Bent legs holding feet
- Legs up together in a pike shape
- Legs up together then straddled apart
- Lying out flat as a ruler

Game Five – Lying on side shapes

When stopping this time, balance on the side of the body, but not for too long as it can become uncomfortable to maintain. If possible, use matting. Try a tuck position first, and then you could try:

- Rest on side with legs slightly bent
- Rest on side and make a banana shape
- Pike with hands touching legs

Game Six – Face down shapes

When participants are more confident you can try a face down position like a star. You could also try:

- Stretch out long and flat
- Tucked legs under body
- Hands and knees
- Hands and feet squatting, looking at the floor
- Hands and feet some distance apart, with the rest of the body off of the floor

Game Seven – Moving on the spot

When the call is given to stop, give plenty of processing time before an action is called, or running commences.

Some movements to try on the spot are bobbing, rocking, marching, running, jumping in shape, hopping, touch ground and jump, and spot the dog.

Game Eight – Standing still, moving upper body

When the leader calls "stop", the body part should be called next, and then the action. This might help give a clearer understanding to the player. Try the following actions:

- Shaking or waving hands in the air
- Wiggling fingers
- Clapping hands together, or on knees or thighs or on sides or on opposite shoulders
- Rubbing hands together
- Patting the ground
- Swinging arms up and down
- Punching the air
- Lifting arms out to the side and return
- Small or large arm circles
- Rubbing own thighs or knees or shins or feet or arms
- Touching and counting toes and feet

Game Nine - Spinning and turning

When "stop" is called, try turning and spinning on different parts of the body.

You could try this when standing or sitting, or when on the front or back. Wait until everyone has stopped spinning before you commence running again.

Game Ten –
Balancing while some parts of the body are in view

Once body shapes and balances have been practised, they can become quicker for the player to initialise. Eventually, this can give more scope for an individual to improve shape, as opposed to creating the basic move.

Try balancing while part of the body is in view, such as when sitting down with feet held up off the floor. As confidence builds, try other balances when running stops such as:

- Lie down on side with one leg elevated
- Sit on the ground and raise one leg upward
- Lie on back and raise one leg upward

Game Eleven –
Balancing while some parts of the body are not always in view

These exercises can be very challenging. Keep your instructions simple and demonstrate wherever possible. Use agility mats for safety and also for prompting which part/s of the body should be touching the mat.

- Balance on knees
- Balance on hands and knees
- Hands and feet with one leg elevated

- Stand on one leg with free leg to the front, side or back
- Lie down on back, bend knees and lift seat up

Game Twelve – Sequences on one level

When the players stop running this time, encourage them to use shapes that are on the same level and that flow easily from one to the other, such as a star, then move feet together and place arms by sides. Try these:

- Head shoulders knees and toes
- Tuck, pike, and straddle
- Lie down on back, without getting up, make a star shape and then hold knees to chest in tuck

Game Thirteen – Sequences on different levels

Do not make the sequence too long or complicated. Give participants time to change shape. Some sequences could be:

- Stand tall then squat in a tuck
- Stand on one leg, then place two feet down and jump
- Star face down on ground, hands and knees, stand up tall and turn around on two feet

Game Fourteen – Music

There is much discussion about what type of music individuals with ASD prefer but it seems there is no one type that suits everyone. Care should be taken to keep the volume to a level that is comfortable for all. You can use music throughout Jog and Stop either while the players are running, or when they have stopped for the following:

- Starting and stopping to music, instead of calling stop and go
- Playing music when the participants are running and when the music stops, encourage participants to stop and make a shape
- The music is not played while every one is running, but when "stop" is called, the music starts and everyone makes actions to the music played. This could be action music or pop party music

Different ways to travel around the room before and after stopping

Try more challenging ways to travel until asked to stop. When you restart, repeat the same action. Move on to other ways of travelling when players are ready:

- Walking quickly
- Knees up high while walking
- Hands and feet walking
- In 'The Conga' formation but walking

This time jog first, then stop and then try a group activity such as:

- All hold hands, make a circle then move clockwise or anticlockwise
- The group sits on the ground in a straddle position all in a line and facing in the same direction
- Sit side by side in a pike position
- Hold hands and move as a group in a wavy line

Cooling down

Encourage the group to walk around the room as slowly as possible. Stop and ask everyone to stop and look at what you are doing. Give time for participants to stop. Some individuals may not seem as if they are taking notice of what you are saying but this is not always so.

Ask everyone to stretch their neck from side to side. Bring your arms across the chest in a big hug and stretch the arms out wide. Sit down on the floor and tuck up into a ball then stretch out again into a straddle shape.

While your legs are still apart, lean out slightly and touch the floor on one side and then the other, bring your legs together and place your hands on your legs. Shake your legs out gently against the floor.

Congratulate the group for all efforts made throughout Jog and Stop. This game is a very good way to improve cardiac fitness.

Roll Ball

Roll Ball (*Visual Aid*)

Introduction

Roll Ball is a 'hands on' ball rolling game for one or more players. The ball is rolled along from one end of the play area to the other where it is then pushed onto a ball rest.

To start Roll Ball, a player is chosen to start the game and the ball is placed on a marker. When the referee calls out "Ready, steady, roll!" the ball is rolled off the marker onto the play area, where any player can then try and roll the ball. The game stops when the ball is placed on the rest.

A player can play the game on an individual basis or within a group which works to transport the ball onto the ball rest. Roll Ball has few rules (it is advisable to use the hands only). There are no teams.

For Roll Ball, you will need a clear space that will safely accommodate the number of children that are playing (indoors or outdoors), a marker or line to start the game from, a ball rest, and a large clear inflatable ball.

Points to consider with Roll Ball

- Complete a risk assessment before playing
- It might be beneficial to include siblings
- Some children might find it beneficial to see a picture sequence of the game first

- If some children do prefer visual clues, have a red, orange and green card ready that can be shown alongside the words, stop, ready, steady, roll!
- Try not to choose a ball that bounces too high, or that is too brightly coloured
- You may find that the larger the ball, the less likely players are to tumble over the top
- Sometimes players find a clear ball easier to manoeuvre as the room can be seen through it
- Some players may participate more when there are less players playing
- You may want to arrange a game for players who are the most competitive for possession of the ball

Warming Up

It is advisable that everyone should be dressed in comfortable clothes that are suitable to exercise in, and all jewellery removed. Individuals should be in good health and if any players have specific needs these should be made known to staff.

Try keeping the warm up routine the same each time you play Roll Ball for a number of weeks. If the players know what to expect, this can help to reduce anxiety.

Start the warm up with walking. Encourage players to walk in the same direction. Then, encourage the players to jog.

Finally, ask the players to stop jogging and to stand in a designated area. Encourage players to copy the set of exercises below while you demonstrate:

- Neck stretches side to side
- Wave hands
- Backward arm circles
- Run on the spot
- Touch the floor and stretch up
- Touch the floor and jump up
- Touch stomach then knees then feet

Game one - Stages

Stage One - Introduce the basic action
Roll Ball can be introduced in stages on an individual or group basis. Firstly, put the ball very close to the ball rest. Call "Ready, steady, roll!" Roll the ball onto the rest and call "stop".

Stage Two - Introduce a marker

Now place the ball on a flat marker in front of the ball rest. Call "Ready, steady, roll!" and roll the ball onto the ball rest.

Stage Three - Increasing the distance the ball will travel to the ball rest

Each time you play, place the marker further away from the ball rest, until finally the marker is positioned where you wish to start the game from. Praise players individually for rolling the ball well or rolling the ball onto the ball rest.

Game Two- Focusing on direction

If players find it difficult to focus on rolling the ball in the direction of the ball rest, place two benches turned on their sides and place either side of the ball rest to form a V shape channel. Encourage the players to take it in turns to roll the ball on the floor between the benches and up onto the ball rest.

Game Three – Spatial awareness and directionality

To encourage use of space, and greater manipulation of the ball, start the game from any point in the room, (this could also be a corner, or side). You may even choose to start the game with the ball placed on a piece of equipment such as a low agility table.

Once you have started the game from a variety of places then ask the players where they would like to start the game from. If you do not get a response still give options, either verbally or by visual aid.

Game Four – Challenging the sensory system with texture

Before you play, you will need to have various bands (13cm wide) of textured material to wrap around the ball and fasten with Velcro. Materials you could use are fake fur or netting.

Start play from a marker. Encourage the players to roll the ball. Not all players will feel comfortable with the different textures, and may take a while to get used to them, or for some, not at all.

When all of the textures have been explored, place a variety of different textures and shapes on the ball. If resources are limited, you could use a pre formed textured ball instead.

Game Five – Handling different sized balls

For this game you will need four different sized balls, along with a suitable ball rest for each. Start play with the largest ball and rest first. Call out "Ready steady roll!" Once the ball has been rolled and placed on the ball rest, start play again, but this time with the ball and rest which is the next size down. Before the ball is rolled, say "This ball is smaller, bend down to roll the ball". Every time you start play, use a smaller ball and rest.

Game Six – Building up an obstacle course

Always leave a space between each obstacle as you build your obstacle course. For safety reasons, players should take it in turns to play. Place a floor marker before an obstacle such as a wedge. Roll the ball off the marker then up and down the wedge, and finally along the floor onto the ball rest. When the course is completed add another obstacle. You might like to try items such as soft play shapes, a safety mattress, ropes, coits or benches.

At first, make a straight line with the obstacles. Later, try and change the direction of the obstacle course by using right angles and curves.

Game Seven – Following a pathway of markers

Gradually build up a straight pathway of floor markers using various shapes such as arrows, geometric shapes or hand or footprints. Start the game at the beginning on a particular floor marker and end the game with the ball placed on the ball rest.

For a greater challenge, build up a route to roll the ball along that takes different kinds of pathways such as a circular, semi circular, square, rectangular, triangular, zigzag and/or spiral pattern.

- If at any time a player finds it difficult to follow a pathway, using a clear ball might help
- Explore moving along the pathway slowly and another time quickly
- Try counting the markers out loud as you pass the ball over them
- Call out the colour of the markers as the ball passes over them
- Finally, call out the shapes of the markers as the ball passes over them

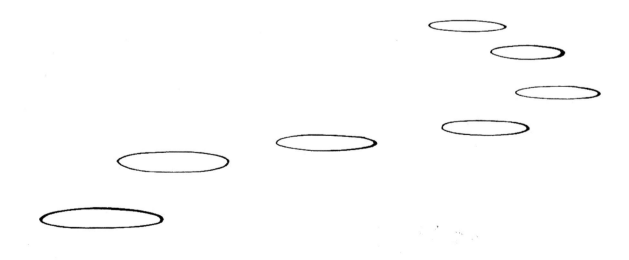

Game Eight – Using benches to challenge individual skills.

Benches can be used in a variety of ways to make Roll Ball interesting and challenging. For safety reasons, players should initially take it in turns.

Variation One

Start the ball from a marker which is placed on the floor. The player walks on floor level, whilst at the same time rolls the ball up onto the surface of a bench which is placed long ways. The player then rolls the ball off the end of the bench down onto the floor and onto the ball rest. More benches could be added to make the route longer.

Variation Two

This time turn the bench upside down and use the narrow side to roll the ball along.

Variation Three

Instead of placing the benches long ways, position three benches in a triangle but leave two benches slightly apart in one corner. Place a marker on the floor in front of one open end, and a ball rest on the floor at the other. Roll the ball from the floor marker up onto the bench, along the bench, and down onto the ball rest to finish. You could also try other shapes such as, an L, U, N, or V shape.

Variation Four

Place two benches side by side approximately half a metre apart. Roll a large ball off a floor marker which is placed on the floor, and upwards to rest in the gap formed between the surfaces of the two benches. The player rolls the ball along and down off the benches onto a ball rest.

Variation Five

Hook one end of a bench up onto the bars of an agility stool or table. On the opposite side of the table hook one end of a narrow plank over the bars. Start the game with the ball on the floor resting on a floor marker in front of the bench. The player stays on the floor, rolls the ball up the bench, over the table and down the plank on the other side. The ball is then rolled down onto the floor and onto the ball rest.

Game Nine – Using motor planning skills and visual processing skills to create a pattern with a number of balls

Place a number of ball rests in a shape chosen from the list below. You will need the same number of balls as ball rests.

- Straight or wavy line
- Triangle or diamond
- Square or rectangle
- Circle, semi circle or oblong
- Any shape with a rest placed on the floor within it

Make sure there is plenty of room to move between the ball rests that are set out. A player rolls each ball from the same floor marker each time in turn until all the ball rests have a ball on them. Try not to knock the balls off their rests while you are rolling the ball. If one does fall off a ball rest, replace it when you have finished placing the ball you were playing with. Once this is successful you might like to try:

- Two players taking it in turns to roll the balls
- A number of players taking a turn to roll a ball each
- Reversing the game by starting the balls on ball rests, and rolling them one at a time into an open pen made from benches

Game Ten – Matching objects

Use the same number of balls as ball rests. Place the ball rests in a line. Place a picture in the bottom of each rest so they can be easily seen. Stick pictures on the balls that match with those inside the ball rests. Players take it in turns to start the ball rolling from the floor marker and onto its matching ball rest. You can choose many themes for matching up the balls to the ball rests such as:

- Colours, numbers or letters
- Photos of expressions or familiar people
- Themes from topic work

Game Eleven – Finding out how different things move

Start the game with one very large clear inflatable ball. The players roll the ball off the marker onto the ball rest. Go back to the start and take some of the air out which will then make it more difficult to push. Each time you take the ball back to the marker to restart the game take a little more air out until it becomes a real challenge to move. Discard the ball when it becomes too difficult to move.

Different objects for you to try to roll or push off a marker onto a rest could be:

- A soft play barrel
- A puck or a large clean floor polishing disc
- A soft play cube
- A large bean bag that you usually use for sitting on
- A round parachute ball
- For a single player playing, they could use a small trolley or trike instead of a ball. Start the game from a floor marker. Move the trolley forward and park it in a designated area
- A player lies down on a body board which is parked on a floor marker, making sure his body weight is distributed safely over the board. The player propels himself off the marker, along the floor, and into a designated floor area

You will need to change the type of ball rest to accommodate the different shapes and sizes of the objects used. Familiarise yourself with how the objects move before the players use them in a game.

Game Twelve – The game of Roll Ball

Place a ball rest at each end of the playing area. Now position a floor marker central to both ball rests. A player chooses which ball rest they will aim towards and starts the game from the marker on the words "Ready , steady, roll!" Encourage different players to have a turn at starting the game.

Cooling down

Regardless of how much players have participated, encourage all players to join in cooling down. Repeat the following exercises from the warm up but at a slower pace:

- Neck stretches side to side
- Wave hands
- Backward arm circles
- March slowly on the spot
- Touch the floor and stretch up,
  then out wide
- Touch stomach then knees then feet
- Sit and stretch gently towards knees

Keep the cool down the same each time you play until the players are comfortable doing it. Build up a more challenging warm up by adding further exercises when they are ready to do so.

Kick

Football

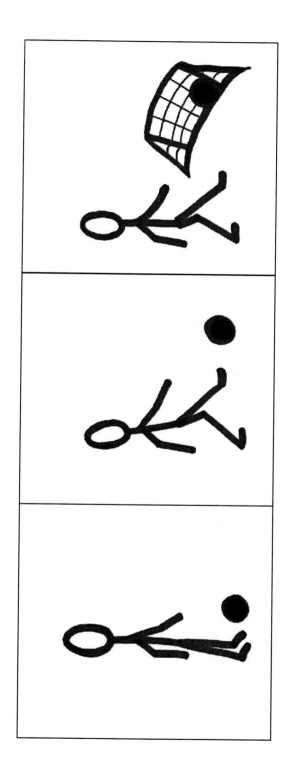

Kick Football (*Visual Aid*)

Introduction

Kick Football is a game based on basic football skills for one or more players. It has few rules, no teams and one goal.

The game of Kick Football starts at the end of the playing area without a goal. The ball is placed on a line or marker and all players can stand where they wish. Someone is chosen to start the game. The referee calls "Ready, steady, kick!" The chosen player kicks the ball off the marker towards the goal end. All players can now try and kick the ball. When the ball enters the goal the referee calls "Goal! Stop the game!" Everyone goes back to the marker and the referee starts the game once again.

For Kick Football, you will need a clear space that will safely accommodate the number and size of children playing (indoors or outdoors), a marker to start the game from, a goal, and a football.

Points to consider with Kick Footall

- Complete a risk assessment before starting
- The floor, walls and ceiling should be clear of any obstructions or projectiles
- It might be beneficial to include siblings
- Some children might find it beneficial to see a picture sequence of the game first

- If some children do prefer visual cues, use an orange card for wait, a green card for go, and a red card for stop
- For those who would like to watch the game, place a bench at the sideline
- Use a ball the size of a football and that does not bounce too high
- Choose a ball that is not too bright in colour and is comfortable on impact
- Choose a ball that is the best size for the needs of the group
- It might be helpful for some players if you mark the ball with a spot the size of a large apple. Players can then aim to kick the coloured spot to commence the game

Warming Up

Everyone, including staff, should be dressed in clothes suitable to exercise in and all jewellery removed. Individuals should be in good health and any special considerations explained to all staff.

Keep the warm up the same each time you play Kick Football for a number of weeks. If the players know what the routine will be each time, this could help reduce anxiety within a busy environment.

Start the warm up with walking. With practice, your aim will be to all walk in the same direction. Next, encourage players to jog.

Finally, call the players to come closer to you and encourage them to copy what exercises you do. You may need to start with one exercise and add one each time you play. You might like to try:

- Nod head up and down slowly
- Lift arms up and down
- Stand and lift knees up one at a time
- Jump on the spot
- Run on the spot
- Jump with arms and legs wide
- Kick feet one at a time
- Touch knees

Game One - Stages

Kick Football can be introduced in the following stages:

Stage One

Place a coloured mat on the ground in front of you. Now put a ball on a flat floor marker close to the mat, call out "Ready, steady, kick!" and kick the ball onto the coloured mat.

Stage Two

Place the coloured mat inside the floor of a goal. Place the ball on the marker close to the mat, and call out "Ready, steady, kick!" When the ball enters the goal, call out "Goal! Stop the game!" Pick the ball up and replace on the marker ready to start again.

Stage Three

Continue to place the marker further and further away from the goal until you reach the desired distance you would like the game to start from. Give praise to players when there is skill shown or a goal is scored.

Stage Four

If kicking the ball in the right direction is proving difficult, as a practice, place two benches either side of the goal on their sides on the ground, and face them into each other to form a channel. When the ball is kicked from the marker, the ball will travel more easily towards the goal. Players can take it in turns to try this.

Game Two - Stationary goalkeeper

Placing a stationary goalkeeper in goal gives the players some predictability while practising shooting for goal. You could use a block first. Next time, try placing a weighted inflatable punch bag in different positions within the goal instead.

Game Three – Moving goalkeeper

Choose a member of staff as a goalkeeper. At first ask the goalkeeper to stand very still while the game is in play, even if goals are scored. Then you could try asking the goal keeper to defend the goal with their feet only, then with just hands, then lastly with hands or feet.

Now, ask or choose a player to have a turn at being in goal. You may need to mark out the area the goalkeeper is allowed to stand in.

Game Four – More than one ball

If play is dominated by any one player, use more than one ball. Line the balls up in a straight line before allowing the player or players to kick the ball at the same time. Leave all the balls in the goal until they have all been kicked into the goal. Place all the balls into a bag and then take them back to the start line to begin the game again.

Game Five - Independence

Select a player to take the ball from the back of the net. Ask them to replace it on the start line, and call out "Ready, steady, kick!" for them to start the game again. It might be helpful for players if you use a set of visual cards that show picking the ball up, then putting it on the line, and then starting play. You may need to use communication support each time you play.

Game Six – Stickers for goals

Place a photo of each player on a board or wall where it can be seen from the playing area. Each time a player scores a goal, place a sticker (that looks like a football) onto the laminated photo.

You could also try a velcro strip under the photo and stick velcro backed football pictures on instead.

Game Seven - Accuracy

Use goals of different sizes. Start with the largest size, then medium and then smallest.

Game Eight – Different goals

If players play Kick Football at a different venue, football goals might not always be available, so try using:

- Collapsible cones for goal ends
- A large open cardboard box against a wall
- Tape marks on the wall to resemble a goal, if playing indoors
- A bench turned on its side

Game Nine – Taking turns

As the game becomes more familiar, have a group of players waiting on the bench for a turn. You may wish to add players one at a time to those already playing, or change everyone who is playing with those who are sitting on the bench.

Game Ten - Recognition

Each time you play Kick Football, keep a total of goals scored by each player. After the game, present a certificate of achievement or stickers to players for trying, playing well, or scoring goals.

Congratulations!

David Jones

Scored 2 goals!

Playing Kick Football

On Wednesday June 22nd / 2010

Basic Skills

You might like to try the following without actually playing a game of Kick Football. Learning new skills and improving old ones is a helpful way to improve both body and ball control.

Walking without the ball

- Slowly
- Quickly
- Walk and stop
- Walking in and out of cones
- Walking between cones
- Walking backwards around a cone or cones
- Walking sideways around cones

Running or moving quickly without the ball

- Jogging forwards
- Jogging backwards
- Fast running forwards
- Run, stop and run
- Jogging in a circle
- Chasing a player who has a tag attached to them and trying to take it away

Kicking the ball practice

Moving, or even standing still while manipulating an object such as a ball, can be very challenging. Practice is important in order to gain skill and is an opportunity to increase self esteem through achievable targets.

Ideas for practicing control of the ball

- Use a football which is attached by string to a weighted base
- Place a soft ball into a net bag. Attach a piece of strong elastic to the bag and fix it to a hook in the ceiling. Emphasise careful kicking
- Kick a balloon that is attached or not attached to a piece of string
- Make a gutter out of strong cardboard to kick and send the ball along
- Stand on a low platform and kick the ball down a gentle slope

- Make a long narrow pathway with raised sides, (you could turn benches on their sides) to practice moving forwards with the ball in front of you
- Kick a ball against a wall or rebound net
- Place a number of cones in a line across the play area. The player kicks the ball from the start line towards the cones. The player moves between them, and continues on towards the goal

Stopping the ball practice

- Practise foot control by pushing your foot down onto a whoopee cushion
- Sit on a chair and lift up your foot then place it down onto a ball that is rolled towards you

- To practise balance, place a number of coloured spots on a bench. Call a colour such as red. The player moves to where it is and then puts one foot up onto the red spot

Cooling down

Regardless of how much players have participated, encourage all players to join in cooling down. Repeat the following exercises which are similar to the warm up but should be done at a slower pace.

- Nod head up and down
- Lift arms up and down
- Stand and lift knees up one at a time
- Bend knees while standing on the spot
- Walk or march on the spot
- Stretch out with arms and legs wide
- Shake feet one at a time in front of you
- Touch knees or toes
- Sit and stretch towards knees and shins

Useful addresses

Disability Sport England
Solecast House
13-27 Brunswick Place
London
N1 6DX

Disabled Sports U.S.A
451 Hungerford Drive
Suite 100
Rockville
MD 20850

Sport Canada
Canadian Heritage
15 Eddy Street
16th Floor
Gatineau
Quebec
K1A OM5

Australian Athletes With A Disability
6 Figtree Drive
Sydney Olympic Park
NSW 2127

The National Autistic Society
393 City Road
London
EC1V 1NG

Scottish Society for Autism
Hilton House
Alloa Business Park
Whins Road
Alloa
Scotland
FK10 3sA

The National Autistic Society Cymru
6-7 Village Way
Greenmeadow Springs Business Park
Tongwynlais
Cardiff. CF15 7NE

Irish Society of Autism
Unity Building
16-17 Lower OConnell Street
Dublin 1
Republic of Ireland

Denmark
Landsforeningen Autisme
Kiplings Alle 42
DK-2860 Soborg
Denmark

Autism Society of America
7910 Woodmont Avenue
Suite 300 Bethesda
Maryland 20814
United States of America

Autism Association Queensland
P.O Box 354
Sunnybank Hills
Queensland 4109. Australia

Autistic Association of New Zealand
1st Floor, 257 Lincoln Road
Addington, Christchurch
New Zealand

Equipment and resources

Davies Sports Equipment Cheshire
United Kingdom SK14 4LL

TFH Toys Worcestershire
United Kingdom DY13 9HT

SpaceKraft Ltd Toys West Yorkshire,
BD18 3HH
United Kingdom

Coachwise 1st4sport Leeds
LS12 4HP. United Kingdom
(Teaching and coaching publications)

THE URUK
WORLD SYSTEM

SECOND EDITION

THE DYNAMICS OF
EXPANSION OF EARLY
MESOPOTAMIAN
CIVILIZATION

· GUILLERMO ALGAZE ·

THE UNIVERSITY OF CHICAGO PRESS

CHICAGO | LONDON

The University of Chicago Press, Chicago, 60637
The University of Chicago Press, Ltd., London
© 1993, 2005 by The University of Chicago
All rights reserved. Published 2005
Printed in the United States of America

10 09 08 07 06 05   5 4 3 2 1

ISBN: 0-226-01382-0 (paperback)

Library of Congress Cataloging-in-Publication Data

Algaze, Guillermo, 1954–
    The Uruk world system : the dynamics of expansion of early Mesopotamian
civilization / Guillermo Algaze.—2nd ed.
        p. cm.
    Includes bibliographical references and index.
    1. Iraq—Civilization—To 634. 2. Middle East—Civilization—To 622.
I. Title.
    DS73.1.A44 2005
    935—dc22

                                                                    2005002709

⊗ The paper used in this publication meets the minimum requirements of
the American National Standard for Information Sciences—Permanence
of Paper for Printed Library Materials, ANSI Z39.48–1992.

Contents

Illustrations

Prologue

A decade has passed since the publication of the original edition of *The Uruk World System*.[1] Normally, that is more than enough time for new archaeological data bearing on important problems of interpretation to emerge, forcing theories crafted on earlier evidence to undergo substantial revision. Alas, political developments in the Near East in general and Iraq and Iran in particular have substantially slowed or altogether stopped the pace of archaeological research in the core areas of early Mesopotamian civilization that are the most crucial to refining our understanding of the processes and dynamics of expansion of Uruk societies. Accordingly, new data shedding light on the Uruk phenomenon is largely limited to developments in portions of Syro-Mesopotamia now located within Syria and southeastern Turkey that are still open to archaeological research.

Given the narrow scope of the relevant new data at hand, new insights pertaining to the Uruk Expansion center around the nature of preexisting societies in the areas of the periphery into which Uruk polities intruded. To a lesser degree, however, the new data also clarifies specific points of interpretation about the nature of the intruding sites. Chapter 8, which is newly written for this edition, therefore updates and expands pertinent information about specific Uruk and indigenous

sites in the northern periphery of Mesopotamia previously dealt with in chapters 3, 5, and 6. Chapter 8 also outlines recent discussions by various scholars about the meaning of these developments and specifically highlights areas where, I believe, some of my earlier interpretations need to be expanded, modified, or reconsidered altogether.

The new work presented in chapter 8 indicates that I had earlier underestimated the level of social complexity of indigenous societies in areas of the Mesopotamian periphery into which Uruk societies intruded. In fact, it now seems that until the onset of the fourth millennium B.C. southern Mesopotamia was but one of several competing regions across the ancient Near East where parallel strides toward social complexity were taking place. This makes the emergence of multiple competing city-states across southern Mesopotamia in the fourth millennium all the more noteworthy, as this was the first time that the southern polities, both singly and in the aggregate, surpassed contemporary societies elsewhere in southwest Asia in terms of their scale and degree of internal differentiation, both social and economic.

The Uruk period in the Mesopotamian alluvium, therefore, represents a dramatic "take-off"—a decisive shift, in favor of southern Mesopotamia, of the balance of urbanization,

socio-political complexity, and economic differentiation that had existed across the ancient Near
East until the onset of the fourth millennium. The
roots of the Uruk takeoff are explored in detail in a
separate article recently published in the journal
Current Anthropology (Algaze 2001a). This book
focuses instead on how disparities in power and
prestige created by the takeoff allowed for the

Uruk Expansion. More specifically, it explores the
ways in which that expansion affected areas at the
periphery of southern Mesopotamia in the fourth
millennium. Additionally, it documents the varying strategies that Uruk societies used in unwit-
tingly creating what, with some caveats, can be
considered as the world's earliest "world system"
and, possibly, its first imperial venture.

Note to Prologue

1. For scholarly reviews of the original 1993 En-
glish edition, see P. Amiet, *Revue d'Assyriologie* 88
(1994): 92–93; P.-A. Beaulieu, *Classical World* 88 (1995):
235–36; C. Broodbank, *Antiquity* 67 (1993): 645; T.
Cuyler Young, Jr., *Bulletin of the American Schools of
Oriental Research* 297 (1995): 84–85; A. Joffe, *Journal
of Field Archaeology* 21 (1994): 512–15; K. Keith,
American Journal of Archaeology 99 (1995): 152–53;
C. C. Lamberg-Karlovsky, *The International History Review* 17 (1995): 767–68; R. J. Mathews: *Bibliotheca Ori-
entalis* 51 (1994): 665–71; S. Pollock, *Science* 264 (1994):
1481–82; N. Postgate, *Journal of the American Oriental
Society* 116 (1996): 147–48; and H. T. Wright, *American
Anthropologist* 97 (1995): 151–52.

Preface

Only recently has it become possible to conduct systematic research bearing on the archaeological development and early history of areas in the northern and eastern periphery of the southern Mesopotamian alluvium. Numerous investigations are now underway in the plains of northern Syria, northern Mesopotamia, and southeastern Turkey as well as in the nearby highlands. Combined with what information was obtained from intensive research in the alluvial lowlands of Khuzestan in the 1970s, the emerging corpus of data from the north and northeast allows us for the first time to explore a number of questions of major import for the early historical development of ancient Near Eastern societies. One of those questions constitutes the focus of this study: that of the extent and magnitude of the processes of external expansion that accompanied the crystallization of Sumero-Akkadian civilization in the Mesopotamian alluvium during the Uruk period in the second half of the fourth millennium B.C.

The development of sociopolitical and economic complexity in communities in the alluvial lowlands of southern Iraq during the Uruk period has been, of course, the object of considerable recent research, and in many ways this study should be conceived as part of that ongoing effort. However, instead of examining the emergence of civilization in the alluvium from the point of view of

changes in the Mesopotamian core itself, I focus on the external manifestations and consequences of that process. These include the colonization of the neighboring Susiana plain of Khuzestan and the establishment of a variety of specialized settlements at strategic locations across the northern plains and in the surrounding highlands. These phenomena are analyzed from the perspective of models of cross-cultural interaction derived in great part from historical literature on the penetration of relatively undeveloped peripheral areas by highly organized modern European societies. In spite of obvious temporal and geographic differences involved in the transference of eurocentric conceptual frameworks to an ancient Near Eastern context, the models are relevant in that in each case interaction between societies at significantly different levels of socioeconomic development appears to have been the norm. More specifically, I explicitly assume (1) that for a variety of endogenous reasons not yet fully understood, Uruk societies of southern Iraq had achieved levels of sociopolitical organization that were significantly more advanced than those of contemporary communities on their periphery and (2) that differences in the resource endowments of the lowlands of Mesopotamia and the surrounding highlands ensured that highly stratified societies such as emerged in the alluvium during the Uruk period could neither develop further nor maintain themselves in the long term unless they had access to a resource base significantly wider than the alluvium itself.

It could be argued with some justification that the corpus of available information from the Mesopotamian periphery bearing on the expansion of Uruk societies remains much too fragmentary, ambiguous, and incompletely published for a systematic attempt at interpretation at this time. Nevertheless, enough data have already appeared so that an initial approximation can be attempted. This study, an extensive revision of my doctoral dissertation presented to the University of Chicago in 1986, represents such a preliminary assessment. Since much

pertinent research remains unreported and even more remains undone, it is expected that significant modifications to the construction presented here will become necessary as new data are made available from ongoing research projects in northern Syria, northern Iraq, and southeastern Turkey and by the publication of final results of previous work in southwestern Iran. In the meantime, it is hoped that this assessment will help bring into sharper focus problems still remaining in our understanding of the processes of expansion outward that formed an integral part of the emergence of city-states in the alluvial lowlands of southern Iraq during the Uruk period.

Acknowledgments

Few authors do not owe a significant debt to a great number of their colleagues and teachers. I count myself fortunate in that mine is greater than most. Among those who have had a major impact on my professional and intellectual development are a number of professors and friends presently or formerly at the University of Chicago: Robert McC. Adams, McGuire Gibson, Helene Kantor, and Leon Marfoe. Whether consciously or not, the better part of my ideas concerning the development of Mesopotamian civilization is derived from lectures, classes, and numerous conversations with each of them. More specifically, many of the points developed in this monograph are ultimately derived from seeds planted at some point or another during my student years by these scholars. Kantor, Gibson, and Adams also read earlier drafts of this book and offered valuable suggestions, both substantive and editorial. In terms of approach, my greatest obligation is to Marfoe, from whom I learned that it is impossible to understand any social system in isolation.

Long conversations with colleagues in diverse disciplines have contributed to the development of ideas introduced in this work. Particularly influential were Peter Akkermans of the University of Amsterdam, Virginia Badler of the University of Toronto, Douglas Esse of the University of Chicago, Glenn Schwartz of Johns Hopkins University, Joanne Scurlock of the University of Chicago, Dietrich Sürenhagen of the University of Heidelberg, Maria Trentin of the Institute of Archaeology of the University of London, Patricia Wattenmaker of the University of Virginia, Harvey Weiss of Yale University, Aslıhan Yener of the Smithsonian Institution, and Richard Zettler of the University of Pennsylvania. Others contributed to my understanding of the Uruk phenomenon by allowing me to follow the progress of their excavations in the field or by kindly permitting me access to pertinent, often unpublished, archaeological materials. Special thanks are due to Manfred R. Behm-Blancke (Hassek), Rudolph Dornemann (Hadidi), Richard Ellis (Gritille), Harald Hauptmann (Lidar), Joan Oates (Brak), Mehmet Özdoğan (Karababa Survey), Alba Palmieri (Arslan Tepe), and Mauritz van Loon (Hammam et-Turkman). Equally important were the contributions of others who kindly commented on earlier drafts of this monograph and on the doctoral dissertation on which it is based: Maggie Brandt, Mary Evins, Ronald Gorny, and Donald Whitcomb of the University of Chicago, Elizabeth Carter of the University of California, Los Angeles, Mario Liverani of the University of Rome, and Philip Kohl of Wellesley College. My most immediate debt, however, is to Henry T. Wright of the

University of Michigan and Gil Stein of Northwestern University, who reviewed the final versions of the manuscript. Each offered insightful and detailed criticism, crucial missing references, and important editorial comments that in many cases have been incorporated into the present work. Also incorporated are points made by colleagues who commented on an earlier summary of my views that appeared in *Current Anthropology* (1989). The substantial contributions of the scholars and friends just listed are acknowledged with gratitude, but remaining errors of omission and interpretation are entirely my own.

Over the years, a number of institutions have provided financial support that was directly or indirectly related to this study. The University of Chicago supported my years as a graduate student with a variety of generous fellowships. The Oriental Institute, in particular, paid for the costs involved in the analysis of data from excavations at Kurban Höyük, some of which is incorporated into the present work. Much pertinent information from my own surveys along the Tigris and Euphrates rivers in Turkey during 1988, 1989, and 1990 has also found its way into this monograph. Those surveys have been financed by the Smithsonian Institution, the National Geographic Society, the National Endowment for the Humanities, the American Philosophical Society, the American Council of Learned Societies, the American Research Institute in Turkey, the British Institute of Archaeology at Ankara, and by several private donors. Final revisions to the manuscript were made possible, in part, by a Mellon Foundation Postdoctoral Fellowship at the University of Pennsylvania. The contributions of these various institutions are greatly appreciated.

The majority of the illustrations were produced with admirable skill by Carlene Friedman of Chicago. A final note of recognition goes to my wife, Elise Auerbach, who offered insightful criticism and needed support throughout.

1

Introduction

Archaeologists have become increasingly critical of neo-evolutionary formulations for the development of complex society that stress internal . . . factors to the exclusion or near exclusion of interaction and exchange among disparate societies at different levels of cultural development. . . . The basic fact remains that the . . . cultural evolution of any society is dependent upon relations with other societies; that cultures are open, not closed, systems; and that studies . . . that fail to consider broader patterns of interaction are necessarily incomplete and partial. —P. L. Kohl, "The Use and Abuse of World Systems Theory"

A SUPRAREGIONAL PERSPECTIVE

The marked geographic, environmental, economic, and cultural contrasts between the alluvial lowlands of southern Mesopotamia and the high plains and highlands of its periphery imposed a number of enduring constraints on the development of societies in each of those areas. One crucial constraint was that in the Mesopotamian alluvium, a land devoid of most resources other than the basic ones provided by agriculture and animal husbandry, a substantial proportion of the material requirements needed to sustain highly stratified social systems had to be imported (Oppenheim 1976). The needed resources were largely to be found in distant highland areas whose communities, to judge from existing historical and archaeological evidence, were characterized by significantly lower levels of sociopolitical and economic integration than those of city-states in the Iraqi alluvium, at least before the third millennium B.C. What, then, is the proper framework for the study of societies in these contrastive areas and, more specifically, for understanding the genesis of Sumerian civilization in southern Mesopotamia during the second half of the fourth millennium B.C.?

Recent approaches to this question have explored the role of sources of disequilibrium within communities in the alluvium as causative in the evolutionary processes that culminated in the rise of Uruk city-states. Individual studies have focused on the growth of urban polities (Adams 1981; Adams and Nissen 1972), the emergence of complex hierarchical administrative structures (Johnson 1973, 1987; Wright and Johnson 1975), the accretion of social stratification and political differentiation (Zagarell 1986), the transition form reciprocal to redistributive economies (Polanyi 1957), and, finally, the impact of specific "prime movers," such as agricultural intensification and population growth (Smith and Young 1972), warfare (Wright et al. 1975), or the development of intraregional trade (Johnson 1973; H. T. Wright 1972; Wright and Johnson 1975).

Important as each of these various factors must have been, the complex modifications and innovations in internal social, political, and economic organization resulting in the initial elaboration of Mesopotamian civilization surely did not occur in a vacuum. Rather, the processes leading to the emergence of city-states in the alluvium could have only taken place against a much wider background, one in which cross-cultural contacts and interregional exchange occupied a prominent position. This is underscored by later documentation from Mesopotamia itself. From at least the third millennium onward, a diverse corpus of historical evidence allows us to trace the changing roles of exchange and coercion, as well as public institutions, both secular and religious, and private entrepreneurs in the procurement of the required resources (Larsen 1987).[1] The relative importance of each of these factors varied considerably from period to period. In spite of the considerable differences in the types of goods exchanged and the changing nature of resource procurement strategies through time, however, one thing remained constant: the maintenance over the long run of complex political organizations in the Mesopotamian alluvium is incomprehensible outside the framework of a broader universe, a wider system of economic and, on occasion, political relationships between it and areas with complementary resources and societies at significantly different levels of socioeconomic integration.

The only proper framework for the study of the phenomena connected with the rise of Mesopotamian civilization, then, is one that takes into account the likelihood that sources of disequilibrium external to the alluvial system of southern Iraq were as influential in explaining the development of the particular political economy of civilization there as the internal sources illuminated by recent research. In a sense, the processes generated by those internal variables may be seen as a sort of "head start" that allowed successive societies in the south to respond actively and creatively to the conditions of disequilibrium imposed on them by the physiographic and cultural framework in which they were embedded.

One such response that has until now not received the attention it deserves was the development of long-distance exchange and cross-cultural contacts between Uruk societies in southern Mesopotamia and surrounding communities of the periphery in an attempt to secure and regularize the flow of desired resources (but see now Marfoe 1987 and Zagarell 1986). This relative lack of attention is puzzling, since long-distance exchange and state formation have been repeatedly shown to be intricately connected, whether directly through state control of the trade itself or indirectly through state control of the commodities to be exchanged and of the means (labor) for their production (Adams 1974; Alagoa 1970; Eisenstadt 1979; Terray 1974). Moreover, in the Mesopotamian case this insufficient consideration is problematic, since evidence for close contacts between societies in the southern alluvium and communities in the plains of northern Mesopotamia predating the emergence of Uruk city-states by a millennium or so has been available for almost half a century (Tobler 1950), and more recent research has consistently supported the validity of the earlier data on this point (e.g., Akkermans 1989; Breniquet 1989; J. Oates 1983).

RESOURCE PROCUREMENT STRATEGIES AND THEIR IMPACT

Although contacts between societies in the Mesopotamian alluvium and communities in the surrounding areas had existed in one form or another since prehistoric times, their intensity varied considerably through the ages. Historically, however, some factors recurred. Periods of internal coherence and centralization in the alluvium were commonly preceded by an increase in resource procurement activities and were generally followed by more or less successful processes of expansion that can be interpreted as attempts to control the critical routes of trade through which flowed needed resources.

A particularly clear and well-documented example of this phenomenon is that of the Akkadian period in the second half of the third millennium, when the sporadic raids and trade expeditions of late Early Dynastic kings were institutionalized by diverse means. These included (1) the establishment of a network of strategically located enclaves and garrisons at focal nodes along the lines of communication and transportation crisscrossing the northern Mesopotamian plains (Brak, Mari, Nuzi); (2) the extension of direct political control into the neighboring Susiana plain of Khuzestan (Susa) and the Upper Tigris area (Nineveh, Assur); (3) the intensification and regularization of trade contacts with an ever-widening circle of peripheral communities ranging from the Persian Gulf coast and beyond (Magan, Meluhha, Dilmun) to the Taurus/Anti-Taurus highlands (Silver Mountain, Purushkhanda) and still further to the coastal upland ranges of Lebanon and Syria (Cedar Forest); and (4) periodic military expeditions and raids directed against local polities not amenable to trade, such as Ebla, Armanum, Subartu, Lullubu, and Simurrum (Hirsch 1963; Larsen 1979; Foster 1977; Maeda 1984). The close correlation between sociopolitical centralization in the alluvium and expansion outward has been noted by Larsen (1979:97), who suggests that the recurrent imperial phases in Mesopotamian history may be seen simply as episodes when societies in the Mesopotamian alluvium took an especially active role in ensuring a reliable flow of resources.

The reasons why a flow of resources had to be maintained in all periods and sometimes ensured by force in specific periods are explained by contrasts in the natural resources available in the Mesopotamian alluvium and those obtainable in its periphery, as well as by differences in the sociopolitical and economic structures of societies at either end of the geographical spectrum. These differences are illuminated by diverse documentary sources dated to the third and second millennia which suggest that, for most periods, contacts between the two groups of communities were based on the flow of raw materials and, occasionally, dependent labor (slaves and prisoners of war) from the highlands to the lowlands. These peripheral resources were obtained through tribute or plunder or in return for labor-intensive processed and semiprocessed goods from the alluvium (Leemans 1960; Larsen 1987; Yoffee 1981).

If modern historical and sociological studies on development and underdevelopment may be used as a guide, conditions of asymmetrical exchange such as described would result in two parallel and closely related long-term processes: In the alluvium, the onset of contacts would have strengthened the economic, social, and political base of the communities involved. In the periphery, however, it should be expected that after an initial period of vigorous growth, a significant weakening of the socioeconomic structures of local communities would occur. The dichotomy in the impact of contacts on alluvial and peripheral societies is explained by the "spin-off" effects of the contacts on the polities involved. In the periphery, no positive spinoffs could come from having to pay tribute, having a portion of the able-bodied population deported as prisoners of war, or being plundered. Economic contacts, however, were another matter altogether. Initially at least, the onset of exchange would have represented a powerful stimulus for the emergence of more complex sociopolitical structures, particularly if the indigenous societies affected were themselves on the threshold of a social evolutionary process fueled by internal pressures.

A number of studies provide clues as to these processes. It is often the case that native elites controlling either the actual resources being exploited or access to those resources take advantage of their natural role as organizers of the means of production and (at times) mediators of the exchange to consolidate and extend their power, both in the context of their own societies and vis-à-vis their local rivals (Paynter 1981). Moreover, the destabilizing effects of exchange often lead to the further delineation of preexisting tendencies toward class differentiation within indigenous societies as a consequence of occupational specialization, whether voluntary or coerced. In many instances, the onset of contacts leads to the consolidation of elite control over labor supplies and the emergence of a class of fully or semicoerced individuals involved directly on a seasonal or permanent basis in both the extraction of resources required for the exchange and the provision of the minimal security that is a precondition for it (Terray 1974). Another common result is the growth of a specialized class, usually organized along kin lines, whose role is to act as mediators and brokers of the exchange (Daaku 1970). To summarize, in the short run, the onset of asymmetrical exchange relationships with the more advanced polities of the Mesopotamian alluvium would have unleashed substantial pressures within peripheral societies leading toward a new social order, one allowing for improved storage and distribution facilities, for exponentially more complex administrative structures, and for the ritual displays needed to validate the changes taking place in the realm of social relationships (Adams 1974).

However, the initial phase of vigorous growth in peripheral communities could not last long, since, in contrast to the sociopolitical effects just enumerated, the economic spinoffs of the exchange would have been relatively negligible: the trade itself did not involve the creation of any significant new means of production, but rather the extraction of finite unprocessed resources. A further consequence of this would be the loss of flexibility and viability of the economy of peripheral communities as those societies became increasingly overspecialized in the procurement of only a limited number of specific goods for export. In so doing, their economies would become increasingly vulnerable as they grew more and more dependent on a single market (Galtung 1971).[2] In the long run, then, the onset of contacts with more highly integrated polities in the alluvium would have resulted in two diametrically opposed processes within peripheral communities: sociopolitical structures already in place would be consolidated and strengthened and, at the very same time, the economic base needed to sustain those increasingly complex and differentiated structures would be weakened and made progressively more susceptible to eventual collapse.

In contrast, in the alluvium all of the social, political, and economic spinoffs would have been positive. Benefits to societies at the receiving end of tribute and plunder are immediately obvious, since those resources strengthen the power base of military elites in direct proportion to the weakening of the forces arrayed against them. Benefits from economic contacts, however, although similar to those already discussed for peripheral societies, would be even more far-reaching and pervasive. This is explained by the prevailing pattern of trade, which, as will be recalled, was largely based on the exchange of wholly or partially manufactured goods from the alluvium for unprocessed raw materials from the periphery. As noted by the economist Jane Jacobs (1969), asymmetrical export-driven economies such as described have important "multiplier effects" on the societies practicing them. One such effect would have been increased employment and economic expansion at the core as imports were processed and distributed and as local production for export was diversified and intensified. Jacobs's point is particularly pertinent to the Mesopotamian case, since many of the resources traditionally imported into the alluvium, such as timber, metal ores, various exotic, semiprecious, and utilitarian stones, and bitumen, required a significant degree of processing before they could be converted into usable form and incorporated into the economy (below, chap. 4). Exports, in turn, whether destined for distribution within the alluvium or for faraway markets, were labor-intensive and consisted principally of surplus grain, leather products, dried fish, dates, and textiles (Crawford 1973). The production of an exportable agricultural surplus, for example, involved the employment of armies of laborers and contingents of supervisors in order to create, maintain, and operate the necessary irrigation networks; and to harvest the grain, winnow it, store it, and finally, bale it for shipment. Similarly, the production of dried fish, dates, and leather products also required considerable manpower resources: fish have to be caught, salted, and packaged; date palms have to be pollinated and dates gathered and packaged; sheep and goats must be fed, herded, sheared, killed, and their skins have to be cut, tanned, and otherwise processed. Moreover, the production of other processed goods for export demanded an even greater investment in manpower and time. A case in point was the production of textiles, the industrial scope of which is underscored in third and early second millennium economic texts. Each major city-state had a palace-organized weaving establishment where thousands of dependent women (and, on occasion, their children) labored to process wool into finished fabrics and garments (Jacobsen 1953; Maekawa 1980; Waetzoldt 1972). The amount of time and effort spent in the production of these fabrics earmarked for foreign markets was astonishingly high. According to Larsen (1987), simple fabrics took almost a month to complete, while particularly elaborate pieces took, on occasion, well over three years.

In the Mesopotamian case, however, a further and equally important multiplier effect existed. The various activities connected with export production required scores of bureaucrats to record, store, and redistribute the output, and also to supervise the housing of laborers and the distribution of subsistence rations. Once in place, the pressures for such a bureaucratic apparatus to become self-perpetuating would have been overwhelming, since exclusive access to the imported resources and luxury goods acquired in exchange for the products manufactured by the encumbered laborers would surely be invested with significant social, political, and religious meaning and used to secure the hegemony of the bureaucratic and administrative elites (Terray 1974). A reliable flow of resources had to be ensured at all costs, then, since interruptions would have resulted in politically unacceptable socioeconomic dislocations: the reproduction and growth of the social order was predicated on the production of the exportable surpluses that, short of war, assured access to resources not available in the Mesopotamian lowlands. It is therefore clear why expansion phases occurred only at particular junctures in Mesopotamian history—in those periods when a growing economy required the taking of active and expensive steps for its maintenance.

It hardly needs to be stressed that the sort of economic spinoffs just described for the alluvial core would have been absent in the periphery. While admittedly, the extraction of specific raw materials may require potentially significant manpower expenditures, the end result of that exploitation is not further down-the-line processing employment and administrative complexity, but rather a hole in the ground or a hillside barren of trees. In brief, the asymmetrical nature of the exchange between the less developed peripheral societies and the more highly integrated communities of

the alluvium would have, over time, tended to perpetuate and magnify preexisting differences between societies at opposite ends of the exchange spectrum (Galtung 1971).

"MOMENTUM TOWARD EMPIRE" IN THE URUK PERIOD

But when exactly did an interaction system based on the ability of highly integrated societies in the Mesopotamian alluvium to mobilize and accumulate resources drawn from a far-flung periphery first develop, and moreover, how far back into Mesopotamian history can the closely associated phenomenon of recurrent imperial phases be traced?

These questions can now be addressed by reference to a growing corpus of new and reinterpreted evidence for the archaeological history of several areas on the periphery of the Mesopotamian alluvium. In the last two decades or so, archaeological research has begun to focus systematically both on the fertile alluvial plains of southwestern Iran directly east of the Mesopotamian alluvium and in the high plains of northern Mesopotamia, northern Syria, and southeastern Anatolia (hereafter Syro-Mesopotamia) directly north and northwest. Although many excavations and surveys (in the northern plains) are still in progress and much of the relevant material remains unpublished or only incompletely published, a considerably clearer picture of the archaeological development of significant sections of the Fertile Crescent outside of the Mesopotamian alluvium is beginning to emerge. For the later fourth millennium, these data have contributed to a more precise realization of the nature, intensity, and variety of contacts between polities in the Mesopotamian alluvium and communities in its periphery.

This emerging corpus of data will be the object of detailed discussions in following chapters. However, my conclusions may be anticipated by my suggesting that the data show a complex, albeit loosely integrated, supraregional interaction system similar to that described above for the Akkadian period already in place by Uruk times, almost a millennium earlier. The existence of this system can be shown directly by tracing the settlement patterns of Uruk sites outside of the Mesopotamian alluvium and the presence of typical Uruk artifacts in indigenous peripheral sites. Indirectly, its existence can be inferred from the demonstrable impact that contacts with Uruk societies had on communities in the periphery. This impact may be understood in the context of historical and ethnographic studies noted above.

The full significance of data bearing on contacts between Uruk societies of southern Iraq and Khuzestan and communities in the high plains of Syro-Mesopotamia and the highlands of Iran and Anatolia cannot be properly assessed unless the evidence from those disparate regions is looked at as a whole. Only then can a coherent pattern be discerned: by the second half of the fourth millennium, societies of the Mesopotamian alluvium were already in the midst of an intense process of expansion that took diverse forms and affected a number of areas differently. This process may be considered to represent the earliest well-attested example of the cyclical "momentum toward empire" that was to become a recurrent phenomenon throughout millennia of Mesopotamian history (Gibson 1974; Larsen 1979).

A CONCEPTUAL FRAMEWORK FOR THE ANALYSIS OF THE EVIDENCE

It is probably safe to say that archaeologists and historians have largely failed to recognize the beginnings of this cyclical "momentum toward empire" in the fourth millennium B.C. Rather, most scholars have tended to characterize the formative period of Mesopotamian civilization in terms of a progression toward increasingly centralized and complex social and political systems. This progression is seen as reaching its peak only by the second half of the third millennium with the emergence of the Akkadian empire, which is conceptualized as the first successful instance of a well-defined nexus of formal relationships of economic and political dependency encompassing a number of distinct geo-

graphic, ecological, cultural, and ethnic boundaries (Larsen 1979; Jacobsen 1957).

That the growing corpus of data bearing on the impact of Uruk societies on surrounding communities is not readily taken as evidence for a system of relationships of dependency and domination on an imperial scale comparable to that of the Akkadian period can be explained by a number of factors. First, empires and supraregional interaction systems are as diverse as the kaleidoscope of historical and geographic circumstances within which they develop. As a result, no real agreement on a definition of such phenomena has gained common currency among historians and sociologists, much less among scholars investigating the origins and development of Near Eastern civilizations. Second, scholars in the field have tended to focus primarily on processes in the cores, for which some amount of historical documentation is usually available, and have paid scant attention to processes in the periphery, often poorly documented if documented at all (Adams 1984:81). In addition, and partly as a result of this bias, those definitions that have been applied to ancient Near Eastern data have tended to overemphasize the formal aspects of territorial and political dominion over previously independent polities as the key characteristic of imperial relationships. The purely economic aspects of cross-cultural relationships of dependency and dominance are either not treated or are dealt with as important but nevertheless secondary manifestations of what is primarily conceived of as a political process.

What is needed in order to make sense out of the mass of seemingly disparate data connected with the impact of the Uruk expansion into the periphery is an interpretive scheme that is as broad as the data themselves and as flexible as they are varied. A flexible enough framework that falls well within the parameters of the supraregional perspective put forward in the preceding section is that of scholars who study issues of development and underdevelopment in the modern world (e.g., Amin 1976; Baran 1957; Emmanuel 1972; Frank 1967).

While their positions vary considerably in emphasis and methodology, their work shares a common theme: given a system of cross-cultural interdependency—as surely was required in light of the constraints, noted above, involved in the Mesopotamian case—understanding the transformations occurring in any particular subset is impossible unless related changes taking place in the other interdependent subsets are taken into account as well. These researchers have thus adopted what may be characterized as a global approach to historical change that is of considerable heuristic value to the study of the processes connected with the emergence and maintenance of civilization in the Mesopotamian alluvium. Transferring the Marxist notion of social totality (whereby all elements within a single social system exist in a matrix of mutual determinations) to a broader cross-cultural canvas (Aronowitz 1981:505), these scholars contend that social systems and their transformations must be analyzed within the context of a dynamic structure of asymmetrical relationships of interdependency, principally (but not solely) economic in nature, that in many cases originate outside of any particular region or any specific group.

Typical of this perspective is the work of the sociologist Immanuel Wallerstein (1974), who explores the widespread transformations resulting from the emergence of capitalism in Europe and the closely related phenomenon of European colonial expansion. He argues that by the late fifteenth and early sixteenth centuries A.D. the growth of capitalism in Europe had given rise to a new and enduring form of cross-cultural interaction encompassing several distinct modes of production and political formations, which he termed a "world system" or "world economy":

> It is a "world" system not because it encompasses the whole world, but because it is larger than any political unit. And it is a "world economy" because the basic linkage between the parts of the system is economic, although this was reinforced to some extent by cultural links, and eventually . . . by political arrangements." (Wallerstein 1974:15).

According to Wallerstein, this interaction system was based on a hierarchically organized division of labor that allowed a small number of politically centralized northern European core groups, often in fierce competition, to expand well beyond the boundaries of Europe and to accumulate resources drawn from a vast periphery, principally portions of the New World, Africa, Asia, and Eastern Europe. Depending on local circumstances, these peripheral areas were characterized either by weak, partially dependent, local governments or by outright colonial domination. The bond that held the various elements of the hierarchy together at any given time was economic interdependency. Cores exported manufactures to the periphery, while the latter supplied core groups with agricultural staples, bullion, and other required raw materials, whether extracted directly by coercive means, by way of tribute or taxation, or indirectly by the inherently asymmetrical nature of the exchange between the two groups.

Wallerstein's work has been reviewed extensively from widely varying methodological and theoretical viewpoints. From the perspective of those interested in reconstructing cross-cultural interaction systems that developed well before the modern age, a number of crucial points emerge from these reviews. Perhaps the most important is that Wallerstein does not recognize that the processes of asymmetrical exchange and cross-cultural interdependence that he documents for areas of the Third World transformed by modern European imperialism apply also to earlier periods and non-Western peoples (Chase-Dunn and Hall 1991; Kohl 1979; Schneider 1977). This failing is traceable to his rigid conceptualization of both ancient trade and ancient empires.

Concerning trade, Wallerstein (1974:20–21) establishes a dichotomy between what to him is largely immaterial ancient exchange based principally in "preciosities" and what he considers to have been profoundly destabilizing modern trade founded on bulk staples, bullion, and other essentials. However, this dichotomy is both false and irrelevant. It is false because, initially at least, the economic impetus for the early European voyages of discovery was not provided by demand for staples, but by the appetite of increasingly affluent European elites for exotic commodities, such as spices, sugar, and precious metals (Scammell 1989:53). And while some of these commodities (e.g., sugar) were eventually transformed into staples (Mintz 1985), that transformation was itself a consequence of the expansion. Moreover, early exchange was by no means limited to what Wallerstein would categorize as preciosities. In the case of ancient Mesopotamian civilization, for instance, evidence derived from archaeological and textual sources indicates that imports historically consisted not only of "luxuries" for elite consumption, but also of commodities such as copper and wood that must by all accounts be considered essential to the maintenance of complex social organizations in the resource-impoverished alluvial environment of southern Iraq (below, chap. 4).

At a more basic level, however, Wallerstein's dichotomy is irrelevant because the substantial impact of external exchange on the social evolution of core and peripheral societies can be shown to obtain even if the trade is largely founded on the exchange of luxury commodities. This was noted by Jane Schneider (1977), who suggests that by helping cement patron-client relationships within a single kin group and by contributing to the creation of alliances between diverse social groups, ancient trade in prestige items had a crucial role in the formation and consolidation of social inequalities. More specifically, in the context of core-periphery relationships, the export of core-manufactured prestige goods is often directly related to attempts by the core to expand its territorial or economic control in specific portions of the periphery by winning and maintaining the loyalty of subordinate local lineages (Friedman and Rowlands 1977). Conversely, in the periphery, political advantage gained through monopoly control of status-validating imports is commonly instrumental in the establishment, maintenance, and reproduction of state-level power relationships (Ekholm 1977; Frankenstein and Rowlands 1978). The Abron kingdom of Gyaman,

northeast of Ivory Coast, in Africa, is an instructive case. Using available historic data, Terray (1974) was able to show that the growth of the Abron state in the eighteenth century A.D. was intimately connected to long-distance trade in prestige items—not directly by means of control of the exchange itself, but indirectly by means of the elites' acquisition of slaves and captives for the specific purpose of producing an exportable surplus to be exchanged for the luxury goods they required.

A second and possibly more important reason why Wallerstein does not grasp the validity of his model of social change for periods significantly preceding the emergence of capital imperialism is his view of ancient empires as essentially homeostatic institutions" in which," he contends, "there is a single political system over most of the area, however attenuated the degree of its effective control" (Wallerstein 1974:84–85). Given this definition, Wallerstein differentiates between modern "world systems" and earlier "world empires" by suggesting that while in the latter the boundaries of political and economic hegemony are coterminous, in the former the extent of economic hegemony far outreaches that of political control. But here again Wallerstein's definitions are unnecessarily restrictive. A close look at some ancient empires leaves no doubt that in many cases the extent of their economic hegemony far outreached the boundaries of their political control. An extreme but by no means unique example is the "trading post empire" of Carthage in the Western Mediterranean prior to the third century B.C. Controlling little in the way of territory, the seafaring Carthaginians managed to exert an overwhelming influence in the economic life of the Western Mediterranean world by means of a number of strategically located enclaves and a network of alliances with otherwise independent local rulers (Whittaker 1978).

There is, however, an alternative to Wallerstein's approach that also falls well within the intellectual framework of studies of development and underdevelopment, avoiding some of the pitfalls of his scheme and retaining its strengths. I am referring to the work of a number of historians who have challenged explicitly and in a systematic manner the traditional views of empires as systems of primarily political relationships and of imperialism as a product of processes at work only within the imperial cores. In so doing, these scholars have adopted a broad perspective of empires and imperial phenomena that is particularly suited to the analysis of the fragmentary evidence available on the impact on the periphery of the southern Mesopotamian expansion during the Uruk period, since, as will become apparent later in the discussions, that evidence is derived almost entirely from peripheral sites and reflects contacts that are primarily economic in nature.

The view of an empire as a nexus of primarily political relationships (which mars Wallerstein's analysis and which appears to be prevalent among many orientalists) was called into question by the publication some forty years ago of a controversial review of British imperialism in the nineteenth century written by Jack Gallagher and Ronald Robinson (1953). They dispute the basic tenet of the more traditional interpretations of the nature of empires and imperial phenomena by contending that those interpretations neglect a whole range of informal, but nevertheless equally influential, types of domination that usually precede, commonly accompany, and on occasion even substitute entirely for more formal political ties. In their view, it is dependency that is at the root of imperial relationships. The actual form that those relationships of dependency take, whether political or economic, is of secondary importance. Formal political rule and territorial dominion are seen only as the most specific and easily defined mode of imperialistic dependency, but by far not the only one, nor even the most common. Furthermore, they argue that formal political ties need not develop in all cases and when those ties do develop it is usually only after a process of "informal" economic penetration that is in effect also a mode of imperialistic domination.

For Gallagher and Robinson, then, the refusal or failure to use formal methods of control, that is to say, political annexation, has no bearing on the ability of one society to control another. For them,

it is economic dominance that is the irreducible common denominator of imperial systems. The defining characteristic shared by all imperial systems at their onset is the integration of new regions into an expanding economy. Depending on specific local circumstances, some systems may never develop beyond this initial stage, while others may go on to develop more formal political ties. However, these juxtaposed "formal" and "informal" modes of domination are not necessarily mutually exclusive stages in a linear evolutionary process, but represent instead complementary aspects of a continuum.

In a later publication, Gallagher and Robinson (1961) went on to challenge explicitly what they perceived to be another of the failings of the more traditional interpretations of imperialism. In their view, theories that attempt to understand relationships of dependency only on the basis of social, political, or economic developments in the core are ignoring a whole range of equally vital factors at work in the periphery (Robinson 1976). In particular, the authors noted that the onset of relationships of economic dependency (i.e., informal empire) will in the long run result in one of two mutually exclusive responses in the periphery: most frequently, the collapse of the preexisting political order requiring the imperial power to step in formally to fill the power vacuum or else to abandon the area altogether; less frequently, the strengthening of indigenous sociopolitical structures until local communities become expansive in their own right.

The conceptual underpinnings of Wallerstein's work, with modifications as noted above, and the broader view of imperial systems propounded by Gallagher and Robinson have an important bearing on the interpretation of emerging data on the dynamics of expansion of Uruk societies. From the perspective of the core, those dynamics may be profitably visualized within a framework of cross-cultural interdependency, largely economic in nature, and competition between rival polities. From the perspective of the periphery, however, the expansion of Uruk societies can be conceptualized in terms of a continuum from more formal to more informal modes of imperial domination. External contacts in the Uruk period followed a number of different approaches that were conditioned by varying geography, ecology, and previous settlement history. A more formal mode involving an actual process of colonization is evinced in nearby areas, such as southwestern Iran, where indigenous settlement was in decline and where, as in the Mesopotamian alluvium itself, irrigation agriculture was practicable. However, in more distant areas where the economic subsistence base was different from that of the alluvium and where native settlement was not in decline, such as the plains of Syro-Mesopotamia, Uruk settlements appear only at strategic locations, principally at the juncture of the most important overland routes and waterways. The policy that can be inferred is one of "informal" economic control.

The evidence for these complementary contact strategies will now be discussed in detail. Chapter 2 will explore the context and nature of Uruk settlement in southwestern Iran, and chapters 3 to 6 are devoted to the different strategies and consequences of contacts between Uruk societies and indigenous communities in the plains of northern Mesopotamia, northern Syria, and southeastern Anatolia. In particular, chapter 3 examines the character of southern Mesopotamian settlements in the north, the strategic rationale that underlies their locational pattern, and their chronology, and chapter 4 focuses on their function. Chapter 5 presents available evidence for the nature of indigenous societies in the periphery and explores how preexisting conditions helped shape the strategies of Uruk contacts with those societies. Chapter 6 goes on to review the range of archaeological evidence from peripheral sites attesting to possible changes in the social texture of local communities unleashed by the intrusion of southern Mesopotamian elements into the area. The concluding chapter looks at the evidence from the eastern and northern periphery as a whole in terms of the conceptual framework put forward here and explores what the data mean in terms of our understanding of the earliest development of southern Mesopotamian civilization. Individual subsections briefly examine remaining problems in our comprehension of processes relating to the Uruk expansion and offer some suggestions for further research.

2

Uruk Sites in the Susiana Plain of Khuzestan

Recent research has made the archaeological history of the various plains of southwestern Iran one of the best understood in the ancient Near East. The pioneering framework of Le Breton (1957) for Susiana, historically the most important of those plains, has now been amplified and clarified by new excavations at the important centers of Susa (Le Brun 1971, 1978a) and Chogha Mish (Delougaz and Kantor, n.d.), by excavations at various smaller nearby sites (Johnson 1976; Wright et al. 1980), and by numerous surveys (Adams 1962; Alden 1987; Johnson 1973, 1987). Moreover, a variety of complementary research also exists for the surrounding plains (H. T. Wright 1979, 1981a, 1987). This evidence leaves no doubt that throughout the second half of the fourth millennium B.C., in the Uruk period, communities in southwestern Iran developed in ways that were increasingly analogous to those of the alluvial lowlands of southern Iraq, the Sumerian heartland. This convergence represented a sharp reversal of a millennia-old trend toward increasing regional differentiation in the cultural assemblages of the two areas and, I would argue, indicates an outright process of colonization of the plains of Khuzestan by settlers from the Mesopotamian alluvium. To some degree, this process may be conceptualized within the framework of the more formal modes of imperial relationships discussed in the preceding chapter.

GEOGRAPHICAL FRAMEWORK

Hemmed in between the Zagros highlands to the east and the Tigris-Euphrates lowlands to the west are the closely connected plains of southwestern Iran, from west to east: Deh Luran, Susiana, Ram Hormuz, Behbahan, and Zuhreh. The largest and most fertile of these is the Susiana plain. It represents an extension eastward, at a slightly higher elevation, of the alluvial plains of southern Mesopotamia (fig. 1). More specifically, Susiana is formed by alluvial deposits from the Karun, Karkheh, and Dez rivers, which collectively drain the Luristan highlands to the north and much of the south-central Zagros to the east. The plain receives varying amounts of rainfall, with precipitation increasing as the Zagros piedmont is approached and decreasing toward the southwest in the direction of the Tigris-Euphrates basin and the Persian Gulf. Historically, settlement in Susiana concentrated in the area north of the Haft Tepe ridge, which is closest to the Zagros and is also the best watered. Here, average annual precipitation is in the 250–400 millimeter range, and successful rainfed agriculture is the norm in all but the driest years (Fischer 1968;

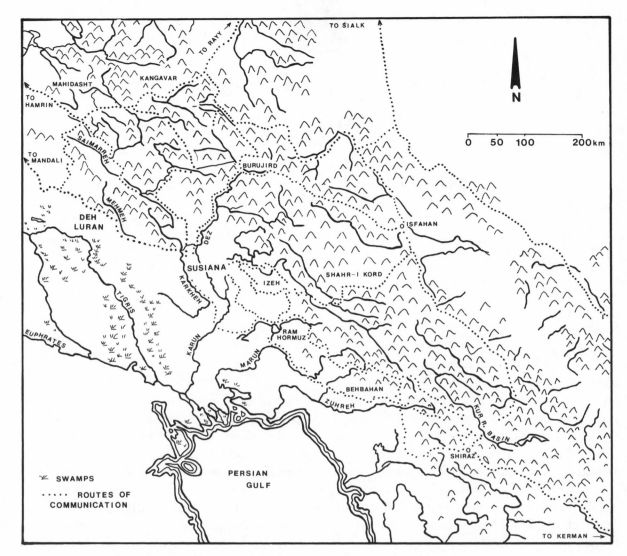

Fig. 1. Southwestern Iran: principal plains, rivers, and routes of communication.

Kirkby 1977). Moreover, until relatively recent times, aggradation rather than incision was the principal feature of river regimes in southwestern Iran, so that both winter and summer irrigation would have been possible across Susiana with minimal effort in the past (Kirkby 1977).

Although bounded to the north and east by successive folds of the Zagros Mountains, access between the Susiana lowlands and the central plateau of Iran is possible via an array of routes that cut across high intermontane plains in the Zagros and mountain passes farther inland (fig. 1). Routes along the Ram Hormuz and Behbahan plains lead southeast and eventually emerge in the Kur River basin of Fars (Hansman 1972; Stein 1940). To the east, routes traversing the Izeh (Malamir) plain and the Bakhtiari Mountains permit passage onto the environs of Isfahan and ultimately into the mineral-rich region in the vicinity of Qum and the Dasht-i Kavir, the Great Salt Desert (Zagarell 1982). Communication northward is made possible by tracks up the various tributaries of the Dez and Karkheh rivers which cross the mountain ranges of Luristan and come out in the Hamadan plain. Susiana is separated from the Mesopotamian alluvium to the west by seasonal and highly variable marshes and lagoons into which the Karkheh River drains and by a series of barren sandstone and gypsum hills with few permanent sources of water (Goff 1971; Stein 1940). Nevertheless, contacts between the two areas were relatively easy, a factor that may account for the close cultural connections that may be discerned between them in some periods. Historically, the most important land route connecting the two regions keeps to the north of the Karkheh marshes and crosses the Deh Luran plain diagonally before skirting the western flank of the Kabir Kuh range and emerging in the Diyala River basin (H. T. Wright 1981a:264).

MESOPOTAMIAN COLONIZATION

The Susiana plain constituted the core of Uruk settlement in southwestern Iran. While Uruk sites are also found in the neighboring plains, by and large settlement in those plains appears to have fluctuated in direct proportion, and possibly in response, to developments in the more central Susiana region (Wright 1987), which is therefore the focus of the discussions that follow.

The results of the various surveys and excavations in Susiana show that by the later part of the Uruk sequence (Middle/Late Uruk in local terminology) the plain had become part and parcel of the Mesopotamian world, an extension eastward of the culture and institutions prevalent in the lowlands of southern Iraq. The surveys of Wright and Johnson, in particular, document with precision the pattern of Uruk settlement in Susiana at this time: in the Middle Uruk period the principal centers were Susa and Chogha Mish on opposite ends of the plain. The former is situated on the Shaur River, a small tributary of the Dez, and at some 25 hectares commanded the western portion of the plain. Chogha Mish was also positioned along a tributary of the Dez, the Shureh River. At 18 hectares, Chogha Mish was only slightly smaller than Susa

and dominated the eastern portion of the Susiana plain (Johnson 1973, 1987). Surrounding these central occupations and scattered across the plain were numerous subsidiary sites and villages (fig. 2). By the final phase of the Uruk period, however, important changes had taken place. Overall regional settlement density declined as many villages were abandoned along a 15-kilometer-wide band of territory roughly equidistant to each of the two principal centers, resulting in sharply polarized settlement clusters at either end of the Susiana plain. Johnson (1987) interprets these changes as reflecting the onset of intraregional conflict in Susiana. The size of Susa may have declined at this time, but this is unclear.[1] Just before the very end of this phase, however, Chogha Mish was either abandoned or contracted significantly (Dittmann 1986a:344).[2]

In spite of the settlement pattern changes just noted between the Middle and Late Uruk phases, there is little change in the size range attested for Uruk sites across Susiana. Included in each phase are numerous small agricultural villages 1–2 hectares in size, larger villages averaging 5–7 hectares, small "towns" in the 10–12 hectare range, and the small urban centers of Susa and Chogha Mish (Johnson 1973). The material culture of these sites is homogeneous throughout the plain. Excavations at both the largest centers and smaller sites in their vicinity indicate that the artifactual assemblages of Middle/Late Uruk sites across Susiana and contemporary sites in the Mesopotamian alluvium are analogous (Amiet 1986), allowing us to equate the Susa Acropolis I (Levels [20?]19–17) and Chogha Mish (Protoliterate B) sequences in Susiana with the Eanna VI–IV (Warka) and Inanna XX–XV (Nippur) sequences of southern Iraq (Strommenger 1980b:486).[3] Parallels between the two areas are not limited to ceramic assemblages that are largely identical (e.g., fig. 3A–H)—although a few types in southwestern Iran do betray contacts with the nearby highlands—but include conspicuous similarities in glyptic practices, accounting procedures (tokens, balls, bullae, and tablets), and iconogra-

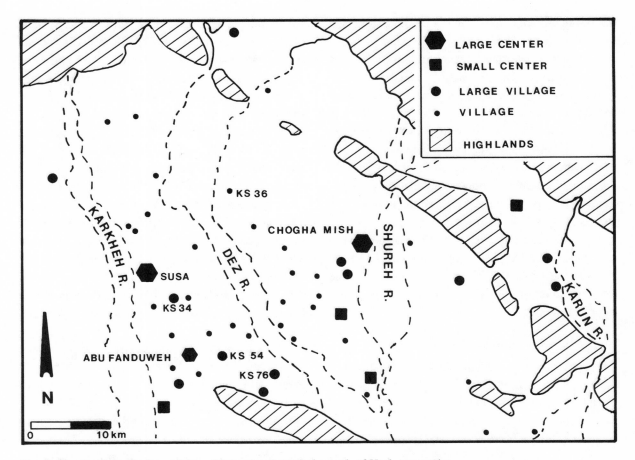

Fig. 2. The northern Susiana plain: settlement pattern at the peak of Uruk occupation.

phy as well. Moreover, if we may extrapolate from depictions in Uruk glyptic in Susiana, traditions of monumental and religious architecture also appear to have been uniform across the two areas (fig. 3Y–BB).[4]

The striking parallels that may be observed between the material culture of the Mesopotamian alluvium and the Susiana plain in the later part of the Uruk period have important implications for our conceptualization of the development of Susiana in the second half of the fourth millennium. Equivalent sealing and accounting practices in each of the two regions indicate uniform record keeping and administrative procedures (Schmandt-Besserat 1986) (fig. 3S–X). In turn, this may suggest the existence of largely analogous institutions—particularly if Nissen (1977) is correct in seeing the schematic seals that are common to both areas (often depicting pigtailed women at work, e.g., fig. 3N, Q) as lower-level institutional seals. Comparable modes of social organization are also suggested by iconographical similarities in the fully modeled glyptic repertoires of each area: in each case it is the same larger-than-life male figure wearing his hair in a chignon who is depicted at the apex of the administrative and religious hierarchy (e.g., fig. 3M, P).[5] Other iconographic parallels evince a shared mythology (e.g., fig. 3I–L), and possibly even the existence of common religious rituals, as may be inferred from representations of apparently identical offerings brought into temples (e.g., fig. 3O, R).[6]

The evidence just outlined leaves little doubt that in the later part of the Uruk period Susiana was culturally as much a part of the Mesopotamian world as the alluvium itself. Any consideration of the emergence of Uruk civilization, therefore, must

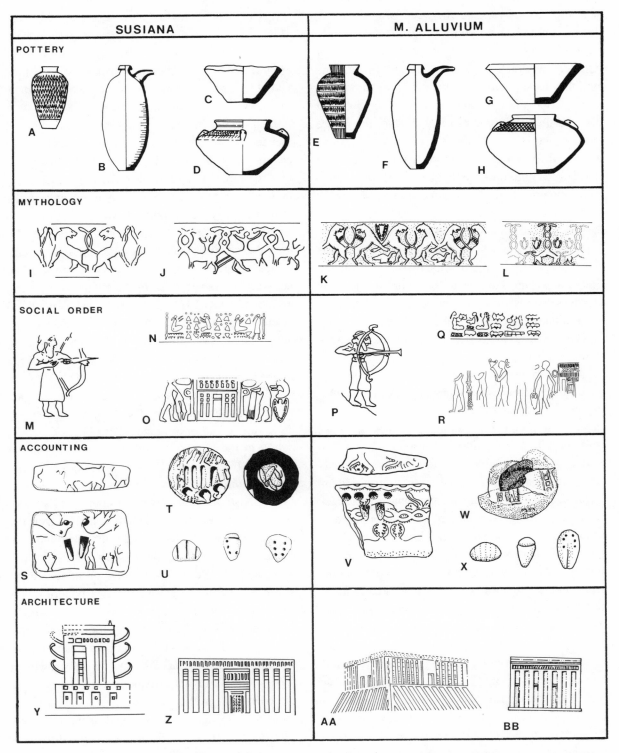

Fig. 3. Selected parallels between the cultural assemblages of the Susiana plain and the Mesopotamian alluvium in the Late Uruk Period (not to scale).

take into account the role of Susiana in that process. How did this convergence between two previously distinct culture areas come about? Henry Wright and Gregory Johnson see it as the natural result of long-term interaction between societies in Susiana and the Mesopotamian alluvium throughout the Uruk period (Wright and Johnson 1985; Johnson 1987, 1988/89). While this is plausible, the nature of the proposed interaction is yet to be defined, and the social mechanisms at work within societies in Susiana leading to the remarkable processes of acculturation must still be clarified. In the meantime, another possibility may be suggested to account for the convergence in material culture between the two areas: that the pervasive Uruk elements in Susiana denote a process of colonization by settlers from the nearby alluvium. I use the term "colonization" in its classic sense as implying an actual movement of population for the purpose of acquiring and holding territory and exploiting its economic resources (Finley 1976).

The colonization hypothesis is defended by an increasing number of scholars (e.g., Amiet 1986; Lamberg-Karlovsky 1985; Nissen 1983; Sürenhagen 1986a) and in my opinion fits best the data available. First, it explains the overwhelmingly Sumerian character of elite activities and material culture in Susiana by the later half of the fourth millennium. Second, it accounts for the apparently longer evolution of the Uruk tradition in Iraq as opposed to Khuzestan. Traditionally, the Late Susiana sequence of southwestern Iran has been thought to overlap with the very beginnings of the Early Uruk period in the alluvium. This was suggested initially by Le Breton (1957:94) more than thirty years ago on the basis of intuitive stylistic comparisons. His insight now appears supported by the absence in Susiana of a variety of pottery types that are found only at the onset of the Early Uruk sequence at Warka and disappear shortly thereafter (Adams 1981:60).[7] Another indication of a time lag between the start of the Uruk tradition in the two areas is provided by a comparison of available clusters of radiocarbon dates from Late Susiana levels at Susa and Jaffarabad in Susiana, from Bayat-phase con-

texts at Tepe Sabz in Deh Luran, and from Ubaid 4 levels at Tell el'Ouelli in the alluvium (J. Oates 1983: fig. 9). Recalibrated under a single standard, the Late Susiana dates from Khuzestan are consistently later by a few centuries than those from Late Ubaid levels in the alluvium, which actually equate instead with the earlier Bayat range.

Third, the colonization hypothesis explains the archaeological break in the Susiana sequence preceding *and* following the Uruk period. This break is discernible in significant changes in the settlement pattern of the Susiana plain at the onset of the Uruk tradition that would otherwise be difficult to account for. These changes contrast dramatically with the situation in the Mesopotamian alluvium, where cultural continuity appears to have been the norm at the transition from the Ubaid to the Uruk periods (Adams 1981:59). This is best exemplified at the southern site of Eridu, where earlier Ubaid temples give way without interruption to ever more massive Uruk structures built along the very same lines (Safar, Lloyd, and Mustafa 1981). Not so in southwestern Iran. At Susa the massive stepped platform on the center of the acropolis was abandoned at the end of the Late Susiana period. Occupation at the site continued into the Uruk period (Canal 1978; Wright 1984b), but extended only over a diminished area of the acropolis (Johnson 1973). Also abandoned were a number of smaller dependent settlements in its environs (G. Dollfus, quoted in Weiss 1983:42). A parallel abandonment can be observed at Chogha Mish (H. J. Kantor, pers. comm., 1987). The dislocation of settlement at Susa and Chogha Mish reflects a pattern of regional significance. The onset of the Uruk tradition in Susiana was marked by a large jump in the number of settlements, and total occupied area trebles in the earliest Uruk phase—a substantial growth in population that reversed demographic trends of the preceding half millennium in the area (Wright and Johnson 1975: table III). The end of the Uruk tradition in Susiana is as disjunctive as its onset, and this serves to emphasize again the intrusive character of the Uruk presence in the area. Chogha Mish is once again abandoned, the size of Susa diminishes significantly for a second time (Alden 1987), and, in at least some portions of the site, there is a clear break in the archaeological and artifactual sequence (Acropolis I, Levels 17 and 16; see Le Brun 1971). Regionally, these changes are accompanied by a precipitous decline in total occupied area: settlement declines by a factor of three in comparison to the end of the Uruk period and by a factor of six in comparison with the earlier peak of Uruk settlement (Alden 1987).

Fourth, the colonization hypothesis explains the settlement pattern of the Susiana plain in the still little understood Early Uruk period, when settlements concentrate around Susa and Abu Fanduweh on the western portion of the plain—the one closest to the alluvium. In contrast, the eastern portion of Susiana, where Chogha Mish would eventually emerge as an important regional center, appears only lightly settled at the time, in spite of an agricultural potential that equaled that of the environs of Susa (Johnson 1987: table 21). Finally, the colonization hypothesis explains the full spectrum of Uruk site sizes and concomitant functions across the plain as well as the homogeneity of Uruk material culture throughout the region. Mesopotamian materials are found at all sites, from major administrative centers to the smallest hamlets whose location and size leave no doubt as to their rural orientation. If the Uruk presence in Susiana did not represent a process of wholescale regional colonization as has been argued, then we should expect to find archaeologically identifiable and spatially segregated traces of a different but contemporary tradition in the area. Such a pattern is in fact discernible in the environs of specialized Uruk outposts across the Mesopotamian periphery (below, chap. 3) but has not been recognized in the Susiana region—arguably one of the most intensively surveyed of the Near East.

The evidence for a colonization of the Susiana plain by settlers from the alluvium in the Uruk period is, I believe, compelling. Yet we know little about the actual mechanics of the process and less still about what happened to the supposedly few indigenous inhabitants of the area at the time of the Uruk intrusion. Two possibilities could help account for the lack of pertinent evidence. One is that a portion of the original population may have shifted into a more nomadic existence, largely undocumented in the archaeological record. The second is that the remaining population was partially assimilated. As Amiet (1979a, 1979b) has perceptively noted, this last assumption finds some support in artifactual evidence from Susa, where numerical notation tablets with a single pictogram,[8] possibly in Proto-Elamite script, suggest the existence of a native substratum under the broad layer of elite Uruk culture revealed by the archaeological evidence reviewed above.

CHRONOLOGY AND CONCLUSIONS

Until the still relatively unknown Early Uruk sequences of the Mesopotamian alluvium and the Susiana plain become better documented, it will not be possible to ascertain exactly at what point in the Uruk sequence the colonization of the latter area started. It will be recalled that a number of ceramic types that appear early in the Uruk sequence at Warka and disappear soon thereafter are absent from Susiana, suggesting the existence of a time lag between the onset of the Uruk tradition in southern Iraq and its introduction into southwestern Iran. The problem of equating the two sequences is compounded further by the fact that many of the types that have been identified as "Early Uruk" in the seriation of surface survey collections in Susiana have no parallels in the deep sounding at Warka, which unfortunately remains our only guide to the earlier portion of the Uruk sequence in the alluvium.[9] Moreover, while the remaining Early Uruk Susiana types do appear early in the Eanna sequence, most also continue into later levels.[10]

The chronological difficulties in correlating the earlier portions of the Uruk sequences in Susiana and the alluvium mean that we cannot properly assess at this time the original impetus behind the Mesopotamian intrusion into Susiana. A tantalizing hypothesis, however, may be suggested for future testing. This is that the colonization of Susiana may be a collateral result of settlement dislocations and north-south population shifts taking place within the Mesopotamian alluvium during the earlier half of the Uruk period as a result of the drying up of a major channel of either the ancient Tigris or Euphrates (Adams 1981; Gibson 1973, 1976).

Whatever its roots, it seems clear that the Mesopotamian intrusion did not cause the collapse of the indigenous prehistoric cultures of the Susiana plain. Rather, it merely took advantage of an internal process of disintegration that was at the time well advanced. The various Susiana surveys indicate that population and settlement densities peaked in the last half of the fifth millennium (Middle Susiana 3) and declined throughout the earlier half of the fourth millennium (Susa I or Late Susiana period) (Wright and Johnson 1975: table III). This endogenous process is still poorly understood but parallels similar developments in the Kur River basin of Fars (Sumner 1977, 1986) and the various highland plains surrounding Susiana (H. T. Wright 1987). Paradoxically, Susa emerged as an important center precisely while regional population densities slumped (H. T. Wright 1984a, 1986). Nevertheless, surveys show that by the very end of the Late Susiana period (Transitional Susa A), Susa too had declined and no single preeminent site existed in Susiana (Johnson 1973: fig. 15).

In terms of its economic and political potential, then, Susiana was largely undeveloped at the onset of the Uruk period. Uruk settlers were thus drawn into a fertile and potentially quite productive area that was only lightly settled and could surely mount only minimal resistance. However, to speak of an Uruk intrusion and of the colonization of the Susiana by Uruk settlers is not to imply the existence of a well-coordinated effort by a single Uruk community holding sway over the whole plain. This is incompatible with the evidence presented by Johnson for interregional warfare within Susiana in the final phase of the Uruk period. Susa and Chogha Mish thus appear to have been independent from each other, and almost certainly were also independent from contemporary polities in the Mesopotamian alluvium.

The Mesopotamian intrusion in southwestern Iran was by no means an isolated phenomenon. Rather, it should be understood within a wider framework of analysis that takes into account other processes of expansion of societies in the Mesopotamian alluvium in the Uruk period that the move into Susiana may have helped spur. However, these varying processes appear to have been of a significantly different nature and did not involve the taking over of large expanses of territory. One such process was the establishment of a number of strategically located Uruk enclaves in areas of the north and northwestern periphery of the alluvium, which represented a critical geographical link between the resource-starved Mesopotamian lowlands and large portions of the surrounding highlands where coveted resources were obtainable.

3

Uruk Settlements in the Syro-Mesopotamian Plains and Surrounding Highlands

The settlement pattern of Uruk sites in the high plains of northern Mesopotamia, northern Syria, and southeastern Anatolia, the area that here for the sake of convenience is referred to simply as Syro-Mesopotamia, differs markedly from that just described for the Susiana plain. Whereas in Susiana Uruk sites are found in a whole range of sizes spread more or less evenly over the landscape, in the Syro-Mesopotamian plains only a small number of urban-sized enclaves are found. In those cases where the evidence is most coherent, it can be seen that these centers were surrounded by a cluster of immediately dependent villages and that they were established at locations of considerable strategic importance. When Uruk sites are found away from these clusters, they are always small, isolated, and appear to have been closely linked to overland routes in and out of the northern plains. This varying settlement pattern is indicative of a set of relationships with indigenous communities that may be profitably conceptualized within the framework of the more informal (i.e., economic) modes of imperial relationships discussed in the introductory chapter and is surely attributable to a number of factors, including distance away from the alluvium and the previous settlement history of the intruded areas. However, another element that was of considerable importance in shaping the pattern of Uruk

settlement in the northern plains was the historical role of the region as a land of passage, a bridge connecting a number of disparate but complementary environmental and cultural areas. Thus, before proceeding to an examination of the nature and intensity of contacts between southern Mesopotamia and its north and northwestern periphery in the Uruk period and how those contacts affected the subsequent development of preexisting polities, it is necessary to review the evidence for the geography and climate of the Syro-Mesopotamian plains, factors that more than anything else are responsible for the historical role of the area as a hub of overland communications.

GEOGRAPHICAL FRAMEWORK

Even a cursory review of the physical geography of the Near East reveals that the high plains of Syro-Mesopotamia constitute an unusually coherent unit of study. In great measure, this coherence is derived from the fact that the area is characterized by a distinctive topography, hydrology, and climate that stand in sharp contrast to the corresponding features of immediately surrounding regions. In simplified fashion, Syro-Mesopotamia may be characterized as a series of undulating plains directly south of the massive Taurus/Anti-Taurus range of Anatolia and extending from the Assyrian foothills of the Zagros range in the east to the Amanus Mountains and the Jebel Zawiyah paralleling the Mediterranean coast in the west. Within this broad area, terrain elevation and precipitation vary considerably, both being higher toward the north and northeast in the direction of the Taurus/Zagros piedmont. The elevation and rainfall gradients diminish slowly toward the south as the plains become progressively lower, drier, and more marginal. The effective southern limit of the Syro-Mesopotamian plains is thus marked more by the decline in rainfall than by geographical relief and accordingly varies from year to year. In average years, however, a range in the 300–350 millimeter isohyet may be considered as the minimum necessary to safeguard against catastrophic crop failure.[1] That range falls somewhere along an imaginary arc immediately south and east of Aleppo, just south of Carchemish on the Euphrates, north of Hassaka on the Khabur, and south of Mosul on the Tigris (fig. 4). Settlement and agriculture concentrate north of this arc, and the combination of relatively abundant precipitation, Irano-Turanian steppe vegetation, and deeply incised rivers means that there is a heavy emphasis on extensive dry-farmed grain cultivation in the vicinity of settled areas and pastoralism elsewhere. South of this arc, human occupations become increasingly rare and are restricted to small patches in the immediate vicinity of the floodplains of the perennial waterways, where local irrigation is possible if weirs are built and canals dug.

In somewhat greater detail, it is possible to subdivide the Syro-Mesopotamian plains into three subregions. From west to east these are: the Syrian Saddle, the northern Mesopotamian plains (el-Jezira), and the Transtigridian Plains. These subregions will now be examined in greater detail (fig. 4).

The Syrian Saddle

West of the Levantine coast and the Amanus and Jebel Zawijah ranges are the high plains of the Syrian Saddle, the area that may be identified entirely with the Syria of classical sources.[2] On their northwestern end and wedged between the Amanus and the Jebel Ansariyah are the plains of Antioch and Islahiyeh, traditional gateways between Syria and southern Anatolia. Because of their proximity to the surrounding mountains and the Mediterranean climatic region, annual average precipitation in the Antioch/Islahiyeh areas is high (400–500 mm), and this ensures reliable rainfed crops even in unusually dry years (Braidwood 1937). The rest of the Syrian Saddle is composed primarily of fertile Terra Rosa soils and represents an easily traversed region devoid of sharp internal subdivisions. It is best described as a broad, relatively well-watered upland plain interrupted by low undulating hills and shallow valleys, which slope gently from north to south away from the Taurus/Anti-Taurus and from west to east in the direction of the Euphrates. The northern portion of this area, in the environs of Gaziantep, is formed by rolling plains cut by a number of small rivers, including the Suban Su, the Afrin Su, the Nizip Su, and the upper reaches of the Sajur Su. To the south is the plain of Aleppo, watered by the Qoueiq River. Arguably the most important and agriculturally most productive region of modern Syria, the Aleppo region receives adequate precipitation, averaging some 300–400 millimeters per year (Dorrell 1981). East and southward from Aleppo in the direction of the Euphrates, however, the Syrian Saddle becomes progressively drier, more eroded, and more marginal as it approaches and gently blends into the northern reaches of the Syrian desert (Grant 1937). Historically, this area has been exploited primarily by nomadic or semi-nomadic pastoralists, although some dry-farmed cereals may be grown in good years, particularly in the environs of the Sajur basin (British Admiralty 1919, 1943; Wirth 1971).

The Jezira of Mesopotamia

Separated from the Syrian Saddle by the Euphrates River and extending eastward up to the Tigris are the high plains of northern Mesopotamia, often referred to by their Arabic name el-Jezira. The Jezira plains slope gently in a southeast direction away from the Taurus to the north and the Euphrates in the west. In addition to the Euphrates and

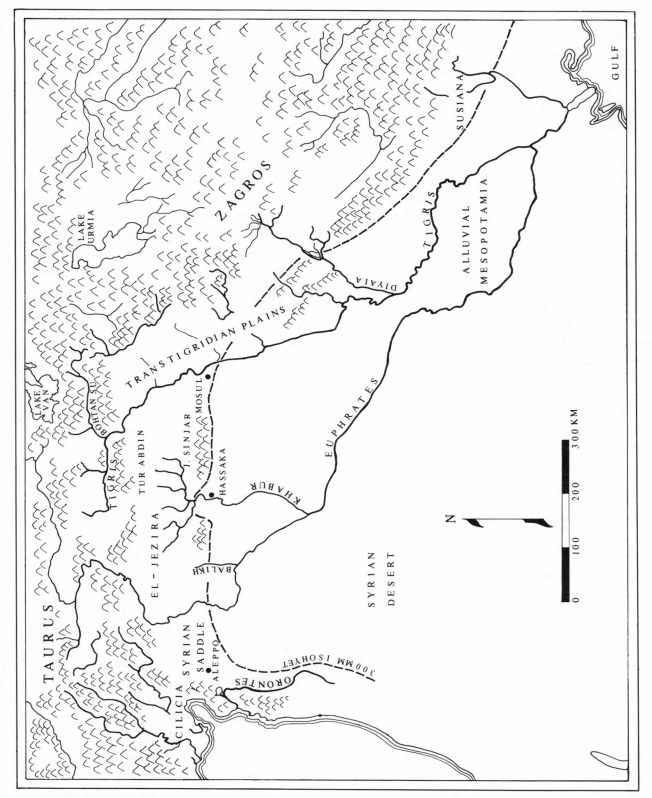

Fig. 4. Northern Syria, northern Mesopotamia, and southeastern Anatolia: principal geographic features and sub-divisions of the Syro-Mesopotamian plains.

Tigris rivers, the Jezira is also cut by the Balikh and Khabur rivers, the two principal east bank tributaries of the Euphrates. The area is also interrupted by two parallel mountain chains, the Karacadağ/Tur Abdin to the north and the Jebel abd el-Aziz/Jebel Sinjar to the south. The Tur Abdin group, some 200 kilometers in length, is the most massive of the two. The southern chain is more modest and is broken by the Lower Khabur River. Both sets of mountains run roughly parallel to the Taurus along an east-west axis and effectively divide northern Mesopotamia into two parallel sets of plains (Wirth 1971; British Admiralty 1943, 1944). The main and historically most important of these plains is that traditionally referred to as the High or Upper Jezira: an irregular band of gently undulating terrain located entirely north of the abd el-Aziz/Sinjar ranges (Dillemann 1962; van Liere and Laufrey 1954/55). Average yearly precipitation is high and the degree of interannual variability is relatively low. A range of 400–500 millimeters per year is common at the foot of the Tur Abdin, while averages of 200–250 millimeters are the norm in the environs of the Jebel Sinjar (Wirth 1971: map 3). Toward the west in the direction of the Euphrates, the Upper Jezira is relatively barren except in winter and spring and is characterized by gentle limestone ridges interrupted by deeply incised seasonal wadis and, occasionally, by relatively extensive alluvial plains such as that of Harran (Erinç 1980). The eastern sector of the Upper Jezira, however, is well watered, since the area is cut by a number of perennial streams which drain the southern flank of the Tur Abdin massif and form the funnel-shaped headwaters of the Khabur River. The plains in this region flatten out toward the south and southeast as the abd el-Aziz/Sinjar ranges are approached and in general are covered with fertile alluvial soil (Dobel 1978).

In contrast to the agriculturally rich Upper Jezira, the Lower Jezira is formed by a dry, flat, and relatively featureless steppe extending southward from both the 200–250 millimeter isohyet and the abd el-Aziz/Sinjar range down to the flat alluvial plains of Babylonia. With few exceptions—such as the area immediately south of the Jebel Sinjar, which receives higher precipitation rates on account of the nearby mountains, and specific low-lying portions near the confluence of the Balikh and Khabur and the Euphrates, where gravity-flow irrigation becomes practicable—habitation in the Lower Jezira is only possible in relatively narrow strips immediately adjacent to the perennial watercourses (British Admiralty 1943, 1944).

The Transtigridian Plains

East and northeast of the Tigris rise the Transtigridian Plains, a crescent-shaped extension of the northern Mesopotamian plains in the direction of the eastern Taurus and the Kurdish sector of the Zagros highlands. The region is characterized by grassy rolling hills and depressions, which become increasingly sharper as the lower mountain folds are approached. The Transtigridian Plains are cut by a number of east bank tributaries of the Tigris draining the western flank of the Zagros, the most important being the (eastern) Khabur/Hezil Su, the Khosr, the Greater Zab, the Lesser Zab, the Adhaim, and the Diyala. Together, these tributaries divide the area wedged between the Tigris and the highlands into five distinct sections, each characterized by a relatively broad upland plain extending southwestward from the point the rivers emerge from the mountains. From north to south these are the Cizre-Zakho, the Mosul, the Erbil, the Kirkuk, and the Diyala/Hamrin plains. Each of these plains, in turn, controls access to the principal highland passes across the surrounding highlands. Average yearly precipitation decreases toward the southwest but is on the whole abundant, with the greater portion of the Transtigridian Plains in the 300–400 and 400–500 millimeter isohyet range (British Admiralty 1944; Weiss 1983: 39–42, figs. 2–3).

The role of the Syro-Mesopotamian plains as a land of passage uniting otherwise distinct regions derives in great measure from the topography and climate of the area. The relatively well-watered plains and their significant agricultural potential ensure the availability of natural grasslands for use as fodder as well as other needed supplies. Unless outweighed by political considerations, these environmental factors make of the Syro-Mesopotamian plains a natural thoroughfare for east-west and north-south communication across the Near East. They represent the only juncture where overland routes from the Anatolian and Iranian plateaus, the Mediterranean coast, the Mesopotamian alluvium, and the Persian Gulf unite into a single network (Semple 1930). Prior to the extensive use of the camel for transportation and the opening of long-distance routes across the more barren sectors of the Syro-Arabian desert sometime in the later half of the second millennium B.C., overland routes in and out of the Mesopotamian alluvium had to follow either the Tigris or the Euphrates northward into Syro-Mesopotamia. The strategic importance of the area was not lost on societies of southern Mesopotamia in the Uruk period, which attempted with some success to dominate the critical lines of communication crisscrossing the region.

URUK ENCLAVES IN SYRO-MESOPOTAMIA

Discovery and Background

Only recently, as research has begun to be focused in a systematic manner on the Syro-Mesopotamian plains, has it become possible to characterize the settlement pattern of Uruk sites in the area. The last two decades or so, in fact, have witnessed a veritable revolution in our understanding of the archaeological history of Syro-Mesopotamia, as the number of surveys and excavations has grown exponentially. Much of the impetus for this research has been provided by the construction of dams on the principal waterways of the Syro-Mesopotamian plains. Along the Euphrates, for example, the construction of the Keban Dam in the late 1960s and early 1970s opened significant portions of the nearby Anatolian highlands to archaeological exploration, in particular the Malatya, Altınova, and Elazig plains (Whallon 1979). Just south of the Keban area, two additional dams

were erected during the 1980s, the Karakaya and Atatürk (formerly Karababa) dams. The latter is the largest in Turkey and is now in the final stages of construction. The building of these dams, in turn, resulted in the exploration of large portions of the Taurus piedmont and considerable stretches of the terraces flanking the upper elbow of the Euphrates bend in southeastern Turkey (Özdoğan 1977; Wilkinson 1990a). Similarly, plans for two further dams south of the Atatürk region, the Birecik and Carchemish dams, have resulted in recent surveys of most of the remaining stretch of the Euphrates in Turkey up to the Syrian border (Algaze 1989a; Algaze et al. 1991). This growing corpus of archaeological information from southeastern Anatolia is complemented by excavations and surveys downstream in northeastern Syria resulting from the construction of the Tabqa and Tishreen dams. The latter is now being erected near Menbij, while the former was built two decades ago in the lower elbow of the Upper Euphrates bend (van Loon 1967).

To the east along the Khabur and Tigris rivers the situation is similar, although research efforts have been to date less intensive. A dam now under construction on the Lower Khabur has resulted in surveys and excavations in the environs of Hassaka (Monchambert 1984). The Upper Tigris, too, has recently been explored largely as a consequence of ongoing or planned dam projects. Two new dams (İlısu and Cizre) scheduled to be built along the Tigris within southeastern Turkey have opened for survey the affected areas along the Tigris itself and several of its tributaries (Algaze 1989a; Algaze et al. 1991). Downstream and just across the border from Cizre, the recent construction of the Eski Mosul Dam in northern Iraq similarly resulted in surveys and excavations in the Tigris basin just north of Mosul (Demirji 1987). Of equal importance are associated surveys of areas earmarked for intensive agricultural development that have taken place in the Tell Afar area of the Upper Jezira just west of the Tigris (Ball, Tucker, and Wilkinson 1989; Wilkinson 1990b). Finally, the construction in the 1960s of dams in the Dokan area of the Lesser Zab

and the Darband-i Khan gorge on the Diyala headwaters, both in Iraqi Kurdistan, allowed some research to be conducted in highland plains that are
now largely inaccessible to archaeologists (Abu al-
Soof 1964).

As knowledge of the archaeology of Syro-
Mesopotamia has increased, interest in the area as a
whole has also grown. Partly as a result, a variety
of complementary surveys and excavations have
been undertaken, principally in northern and northeastern Syria and northern Iraq. Areas explored include (1) the Qoueiq River basin in the vicinity of
Aleppo (Matthers 1981); (2) portions of the Sajur
River in Syria south of the Turkish border (Sanlaville 1985); (3) portions of the Euphrates basin
within Syria south of the Tabqa Dam and north of
the Iraqi border, in particular between Lake Assad
and Raqqa (Kohlmeyer 1985), in the vicinity of Ashara (ancient Terqa) (Simpson 1983), and between
Deir ez Zor and Abu Kemal in the environs of Mari
(Geyer and Monchambert 1987); (4) the Balikh basin north and south of the Turkish border (Yardımcı
1991; Akkermans 1984; van Loon 1988); (5) the
Lower Khabur basin (Röllig and Kühne 1977/78;
Monchambert 1984); (6) the Wadi Jarrah (Weiss
1986; Wattenmaker and Stein 1989) and Wadi Jaghjagh (D. Oates 1977, 1983) branches of the Upper Khabur; and (7) parts of the Upper Jezira in
northeast Syria (Meijer 1986) and northern Iraq
(Wilkinson 1990b).

Many of the excavations and some of the surveys are still in progress, much of the relevant material remains unpublished or only incompletely
published, and whole areas remain unexplored,
principally portions of the Balikh, Khabur, and Tigris basins within southeastern Turkey. Nevertheless, an intelligible picture of the history and archaeology of large sections of Syro-Mesopotamia is
beginning to emerge, especially for developments
alongside the principal waterways. Particularly important are the results bearing on the Late Chalcolithic period in Syro-Mesopotamia (second half
of the fourth millennium B.C.) and the transition
to the Early Bronze Age. Most startling has been
the evidence for intense contacts between the
civilization of Uruk-period Mesopotamia and

contemporary cultures of the north. That such
contacts had taken place had, of course, been
common knowledge for a long time; what was
not apparent until now was their intensity and
nature.

The Location of Uruk Enclaves

In terms of the long-term development of the
Syro-Mesopotamian plains, the presence of urban-
sized sites with an assemblage that is wholly of
southern Mesopotamian Uruk derivation represents, not a break in the sequence—local sites were
not replaced to any great extent—but rather a
highly selective intrusion. This intrusion took place
within the context of an indigenous Late Chalcolithic culture with a long *in situ* development that
was by all accounts flourishing. Characterized by
chaff-tempered ceramics of the type first defined by
Braidwood for Phase F of the Amuq sequence (below, chap. 5), this preexisting assemblage has been
shown by surveys and excavations to have had a
broad distribution extending from coastal Syria
through to the Transtigridian Plains and into the
southern flanks of the Anatolian highlands. Within
this extensive geographical horizon, Uruk sites are
few in number and are only found at very selective
locations, invariably on or near the junctures of the
main north-south waterways and the principal east-
west overland routes. At those locations, to judge
from a variety of complementary excavation
and survey evidence, southern sites are typically
composed of a central "enclave" of sizable proportions surrounded by a varying number of much
smaller satellite villages. The latter may have served
to supply the central sites with agricultural
and pastoral products, but this is yet unconfirmed
by detailed paleobotanical and paleozoological
analyses.

Uruk enclaves and associated clusters of the
type described have been found along each of the
three principal rivers of the Syro-Mesopotamian plains. The evidence is clearest along the Euphrates, where minimally three enclaves existed:
the Habuba Kabira-süd/Tell Qannas/Jebel Aruda
complex in the lower elbow of the river bend within
the area now flooded by the Tabqa Dam in north-

eastern Syria, Carchemish and several sites in its immediate vicinity just north of the border between Turkey and Syria, and Samsat on the upper elbow of the river bend within the area submerged by the Atatürk Dam in southeastern Anatolia. One enclave has been identified thus far along the Upper Khabur, Tell Brak on the Wadi Jaghjagh, and another existed at the site of ancient Nineveh, on the Upper Tigris near Mosul.

Upper Euphrates Enclaves.   Of the several Euphrates enclaves, the clearest case is that recently excavated in the Tabqa area. This enclave was centered at the site of Habuba Kabira-süd/Tell Qannas some 15 kilometers north of Meskeneh. The Uruk settlement at this location was perched on a low terrace 7–10 meters directly above the river floodplain and was excavated jointly by a German team in the lower parts of the site (Habuba Kabira-süd) and a Belgian team in the associated acropolis (Tell Qannas). As the site was largely unoccupied after the Uruk period, extensive horizontal exposures of Uruk levels were practicable, totaling well over 20,000 square meters. These unparalleled exposures revealed that an earlier, apparently small and short-lived occupation (judging from the limited number of replasterings of its walls) was replaced by a well-planned urban-sized settlement with carefully laid-out streets and well-differentiated residential, industrial, and administrative quarters—all apparently constructed as part of a single master plan (fig. 5). The administrative/religious center of the city was located at Tell Qannas, where a series of monumental buildings of tripartite plan was uncovered. These structures are of a type characteristic for public architecture of the Uruk period in southern Mesopotamia.

Immediately north of the Qannas acropolis and connected to it by a long avenue running parallel to the river along the length of the settlement was the main residential area of the city. Although only partially excavated, this quarter was impressive in its extent. Regularly laid out on either side of the main thoroughfare were numerous houses, all in variations of the tripartite plan common for the more massive structures of Qannas. The whole settlement was surrounded by a sturdily built fortification wall, which is preserved on its northern and western sides. This wall was 3 meters wide and was studded with regularly spaced rectangular towers on its exterior. At least two gateways into the city were found, both on its western side (Finet 1979; Ludwig 1979; Strommenger 1980a; Sürenhagen 1986a). Directly southwest of Tell Qannas was an extended low mound area that has been shown by surveys and a few limited probes to be contemporaneous with the walled settlement to the north (Heinrich et al. 1973:9). This area was never exposed to any great extent, and it is uncertain whether or not it was encompassed within the city walls (fig. 5).

Dutch excavations at Jebel Aruda, about 8 kilometers north of the Habuba/Qannas city, have exposed another important Uruk settlement, apparently of a different nature and significantly smaller than the Habuba/Qannas settlement. Strategically situated on a limestone ridge towering some 60 meters above the level of the surrounding plain, the Uruk installation at Jebel Aruda had as its center two monumental niched and buttressed buildings of the usual tripartite type and associated raised terraces similar to those uncovered at Tell Qannas. However, the Aruda structures did not stand isolated from the rest of the nearby settlement as was the case at Qannas. Flanking the central Temenos area at either side were associated structures, apparently residential in character (van Driel and van Driel-Murray 1979, 1983). Once again, individual compounds are similar in plan to those characteristic for Habuba Kabira-süd, but some are larger, suggesting elite housing connected in some way to the nearby monumental structures (fig. 6). The relationship of the small Aruda settlement to the much larger Uruk city downstream remains enigmatic. However, it is likely that Strommenger (1980a) is correct in that Aruda functioned as the overall administrative center for Uruk sites nearby. This assumption is supported by the defensible position of the hilltop settlement and the elite character of its structures.

The scale of the Uruk cluster in the Tabqa area may be inferred from the main enclave at Habuba-

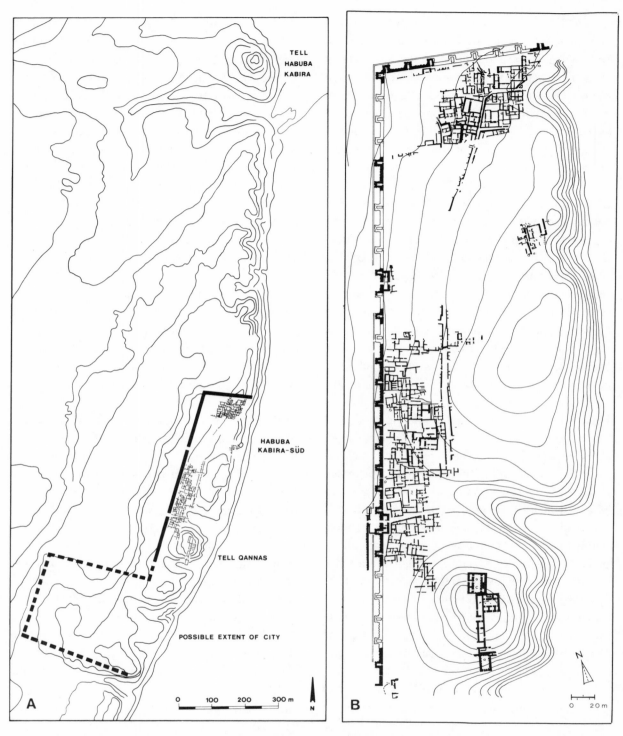

Fig. 5. Plan of Habuba Kabira-süd and Tell Qannas. (A) Possible extent of the city; (B) detail of excavated areas.

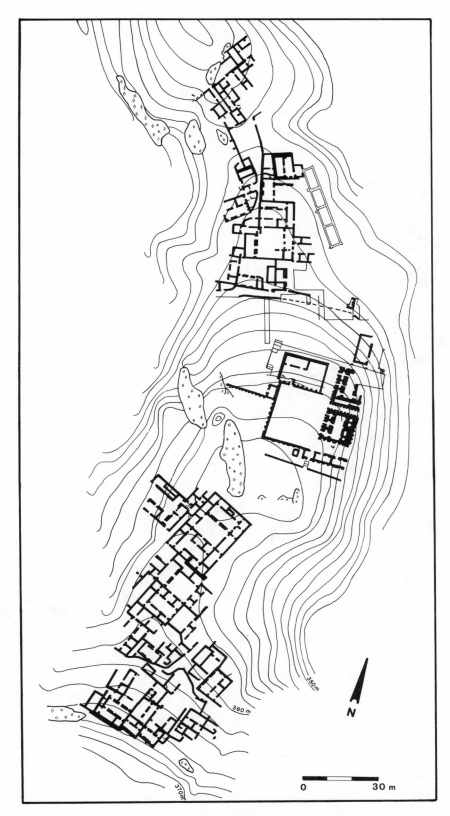

Fig. 6. Central Temenos and associated Uruk structures at Jebel Aruda.

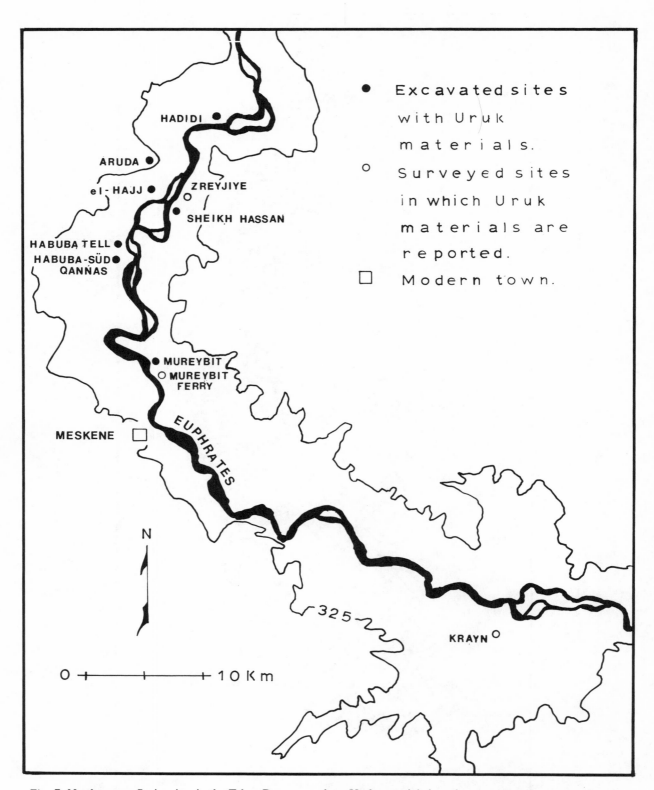

Fig. 7. Northeastern Syria: sites in the Tabqa Dam area where Uruk materials have been recovered or reported.

süd/Tell Qannas. The area encompassed by the city wall as preserved is about 10 hectares (600 × 170 m). The settlement is sure to have been larger than the walled portion, however, since the southern sector of the fortification wall has eroded away and, as will be recalled, directly southwest of Tell Qannas existed a substantial settled area of the Uruk period not encompassed by the city wall. Thus the minimum extent of the settlement must have been close to 18 hectares (Strommenger 1980a:33). Moreover, a larger size of about 40 hectares is not impossible, since surface traces of Uruk ceramics were also found across a 200-meter-wide band extending north of the walled settlement for a further distance of about 1 kilometer (Sürenhagen 1974/75:45) (fig. 5). To this must be added the roughly 2 hectares of settled area at Jebel Aruda.

Additionally, it is clear that Habuba/Qannas and Aruda were not the only Uruk settlements in the lower elbow of the Euphrates bend. Uruk assemblages have been identified with certainty in five other excavated sites in the area surrounding the Habuba/Qannas enclave. These are (1) Tell Habuba Kabira, 1 kilometer north of Habuba (Strommenger 1980a:69); (2) Tell el-Hajj, about 5 kilometers north of the latter (Stucky et al. 1974: 45–49); (3) Tell Hadidi, some 9 kilometers upstream of el-Hajj (Dornemann 1988:18); (4) Tell Mureybit, about 10 kilometers downstream from Habuba and on the opposite (east) bank of the river (van Loon 1968:277); and (5) Tell Sheikh Hassan, a small occupation directly opposite Habuba that has yielded a surprisingly long sequence of Uruk deposits (Boese 1986/87). Uruk ceramics are also reported in at least three other nearby mounds, but this is unconfirmed by excavations.[3] Whatever the total number of occupations at the time, it is apparent that in the Tabqa area we are dealing with both a central Uruk settlement of considerable size and a cluster of possibly dependent smaller settlements in its immediate vicinity (fig. 7).

The other Uruk enclaves along the Euphrates have been exposed to a much lesser extent and are only poorly understood. However, extrapolating from available excavation and survey data, they too must have represented impressive settlements equal to their Tabqa counterparts. Another cluster of Uruk sties existed some 80 kilometers upstream from the Tabqa area, at a point where the terraces flanking the Euphrates become wider, creating broad patches of level, often irrigable, land. Only recently defined by surveys in southeastern Turkey (Birecik and Carchemish Dam areas) and northeastern Syria (Tishreen Dam area), this cluster stretches from the vicinity of the modern town of Birecik in Turkey to the neighborhood of Jerablus, just across the border in Syria and about 30 kilometers to the south (fig. 8).[4] Eighteen Uruk sites have been recognized thus far, each yielding beveled-rim bowls and, depending on the size of the sample, all or portions of a typical grit-tempered Uruk ceramic repertoire that contrasts markedly with the chaff-tempered assemblage of nearby Late Chalcolithic sites. Most of the Uruk sites in the Birecik-Jerablus area are relatively small, not larger than village-sized, and are located on low terraces bordering the river, usually on the edge of the first contour line overlooking the floodplain. Four sites just north of the Turkish-Syrian border, however, are more substantial (Algaze et al. 1991). These larger sites form part, no doubt, of one or more enclaves comparable to those uncovered in the Tabqa area.

One component of the Uruk settlement complex in the Biercik-Jerablus area was the important site of ancient Carchemish (fig. 9). Early British soundings into the acropolis of the mound revealed a variety of Uruk ceramics (fig. 10), at least one typical cylinder seal in geometric style depicting three superimposed rows of fish with numerous parallels at Uruk sites elsewhere,[5] and traces of what appears to have been a long-lived Uruk occupation, minimally 3 meters in depth, superimposed on Late Chalcolithic levels.[6] However, the limited exposures obtained at Carchemish and the limitations inherent in the excavation methodology employed do not allow for a good approximation of the site's Uruk-period extent or for an understanding of its nature at the time.

More reliable data are available for several newly discovered Uruk settlements in the immediate vicinity of Carchemish. Three such sites were

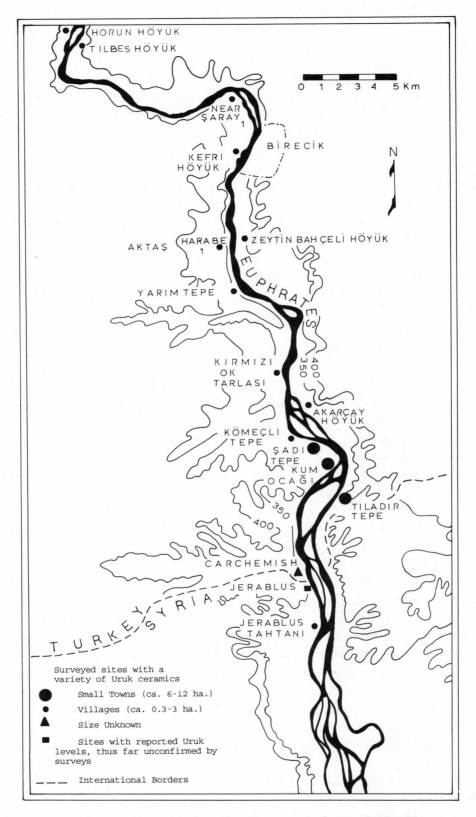

Fig. 8. Southeastern Anatolia and northeastern Syria: sites in the Birecik-Jerablus area where Uruk materials have been recovered or reported.

Fig. 9. Acropolis of Carchemish and nearby lower terrace: view from the north.

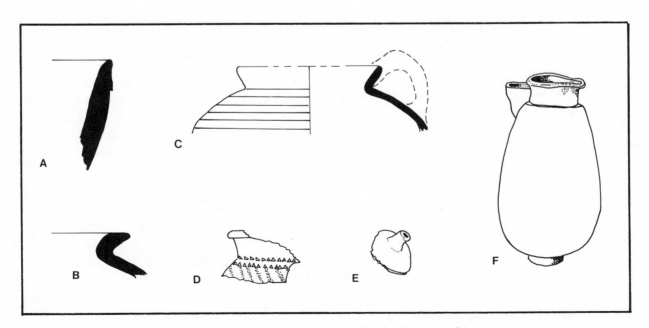

Fig. 10. Selected Uruk ceramics from the acropolis mound at Carchemish (not to scale).

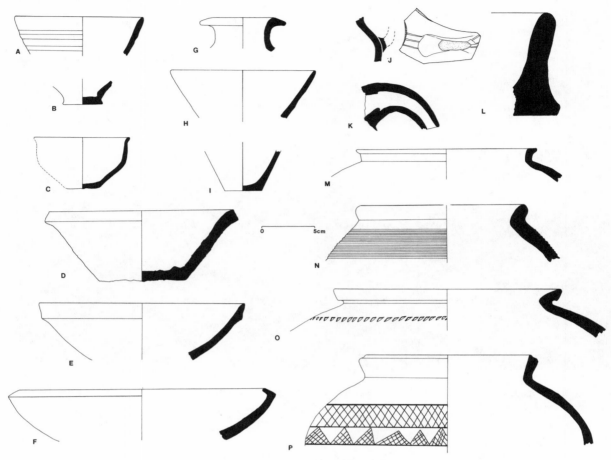

Fig. 11. Uruk ceramics from Tiladir Tepe (A, J), Şadi Tepe (G, K), Komeçlı Höyük (B–C, F, L, N, O), and Kum Ocağı (D–E, H–I, M, P).

identified in a single group on the west bank of the river some 6–9 kilometers upstream of Carchemish. At the center of this agglomeration was Şadi Tepe, the largest and most important of the three. The Uruk settlement at this location was about 8 hectares in extent (320 × 200 m plus a higher contiguous area of 100 × 100 m) and was established on top of a high limestone ridge rising 40–50 meters above the level of the surrounding plain (fig. 12). It thus occupied a defensible position that is closely comparable to that of Jebel Aruda. Şadi Tepe was abandoned after the Uruk period and numerous beveled-rim bowls and other Uruk pottery types littered its surface (e.g., fig. 11G, K). The chipped stone assemblage was also typical, and included Canaanean-type blades and flake flint scrapers. Like Aruda, Şadi Tepe seems to have been the

locus of an occupation that was possibly administrative in character. This may be surmised from its strategic position over the nearby plain and, more directly, from the presence of bitumen-covered terra cotta wall cones (Algaze 1989a:281, fig. 36, bottom left) and cylindrical pottery drainpipes on its surface, indicating the existence of substantial public buildings.

Flanking Şadi Tepe to the north and south were two further Uruk settlements, each situated on the lowest terrace overlooking the Euphrates floodplain. Each also produced evidence for a full repertoire of Uruk ceramics (fig. 11B–F, H–I, L–P). The largest of the two was Kum Ocağı, about 2 kilometers due south of Şadi Tepe. Unfortunately, Kum Ocağı had already been largely destroyed by a gravel quarry by the time the site was first discovered in 1989, but its extent was still traceable: 6.3 hectares (420 × 150 m). It could be observed that the settlement was founded on virgin soil and that it was relatively short-lived, since only 1–1.5 meters of deposition were visible in a disturbed section. The second site was Komeçlı Höyük, less than a kilometer north of Şadi Tepe. Like many other sites flanking the Euphrates in the Carchemish-Birecik Dam areas, Komeçlı too has now been bulldozed to make way for a cotton field, but in 1989 it could be observed that the site was about half the size of Kum Ocağı (250 × 110 m) and was similar in its elongated shape and position along the riverbank. Moreover, it too represented a short-lived occupation, since only about 2 meters of deposition could be observed on the eastern section of the site, which had been cut by the river (Algaze et al. 1991).

The largest Uruk enclave identified in the neighborhood of Carchemish was Tiladir Tepe. The site is roughly equidistant between Carchemish and Şadi Tepe, but is situated on the opposite (east) bank of the Euphrates at the edge of a steep bluff overlooking the river floodplain (fig. 13). Although much of Tiladir Tepe was overlain by Middle Bronze Age levels, its Uruk-period extent was clear. Numerous beveled-rim bowls and other characteristic Uruk types (fig. 11A, J) eroding from the steep western section of the settlement revealed that all of its 600-meter length was occupied in the earlier period, and scattered Uruk sherds from the site's surface indicate that this occupation extended over much of the 200-meter width of the bluff on which it is located. Tiladir Tepe was thus about 12 hectares in size. About 4 meters of deposits could be observed in the Tiladir section. However, because of later overburden, the Uruk contribution to this depth could not be ascertained (Algaze et al. 1991).

North of Birecik, the Euphrates flows in a narrow gorge for about 100 kilometers or so. It opens

Fig. 12. Şadi Tepe: view from the west.

Fig. 13. Tiladir Tepe: view from the northwest (extent of site indicated by arrows).

again just north of the point where the Atatürk Dam was erected, not far from the ancient Hellenistic/ Roman metropolis of Samosata/Samsat (fig. 14). It is here that another Uruk enclave is found. The extent of the Uruk occupation at Samsat has been documented by Özdoğan's survey (1977), which recorded numerous beveled-rim bowls and occasionally other Uruk pottery types eroding from every slope around the circumference of the high mound. At a minimum, this suggests that the Uruk occupation may have extended over the full 17.5 hectares (350 × 500 m) of the mound. But this does not take into account the possibility of contemporary settlement in the surrounding lower terrace, which was buried by overburden of the classical periods and was never sounded. Uruk levels at Samsat were exposed in a small test trench on the west slope of the mound, and some preliminary observations on the finds can be made on the basis of the available reports. Traces of a fortification wall surrounding the settlement were detected in the trench

(Mellink 1989:114), and it is likely that substantial Uruk (public) architecture existed at the site, since clay wall cones of Uruk type were recovered in the sounding, unfortunately not *in situ*. Some details are known of the associated assemblage, which included numerous beveled-rim bowls (Mellink 1988:110), one typically Mesopotamian carinated jar with a burnished red slip (Özten 1984: fig. 1), and a handful of cylinder seals, at least one of which depicts a row of recumbent animals with heads turned backward within ladderlike filling motifs, possibly representing a fence or net (Özgüç 1987: fig. 8). Although the engraving of the seal appears provincial (H. J. Kantor, pers. comm., 1988), the motif itself is wholly characteristic for Late Uruk glyptic.[7]

Surveys show that several small sites in the vicinity of Samsat produced materials of the Uruk period. In the Atatürk region, however, those materials often occur in sites with mixed indigenous chaff-tempered and exogenous Uruk assemblages.

Fig. 14. The high mound of Samsat: view from the west.

Included in this group are six village-sized mounds in the immediate environs of Samsat and a small occupation near Bozova, some 25 kilometers away (fig. 15).[8] Three of these have not been excavated, and it is thus difficult to say whether they represented newly founded cluster villages surrounding the Samsat enclave, such as those documented in the Tabqa and Birecik-Jerablus areas, or local Late Chalcolithic occupations interacting with Samsat. Those sites that have been excavated, however, clearly appear to represent the latter. The most important of these was Kurban Höyük, which produced an important sequence that helps document changes within indigenous sites in the Atatürk area as a result of the Uruk intrusion. This site will be the focus of detailed analysis in chapter 5. In addition to the sites with mixed assemblages just noted, two further small sites with Uruk materials (Wilkinson 1990a: figs. B6, B26:10–13) have been identified opposite Samsat. Both are situated along the

İncesu, a small east bank tributary of the Euphrates (fig. 15: Sites 15 and 39). Perhaps significantly, neither of these İncesu sites yielded the chaff-tempered Late Chalcolithic repertoire of nearby sites. They may represent part of a cluster of satellite villages surrounding Samsat or, perhaps, may have served as stations aligned with routes from the Samsat area toward the Balikh basin (below). Finally, a further group of three other sites with Uruk and indigenous materials also existed in the northern fringes of the Atatürk region, some 50 kilometers upstream of Samsat.[9] One of these sites, Hassek Höyük, was excavated and proved to be a small isolated Uruk station alongside a river ford. This station too will be described in greater detail below.

Upper Khabur Enclaves.   Remarkable as the scale of intrusive Uruk settlement on the Euphrates might seem to be, that scale is by no means exceptional.

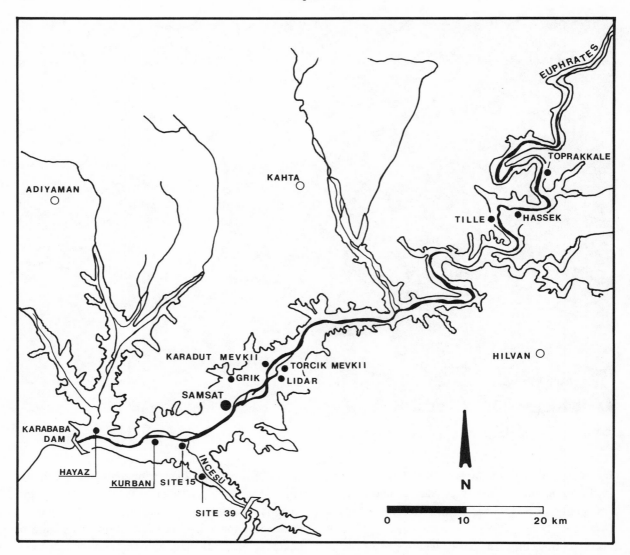

Fig. 15. Southeastern Turkey, Atatürk Dam area: Samsat, Hassek Höyük, and nearby sites where Uruk ceramics have been identified.

This is demonstrated by the results of British excavations and surveys in the Upper Khabur area, where Uruk ceramics are reported to be common at a number of the principal mounds (D. Oates 1977:234), suggesting an intense pattern of contacts with the Uruk world and, possibly, the existence of a number of enclaves. One of those enclaves has been identified at Tell Brak, a large multiperiod mound on the Jaghjagh north of and not far from the modern town of Hassaka. The full extent of the Uruk settlement partially uncovered by Mallowan some fifty years ago at Brak has been

clarified only recently by new British investigations. Their results indicate the presence of Uruk levels over the whole of the site's 40-odd hectares and that the depth of deposits of the period averages some 2 meters across the mound (D. Oates 1982:14). Additionally, the site is surrounded by smaller settlements in which Uruk materials have also been identified. These may represent either an extensive lower city or a number of immediately dependent satellites. In either case, the total size of the Uruk enclave at Brak must have been considerably more than the 40 hectares or so of the site itself. Moreover, the Brak enclave was not isolated, since Uruk materials are reported in eleven sites along the lower portions of the Jaghjagh in Syria (Fielden 1981a:261ff.)—a situation directly comparable to that of the Euphrates enclaves already discussed.

Upper Tigris Enclaves.   The site of Nineveh opposite Mosul on the Upper Tigris seems to have represented a Mesopotamian enclave comparable in both importance and scale to either the Brak or Tabqa examples to the west. The existence of Uruk remains at Kuyunjik, the larger mound of Nineveh, has long been known from the results of Mallowan's deep sounding, where 5–6 meters of deposits of the period were found (Campbell Thompson and Mallowan 1933: pl. LXXIII). That such extensive deposits were not exceptional at the site is now shown by a recent reconsideration of the excavations in the Ishtar Temple area. Central to that reconsideration is the identification of architectural remains uncovered as part of a sizable vaulted-roof building complex, possibly a storehouse (fig. 16). Originally thought by the excavators to represent a series of isolated vaulted tombs of possible third millennium date, this complex can be assigned instead to the Uruk period with some confidence, since beveled-rim bowls were found in the interior of the building at floor level. Even though only portions of two sides were cleared, the scale of this complex was substantial: the building could not have been smaller than the 300 square meters or so exposed and was probably considerably larger (Algaze 1986b). Near this structure were also found portions of another structure of the Uruk period, once again with beveled-rim bowls at floor level. Unfortunately, neither the extent or nature of these remains can be determined from the published report (Algaze 1986b). Nevertheless, the extent of the Uruk occupation at Kuyunjik may be inferred from a number of scattered references throughout the original excavation reports indicating that Uruk deposits, unfortunately of an undetermined depth and nature, were found in several widely scattered areas of the site (Campbell Thompson and Hutchinson

1931:81 n. 2; Campbell Thompson and Hamilton 1932:88–89). Mallowan, in fact, comments that beveled-rim bowls at Nineveh "were deposited over a very wide area from end to end of the city" (1947:222). This suggests that a large proportion of the 40-odd hectares of Kuyunjik may have been occupied in the Uruk period.

While the lack of comprehensive surveys in the vicinity of the site and of excavations on the smaller mound of the Nineveh complex, Nebi Yunus, hamper our overall understanding of developments in the immediate surroundings of Nineveh in the Uruk period, new surveys and excavations in the Eski Mosul Dam area north of the site have revealed what appears to be a pattern comparable to that observed along the Euphrates in the Atatürk Dam area where Samsat is located: a number of apparently local sites showing evidence for contacts with Uruk enclaves in their midst. Most of the pertinent evidence is not yet published, but a preliminary account of excavations in at least two of the Eski Mosul sites, Mohammed Arab and Karana 3, indicates the existence of a locally made ceramic assemblage in which a small number of Uruk types, principally four-lugged jars, are reproduced in association with an otherwise local tradition (Killick 1986; Fales et al. 1987). The same pattern holds further upstream on the Tigris. A recent survey of the Cizre-Zakho plain of southeastern Turkey shows that scattered beveled-rim bowls are commonly found in sites that are otherwise characterized by an indigenous chaff-tempered Late Chalcolithic assemblage (e.g., fig 24; Mehmetçik and Rubaikale). Distinctive grit-tempered Uruk pottery types, however, were only recognized at a single site, Basorin Höyük (fig. 24). In addition to beveled-rim bowls and other typical chaff-tempered local types, Basorin yielded a handful of Uruk conical cups and at least one typical ledge-rimmed jar rim (Algaze et al. 1991).[10]

The Nature of Uruk Enclaves

In the absence of representative exposures, little can be said about the nature of the Uruk occupation at sites such as Samsat, Carchemish, and the newly discovered Uruk emplacements in the

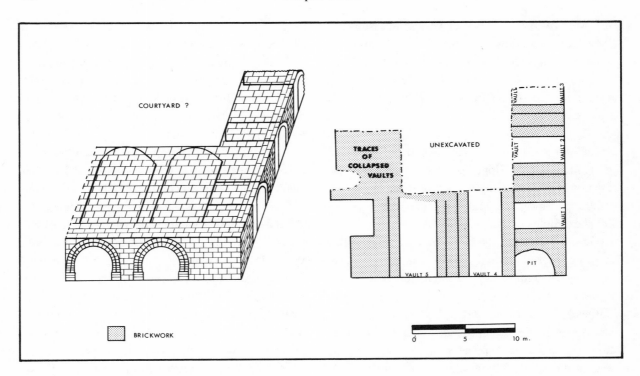

Fig. 16. Plan of the Uruk-period vaulted structure at Nineveh.

Carchemish-Birecik area. However, the evidence summarized above for the Habuba/Qannas/Aruda complex leaves little doubt that at least that settlement cluster represents a colonial outpost of truly impressive urban proportions. Tell Brak and Nineveh would appear to represent something similar (but note Wattenmaker's cautionary comments [1990]). In any event, there can be little doubt that the planners and probably a substantial proportion of the inhabitants of the Tabqa enclave were of southern Mesopotamian origin. This is shown by the familiar southern Mesopotamian architectural plans and construction techniques (Ludwig 1979), diagnostic ceramics and ceramic production procedures (fig. 17A–J), typical small objects, characteristic glyptic practices and iconography, and distinctive accounting and recording systems, including numerical notation tablets and impressed balls (Strommenger 1980a; Sürenhagen 1974/75; Topperwein 1973). This varied evidence is indicative of much more than a process of acculturation. Not only are the structures or the artifacts themselves identical, but more important, the underlying ideology and economy also appear to be identical. The

close parallels in the monumental architecture of the Tabqa Dam sites and similar structures in southern Mesopotamian sites (fig. 17W–Z), for example, are almost certainly indicative of shared administrative practices. No less significant is the shared iconography revealed by the glyptic, which evinces a common mythology and religious beliefs (fig. 17O–V). Finally, the similarities noticed in record-keeping procedures are equally revealing, insofar as they point to the essential uniformity of the economic activities being conducted and of the administrative apparatus in control (fig. 17K–N). In sum, regardless of which of the various estimates discussed for the size of the Habuba/Qannas enclave is accepted, there is little doubt that the apparently rapid transformation of the settlement from a small amorphous village into a well-planned city involved a massive episode of emigration from the alluvium, a veritable case of urban implantation (Schwartz 1988a; Sürenhagen 1986a). The excavators of Habuba-süd, in fact, estimate the population of the site to have been in the range of 6,000–8,000 inhabitants (Strommenger 1980a:34).

The situation at Brak and Nineveh appears sim-

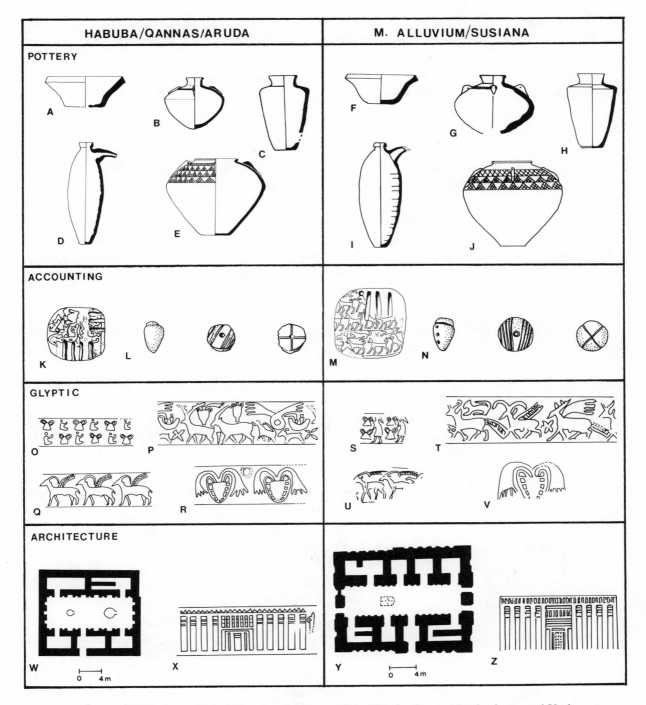

Fig. 17. Selected parallels between the cultural assemblages of the Habuba/Qannas/Aruda cluster and Uruk centers in southern Iraq and southwestern Iran in the Late Uruk period (not to scale unless indicated).

ilar—although available evidence is less comprehensive. A series of monumental structures was uncovered by early British excavations at Tell Brak, all immediately underneath the palace-cum-storehouse of the Akkadian king Naram-Sin. These

structures were originally assigned to the Jemdet Nasr period on the basis of a misapprehension of the chronological range of much of the associated assemblage and of many of the architectural parallels. However, a variety of evidence suggests that they date instead to the Uruk period.[11] Four separate buildings were distinguished, but only the last, the so-called Eye Temple, was excavated to any great extent. Erected on top of a massive platform formed in part by the compacted remains of immediately preceding structures, this building is of unmistakable southern (Mesopotamian) derivation, in spite of its unique eastern wing (but see Weiss 1985:86–89 for a varying view). Particularly telling are its tripartite plan, buttressed exterior façade, and bent-axis approach (fig. 18A), all typical for Uruk monumental architecture. In fact, the arrangement and dimensions of the Eye Temple's central sanctuary match closely those of contemporary temples in the alluvium, for instance at Warka (e.g., fig. 17Y) and Tell Uqair. Equally close parallels can also be drawn with newly discovered temples at Tell Qannas (fig. 17W) and Jebel Aruda (fig. 6). Moreover, the associated objects are also unmistakably southern in style (Mallowan 1947), particularly the striking frieze of gold, silver, and semiprecious stones found over the Eye Temple podium, the wall cones, wall cone imitation plaques, rosettes and related wall decoration (fig. 18H), many of the amulets (figs. 18G; 38F, I), and some

of the glyptic (fig. 18E). A variety of other artifacts of Uruk type were also recovered at the site, albeit not in context. Included in this category are cylinder seals and impressions (e.g., fig. 18F), an unsealed numerical notation tablet (fig. 18J), two unique pictographic tablets (fig. 18I), and a full repertoire of characteristic Uruk pottery types (e.g., fig. 18B–D).[12]

Like the Tabqa and the Khabur enclaves, Nineveh too has a full complement of material culture typical for the Uruk period, though the contemporary vaulted building already discussed has no known parallels in southern Mesopotamia and represents a northern architectural tradition. Excavations in the Ishtar Temple area yielded a typical repertoire of characteristic Uruk ceramics (e.g., fig. 19A–H), as well as a variety of other evidence showing that glyptic practices, iconography, and accounting procedures at the site were also of southern Mesopotamian derivation. A recently republished bulla found inside a pit full of beveled-rim bowls, for example, bears an impression depicting a lion attacking a pair of bulls standing back to back—a motif exactly paralleled in Uruk glyptic at other sites (fig. 19J).[13] A second impression of

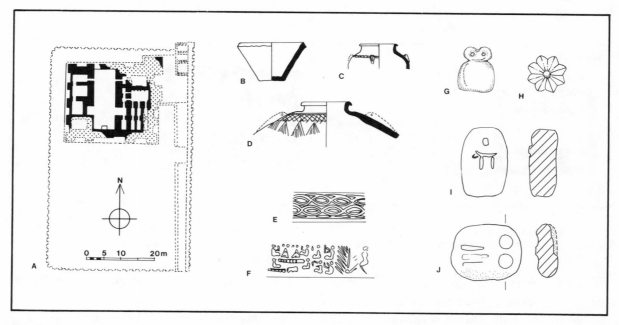

Fig. 18. Selected elements of Uruk culture at Tell Brak (not to scale unless indicated).

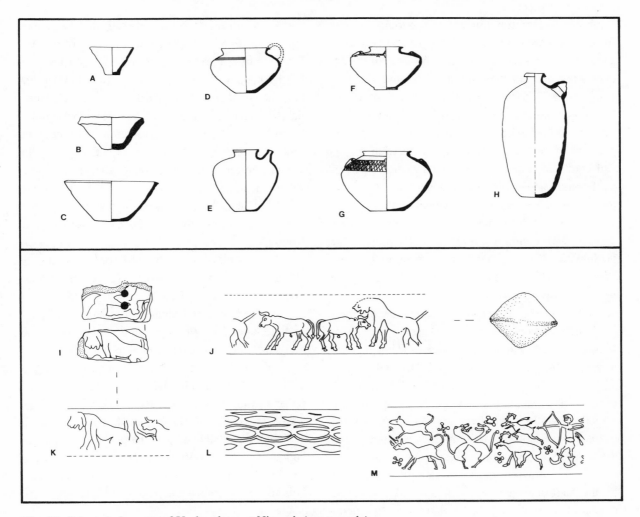

Fig. 19. Selected elements of Uruk culture at Nineveh (not to scale).

possibly the same seal is found on a numerical notation tablet of well-known Uruk type (fig. 19I, K) from an unknown context with Kuyunjik. Also of uncertain provenance but of similar date are two additional cylinder seals found at the site. One is carved in a provincial style and depicts a stag and an ibex pursued by two dogs and a hunter at either side of a pair of lions with crossed necks (fig. 19M). Although as a composition this seal finds no exact parallels elsewhere, specific aspects of its iconography can be paralleled precisely in the corpus of Mesopotamian glyptic iconography of the Uruk period, particularly the hunting scene itself and the animals with crossed necks.[14] The second seal is of a simple geometrical type depicting rows of ovals

possibly meant to represent fishes or eyes, a familiar motif already noted at Carchemish and with numerous parallels elsewhere (fig. 19L, compare also figs. 18E; 27I–J; 29D).[15]

The nature and reliability of available evidence on the Uruk enclaves and associated clusters are outlined in tables 1 and 2, appended to this chapter.

THE STRATEGIC RATIONALE OF URUK SETTLEMENT IN SYRO-MESOPOTAMIA

The riverine location of the Uruk enclaves described above would seem to suggest that a crucial factor determining their placement was control of the major rivers. That consideration must have been important indeed, since historically the Tigris and

Euphrates rivers functioned as important arteries for downstream commerce (Finet 1969). However, a detailed analysis of the specific position of the enclaves reveals that they are also oriented along an east-west axis focused on the overland routes of communication across Syro-Mesopotamia. This becomes clear when one compares the specific position of each of the enclaves with what historical evidence is available on the structure of overland routes across the Syro-Mesopotamian plains through the ages. An unusually coherent and extensive corpus of information on international trade and routes of communication exists for most of the Hellenistic, Roman, and Byzantine periods, when Western Asia became in effect a land bridge between Europe and Asia. For those periods it is possible to reconstruct the outlines of the network of overland routes crisscrossing the Syro-Mesopotamian plains. These data afford us a better understanding of what Fernand Braudel (1972) termed the "geographic framework of civilization" in Syro-Mesopotamia and the varying ways ancient societies would have been able to exploit that framework, adapt to it, and, at times, circumvent it. The implicit assumption is that the same constraints that can be shown to have had a significant impact on the historical geography of Syro-Mesopotamia during the classical age were also generally operative in the fourth millennium B.C. Thus, before going on to an examination of the locational circumstances of the Uruk enclaves, it is necessary to review briefly the classical evidence for the structures of communication across those sectors of Syro-Mesopotamia in which the enclaves were established.[16]

Overland Routes across Syro-Mesopotamia in the Classical Age

In the classical age, the high plains of Syro-Mesopotamia effectively functioned as the communications hub of the Near East (fig. 20), and the area was crisscrossed by an extensive and well-documented network of routes. The most important east-west routes between the Euphrates and the Tigris were the following (Dillemann 1962; Miller 1962; Poidebard 1934):

1. A northern route crossed the Euphrates either at Zeugma (8 kilometers upstream of modern Birecik) or Samosata (Samsat) and, skirting the southern flank of the Karacadağ/Tur Abdin highlands, headed eastward via Edessa (Urfa), Constantia (Viranşehir), Amuda, and Nisibis (Nuseybin) From Nisibis, two alternate routes are attested. One route continued eastward toward Erbil and the Transtigridian Plains by crossing the Tigris at Bezabde, near Cizre,[17] while the other turned to the southeast and, keeping west of the Tigris, intersected the river in the vicinity of Mosul (fig. 20: Route 2).

2. A central route crossed the Euphrates at either Zeugma or the Europus (Carchemish/Jerablus) area and headed eastward via Carrhae (Harran) on the Upper Balikh and Resaina (Ras el'Ain) on the Upper Khabur. At Resaina three alternative routes are attested. One branch took off northward and joined the northern route already described at Nisibis. A second branch headed due east, crossed the Wadi Khanzir at Chagar Bazar, and eventually joined the Tigris at Mosul, while the third branch proceeded southeastward, intersecting the Jaghjagh in the environs of Brak before crossing the Jebel Sinjar or skirting its southern flank. This route too joined the Tigris at Mosul (fig. 20: Route 3).

3. The southernmost route crossed the Euphrates in the Europus area and proceeded eastward either through Carrhae or Ain el'Arus, both on the Balikh. It differs from the other routes in that it skipped the Upper Khabur basin altogether, keeping to the south of the Jebel abd el-Aziz and the Jebel Sinjar. From the city of Singara on the south flank of the Sinjar range, the route reached the Tigris through one of two possible roads; a northern branch joined the central route mentioned above and intersected the river at Mosul. The other branch cut across the Lower Jezira on a diagonal orientation following the Wadi Tharthar in the direction of Hatra before reaching the Tigris in the neighborhood of Assur (fig. 20: Route 4).

Interspersed with the east-west routes just outlined were a number of north-south routes that clung closely to the rivers. The combination of the

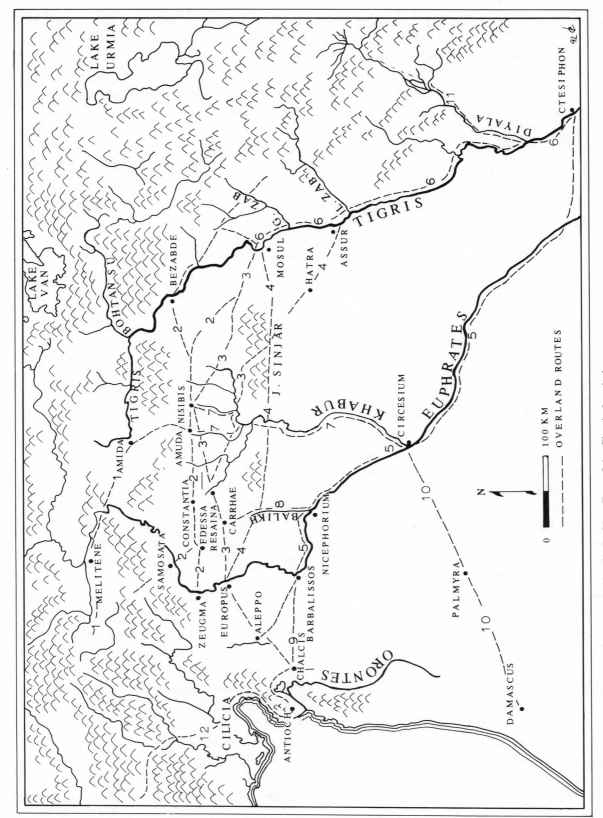

Fig. 20. Major sites and routes of communication in the Near East of the Classical period.

two route systems allowed access between the Mesopotamian alluvium and Syro-Mesopotamia and permitted innumerable permutations in passage throughout the northern plains. The overland north-south route alongside the Euphrates (fig. 20: Route 5) is mapped out in detail in the travel itinerary of Isodore of Charax, who traveled through Parthia along the way to Bactria and China sometime in the late first century B.C. or the first century A.D. (Tarn 1938:53–54). Having crossed the Euphrates at Zeugma, Isodore proceeded eastward toward the Balikh and turned to the south upon reaching that river (fig. 20: Route 8). Downstream from the confluence of the Balikh and the Euphrates, Isodore's route followed closely the course of the Euphrates, first on its left (east) bank down to the confluence of the Khabur and then on its right (west) bank down to the vicinity of Hit, where he crossed the river again and cut across eastward to reach Ctesiphon on the Tigris (Isodore of Charax 1914). Another route is attested by aerial and surface surveys. This route diverged from the Euphrates at the confluence with the Khabur and followed the lower course of the latter river northward up to Hassaka. From Hassaka, a number of subsidiary routes are traceable upward along the various tributaries that form the Upper Khabur watershed (fig. 20: Route 7). Several of the tracks converge on Nisibis, including one along the Jaghjagh where Brak is located. Finally, another subsidiary route leading north from Hassaka is found between the Wadi Awaj and the Wadi Khansir. Skipping Nisibis, it intersected the northernmost of the east-west routes in the vicinity of the Amuda and, crossing the syncline between the Karacadağ and the Tur Abdin massif, headed off northward in the direction of Mardin, Dıyarbakır, and ultimately Malatya (fig. 20: Route 1) (Gregory and Kennedy 1985; Poidebard 1934).

Also connecting into the network of east-west routes across northern Mesopotamia were overland routes alongside the Tigris, which complemented those alongside the Euphrates and were clearly as important (fig. 20: Route 6).[18] These joined the principal east-west routes across northern Mesopotamia by means of three preferred fords across the

Tigris: Bezabde, the terminus of northern routes skirting the Tur Abdin; Mosul, historically the most important of the Upper Tigris fords; and Assur, the target of routes across the Lower Jezira and the Jebel Sinjar alongside the Wadi Tharthar (Dillemann 1962; D. Oates 1968).

The network of routes across the northern Mesopotamian plains was by no means a closed system. To the west, access into the Syrian Saddle and through it to southwestern Anatolia and the Levantine coast was possible through a number of fords across the Euphrates (fig. 20). The northernmost of these was Samosata (Samsat), located on the upper elbow of the Euphrates bend. On the middle stretch, where the river flows along a north-south orientation, were Zeugma, the most important of the classical river crossings, and Europus (Carchemish/Jerablus). The last of the classical fords was Barbalissos (Meskeneh), located far to the south in the lower corner of the river bend just where, pushed by the Jebel Bishri, the Euphrates turns sharply eastward and begins its descent toward the Persian Gulf to the southeast (Jones 1971:231–32).

The location of Samosata, Zeugma, and Europus was far from random. All were situated at points along the Euphrates where the network of east-west routes across northern Mesopotamia intersected the river and crossed over into the Syrian Saddle, commonly by means of bridges (Strabo 1966:16.2.3; Wagner 1976: 107–9). Unlike the crossing further to the north, Barbalissos did not connect with any of the principal east-west routes across northern Mesopotamia. Historically, the lower corner of the Euphrates bend represented the natural terminus of overland caravans alongside the river before cutting across the Syrian Saddle in the direction of Aleppo (Dussaud 1931) (fig. 20: Route 9).

To the north, access to the Anatolian plateau, and ultimately the Meander valley and the Mediterranean, was possible through the natural opening created by the Euphrates River as it emerges from the highlands onto the Malatya plain. As will be recalled, an important route from northern Mesopotamia had Amuda in the Upper Khabur plain as its point of departure and reached Malatya via Dı-yarbakır (fig. 20: Route 1). To the east, the Iranian plateau could be reached by means of a number of passes across the Zagros. Although more massive than the Taurus, the Zagros range actually represents less of a barrier to communication, since its older and more regular folds are interrupted at more regular intervals and are broken-through by a greater number of rivers. In fact, each of the major east bank tributaries of the Tigris creates one inroad into the highlands (British Admiralty 1917; Levine 1973, 1974a). The most important of these routes was the Khorasan Road, which remains to this day the main route linking Baghdad and Kermanshah (fig. 20: Route 11). This route follows the Diyala River into the highlands and snakes its way upward across the central Zagros through a number of intermontane valleys before emerging onto the Iranian plateau in the vicinity of Hamadan (Levine 1974a).

Historical Models and Archaeological Evidence

The preceding discussion on routes of communication and trade in the classical periods is offered as an illustration of possibilities, and as such it is useful in the analysis of the purely archaeological data available on the locational pattern of Uruk enclaves across the Syro-Mesopotamian plains in the late fourth millennium B.C. Before proceeding on to a discussion of the pertinent evidence, however, several points need to be made.

The first point is that a variety of routes are available at any given time and the specific choice of one route over another is governed by two primary considerations: supplies and security. A particular route may be impassable because of depredations of any village, tribe, or state along its course. Alternately, one route may be preferred over another because of logistical considerations. A revealing example of the importance of environmental and logistical constraints on the choice of routes is provided by Alexander's march toward Babylon. Having crossed the Euphrates at Thapsacus on the lower elbow of the Euphrates bend in

Syria in August, at the peak of summer heat, Alexander did not descend along the length of the Euphrates, but rather continued eastward across northern Mesopotamia and turned southward only after having crossed the Tigris. The reasons behind Alexander's "detour" are clearly explained by Arrian (1976:III.7.3), Alexander's later chronicler:

> On setting out from the Euphrates [Alexander] did not take the direct route for Babylon [i.e., down the Euphrates], since by going on the other road [i.e., across the Upper Jezira and down the Tigris] all supplies were easy to obtain for the army, green fodder for the horses and provisions from the country, and the heat was less intense.

In the case of exchange, security represents another important consideration. A particularly clear example is provided by the emergence of the Palmyrene region (the northern reaches of the Syrian desert) as a major thoroughfare of east-west commerce in the early centuries of the first millennium A.D. This role appears closely connected with the disintegration of the Seleucid empire under the combined blows of Romans in the west and Parthians in the east, which resulted in most of northern Mesopotamia and parts of northeastern Syria becoming a sort of buffer zone between the combatants. This opened the door for the creation of a number of petty kingdoms in Syro-Mesopotamia, whose depredations made the desert routes across the Palmyrene more attractive (Rostovseff 1972).

A final point is that although the "geographic framework of civilization" limits the range of the possible, and thus shapes human behavior in similar ways over time, political or technological changes may conspire to alter substantially the range of possibilities. A clear example is provided by Roman attempts to bypass Parthian control of overland routes to India and China by tapping into sea routes toward the east out of Egypt and the Red Sea. In so doing, they initiated a process that came to full fruition only later in the Early Islamic period, when navigation displaced long-distance overland trade across Western Asia in terms of economic importance (Charlesworth 1924; Spuler 1970; White-house and Williamson 1973).

These historical case studies illustrate the complex interplay of geographic, political, and economic factors that ultimately determine something as simple as the selection of one route over another, or even whether an altogether new route is opened along a different orientation. Although specific circumstances must have varied considerably through time, the interplay of factors documented so vividly in historical sources is surely as relevant for the fourth millennium B.C. as it is for the first millennium A.D.

The evidence for the settlement patterns of Uruk enclaves in the Syro-Mesopotamian plains and the relationship of that pattern to the structures of communication of the area will now be discussed in some detail.

Uruk Enclaves at Strategic Nodes of the Lines of Communication

The position of the major Uruk enclaves in the north cannot be attributed to chance: each enclave and surrounding cluster commanded a well-attested strategic juncture where the principal routes intersected the rivers. Samsat, for example, controlled the main river crossing point along the road from the upper plains of the Syrian Saddle and the Kurdish Anti-Taurus (Commagene) into northern Mesopotamia via the northernmost east-west route of the classical age. That route followed the valley of the İncesu in the direction of Urfa, and ultimately the Harran plain and the northern reaches of the Balikh and the Upper Khabur (fig. 20: Route 2; and fig. 21). Downstream from Samsat, the Carchemish/Jerablus area represented another of the historical river crossing points and connected the north Syrian steppe and the environs of Aleppo with the northern Mesopotamian plains east of the Euphrates via the central east-west route of classical times (fig. 20: Route 3; and fig. 21). This route lead across northern Mesopotamia in the direction of Mosul and the Tigris via the middle reaches of the Balikh (Ain el ʿArus) and the Upper Khabur (Ras el ʿAin). And finally, the Tabqa area in the lower cor-

ner of the great bend of the Euphrates represented the last major crossing point before the onset of the Syrian desert—the traditional terminus of overland caravans alongside the Euphrates before cutting across directly west in the direction of Hama on the Orontes or, alternately, toward the northwest across the Syrian steppe in the direction of Aleppo, the Amanus, and ultimately Cilicia and southwestern Anatolia (figs. 20–21).

Similarly, the location of Mesopotamia enclaves along the Upper Khabur and Upper Tigris basins is also best understood in terms of a strategic rationale designed to ensure control of overland routes of communication. Barely 100 kilometers south of the Jaghjagh headwaters and the mineral-rich highlands in the Dıyarbakır region, Tell Brak was well situated to control overland north-south traffic from the Euphrates alongside the Khabur (fig. 20: Route 7; and fig. 21). Traces of a Roman road alongside the Jaghjagh not far from Brak have, in fact, been detected in surveys (Gregory and Kennedy 1985), and there is a Roman *castellum* near the site itself (Poidebard 1934: pls. CXXII–CXXXVIII). However, of equal importance for understanding the location of Brak is the strategic position of the site near one of the few passageways through which it was possible to cross from the Upper Khabur basin into the Sinjar plains to the east without undue difficulty (D. Oates 1977:236). It comes, thus, as no surprise to find that the Uruk enclave at Brak lay at the juncture of the Jaghjagh and one of the main routes across the northern Mesopotamian plains, the one that cut across toward Ras el ʿAin in the direction of the Tigris via the Jebel Sinjar (fig. 20: Route 3; and fig. 21).

Along the Upper Tigris, the placement of an Uruk enclave at Nineveh was also by no means coincidental. Historically, the Nineveh/Mosul area represented the most important of the Tigris fords, and Nineveh was situated at the intersection of the river and several of the main east-west overland routes from the Euphrates via the Balikh, Upper Khabur, and the Jebel Sinjar. Moreover, traditionally the Tigris was an important thoroughfare for downstream navigation. The convergence of these

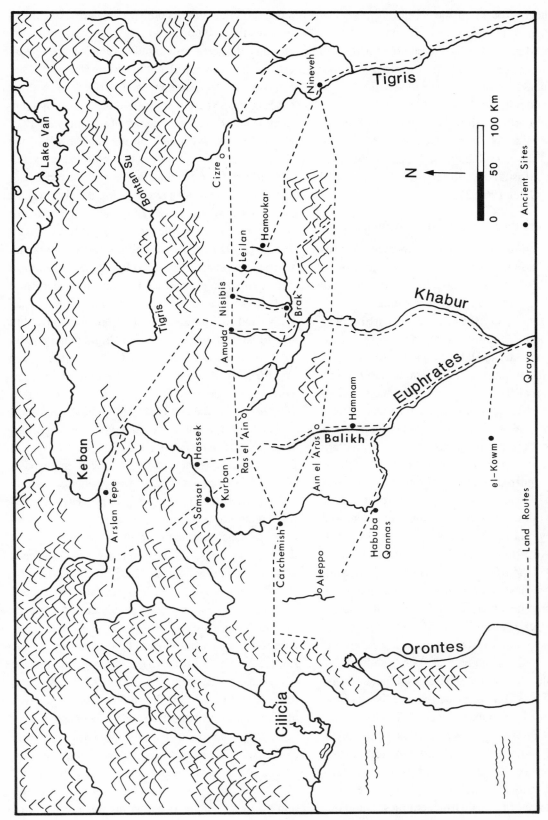

Fig. 21. Major sites and routes of communication discussed in text.

complementary routes made Nineveh an ideal transshipment point where the overland traffic from the west could be easily and cheaply funneled south downstream on the Tigris. In the drier summer months, when the river level was lower and navigation more difficult, routes from the west could join the overland north-south route in and out of the alluvium alongside the Tigris. This route kept to the east bank of the river and crossed it precisely in the environs of Mosul/Nineveh (fig. 20: Route 6; and fig. 21) (D. Oates 1968:21).

Uruk Stations along the Lines of Communication

In addition to the strategically located enclaves already discussed, much smaller Uruk outposts or "stations" also existed alongside the principal waterways of the Syro-Mesopotamian plains, which historically constituted the principal means of north-south communication across the area. Downstream from the Habuba/Qannas/Aruda complex along the Euphrates, for example, are found a number of small Uruk sites lining the banks of the river. These sites no doubt represent links along a north-south Uruk route, which precisely parallels later classical routes (fig. 20: Route 5). No pattern is yet apparent in the spacing of the Uruk stations thus far recognized along the Euphrates, but this could well be due to the uneven nature of survey coverage. Four of these occupations were identified by Kohlmeyer (1985) in a recent survey of the Euphrates basin between the Tabqa Dam and Raqqa (fig. 22: Sites 99, 96, 55, 1).[19] As these sites are all located on the east bank of the river, it is likely that at least from the juncture with the Balikh northward, the Uruk route followed the left bank of the Euphrates and crossed the river near Meskeneh. Other Uruk stations can be traced on both banks of the Euphrates below the Balikh confluence. One such station was Tell Qraya on the west bank of the river, just north of Ashara (ancient Terqa). About 1.8 hectares in extent, the site is isolated on a bluff overlooking the nearby river valley. At least 3 meters of deposits of the Uruk period were recognized during excavations, which yielded evidence for a wide repertoire of typical Uruk ceramics, small ob-

jects, glyptic, and accounting devices. Excavated remains include portions of at least two rooms, apparently domestic in character, and an open work area with a number of pottery kilns (Reimer 1989; Simpson 1988). Another small Uruk station along the Euphrates route was Tell Ramadi, recently identified in surveys in the vicinity of the ancient city of Mari. The site is located on the same bank of the river as Qraya, but some 50 kilometers downstream, not far from the Iraqi border. It too is isolated on a promontory overlooking the river valley, and on its surface a variety of typical Uruk ceramics were recovered (Geyer and Monchambert 1987:318, figs. 8, 10). Finally, a further Uruk station site is reported about 100 kilometers south of Tell Ramadi on the east bank of the river near Rawa in Iraq (M. van Loon, pers. comm., 1986). Like Qraya and Ramadi, the small site also sits on a bluff overlooking the river (fig. 22). Immediately south of Rawa, however, no further Uruk sites have been documented in surveys of the Haditha Dam reservoir area that covered the 60 kilometer stretch of the river between Ana and Haditha (Abdul Amir 1988).

Feeding into the routes alongside the Euphrates were complementary routes beside the Balikh and Khabur rivers. These can also be traced on the basis of recent survey and excavation evidence. Along the Balikh within modern-day Syria, Uruk ceramics, apparently not in association with contemporary Late Chalcolithic materials, were discovered in three small sites, all near the river (Akkermans 1984) (fig. 22:BS 265, BS 182, BS 35). Since the Balikh often served as a link between the central and northernmost east-west routes across northern Mesopotamia (fig. 20: Routes 2–3) and the overland route in and out of the alluvium alongside the Euphrates (fig. 20: Route 5), it is possible that some or all of these sites represent further stations such as those identified on the Euphrates itself, although none of the sites in question has yet been excavated. Intriguingly, as Akkermans (1988b) has noted, each of these Balikh sites with Uruk remains was situated near a larger indigenous Late Chalcolithic site. Thus, in addition to their hypothesized role as "stations," these small occupations may have also

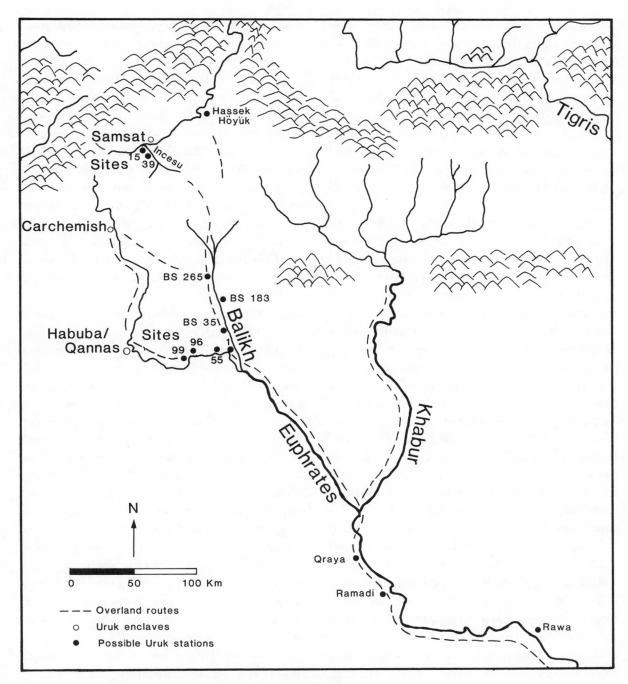

Fig. 22. Possible Uruk stations along the Euphrates and Balikh rivers.

played some role in mediating contacts between indigenous regional centers and faraway Uruk enclaves along the Euphrates and the Upper Khabur. Other Uruk stations aligned toward the Balikh may have existed along the Incesu valley, which, as will be recalled, traditionally served as a corridor from the Samsat area to the southeast. Possible candidates for this role are the two previously discussed small sites with Uruk ceramics near the mouth of the stream opposite Samsat (fig. 22: Sites 15 and 39).

Also oriented toward the Balikh route is an Uruk station uncovered by German excavators at Hassek Höyük, part of the already noted group of sites with Uruk materials along the Euphrates in the northern fringes of the Atatürk Dam region. Situated some 50 kilometers north of Samsat, Hassek controls what must have been and continues to be an important crossing of the Euphrates allowing passage from the Anti-Taurus piedmont into the northern Mesopotamian plains east of the Euphrates (figs. 15, 22). Like the possible Balikh stations in Syria, Hassek Höyük appears to have been relatively small, about 1.5 hectares in extent. As overburden of later periods was light and spatially restricted, comparatively broad exposures of fourth millennium levels were practicable at the site. Those exposures revealed a small fortified settlement, roughly oval in shape, centered around two abutting tripartite houses of the Mittelsaal type (fig. 23B), closely resembling examples from Habuba Kabira-süd (fig. 23A). This composite building was surrounded by a number of monocellular structures, work areas, and grain storage facilities. Like the much larger Uruk enclave in the Tabqa Dam area, the small Uruk station at Hassek was short-lived: founded on virgin soil, it was built largely in a single coherent effort, although some minor modifications and subphases can be traced. Unlike at Habuba, however, where the associated assemblage was purely of Uruk type, at Hassek the Mesopotamian architectural scheme appears in the context of an assemblage in which Uruk artifact and pottery types and indigenous chaff-tempered ceramics are found side by side (Behm-Blancke 1989; Behm-

Blancke et al. 1981, 1984). This assemblage is relevant for issues of chronology and will be discussed in greater detail in chapter 5.

Whether stations such as those already discussed for the Euphrates and Balikh rivers may have existed along the various branches of the Khabur River is less clear. As will be recalled, new British surveys show that Uruk materials are common along the Wadi Jaghjagh and areas immediately to the west, but precise information on the actual number of sites involved, their exact location, their size and configuration, the range of Uruk types found, and the associated assemblage is still lacking. Uruk pottery has also been identified at a number of small sites alongside the various branches of the Upper Khabur east of the Jaghjagh, but there too we lack sufficient information (Meijer 1986:6, 8, fig. 16h–i) (fig. 24).

The situation along the Lower Khabur basin, where Uruk materials are also frequently found, is equally lacking in precision, since pertinent surveys and excavations have only been preliminarily published. However, at least four, and possibly five, sites with some Uruk pottery have been identified within the area to be flooded by the Hassaka Dam (fig. 24: Sites 1, 7, 26, 40, and 58).[20] Perhaps significantly, those sites are found in pairs facing each other at opposite banks of the river. One of the east bank sites, Umm Qseir, has been excavated. Preliminary reports indicate that it represents a small occupation about 0.5 hectares in maximum extent. Because of later disturbances, no coherent Uruk-period structures were recoverable. However, a full assemblage of Uruk ceramic types has been identified (Hole and Johnson 1986/87; F. Hole, pers. comm., 1991). Further downstream, Uruk materials are also reported in two other sites, Tell Ahmar-south and Tell Fadgami (Röllig and Kühne 1977/78:125–26) (fig. 24). Moreover, scattered beveled-rim bowls and an Uruk strap-handled cup have been recovered in what seems to have been an ephemeral pastoral encampment along the nearby Wadi ʻAgig (Pfälzner 1984:182, fig. 76:3–4). Of these sites, Tell Fadgami, a small site located on the east bank of the river some 60 kilometers south of Hassaka, is

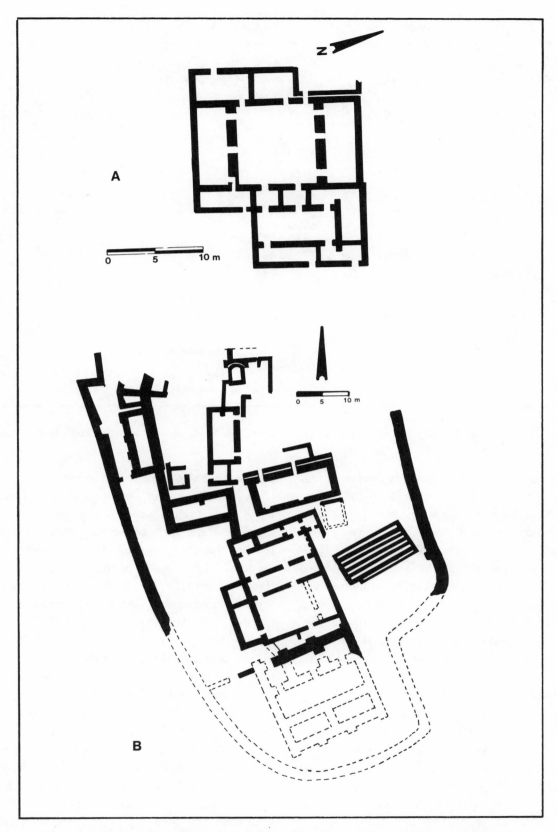

Fig. 23. Plan of Mittelsaal-style house from Habuba Kabira-süd (A) and of Uruk settlement at Hassek Höyük (B).

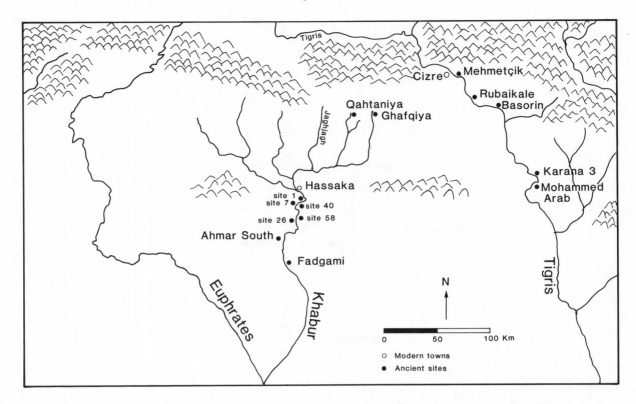

Fig. 24. Possible Uruk stations along the Khabur River and Late Chalcolithic sites in the Upper Tigris basin where Uruk materials have been found.

perhaps the best candidate for a Mesopotamian station in the area. This is suggested by two factors. The first is that numerous beveled-rim bowls and a wide variety of classic Uruk ceramic types were recognized on its surface (Röllig and Kühne 1977/78:125–26; Johnson 1988/89:601 n. 1). The second is that Fadgami occupies a choice location (Musil 1927:85): it lies at the intersection of the overland Roman north-south route alongside the Khabur (fig. 20: Route 7) and the southernmost east-west route (fig. 20: Route 4) from the Euphrates to the Tigris noted above.

However important the overland route alongside the Euphrates may have been, it seems certain that the Tigris route was at least of equal importance. This is demonstrated by the presence of an Uruk enclave in the Nineveh/Mosul area, historically the most important of the Upper Tigris fords. Moreover, as previously noted, a small variety of Uruk ceramics have also been reported at a number of sites along the Tigris north of Nineveh within

Iraq and in least one site within southeastern Turkey (Basorin). These sites are situated along a traditional route from Mosul to Cizre which deviated from the Tigris north of the Eski Mosul area and reached the Cizre region only after crossing the (eastern) Khabur River in the vicinity of Zakho (British Admiralty 1917: Route 90). This evidence suggests a measure of interaction and communication that is compatible with what would be expected if other Tigris fords north of Nineveh/Mosul were to have been in use in the Uruk period. In fact, save for the Habuba/Qannas/Aruda enclave, the location of the Mesopotamian enclaves thus far identified in the north can be easily explained in terms of ties to the Tigris route. The Carchemish/Jerablus area and Samsat, it will be remembered, were not only oriented toward north-south routes alongside the Euphrates (via the Balikh) but were at the same time also the terminus of important east-west routes from the Tigris. Similarly, Brak was also a critical node in east-west routes to the Tigris. In short, whatever other connections they may have afforded, Carchemish and surrounding sites, Samsat, and Brak also formed part of a network of routes whose terminus was Nineveh on the Tigris.

Whether or not other Uruk enclaves and stations may have existed along the east-west overland routes away from the more intensively surveyed rivers can neither be confirmed nor discounted at this point and must remain a subject for future research. To be sure, a number of surveyed sites located along east-west routes crisscrossing the Sinjar plains of northern Syria and northern Iraq have produced some evidence for a limited number of Uruk ceramic types on their surface, and potentially at least some of these sites could represent further Uruk emplacements. However, the majority of such sites were certainly local. Excavations at a variety of Late Chalcolithic sites across the Syro-Mesopotamian plains show that isolated Uruk traits are not uncommon within assemblages that are otherwise wholly indigenous (below, chap. 4). Such traits are best interpreted as evidence for contacts and exchange between indigenous and Uruk societies, contacts that no doubt were mediated through the Uruk enclaves and stations across the north.

Tables 1 and 2, appended to this chapter, summarize the location, orientation, and associations of the Uruk stations thus far identified and outline the nature and reliability of available evidence for them.

URUK OUTPOSTS IN THE PERIPHERY

Outside the geographical horizon of the Syro-Mesopotamian plains delimited by the Tigris and Euphrates river basins, which constitutes in effect the core area of Uruk settlement in the north, large urban enclaves and associated clusters are no longer found. What are found, occasionally, are much smaller isolated outposts located also at critical junctures of the overland routes of communication, in this case those feeding in and out of Syro-Mesopotamia and Khuzestan. These outposts are characterized by a broad range of typical Uruk material culture elements. In terms of size and because of their isolated position in the midst of indigenous communities, they are similar to the Uruk stations thus far recognized, particularly those alongside the Euphrates.

Certainly two and possibly three such outposts have been recognized to date. The two certain cases are in the Iranian highlands, Godin Tepe and Tepe Sialk, while the possible case is in the Palmyrene, a small site in the el-Kowm oasis (fig. 21). Of the Iranian sites, the clearest case is Godin Tepe. The site is strategically located in the southeastern corner of the Kangavar valley, near a natural entrance cut by the Gamas Ab River. On its highest point, a small fortified outpost (fig. 25) of the Uruk period (Godin V) has been excavated. Surrounding this fort was a larger indigenous settlement (Godin VI). The fort itself was built in a non-Uruk style that conformed to local highland canons, and a significant proportion of the pottery contained within was also of local style and manufacture (about 50%). Nevertheless, a wide range of typical Uruk artifacts was found within the structure. These included a variety of ceramic types (fig. 26A–E), glyptic (fig. 26F–G), and numerical notation tablets (fig. 26H–I), all in styles typical for the very end of the Uruk-period sequence as presently understood (Weiss and Young 1975; Young 1986). These intrusive Mesopotamian elements and the commanding position of the fortified structure in which they were found have been interpreted to signify the presence of actual foreigners at the site, presumed to be merchants from Susa by the excavators (Weiss and Young 1975), although their exact provenance remains debatable (Young 1986:220–21). What is unquestionable is that whoever held the fort at the very top of the Godin mound controlled also an important link along the Khorasan Road, which allowed access from the Diyala valley into the Iranian central plateau and points eastward (fig. 20: Route 11; fig. 30). The Uruk fort at Godin appears to have been isolated within the Kangavar valley, since intensive surveys of the valley have failed to produce evidence of further outposts, although isolated beveled-rim bowls have been found in at least three nearby sites (Young 1986:218). Nevertheless, it is likely that outposts similar to Godin may have ex-

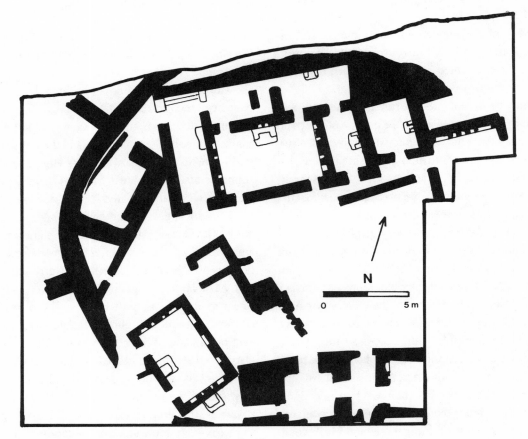

Fig. 25. Plan of the Level V "Fort" at Godin Tepe.

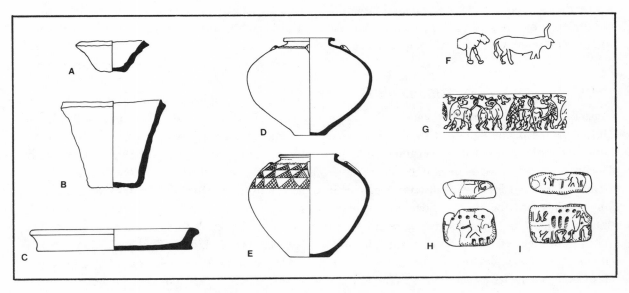

Fig. 26. Selected elements of Uruk culture at Godin Tepe (Level V) (not to scale).

isted elsewhere along the Khorasan Road. Three sites identified in a survey of the Mahidasht valley (west of Kangavar and closer to the Diyala headwaters), for example, yielded numerous beveled-rim bowls, which apparently constituted a sizable proportion of the total recovered assemblage (Levine and Young 1987:40; Young 1986:219).[21]

Farther into the Iranian plateau, just between the inner folds of the Zagros and the edge of the Dasht-i Kavir, near the modern town of Kashan, is another Uruk outpost similar in many respects to that identified in the Kangavar valley. Established at the top of the southern mound of Tepe Sialk in a position that mirrors closely that of the Godin fort, this second outpost may be recognized in the earliest of two phases assigned to Period IV at the mound (IV.1) and is represented by a well-built structure that was only partially exposed (Ghirshman 1938:58–59, pl. LX; Amiet 1985).[22] As at Godin, a variety of typical Uruk pottery was found (e.g., fig. 27B, E–H). Also recovered were equally characteristic small objects (e.g., fig. 27A), cylinder seals (Fig. 27J–L), cylinder seal impressions (e.g., fig. 27I),[23] and numerical notation tablets (e.g., fig. 27M).

Because of the restricted exposures that were practicable in the south mound of Sialk, it cannot be ascertained whether or not the outpost at this location was surrounded by an indigenous settlement, as was the case at Godin. On the contrary, in the published reports, the earliest Sialk IV.1 structures postdate the latest Period III level (7) and the two strata are separated by a thick ash destruction layer (Ghirshman 1938: pl. XLIX). However, if excavations at Godin had explored only the acropolis sequence and not the nearby mound, it would have been logical to conclude that Godin V wholly postdates Godin VI, a demonstrably false assumption. The possibility that Sialk IV.1 too may have been partially contemporaneous with an indigenous settlement in its immediate vicinity is raised by the presence of typical Period III pottery within Period IV.1 structures and burials (Amiet 1986:307–8, figs. 9–11). This precisely parallels the situation within the Godin V fort, where local ceramics were found in association with Uruk types. In brief, the varied evidence for a range of typical Uruk materials at Sialk IV.1 is indicative of its function as an outpost like Godin. This conclusion is reinforced by the location of the site. Like Godin, Sialk is strategically situated at a position commanding an important route across the Iranian central plateau, in

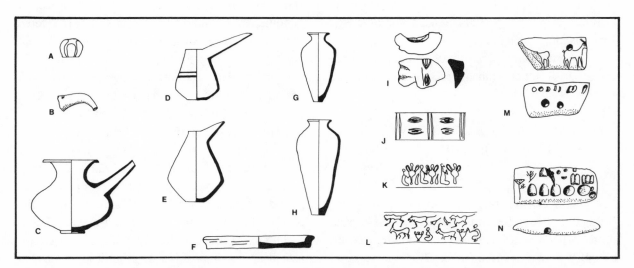

Fig. 27. Selected elements of southwest Iranian Uruk culture at Tepe Sialk: Periods III.7 (C, D, F, K) and IV.1 (A–B, G–J, L–N) (not to scale).

this case the principal north-south route from Afghanistan to Khuzestan (Majidzadeh 1982). This route diverges from the Khorasan Road in the Rayy plain near Tehran and, after crossing Isfahan, emerges in eastern Khuzestan via passes across the southern Zagros (fig. 1).

Also strategically situated is the only Uruk outpost yet identified in Syria away from the Euphrates basin, a small site (el-Kowm 2 Caracol) in the Palmyrene area, where a broad range of Uruk ceramics has been recovered (Cauvin and Stordeur 1985). The site is situated within the el-Kowm oasis, which is a natural stopping point along the traditional caravan route that crosses the northern reaches of the Syrian desert and allows passage (via Palmyra) from the Middle Euphrates to the Orontes and points beyond (fig. 20: Route 10; fig. 21). The el-Kowm outpost is therefore well placed along what must have been an important thoroughfare. However, the Uruk occupation at el-Kowm seems fundamentally different from those already described in the Iranian highlands. One difference is that few traces of structures have been identified and that the small settlement does not appear to have served as much more than a temporary encampment. More important, el-Kowm 2 differs from the Zagros outposts in that it lacked seals and seal impressions, balls, bullae, tablets, and other artifacts implying participation in regional and long-distance exchange.

The nature and reliability of available evidence on the Uruk outposts thus far recognized is outlined in tables 1 and 2, below.

THE CHRONOLOGY OF URUK SETTLEMENT IN THE PERIPHERY

Enclaves

Within the geographical horizon of the Syro-Mesopotamian plains and in terms of their control of the structures of communication and transportation of the area, the urban-sized Uruk enclaves and associated stations effectively constituted nodes in a "network" of surprising breadth. The growth of the network was surely organic, although our under-standing of pertinent chronological data is not yet sufficient to disentangle its details. Nevertheless, its apogee and eventual collapse may be correlated with developments in the Mesopotamian alluvium and Susiana by means of the glyptic and epigraphic evidence from sites such as Habuba-süd/Qannas, Jebel Aruda, Nineveh, and to a lesser extent, Tell Brak. Although existing chronological sequences are not always representative or entirely comparable, the cylinder seals and seal impressions, balls, bullae, and the characteristic numerical notation tablets and complex tokens found in the northern enclaves have a restricted chronological range that can be established in reference to Uruk-period sequences at sites such as Warka and Susa.[24] These parallels suggest a date about the end of the Uruk-period sequence as presently understood for the apogee of the network, roughly equivalent to Levels VI–IV of the Eanna sequence of Warka and Levels (19?)18–17 of the more reliable Acropolis I sequence at Susa (Strommenger 1980b:486; Nissen 1986b:328).[25] If we presume that accounting procedures in the peripheral enclaves would have reflected contemporary practices at the core, the collapse of the network may be dated using the same categories of evidence. Aside from the two unusual and otherwise unparalleled tablets from Brak with a single pictogram (Fig. 18 I), the general absence of pictograms in numerical notation tablets recovered in the northern sites (minimally at Habuba, Aruda, and Nineveh) suggests that the abandonment of the network predates the latest subphase of the Uruk period in the alluvium, Eanna IVa, when the earliest of the Archaic Tablets appear (Nissen 1986b).

However, not all the enclaves need have undergone the same explosive growth that may be documented for the Habuba/Qannas/Aruda settlement. Some may have been established earlier in the Uruk period and grown over a longer period of time. This is apparent even in the Tabqa area. Recent and continuing excavations at Tell Sheikh Hassan have revealed a superimposition of at least eighteen distinct Uruk levels (Boese 1986/87), suggesting a southern Mesopotamian presence in the Tabqa region that significantly predated the Habuba/Qannas/

Aruda emplacements directly across the river. Moreover, some of the Uruk enclaves elsewhere also had fairly long sequences. The clearest cases are Brak and Nineveh, although a fair depth of Uruk deposits can also be inferred for Carchemish. The so-called Eye Temple at Brak, it will be recalled, was only the last of four apparently similar structures in the very same spot. It is certain that even the earliest of those structures ("Red Eye Temple") dates to the Uruk period, since beveled-rim bowls were found in direct association (Mallowan 1947:222). These structures must have been situated on the acropolis of the mound, and their sequence spans at least 6 meters of deposits (Mallowan 1947:50). What exactly the depth of Uruk-period deposits outside of the Brak acropolis was is unknown, but as noted above, recent British surveys suggest an average thickness of about 2 meters across the mound. Similarly, judging by the incidence of beveled-rim bowls in the section, the deep sounding at Nineveh shows that possibly 5–6 meters of deposits of the Uruk period existed at the site (Campbell Thompson and Mallowan 1933: pl. LXXIII). At Nineveh, however, there are no indications in the published material of the functional nature of the area cut by the deep probe.

Outposts

Intriguingly, while some of the urban-sized enclaves in the Syro-Mesopotamian plains evolved over a significant span of time, the much smaller isolated outposts found farther away in the periphery appear to have a much more restricted chronological development, which coincides only with the floruit of the enclave network and could possibly be later. Little can be said about the el-Kowm outpost, as its function is uncertain and only ceramics were recorded.[26] However, greater precision is possible in the case of the Iranian outposts, as both Godin (V) and Sialk (IV.1) produced a broader range of evidence. Particularly important from a chronolog-

ical standpoint are the convex, cushion-shaped numerical notation tablets found in each of the two sites, which date to the very end of the Late Uruk sequence at Susa. With but a single exception inscribed with a pictogram (fig. 26I), the Godin tablets are impressed only with wedge- and dot-shaped numerals, and some bear in addition rollings of a single cylinder seal of Uruk style (Weiss and Young 1975:8–9, figs. 4–5). Identical tablets are also found at Sialk (e.g., fig. 27M).[27] These tablets correlate wholly with examples from Susa that are found only in Level 17 of the Acropolis I sequence (Le Brun and Vallat 1978:30). However, like the one tablet from Godin, some of the Sialk tablets (e.g., fig. 27N) also bear isolated pictograms which place them typologically later than the Susa Level 17 tablets (Amiet 1986:68).[28] The possibility does exist, then, that the occupations of Godin and Sialk could postdate Susa Level 17. However, there is no need to correlate those occupations with the Proto-Elamite period at Susa and the Jemdet Nasr period in the neighboring alluvium, since the one tablet from Godin and the few from Sialk bearing isolated pictograms are definitively earlier than the distinctive Proto-Elamite A administrative tablets of Level 16 at Susa and Period IV.2 at Sialk. Moreover, as Dittmann (1986b:171) has recently argued, the latest subphase uncovered in the Acropolis I sounding at Susa (Level 17A) does not necessarily represent the end of the Uruk-period occupation of the site, but rather a shift in settlement away from the exposed structures, which were left to collapse (cf. Le Brun 1971:210–11). A later occupation predating the Proto-Elamite period is thus likely to have existed, although it is yet to be isolated stratigraphically in the Susa sequence. It is with this ill-defined subphase that the Godin V and Sialk IV.1 occupations should be correlated.[29]

But what was the purpose of the Mesopotamian enclaves, stations, and outposts across the periphery? It is to this question that I turn in chapter 4.

TABLE 1. Types of Uruk Settlement in the Mesopotamian Periphery

Site	Settlement Type	Associated Stations (figs. 22, 24)	Surrounding Cluster (figs. 7, 8, 15)	Size (in ha)	Location	Orientation (fig. 20)	Regions Accessible	Resources Accessible
Habuba/Qannas/ Aruda	Enclave	Site 96 Site 99 Site 55 Site 1 Qraya Ramadi Nr. Rawa	5 sites certain, 3 sites possible	18–40	Euphrates Euphrates Euphrates Euphrates Euphrates Euphrates Euphrates Euphrates	N-S, Route 5 W, Route 9	Syrian Saddle Cilicia	Amanus wood; Bolkardağ minerals, Malatya wood, Keban/Altınova metals
Carchemish area: Tiladir Tepe, Kum Ocaği, Şadi Tepe	Enclave	BS 265 BS 183 BS 35	18 sites	28 +	Euphrates Balikh Balikh Balikh	N-S, Route 5 E-W, Route 3 N-S, Route 8	Syrian Saddle, Northern Mesopotamia, Anatolian highlands	As above
Samsat	Enclave	Hassek Site 15 Site 39 BS 265 BS 183 BS 35	6 sites	17.5?	Euphrates Euphrates Incesu Incesu Balikh Balikh Balikh	N-S, Route 8 E-W, Route 2	Anatolian highlands, Northern Mesopotamia, Syrian Saddle	Malatya wood, Keban silver, Ergani copper
Tell Brak	Enclave	Fadgami? etc.? Qraya Ramadi Nr. Rawa	11 sites?	43 +	U. Khabur L. Khabur L. Khabur Euphrates Euphrates Euphrates	N-S, Route 7 E-W, Route 3	Northern Mesopotamia, Eastern Taurus	Keban silver, Ergani copper
Nineveh	Enclave		?	40?	U. Tigris	N-S Route 6 E-W, Route 2 E-W, Route 3	Northern Mesopotamia	Zagros copper, lapis, gold?, stones; Keban silver; Ergani copper
Godin Tepe (V)	Outpost	N.A.	N.A.	Small	Inland, Kangavar valley	E-W, Route 11 Khorasan Road N-S, Susiana-Rayy	Iranian central plateau	Zagros copper, silver, lead, gold?, lapis, stones
Tepe Sialk (IV.1)	Outpost	N.A.	N.A.	Small	Inland, by Kashan	N-S, Susiana-Rayy	Iranian central plateau	As above
El-Kowm 2 Caracol	Outpost?	N.A.	N.A.	Small	Inland, El-Kowm oasis	E-W, Route 10	Syrian desert Orontes valley	?

Note: N.A. = not applicable.

TABLE 2. Nature and Reliability of Data on Uruk Settlements in the Mesopotamian Periphery

Site	Type	Nature of Evidence	Primary References
		EUPHRATES	
Near Rawa	Station	Survey: ceramics (r?)	M. van Loon, pers. comm.
Tell Qraya	Station	Excavation: ceramics (+), glyptic practices, and iconography, reckoning devices	Reimer 1989; Simpson 1988
Tell Ramadi	Station	Survey: ceramics (+)	Geyer and Monchambert 1987
Sites 1, 55, 96, 99	Stations	Survey: ceramics (r?)	Kohlmeyer 1985
TABQA CLUSTER			
Habuba-süd/ Quannas/Aruda	Enclave	Excavations: architecture, reckoning devices, numerical notation tablets; ceramics (+); glyptic practices and iconography, stone amulets, small objects	Strommenger 1980a; Finet 1979 Sürenhagen 1974/75; Topperwein 1973; Ludwig 1979; van Driel and van Driel-Murray 1979, 1983; van Driel 1982, 1983.
Sheik Hassan	Early Enclave? Cluster Site	Excavations: architecture, reckoning devices, Glyptic practices and iconography, broad range of ceramics	Boese 1986/87
Tell Habuba K.	Cluster site	Excavations: ceramics (r?)	Strommenger 1980a
Tell el Hajj	Cluster site	Excavations: ceramics (+)	Stucky et al. 1974
Tell Hadidi	Cluster site	Excavations: ceramics (−)	Dornemann 1988
Tell Mureybit	Cluster site	Excavations: ceramics (−)	van Loon 1968
Mureybit Ferry	Cluster site?	Survey: ceramics (?)	van Loon 1967
Zreyjiye-south	Cluster site?	Survey: ceramics (?)	van Loon 1967
Tell Kreyn	Cluster site?	Survey: ceramics (?)	van Loon 1967
BIRECIK-JERABLUS CLUSTER			
Jerablus	Cluster site?	Survey: ceramics (r?)	Strommenger 1980a
Jerablus Tahtani	Cluster site	Survey: ceramics (+)	G. Stein, pers. comm.
Carchemish	Enclave?	Excavations: ceramics (+), seal iconography	Woolley 1921, 1952
Tiladir Tepe/ Kum Ocağı/ Şadi Tepe	Enclaves	Survey; terra cotta wall cone, broad range of ceramics	Algaze 1989a; Algaze et al. 1991
Komeçlı Höyük	Cluster site	Survey: ceramics (+)	Algaze et al. 1991
Akarçay Höyük	Cluster site	Survey: ceramics (−)	Algaze et al. 1991
Şavi Höyük	Cluster site	Survey: ceramics (−)	Algaze et al. 1991
Şeraga Höyük	Cluster site	Survey: ceramics (−)	Algaze et al. 1991
Kırmızı Ok	Cluster site	Survey: ceramics (−)	Algaze et al. 1991
Yarim Tepe	Cluster site	Survey: ceramics (−)	Algaze et al. 1991
Zeytin Bahçeli	Cluster site	Survey: ceramics (−)	Algaze et al. 1991
Aktaş H. #1	Cluster site	Survey: ceramics (−)	Algaze et al. 1991
Kefri Höyük	Cluster site	Survey: ceramics (−)	Algaze et al. 1991
Near Şaray # 1	Cluster site	Survey: ceramics (−)	Algaze et al. 1991
Tilbes Höyük	Cluster site	Survey: ceramics (−)	Algaze et al. 1991
Horun Höyük	Cluster site	Survey: ceramics (−)	Algaze et al. 1991
SAMSAT CLUSTER			
Samsat	Enclave	Survey and excavation: ceramics (+); glyptic iconography; terra cotta wall cones	Özdoğan 1977; Özgüç 1987; Mellink 1988, 1989; Özten 1984
Site 15	Cluster site? Station?	Survey: ceramics (+)	Wilkinson 1990a
Site 39	Cluster site? Station?	Survey: ceramics (−)	Wilkinson 1990a
Hassek Höyük	Station	Excavation: architecture, glyptic iconography, terra cotta wall cones, broad range of ceramics, small objects and amulets	Behm-Blancke et al. 1981; Behm-Blancke et al. 1984; Behm-Blancke 1989

(continued)

Notes: (?) data are suspect; (−) data are reliable but the range of types present is small; (+) data are reliable and the range of types present is broad; and (r?) range of types present is unknown.

TABLE 2.   (continued)

Site	Type	Nature of Evidence	Primary References
		BALIKH	
BS 35, 182 BS 265	Stations?	Survey: ceramics (r?)	Akkermans 1988b
		KHABUR	
Tell Brak	Enclave	Excavation: architecture, architectural decoration, broad range of ceramics, glyptic practices and iconography, stone amulets, small objects	Mallowan 1947; Fielden 1981a; D. Oates 1977, 1982, 1983, 1985; J. Oates 1985, 1986
Sites 1, 7, 26, 58	Stations?	Survey: ceramics (r?)	Monchambert 1984
Umm Qseir	Station?	Excavation: ceramics (+)	Hole and Johnson 1986/87
Tell Fadgami	Station?	Survey: ceramics (+)	Johnson 1988/89; Röllig and Kühne 1977/78
		TIGRIS	
Nineveh	Enclave	Excavation: glyptic practices and iconography, numerical notation tablets, broad range of ceramics	Campbell Thompson and Hutchinson 1931; Campbell Thompson and Hamilton 1932; Campbell Thompson and Mallowan 1933; Algaze 1986b; Collon and Reade 1983
		HIGHLANDS	
Godin Tepe (V)	Outpost	Excavation: glyptic practices and iconography, numerical notation tablets, broad range of ceramics	Weiss and Young 1975
Sialk (IV.1)	Outpost	Excavation: glyptic practices and iconography, numerical notation tablets, broad range of ceramics	Ghirshman 1938; Amiet 1985
		SYRIAN DESERT	
El-Kowm 2	Outpost	Excavation: ceramics (+)	Cauvin and Stordeur 1985

Notes: (?) data are suspect; (−) data are reliable but the range of types present is small; (+) data are reliable and the range of types present is broad; and (r?) range of types present is unknown.

4

The Function of Uruk Settlements in the Syro-Mesopotamian Plains and Surrounding Highlands

GATEWAY COMMUNITIES

The pattern of Uruk settlement in the Syro-Mesopotamian plains and in the highlands is indicative of the function of those sites. The isolation of Uruk enclaves within alien hinterlands is often encountered in situations of initial colonial contact between societies at markedly different levels of sociopolitical evolution. Often described as dendritic central places by geographers, such centers are characteristic of vertical distribution systems that cut across political and cultural boundaries and allow well-organized polities maximum access at minimal expense to less developed peripheries (Smith 1976). In fact, the very specific location of Mesopotamian enclaves in the north at focal nodes of the structures of communication crisscrossing the area closely matches models elaborated by geographers to explain the formation and distribution of settlements over nonhomogeneous landscapes in situations where long-distance trade is of primary economic importance. Under these conditions, the models propose that attempts to control access to resources and regularize their flow will likely lead to the creation of "gateway" settlements at natural passage points between contrasting regions involved in the exchange or at locations of "considerable transportational significance," such

as critical nodes along a transportation route or bulk-breaking points (Burghardt 1971; Hirth 1978).

The strategic rationale underlying the location of Uruk enclaves in the Syro-Mesopotamian plains, discussed in the preceding chapter, makes a compelling case for the enclaves as ancient "gateway communities." Their position seems efficiently suited for control of access in and out of the alluvium and of the flow of resources and goods in both directions. Although some of the enclaves could have and most probably did tap into the considerable agricultural potential of their surroundings, the geographically scattered distribution of the enclaves is an indication that neither the acquisition of broad expanses of territory (formal empire) or the effective large-scale exploitation of local agricultural resources were primary considerations (for a contrary view, however, see Schwartz 1988a). The efficient exploitation of Syro-Mesopotamian agricultural resources would have required a radically different configuration than the one observed: a more extensive settlement pattern in areas of high agricultural productivity, such as the Upper Khabur and Upper Tigris basins. In such areas, one would have expected to find a broad range of Uruk sites in various sizes dispersed over a wide landscape away from the rivers and the principal routes—in short, a settlement pattern similar to that observed for the

Susiana plain. Political control would have also necessitated a different settlement pattern than the one actually observed. Although specific circumstances no doubt differed greatly, it is perhaps possible to use what is known of the structure of Neo-Assyrian imperial control over Syro-Mesopotamia in the first millennium B.C. (Malbran-Labat 1982) to infer what effective Uruk political control over portions of the same area would have looked like. Such control would likely have required dispersed Uruk administrative facilities and garrisons within important Late Chalcolithic indigenous centers in the hinterlands of Syro-Mesopotamia, and well as regularly spaced way stations and storehouses along the principal east-west overland routes crisscrossing the area.

Moreover, that control of neither territory nor agricultural resources were primary factors behind Uruk emplacements in the north is underscored by the location of the Habuba/Qannas/Aruda enclave in the Tabqa region, an area where average annual rainfall is at best marginal (150–250 mm) and where river incision precludes irrigation outside of the Euphrates floodplain. In fact, modern studies of the Tabqa region suggest that a good rainfed crop can only be expected once every ten years or so (Métral 1987:112, n. 6). Thus, unless one presumes that the river was significantly less incised in Uruk times than at present, that rainfall was then more abundant, or that shortfalls in the Tabqa area would be made up by better-situated enclaves upstream in Anatolia, in the long run the position of the Habuba/Qannas/Aruda enclave and nearby Uruk sites would have been difficult in the face of local opposition blocking access to grain and other agricultural supplies from the fertile Syrian plains of the Aleppo region to the northwest.[1]

Several clues from the main Uruk settlements of the Tabqa area are consistent with the argument that the cooperation of native groups must have been taken for granted at the time the settlements were established. For one, grain storage facilities were not detected at Habuba-süd, Tell Qannas, or Jebel Aruda, in spite of the substantial exposures that were practicable at each of those sites.[2]

Furthermore, those exposures produced few agricultural implements. Only a few sickles were recorded at Habuba-süd (Strommenger 1980a:55), and at Aruda blades with silica sheen or denticulation such as would be expected for agricultural use were reported to be "almost completely absent" (Hanbury Tenison 1983:27). Instead, as noted by Sürenhagen, what was found were indications that grain from the Syrian hinterland was imported into the settlement. Evidence is provided by a number of storage jars of the chaff-faced Amuq F type found at Habuba, some containing the remains of grain (Sürenhagen 1986a:21–22). These jars are common in contemporary Late Chalcolithic sites across the Syro-Mesopotamian plains and were not produced at Habuba. Some measure of peaceful contact and exchange must have existed in order to ensure continued access to local agricultural resources without which the Tabqa enclave, for all its mighty walls, could not have survived for any extended period of time.

Another case in point is the distribution of apparent Uruk stations on the Balikh alongside what must have been an important overland route. These sites, it will be remembered, were situated in the vicinity of larger indigenous centers, and whatever their function, they could not have existed or operated without the implicit consent of nearby rulers. Most telling in regard to the probable collaboration of local polities and Uruk settlements, however, is the location of Mesopotamian outposts in the Zagros and, possibly, Taurus ranges—of which Godin and Sialk are the only excavated examples. The case of Godin is clearest. In the context of the highland Late Chalcolithic settlement at Godin (Godin VI), the small Uruk fort at the top (Godin V) represents a replica in miniature of the much larger southern Mesopotamian enclaves in the northern plains. In both cases, the intrusive outposts are embedded in an alien hinterland—in the Godin case it is simply all the more immediate. Irrespective of whether the Godin V outpost had its roots in forces originating in the alluvium or, as the excavators have argued, in the at this time closely associated Susiana plain, it is beyond doubt that the position of the hilltop settlement would have been untenable in the face of active local opposition. The survival of outposts such as Godin and Sialk implies that the highland communities in the midst of which they were located were amenable to participation in a wider exchange network tying into the alluvial lowlands of southern Iraq and Khuzestan.

URUK MATERIALS IN THE SURROUNDING PIEDMONT AND HIGHLANDS

The presence of Uruk enclaves in the Syro-Mesopotamian plains and of outposts in the Zagros strongly suggests that highland resources were being exploited for the alluvial market. Further evidence that this was so is provided by the presence of typical Uruk materials in numerous local sites in the Zagros/Taurus piedmont and highlands. The majority of the sites in question remain unexcavated, and therefore little can be said about the specific intrasite context of many of the objects. At a minimum, however, the intrusive artifacts are indicative of the existence of cross-cultural contacts between highland communities and Uruk polities. Equally important, the distribution of these artifacts furnishes us with important clues as to the intensity and direction of that interaction. It is possible that some of the sites in which characteristic Uruk artifacts are found (in many cases only limited survey evidence is available) might turn out to represent further Uruk outposts in the Godin V or Sialk IV.1 model. However, the majority were surely indigenous occupations. Such sites are often the largest in their localities and are commonly situated at positions commanding either access to highland routes (fig. 30) or to known deposits of highland resources (fig. 35).

Highland Routes

The distribution of Uruk artifacts in sites controlling access to highland routes is most definite in the case of east-west routes across the northern and central Zagros. In those areas, isolated Uruk ceramics are usually found in indigenous sites commanding the valleys leading into and across the mountains. In the northern Zagros piedmont area within Iraqi Kurdistan, for example, Mesopotamian cul-

tural elements have been identified at a variety of sites, all well positioned to control the main routes from the Transtigridian Plains into the highlands. Those routes, it will be remembered, follow the courses of the principal left bank tributaries of the Tigris as they cut across the Zagros (Levine 1973, 1974a). A case in point is the Late Chalcolithic mound of Qalinji Agha (now within the suburbs of Erbil), where two Mittelsaal-type houses flanking an irregularly buttressed platform (fig. 28) suggest some measure of interaction with the Uruk world (Abu al-Soof 1969; Hijara 1973).[3] Such contacts should come as no surprise, since Erbil/Qalinj Agha is centrally located in the Transtigridian plain between the Greater and Lesser Zab rivers and is the traditional terminus of routes into the piedmont following the courses of each of those rivers. Those up the Greater Zab lead toward Ruwandiz and ultimately emerge in the Solduz valley and the Qazvin area, while those up the Lesser Zab cross the Rania plain and eventually reach Hamadan (fig. 30). Surveys and excavations in the Rania area, in fact, have documented at least four Late Chalcolithic sites yielding a small assortment of Uruk ceramics within local assemblages. Uruk types attested include beveled-rim bowls, and characteristic spouted (e.g., fig. 29L–M), pear-shaped (fig. 29K), and strap-handled jars (Abu al-Soof 1985). Interestingly, each of the sites in question (Qarashina, Basmusian, Kamarian, and Tell Shemshara) is located along the principal track across the Rania plain into the Zagros (Abu al-Soof 1970).

Similarly, on the Kirkuk plain not far from where the Adhaim River emerges from the mountains is the site of Nuzi, where layers containing beveled-rim bowls and other typical Uruk pottery types (e.g., fig. 29G, I–J) were exposed in a deep sounding. Also found at Nuzi, but in a different sounding, was a cache of numerous stamp seals with coarse drilled designs (e.g., fig. 29A–B) and four cylinder seals (e.g., fig. 29C–D) (Starr 1939). One of the latter bears the typical late fourth millennium motif of carelessly drilled rows of ovals (fig. 29D), noted repeatedly in the preceding discussions. The stamp seals, in turn, closely resemble

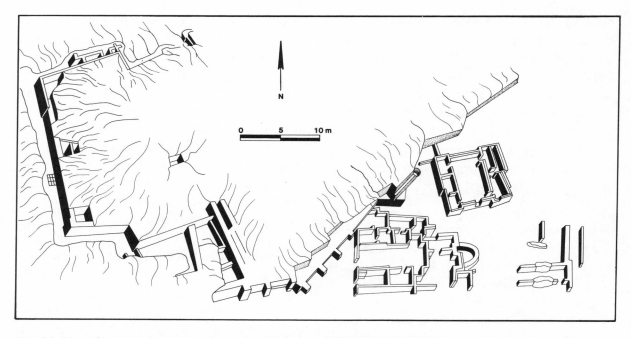

Fig. 28. Plan of buttressed terrace and associated houses at Qalinj Agha (Level IV).

examples from the Eye Temple sequence at Brak.[4] Nuzi, too, is well positioned to control routes into the piedmont, in this case those toward the Shahrizur plain in the Diyala River headwaters and the Sulemaniyah area, which eventually emerge into the Hamadan plain via Sanandaj (fig. 30). Not surprisingly, at least three excavated sites in the Shahrizur area (Bakr-i-Awa, Dwanza Imam, Gerdi Resh) have yielded a limited range of typical Uruk pottery (e.g., fig. 29E, F, H, N), once again, in the context of local assemblages (Abu al-Soof 1985; Hijara 1976).

It is in the central Zagros along the Khorasan Road from the Diyala and Hamrin plains into the Iranian plateau (fig. 30), however, where interaction between Uruk polities and highland communities appears to have been most intense and where the distribution of Uruk materials in strategically situated indigenous sites is most clearly observed. Surveys within the Zagros in Iran show that isolated Uruk ceramics are not uncommon in sites along the various intermontane valleys traversed by the Khorasan Road. Beveled-rim bowls and a limited range of other Uruk pottery types have been identified not only in the Kangavar valley, where Godin is lo-

cated, but in at least eleven sites in the Shahabad and Mahidasht valleys as well, closer to the Diyala (Levine and Young 1987; Young 1986). South of the Khorasan Road, in the intermontane valleys of Luristan, there is less evidence of contacts (Goff 1971; Young 1966), although this may well reflect nothing more than the greater intensity and reliability of surveys to the north. The valleys and plains across Luristan are isolated from Mesopotamia by the imposing Kabir Kuh chain, through which few passes are practicable (Goff 1968). Communications, therefore, are oriented longitudinally toward Khuzestan, and known routes follow the Karkekh and Dez rivers and their tributaries northward (Goff 1971; Stein 1940). Isolated beveled-rim bowls are found in at least two sites in the Hulailan valley (Chia Fatela and Chasmeh Sardeh), which must tie into routes up the Saimarreh River, a tributary of the Karkekh (Goff 1971; Mortensen 1976). Finally, beveled-rim bowls (Dyson 1965) and a single four-lugged jar (Contenau and Ghirshman 1935: pl. 68, top right) are also reported at Tepe Giyan, in the Nehavand valley, which is closely connected to both north-south routes up the Dez and to the Khorasan Road system (fig. 1, above; fig. 30).

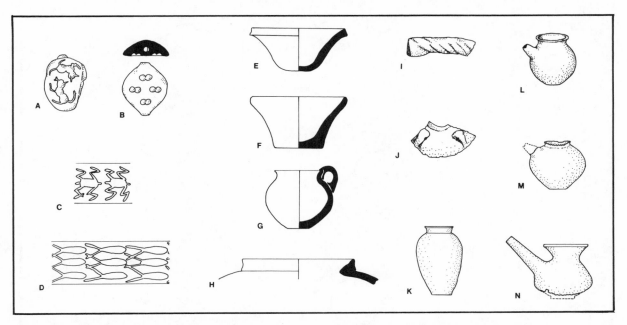

Fig. 29. Selected elements of Uruk culture at sites in the Transtigridian Plains and the Iraqi Kurdistan sector of the Zagros piedmont (not to scale).

Archaeological explorations of southern Zagros passes have been to date less intensive than those of comparable routes to the north. Nevertheless, it is certain that significant highland-lowland contacts also took place across the southern Zagros in the Uruk period. A survey of the Shahr-i Kord plain in the Bahtiyari region just northeast of Khuzestan, for example, revealed two sites barely 1 kilometer from each other (possibly successive occupations) with some Uruk ceramics on their surface (Zagarell 1982:39, 64, figs. 7, 25, 27–28). Both sites are located along an important road from Susiana (via the Izeh plain) into the central plateau, the same route that connects eventually with the Sialk outpost. Further still to the south, routes across the Zagros toward Fars and eventually Kerman and Sistan (fig. 1) remain largely unknown, save for the early surveys of Stein (1936, 1940). These routes must have been important, however, since Uruk materials were commonplace in surveyed Early Banesh sites in the Kur River basin of Fars (Alden 1979; Sumner 1986). Types attested include beveled-rim bowls (fig. 31A), storage-sized jars with undercut rims, four-lugged jars with characteristic shoulder incisions (fig. 31E–F), spouted

bottles with band rims (fig. 31G), an assortment of typical drooping or trumpet-shaped spouts (fig. 31H), pear-shaped bottles (fig. 31I), wall cones (fig. 31J), and stone weights (?) with cruciform grooves (fig. 31B).[5]

Alden (1982) interprets the Uruk materials in Fars as signifying an actual process of colonization by settlers from Khuzestan. In the absence of coherent exposures of Early Banesh levels that would reveal the nature of the associated cultural assemblage, however, available evidence could as well be taken to indicate a process of acculturation caused by the onset of intense contacts with Uruk societies in the Susiana plain, possibly related to the opening of routes toward the southeast. In either case, however, interaction between Fars and the Uruk world can be shown to have been a long-term process, since beveled-rim bowls are found already in excavated Terminal Lapui–period levels in at least one Kur River basin site, Tal-i Kureh (Alden 1979:155). Perhaps significantly, Early Banesh sites cluster in the western portion of the basin (Alden 1982:620; Sumner 1986), at the head of routes from Khuzestan via the Ram Hormuz and Behbahan plains (Hansman 1972; Stein 1940). Nevertheless, a cache

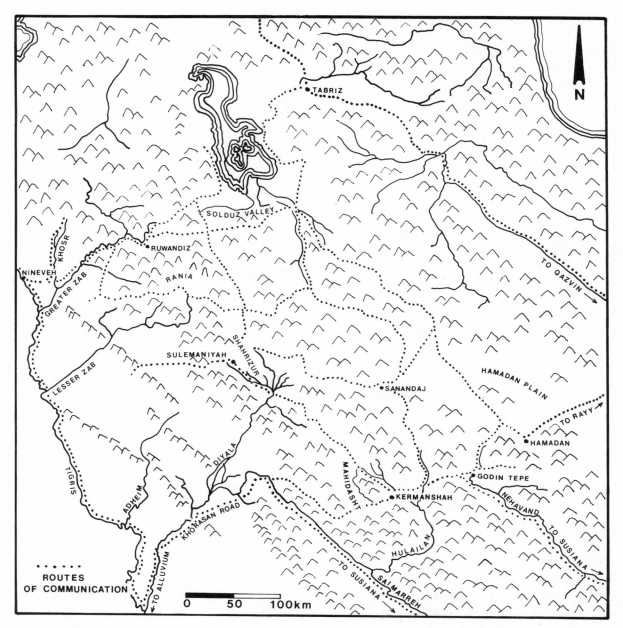

Fig. 30. Sites in the Transtigridian Plains and intermontane valleys of the northern and central Zagros where Uruk materials have been found.

of vessels among which were several unmistakable Uruk types (e.g., fig. 31C–D) was found by Stein in the opposite (northeast) end of the Kur River basin, in a narrow defile that appears to mark a track northward toward the Isfahan area.[6] Whether or not these vessels indicate an actual occupation or simply one or more burials cannot, however, be ascertained from the published information.

A similar distributional pattern of Uruk materials within local sites is found in southeastern Anatolia and the Taurus region. There, too, sites with evidence of southern Mesopotamian cultural elements appear to stand at the top of local settlement hierarchies and are commonly found at locations controlling access to highland routes. One such route appears to have been the Tigris River itself and its various tributaries. Beveled-rim bowls have been recognized at the site of Çattepe at the confluence of the Tigris and the Bohtan Su, an important Tigris tributary southeast of Siirt (Algaze 1989a: 254). The strategic position of this site astride a traditional route following the Bohtan into the eastern Taurus and the Bitlis Pass (British Admiralty 1917; Route 85) is demonstrated by the fact that Çattepe later became the locus for a sizable Late Roman *equites* fort on the eastern border of the Roman empire (Lightfoot 1986), large portions of which are still visible today. Further upstream on the Tigris catchment, beveled-rim bowls have also been recovered at Gre Migro, an imposing (45 meters high) mound on the Batman River. Located 22 kilometers north of the confluence with the Tigris, Gre Migro is the most important multiperiod mound in the Batman basin (Algaze 1989a). Moreover, traces of a classical period(?) bridge by the foot of the mound indicate that this site too is well positioned in relationship to traditional routes in the region (fig. 32).

The best example yet known from Anatolia of the correlation between Uruk materials and strate-gically located native sites is Arslan Tepe in the Malatya area of the eastern Taurus (fig. 32). Recent Italian excavations at this site have uncovered a massive Late Chalcolithic architectural complex (see fig. 45 below) characterized by a largely indigenous assemblage (Arslan Tepe VIA) that will be discussed in greater detail in the chapters that follow (Frangipane and Palmieri 1988). For the moment, it is sufficient to note that within this complex was found a small number of imported Uruk artifacts and locally made copies of Uruk pottery types and seals. Particularly important are a variety of spouted jars and bottles of unmistakable Uruk ware and type (fig. 33D–E) recovered *in situ* in storerooms (Palmieri 1989: fig. 3:5–7). Other Uruk or Uruk-like types in the complex include a handful of beveled-rim bowls (fig. 33C), an ovoid jar with a crosshatched band and diagonally reserved slip shoulder decoration (fig. 33 G), small four-lugged jars (fig. 33A), drooping spouts (Palmieri 1973: fig. 72:10), and globular storage-sized jars with winkel-haken-like impressions and diagonally reserved slip on their shoulders (fig. 33F). Also found in the complex were impressions made from a limited

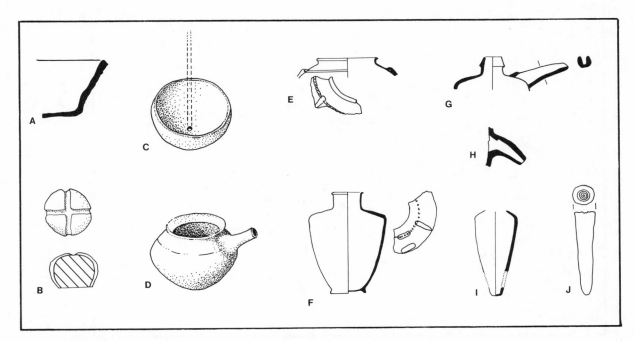

Fig. 31. Selected elements of southwest Iranian Uruk culture in Fars Province (not to scale).

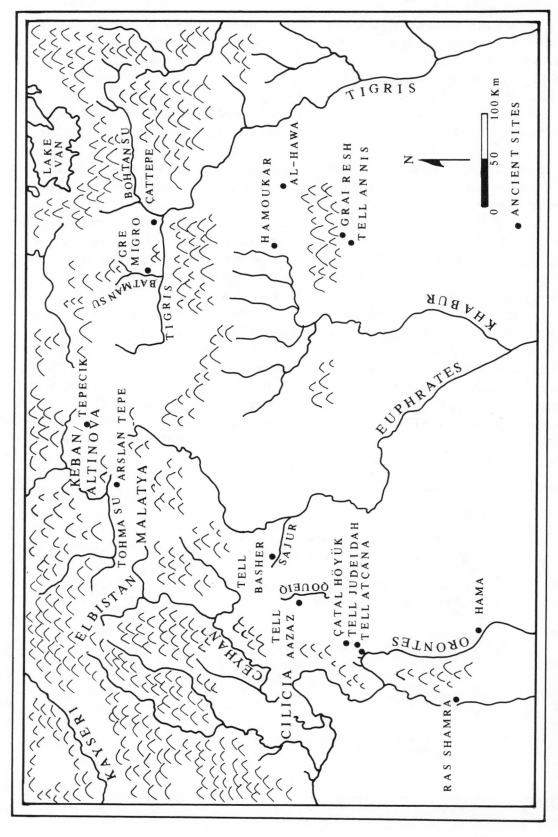

Fig. 32. Late Chalcolithic sites in the Syro-Mesopotamian plains and southeastern Anatolian highlands where Uruk materials have been found.

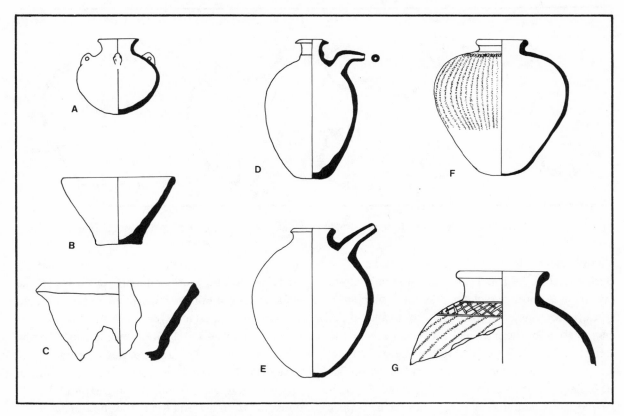

Fig. 33. Selected ceramics of Uruk origin or Uruk type from Period VIA levels at Arslan Tepe (not to scale).

number of locally produced cylinder seals with an iconographical repertoire strongly reminiscent of Uruk glyptic styles (e.g., fig. 44A–D below). The presence of Uruk-related artifacts at Arslan Tepe is certainly not coincidental. Surveys indicate that the site is the largest in the Malatya plain and the nearby Tohma Su basin. Moreover, the Malatya area commands an important pass across the Taurus range and has historically represented the natural meeting point of routes from the Kayseri plain and central Anatolia (via Elbistan or the Tohma Su) and routes from eastern Anatolia and the Syro-Mesopotamian plains (Yakar and Gürsan-Salzmann 1979).

Highland Resources

In addition to sites controlling access to important highland routes, Uruk materials are also often recognized in indigenous sites exploiting known deposits of valued highland resources. Typically, those sites are also located within easy reach of im-

portant routes of communication. This pattern is clearest in the case of metals, particularly copper. In the Taurus highlands, for instance, traces of copper smelting have been uncovered in Late Chalcolithic levels of sites in the Keban region, near the important Ergani copper mines and accessible to the Upper Khabur area of northern Mesopotamia via routes across the Karacadağ/Tur Abdin massif. Two of the sites, Tepecik and Norşuntepe, produced sizable amounts of copper slag (Esin 1975; Hauptmann 1975), indicating the existence of a flourishing native industry which probably predated and was surely contemporaneous with the network of Uruk enclaves in the north. Intriguingly, Uruk ceramics have been reported in one of those sites, Tepecik (fig. 34). These materials were not found in the main settlement itself, where smelting was performed, but were concentrated instead on an isolated structure on the southwest slope of the mound (Esin 1982).

Important copper deposits also exist in the Ira-

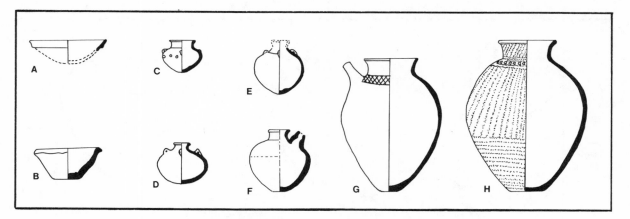

Fig. 34. Selected ceramics of Uruk type from the structure on the southwest slope of Tepecik (not to scale).

nian plateau (J. R. Caldwell 1967; Wertime 1973; Berthoud et al. 1982). There, too, it is possible to document the presence of a handful of Uruk pottery types in the context of local sites commanding access to some of the principal copper sources in the area (fig. 35). At Tepe Ghabrestan (Level IV.1–3), for example, numerous beveled-rim bowls and occasional conical cups of Uruk type (Majidzadeh 1976a) were found. The site lies near copper sources in the Qazvin plain and appears to have been an important metallurgical center since at least the fifth millennium B.C. (Majidzadeh 1979). Ghabrestan was accessible to Uruk societies through either the Khorasan Road or through an east-west road of lesser importance into northern Mesopotamia via the Solduz valley and the Lesser Zab.

A comparable case is found at Tepe Sialk where, as will be recalled, an Uruk outpost was established astride the principal north-south route across the Iranian plateau. Two distinctive Uruk spouted bottles (e.g., fig. 27C) were found in a level predating the outpost,[7] and a recent reevaluation of the evidence by Amiet (1985, 1986) suggests that other Uruk artifacts assigned in the original publication to Sialk IV may have been found instead in earlier levels (fig. 27D, F, K). Like Ghabrestan, Sialk was located close to important copper sources (fig. 35), and it was an important metallurgical center long before its first contact with Uruk societies is documented at the site (Majidzadeh 1976a). Sources in the Veshnoveh area in the im-

mediate vicinity of Sialk may have been mined already in the late fourth millennium, although the evidence is not conclusive (Holzer, Momenzadeh, and Gropp 1971). However, analyses of copper objects from Susa and Sialk show that the Anarak mines, which are the largest in Iran and are located some 100 kilometers due east from Sialk in the Dasht-i Kavir, were certainly being exploited at the transition from the fifth to the fourth millennium, if not before (Berthoud et al. 1982).

Finally, important copper sources are also found in the Kerman region (Berthoud et al. 1982; J. R. Caldwell 1967). Once again a small variety of Uruk materials are found at strategically located sites near those sources. Cases in point are Tal-i Iblis in the immediate vicinity of a major deposit and Tepe Yahya near less substantial mines (fig. 35). The case of Iblis is clearest. Situated in the Bardsir valley some 80 kilometers southwest of Kerman, Iblis was by the fifth millennium an important indigenous metallurgical center comparable to either Ghabrestan or Sialk (J. R. Caldwell 1967). Beveled-rim bowls, four-lugged jars, and other Uruk types were identified in late fourth millennium deposits (Iblis IV) at the site (J. R. Caldwell 1967:23–25, figs. 24, 26, 45:5). The case of Yahya, a little over 200 kilometers directly south of Kerman, is more ambiguous, as the only Uruk type recovered in contemporary levels (Yahya Va) was the beveled-rim bowl, and only a handful of small sherds of the type were represented (Beale

1978:301).[8] The Kerman-area resources processed at Iblis or Yahya were accessible to Uruk societies in Khuzestan, either directly through routes across the south-central Zagros and the Kur River basin or indirectly from the Sialk/Kanshan area via routes bordering the western edge of the Dasht-i Kavir and Dasht-i Lut (J. R. Caldwell 1967:26).

The distribution of Uruk artifacts in the Zagros/Taurus ranges indicates that while Uruk enclaves in Syro-Mesopotamia and Uruk states in Khuzestan controlled the flow of resources and goods in and out of the alluvium, by and large control of the sources of raw materials themselves and of the routes that fed into the lowlands was held by indigenous communities that were willing to trade. Excavated archaeological evidence of one such community is available from the site of Tepe Gawra, situated some 20 kilometers northeast of Nineveh alongside one of the tracks across the Transtigridian plain that follows the length of the Khosr River into the Zagros (British Admiralty 1917: Route 67a).

The evidence from the site is somewhat ambiguous: in the context of what was published as a small mound, about 2 hectares in extent, were found significant indications of spatial and social differentiation not entirely compatible with our preconceptions of the social structure of settlements of Gawra's alleged size. The unique round structure uncovered in Level XI and the large tripartite structures of Levels IX and VIII (Tobler 1950), for example, suggest a measure of labor mobilization beyond the resources usually associated with small villages. An analogous conclusion is indicated by the presence of numerous sealings at the site suggesting the receipt of commodities from the surrounding area (Rothman 1988). Similarly, the substantial amounts of exotic resources recorded in some of the Late Chalcolithic tombs at Gawra are unexpected in the context of such a small settlement (Tobler 1950).

One possible explanation for the observed discrepancies at Gawra is that a lower terrace sur-

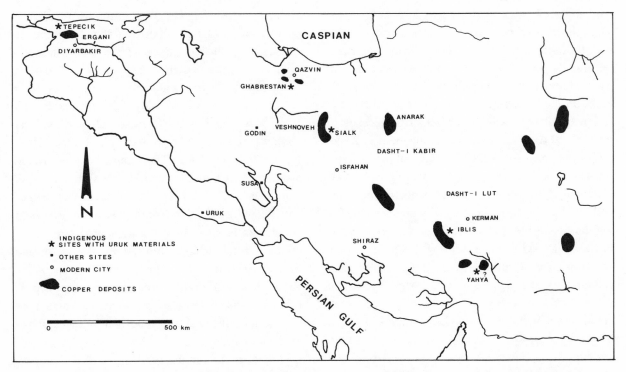

Fig. 35. Principal copper-bearing deposits in southeastern Anatolia, the Iranian plateau, and western Afghanistan and indigenous sites in their vicinity where Uruk materials have been found.

rounding the mound may exist that was neither dug nor recognized by the excavators (McG. Gibson, pers. comm., 1986). It is thus possible that Gawra as presently known represents but the acropolis of a significantly larger site. However, other scenarios (which need not exclude the preceding) are also possible. One is that suggested by Rothman (1988), who sees Gawra as a small independent ceremonial and administrative center servicing seminomadic groups in the Transtigridian Plains and the Zagros piedmont. Another is that Gawra represented a specialized settlement, perhaps an important link in the chain of local communities involved in highland-lowland trade. What role, if any, seminomadic groups would have had in the exchange is uncertain, but this last hypothesis would serve to explain the relative wealth of Late Chalcolithic levels at the site in terms of exotic imported resources such as precious and semiprecious stones (turquoise, jade-ite, hematite, lapis, carnelian, diorite, marble, alabaster, gypsum, serpentine, steatite, quartz), sea shells, ivory, obsidian, copper, silver, and gold (Rothman 1988; Tobler 1950). Moreover, this exchange-link hypothesis would also help to explain the close connections with the highlands that may be discerned across a wide spectrum of the material culture of Late Chalcolithic levels at Gawra. This relationship is particularly close in the glyptic and ceramic repertoires of the site. The glyptic tradition of Gawra, with its characteristic scenes of horned and tête-bêche animal arrangements (Tobler 1950), has precise parallels in the stamp seal tradition of contemporary sites in the Zagros (D. H. Caldwell 1976) and highland Anatolia (Frangipane and Palmieri 1988). Also closely matched in the highlands are the distinctive fine impressed wares of Levels IX–XI (Tobler 1950: pl. LXXXa), which are attested at a number of Anatolian sites, most prominently at Norşuntepe in the Altınova area of the eastern Taurus (Hauptmann 1979: pl. 30). Other connections with the Altınova area are documented by the mortuary practices of the Late Chalcolithic inhabitants of Gawra. A case in point is provided by the rectangular mud-brick tombs of Levels VIII–XI (e.g., Tobler 1950: pl. XLVIa), which find pre-

cise correspondence at Korucutepe (van Loon 1978:10–11, pl. 9).

URUK MATERIALS IN THE SYRO-MESOPOTAMIAN PLAINS

Scattered Uruk ceramic types and, more rarely, seals have also been recovered at numerous Late Chalcolithic sites across the Syro-Mesopotamian plains. Such materials provide our only indication for the extent and direction of contacts between Uruk emplacements along the rivers and communities in the immediately surrounding plains.

East of the Euphrates (fig. 32), for instance, isolated Uruk pottery types are reported at (1) the important site of Tell Hamoukar in northeastern Syria (Sürenhagen, cited in Weiss 1983:44); (2) a variety of small sites surveyed on the plains north of the Jebel Sinjar in northwestern Iraq (Wilkinson 1990b); (3) the large site of Tell al-Hawa; also in the Sinjar plains of Iraq (Ball, Tucker, and Wilkinson 1989); and (4) at several sites on the southern flank of the Jebel Sinjar in Iraq, including Tell Gudri (Abu al Soof 1985), Tell an-Nis (Lloyd 1938), and Grai Resh (Lloyd 1940). West of the river (fig. 32), beveled-rim bowls are reported at the important site of Hama on the Orontes River, where a long sequence of the bowls was attested (Thuesen 1988:114, table 26), and in three sites in the plain of Antioch, Alalakh (Woolley 1955b), Çatal Höyük (fig. 36A), and Tell Judeidah (Braidwood and Braidwood 1960:234). A handful of other Uruk types (e.g., fig. 36B–C) have also been excavated at Judeidah, where they concentrate in late Phase F and early Phase G floors (Braidwood and Braidwood 1960). Uruk spouted jars with drooping spouts can be identified in a plundered Late Chalcolithic burial at Eski Ören (Archi, Pecorella, and Salvini 1971: fig. 90), a small mound on the Afrin River in the Gaziantep area. Finally, unspecified types of Uruk pottery are reported at a small Late Chalcolithic site near Karatepe on the Ceyhan River in the southern piedmont of the western Taurus (M. Özdoğan, pers. comm., 1988).

Less common but also attested in the plains west of the Euphrates in southeastern Turkey and

Syria (fig. 32) are cylinder seals carved in provincial versions of Uruk glyptic styles depending heavily on the use of the drill. The majority are of unknown provenance, having been acquired in the antiquities market (e.g., fig. 36E).[9] A few of the seals, however, can be assigned with varying degrees of certainty to specific sites. Particularly noteworthy among the latter are (1) a seal depicting a row of horned animals within ladderlike motifs (fig. 36D), allegedly excavated at Ras Shamra (ancient Ugarit); (2) four seals with varying motifs from Tell Judeidah and Çatal Höyük (e.g., fig. 36F);[10] (3) one seal depicting a herd of animals in front of a shrine in a manner strongly reminiscent of seals from Warka (Buchanan 1966: no. 22: cf. Heinrich 1936: pl. 19c), alleged to be from tell Aazaz in the Qoueiq basin north of Aleppo; and (4) two seals engraved in provincial versions of the Uruk animal-file motif (Buchanan 1966: nos. 707, 715) from Tell Basher, a large mound along the Sajur River midway between Gaziantep and Carchemish (Archi, Pecorella, and Salvini: 1971:95–97).

As a whole, the distribution of Late Chacolithic sites in the Syro-Mesopotamian plains in which isolated Uruk artifacts are documented is less easy to characterize than that of Uruk materials in the highland and piedmont sites already discussed. The clearest pattern emerged east of the Euphrates, where some of the sites appear to have been relatively important within their respective localities and others were certainly positioned along established overland routes. This is most obvious in the case of the Sinjar sites. Those on the southern flank of the Jebel Sinjar are clearly aligned with the southernmost of the main routes between the Upper Tigris and the Upper Euphrates (fig. 20; Route 4; and fig. 21), while those on the plains north of the Jebel are aligned with more northerly routes (fig. 20; Route 3; and fig. 21). This is confirmed by Wilkinson's recent survey in the northern Sinjar plains. He found that while Late Chalcolithic settlements were numerous, only a minority of those sites yielded a small range of associated grit-tempered Uruk sherds. More significant, sites in which Uruk materials were recovered were generally aligned with east-west overland routes across the area (Wil-

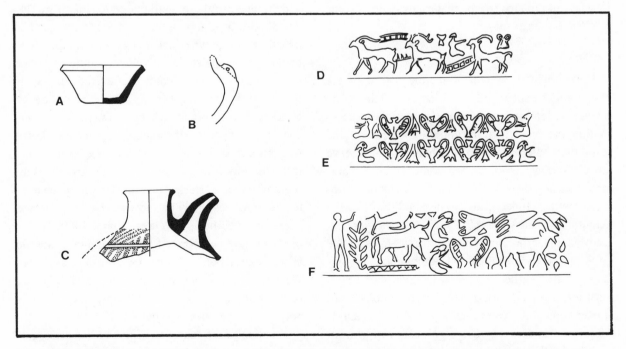

Fig. 36. Selected ceramics of Uruk type from the plain of Antioch and samples of peripheral Uruk seals from northern Syria (not to scale).

kinson 1990b: fig. 6, underlined sites). West of the Euphrates River, however, the distribution of local sites with Uruk materials is less clear because of the wide geographical dispersal of the sites in question, and because in many cases comprehensive surveys in their vicinity are lacking. The nature of indigenous settlements in Syro-Mesopotamia at the time of the Uruk intrusion will be discussed in detail in chapter 5.

THE COMMODITIES EXCHANGED

In the long term, cross-cultural exchange and some measure of indigenous collaboration are the only hypotheses that satisfactorily explain available evidence for the Uruk presence across the Mesopotamian periphery. In particular, these hypotheses account for (1) the locational pattern of Uruk enclaves in the Syro-Mesopotamian plains, (2) the otherwise marginal position of the Habuba/Qannas/Aruda cluster, (3) the small Uruk sites near large local centers along the Balikh route, (4) the isolated position of Uruk outposts in highland valleys of the Zagros, (5) the distribution of scattered Uruk artifacts within indigenous highland sites near metal resources, and finally, (6) the material wealth of some local sites such as Gawra.

Exports

Not much is known about the nature of the commodities exchanged, but if later third and early second millennium documentation may be used as a guide, the majority of the goods exported from the alluvium would have been perishables, which leave few or no traces in the archaeological record. Paramount among these would have been elaborate finished textiles. Indeed, all the preconditions for the manufacture and export of such textiles were already in place in Mesopotamian city-states of the Uruk period (below, chap. 7), although actual evidence of the textiles themselves in peripheral sites must await the development of more sophisticated archaeological recovery techniques. Less certain is whether surplus grain was a significant export from the alluvium. To be sure, in the Sumerian epic cycle dealing with the kings Enmerkar and Lugalbanda

(Kramer 1952; Wilcke 1969), the city-state of Uruk in the alluvium is portrayed as exporting grain to the city-state of Aratta, located somewhere in the Iranian highlands, possibly in the vicinity of Kerman (Majidzadeh 1976b). This led Kohl (1978:472) to suggest that some highland communities may have come to depend on alluvial grain for their subsistence, but this is disputed by others (e.g., Possehl 1986:85). In any event, long-distance export of grain is not likely to have occurred on a regular basis because the transport of bulk commodities overland between the Mesopotamian alluvium and the Iranian or Anatolian highlands by means of donkeys simply would not have been economical in the long term (Bairoch 1988:11–12).

Whether or not the various types of Uruk ceramics recovered in the highlands were acquired for their contents is unclear. The answer is likely to depend on the function of each of the types involved and this remains largely undetermined. Other than beveled-rim bowls, the most common Uruk forms found in peripheral sites are spouted jars, four-lugged jars, pear-shaped jars, strap-handled jars, and storage-sized jars with undercut rims (figs. 29, 31, 33, 34, 36), although not all sites have this full constellation of types and not every example need be an actual import. Intuitively, it is difficult to see how the coarse but ubiquitous beveled-rim bowls that constitute our most frequent evidence of cross-cultural contacts could have been traded. This inference now appears substantiated by the results of neutron activation analyses of beveled-rim bowls from the environs of Samsat in the Atatürk Dam region of southeastern Anatolia, where the characteristic bowls can now be shown to have been made from site-specific local clays (Evins 1989). More likely to have been prized for their contents are the Uruk spouted bottles found in storerooms at Arslan Tepe VIA. These vessels raise the possibility that valuable liquids (wine or oils?) were one Uruk export, as will be discussed below.

Although the majority of the cylinder seal impressions found at Arslan Tepe with Uruk-related iconography were made from locally produced seals (below, chap. 6), it is possible that some of the impressions may have been of Mesopotamian origin and reached the site accompanying exchange goods. One stopper fitting a bottle of Uruk type, for instance, was found discarded in the same storeroom and bore the impression of an as yet unpublished cylinder seal (Palmieri 1985:32). Inversely, discarded stamp seal impressions found in Uruk enclaves in the north and in Uruk cities in the south may have originated in peripheral sites and arrived accompanying goods of a thus far undetermined nature. A circular impression from the Eye Temple platform at Brak (Mallowan 1947: pls. XXIV:20), for instance, depicts a stag in a style typical for Chalcolithic glyptic in numerous northern sites.[11] Similarly, a number of stamp seal impressions and actual seals from Warka could prove to be of northern or highland origin. The majority of these seals and sealings are of unknown provenance (e.g., Jakob-Rost 1975: nos. 18, 20, 22, 32, 35; Heinrich 1936: pl. 20d), but a few from the Anu Ziggurat area were recovered in levels that can be securely assigned to the Uruk period (e.g., fig. 37A–D).[12]

Imports

But what exactly were the resources funneled into the alluvium as a result of the Uruk control of the structures of long-distance trade in the plains of Syro-Mesopotamia in the late fourth millennium B.C., and moreover, which resources were being acquired through Uruk states in Khuzestan? A number of possibilities may be suggested on the basis of (1) the locational pattern of Uruk enclaves in the north and outposts in the highlands, (2) the observed distributional pattern of Uruk artifacts in indigenous peripheral sites, and (3) direct evidence of resources from the periphery recovered in Uruk sites in the Mesopotamian alluvium and the Susiana plain.[13]

The location of Uruk outposts at Godin Tepe and Tepe Sialk astride the principal east-west and north-south routes traversing the central plateau of Iran is surely indicative of the importance of resources from the plateau and beyond for Uruk societies. One such resource was copper, an essential

commodity that figures prominently in the earliest pictographic tablets (Eanna IVa and III) from Warka (Nissen 1985b:358). Copper artifacts are commonly recovered in Uruk-period contexts. In the alluvium, this was best documented at Warka, where numerous copper vessels and implements were found in Anu Ziggurat area levels underlying the White Temple (Moorey 1985:24–25), in the inventory of the Riemchengebäude (Eanna IV; Lenzen 1958, 1959) and in the Sammelfund hoard (Eanna III, but containing earlier heirlooms; Heinrich 1936:47). Also found at Warka were numerous unworked copper lumps (Heinrich 1938:25) and what by all accounts appears to have been an installation for smelting metals (Nissen 1970:114). Copper implements are also common in Uruk sites in Khuzestan (e.g., Le Brun 1978a). As outlined in the preceding section, significant evidence exists for the exploitation of copper deposits in the Iranian plateau well before the Uruk period. By the late fourth millennium, however, this exploitation must have been at least partially oriented toward satisfying the needs of emerging Uruk urban centers. This may be inferred from the distribution of Uruk ceramics at local sites controlling access to known copper resources and, more tellingly, from the implantation of an Uruk outpost at Sialk. Moreover, the exploitation of Iranian copper sources for Uruk centers can actually be demonstrated at Susa. Analysis of copper artifacts from Uruk-period (and earlier) levels at that site show that the copper used was extracted from the Anarak mines of the Dasht-i Kavir near Sialk (Berthoud et al. 1982).

Other more exotic metals exploited by Uruk societies are also obtainable in the central plateau of Iran. Minimally, these include gold, silver, and lead. Silver and lead commonly associate in the same deposits and, like copper, are obtainable from the Anarak mines. Silver mines are also found in the Dasht-i Lut near the modern city of Yazd (J. R. Caldwell 1967). Silver is attested at Uruk sites. Silver beads, pendants, and bracelets have been found at Sialk in tombs attributable to the Uruk outpost level (IV.1) (Amiet 1985:308), and silver jewelry has also been found in Uruk burials at Susa (Le Bre-

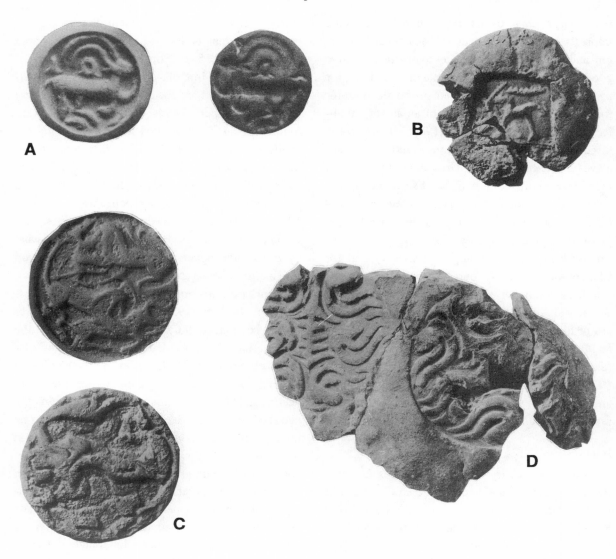

Fig. 37. Stamp seals and stamp seal impressions from Uruk levels at Warka of possible northern or highland origin. A–C: "Kleinfund Schicht" between layers C and D, Anu Ziggurat area; D: Eanna, deep sounding, Level XII (scale 1:1).

ton 1957:109). In the alluvium, silver artifacts have been recovered at Warka, once again, both in the Riemchengebäude (Lenzen 1958, 1959) and the Sammelfund (Heinrich 1936). One important indication that silver from the Iranian plateau was reaching Uruk sites is its presence at the Sialk outpost. Another, is that lead, a by-product of silver extraction, was also found in the Sialk outpost (Amiet 1985:297) and was imported into Late Uruk Susa (de Mecquenem 1943: fig. 14), where it

was fashioned into spouted vessels that imitate contemporary pottery shapes (Le Brun 1978a: fig. 24:9–10).

Less certain, however, is whether gold from the central plateau was being exploited in the Uruk period. Important deposits are located in a zone extending from Qum to Golpayegan, not far from Tepe Sialk (J. R. Caldwell 1967). While there is little evidence to indicate that these deposits were exploited extensively in antiquity, a handful of gold beads have been reported in the Sialk outpost (Amiet 1985:308). Alternately, gold could have been extracted from deposits in the central Zagros in the vicinity of Nehavand and Hamadan—both within easy access to the Khorasan Road and the Kangavar valley (Maxwell-Hyslop 1977:85). A final possibility is that gold, together with lapis lazuli, could have been brought from Afghan sources (Maxwell-Hyslop 1977:85). Gold is attested in Uruk sites in Khuzestan (Johnson 1987:127), but does not appear to have been common. Nonetheless, a small variety of gold artifacts were recovered in contemporary sites in southern Iraq, for instance at Warka in layers underlying the White Temple (Heinrich 1937:53; 1938: pl. 29B), in the Riemchengebäude (Lenzen 1958), and in the Sammelfund (Heinrich 1936:47). Like gold, lapis lazuli also appeared fairly suddenly in the Uruk period, and numerous examples have been reported at Susa (Hermann 1968) and Warka (Heinrich 1936; Lenzen 1958). Lapis is only obtainable from mines in faraway Badakhshan in modern-day Afghanistan, and it most likely reached the Mesopotamian lowlands through either the Khorasan Road or through trans-Iranian routes across Kerman and Fars into Susiana (Majidzadeh 1982). However, more northerly routes across Anatolia are also possible, since unworked chunks of lapis were recovered at Jebel Aruda on the Euphrates (van Driel and van Driel-Murray 1979).

While copper, gold, silver, lead, and lapis from the central plateau and beyond were accessible to Uruk societies through the northern enclaves or Khuzestan, a number of other commodities present in Uruk sites must have been funneled through Uruk states in Khuzestan tapping into routes from southeastern Iran across the south-central Zagros. Such routes are well attested in the third millennium B.C., and their existence already in the late fourth millennium is indicated, as will be recalled, by the presence of Uruk ceramics in the Shar-i Kord plain and in the Kur River basin. One such commodity from the southeast is steatite/chlorite from the Kerman region (Beale 1973; Kohl 1978). It was used for the manufacture of cylinder seals (Asher-Greve and Stern 1983) and for intricately carved ritual

vessels such as those found at Warka and Ur (e.g., Moortgat 1969: pls. 15–16; Strommenger 1962: no. 28). Another was a variety of semiprecious and precious stones, usually worked as inlays, beads, pendants, or amulets. Most prominent among these are carnelian and agate, which could have originated in sources in western India or central Afghanistan (Allchin 1979), but are also found in the central plateau of Iran. The greatest diversity and number were recovered in the Sammelfund (Heinrich 1936:41–41), although exotic stones were also common in earlier contexts at Susa (Le Brun 1978a; Steve and Gasche 1971) and Warka. The contents of the Riemchengebäude, for example, included a unique thronelike chest intricately inlaid with variously colored limestones, alabaster, and lapis (Lenzen 1959). Various exotic stones were also common at Brak, where they were used for small amulets and seals and for architectural decoration in the Eye Temple frieze (Mallowan 1947).

In the same way that the location of Uruk outposts in the Zagros and the distribution of Uruk artifacts in Iranian sites are suggestive of the importance for Uruk societies of resources from the Iranian central plateau, the location of Mesopotamian enclaves in the Upper Tigris, Upper Khabur, and Upper Euphrates areas of Syro-Mesopotamia within easy reach of routes in and out of the highlands of southeastern Anatolia and northwestern Iran is surely indicative of the importance of resources from those regions. No doubt, some of the most important of those resources were timber and wood products—essential though difficult-to-trace commodities. The Kurdish highlands of easternmost Anatolia and Iraq were still heavily forested in the fourth millennium B.C., and exploitable species in the area included pines, junipers, and oaks (Zohary 1973:188–98; Willcox 1992). Zagros timber floated down the Tigris and its various tributaries may help explain Nineveh, although admittedly we still lack direct evidence for the exploitation of wood resources from the Zagros in the Uruk period. We are on firmer ground, however, in the case of Anatolia. Historically, the headwaters of the Euphrates in the southeastern Taurus represented a crucial source of timber for societies in the tree-poor Mesopotamian alluvium. This role is explained by transportational constraints: trunks cut in the Malatya area could easily and cheaply be floated south on the river (Rowton 1967). While we still lack conclusive evidence, it is probable that the export of wood resources from the Euphrates headwaters to the alluvial market may have begun in the Uruk period in order to meet the architectural requirements of rapidly growing Uruk urban centers (Margueron 1992). There is some, admittedly circumstantial, paleobotanical evidence to support this assumption. A recent study of carbonized materials from archaeological contexts in the Keban/Altınova region has concluded that a gradual process of deforestation took place in antiquity and that the process had its onset in the Late Chalcolithic period (Willcox 1974), which correlates with the establishment of Uruk enclaves in the northern plains.

In addition to wood, a number of base and precious metals are also obtainable in the eastern Taurus, including copper, silver, lead, and gold. The importance of the Keban/Altınova and nearby Ergani areas as a potential source of metal ores or finished metal products for southern Mesopotamian societies is underscored by recent explorations into the metallurgical resources available in those areas and their possible exploitation in antiquity (de Jesus 1980; Yener 1983; Seeliger et al. 1985). In fact, recent excavations in the Keban/Altınova region indicate that those resources were being exploited already in the late fourth millennium. As previously noted, substantial evidence for the smelting of copper has been uncovered in Late Chalcolithic levels of excavated sites in the eastern Taurus. An Anatolian origin for some of the copper found in Uruk sites in the alluvium is thus a distinct possibility, particularly since copper implements were common in some of the northern Uruk enclaves, such as Habuba-süd (Strommenger 1980a), Jebel Aruda (van Driel and van Driel-Murray 1979), and Tell Brak, where copper was used for paneling portions of the walls of the central sanctuary of the last Eye temple (Mallowan 1947:32).

Similarly, the important polymetallic mines in the Keban/Altınova area (Yener 1983; Seeliger et al. 1985) constitute a likely source for Mesopota-

mian silver and lead in the Uruk period. Numerous silver objects in Late Chalcolithic graves at Korucutepe, not far from the Keban mines, underscore the fact that the silver sources of the area were being extensively exploited at the time of the Uruk expansion (Brandt 1978; van Loon 1978), and silver is attested in the nearby Uruk enclave at Brak in the Upper Khabur (Mallowan 1947:95). Almost certainly also of Anatolian origin are lead artifacts from northern contexts. One example is a lead bowl from Uruk-period deposits at the small site of Umm Qseir along the Lower Khabur in Syria (Hole and Johnson 1986/87:183). Gold, too, was procurable in the eastern Taurus (Maxwell-Hyslop 1977), and the presence of significant amounts of this metal in the Eye Temple frieze at Brak (Mallowan 1947:93) suggests that Anatolian sources were being exploited for the Uruk market. Finally, another possible import into the alluvium from the eastern Taurus was obsidian. Numerous obsidian bladelets were found in the Riemchengebäude (Lenzen 1959) at Warka. Also dated to the Uruk period is a cache of fine obsidian vessels recovered in layers under the White Temple, also at Warka (Heinrich 1937: pl. 59; Jordan 1932: pl. 20A). A number of those vessels closely resemble examples found in Late Chalcolithic tombs at Tepe Gawra (cf. Tobler 1950: pl. LIIIB–C) and may have been imported as finished products.

While it is likely that both the Habuba/Qannas and the Birecik-Jerablus clusters may have had a role in the control of bulk downstream river traffic from the Anatolian highlands to the alluvium, it should also be remembered that those sites were also oriented toward overland routes across the Syrian Saddle and the west. This orientation suggests the possible exploitation of resources from Southwestern Anatolia and from the Lebanon/Anti-Lebanon and Amanus ranges. The Amanus region was, of course, an important source of wood in the third millennium (Rowton 1967). The great Akkadian king Naram-Sin is the first recorded of many Mesopotamian rulers who sent expeditions to collect prized cedars from Lebanon (Hirsch 1963), but it is not yet possible to ascertain whether the considerable wood resources of the Amanus and Lebanon ranges were already being logged in Uruk times. Recent discoveries of polymetallic mines in the Bolkardağ region of the Taurus near the Cilician gates may also be relevant, particularly since those resources were already being mined in Late Chalcolithic times (Yener et al. 1989:491). Although we have no direct evidence of the exploitation of Bolkardağ metal ores for the Mesopotamian market, the already noted presence of scattered ceramics of Uruk type in the plain of Antioch and along the Ceyhan River basin does suggest some measure of contact between local communities controlling access to the Amanus and western Taurus resources and Uruk settlements on the Euphrates.

In addition to the resources already discussed in connection with specific routes, other imported materials may be documented in the archaeological record of Uruk sites which cannot be tied to any specific source. One such commodity was bitumen, which is obtainable from natural seepages at various locations in southwestern Iran at the foot of the Zagros, in the Middle Euphrates region in the vicinity of Hit, and in the Upper Tigris region near Mosul and Kirkuk (Marschner and Wright 1978). Bitumen was made into asphalt by mixing it with mineral and vegetable matter and used as mortar and for general waterproofing in architectural contexts. Extensive amounts of asphalt were used in Uruk structures at Warka (Heinrich 1937) and Tell Uqair (Lloyd and Safar 1943).

Common stones represent another imported commodity that often cannot be tied to any specific source. One such stone was gypsum, widely available in deposits across the Zagros/Taurus foothills (H. T. Wright, pers. comm. 1992) and in exposed bluffs along the courses of the Tigris and Euphrates rivers in northern Mesopotamia and southeastern Anatolia (H. E. Wright 1955:85). In the Uruk period, but not commonly thereafter, gypsum was heated to make a kind of plaster that was used on the walls of important buildings. More rarely, gypsum plaster was also fashioned into cones and employed as wall decoration in monumental architecture, as at Eridu (Safar, Lloyd, and Mustafa 1981:240). Finally, gypsum plaster was also used for making common bricks and mortar, which were

then used to erect buildings. This peculiar practice is attested at a number of sites (Warka, Eridu, Tell Uqair, Ur, and Mereijib; cf. Hout and Maréchal 1985) and suggests that supplies of imported gypsum were particularly abundant in alluvial centers during Uruk times. Substantial quantities of limestone boulders were also brought into Uruk cities. These boulders were used for building purposes, a practice again only rarely attested after Uruk times. A number of important Uruk public buildings at Warka, for example, had stone foundations and one unique and apparently subterranean structure (Steingebäude) appears to have been built entirely of stone (Boehmer 1985). Similarly, limestone boulders were used for the revetment façade of the platform of successive Uruk public buildings at Eridu (Safar, Lloyd, and Mustafa 1981). Limestone was obtainable from sources in the western desert not far from Warka and Eridu (Boehmer 1985). However, the possibility that limestone could have been quarried from outcrops across the Syro-Mesopotamian plains and shipped down the Tigris or Euphrates cannot be discounted, particularly in light of the advantages of water transport for the movement of goods that are heavy or bulky.

Another stone import was flint. It is widely available as nodules in the western desert and is also obtainable in the Zagros piedmont and across the northern plains. It must have been imported as raw material for the local production of tools. This can actually be demonstrated at Warka, since a number of cores and matching trapezoidal blades were found in the Reimchengebäude (Eichmann 1987). More easily traced, however, are distinctive flint implements imported as finished artifacts. Tabular scrapers, for example, are attested in many contemporary Levantine sites and can be shown to have been manufactured for export in the Negev (Rosen 1983). Scattered examples are reported in such widely separated sites as Jebel Aruda in Syria and Chogha Mish in Khuzestan (Sürenhagen 1986a:19–20). Also reported at Aruda are Canaanean blades of nonlocal manufacture (Hanbury Tenison 1983). These may have been imported from the Upper Euphrates in Anatolia, since specialized workshops producing Canaanean blades for regional distribution were identified at Hassek Höyük, the Uruk station north of Samsat (Behm-Blancke et al. 1984:35). Almost certainly also imported as finished tools were a variety of small blades of rock crystal found as part of the already mentioned cache of chipped-stone artifacts in the Reimchengebäude (Eichmann 1986).

Other exotic stones of uncertain provenance were also imported in the Uruk period. Rarer varieties include colored and bituminous limestones, quartz, chalcedony, amazonite, amethyst, diorite, aragonite, rock crystal, and jasper (Heinrich 1936). More frequent though still rare are translucent stones such as fine alabaster and gypsum, its closely related but coarser variant. At its most spectacular, alabaster was used for carved ritual objects such as the famous vase from the Sammelfund at Warka (Moortgat 1969: pl. 19), the trough from Warka now in the British Museum (Moortgat 1969: pls. 17–18), and the hundreds of "eye" amulets at Brak (Mallowan 1947: pl. XXV:1–9). More common in Uruk sites are cylinder seals (Asher-Greve and Stern 1983) and diverse utilitarian and votive objects made of calcite or marble. These are broadly distributed in sites in the alluvium and Khuzestan and in Uruk enclaves and outposts across the periphery. Included are solid weights or mace heads(?) with characteristic cruciform grooves (fig. 38A–C), various animal-shaped amulets and stamp seals (e.g., fig. 38D–I),[14] and assorted containers and theriomorphic vessels (e.g., fig. 38J–M).[15] The remarkable uniformity of these distinctive artifacts across such widely separated areas is striking and suggests the existence of specialized centers devoted to the production of standardized products for export tailored to the needs of Mesopotamian states in the fourth millennium in a manner reminiscent to the later mid–third millennium trade in carved "intercultural style" chlorite/steatite vessels studied by Kohl (1978, 1979). If so, such manufacturing centers could possibly be located near known calcite and quality gypsum deposits in the central plateau of Iran (Beale 1973), or in sites in Khuzestan such as Susa (Le Breton 1957:109) or Tal-i Ghazir, where Henry Wright (pers. comm., 1992) observed

numerous unfinished stone bowl fragments littering the surface of the site.

Some evidence for cross-cultural trade in finished stone vessels between the Iranian plateau and the Mesopotamian world does exist in the Uruk period. Among the Banesh period sites surveyed by Alden in the Kur River basin was one site (8G38) dated to the Early and Early-Middle Banesh phases which appears to have served as a local distribution center and as a transshipment point for stone vessels between the Iranian east and Susiana in Uruk times. This may be inferred from a number of clues. First, precise parallels may be drawn between vessels found at the site and vessels from Uruk levels in Khuzestan and the Mesopotamian alluvium.[16] Second, on the surface of the site were found hundreds of bowl fragments made of stones not locally available, but there were few joins, suggesting that the bowls were broken elsewhere and discarded haphazardly at the site. Last, traces of debitage were not found at the site, indicating that the bowls were made elsewhere (Alden 1979:114).

Other widely distributed semiprecious and common stones were also imported in the Uruk period for conversion into objects of artistic expression, ritual vessels, utilitarian implements, and the like. Minimally, these include (1) basalt of southeastern Anatolian (Karacadağ area) or northern Syrian (Jebel Haas) origin (Meyer 1981:25–26), which was sometimes used for relief sculpture, for example, the famous Warka Lion Hunt stele (Moortgat 1969: pl. 14), and more frequently, for the manufacture of grinding stones and related ground-stone artifacts; (2) bituminous limestone from oil-bearing layers in the highlands of Iran and northern Iraq, used for ritual vessels, such as are commonly found in association with religious architecture at Warka (e.g., Heinrich 1937: pl. 60; 1938: pl. 29A), and for sculpture in the round, such as a naturalistic ram's head from Warka assignable to the Uruk period on stylistic grounds (Moortgat 1969: pls. 22–23); (3) marble, which is found in the Syrian desert but is more common in the Zagros and the central plateau of Iran (Beale 1973) and was used for ritual vessels (e.g., Lenzen 1958: pl. 40A–B) and, once

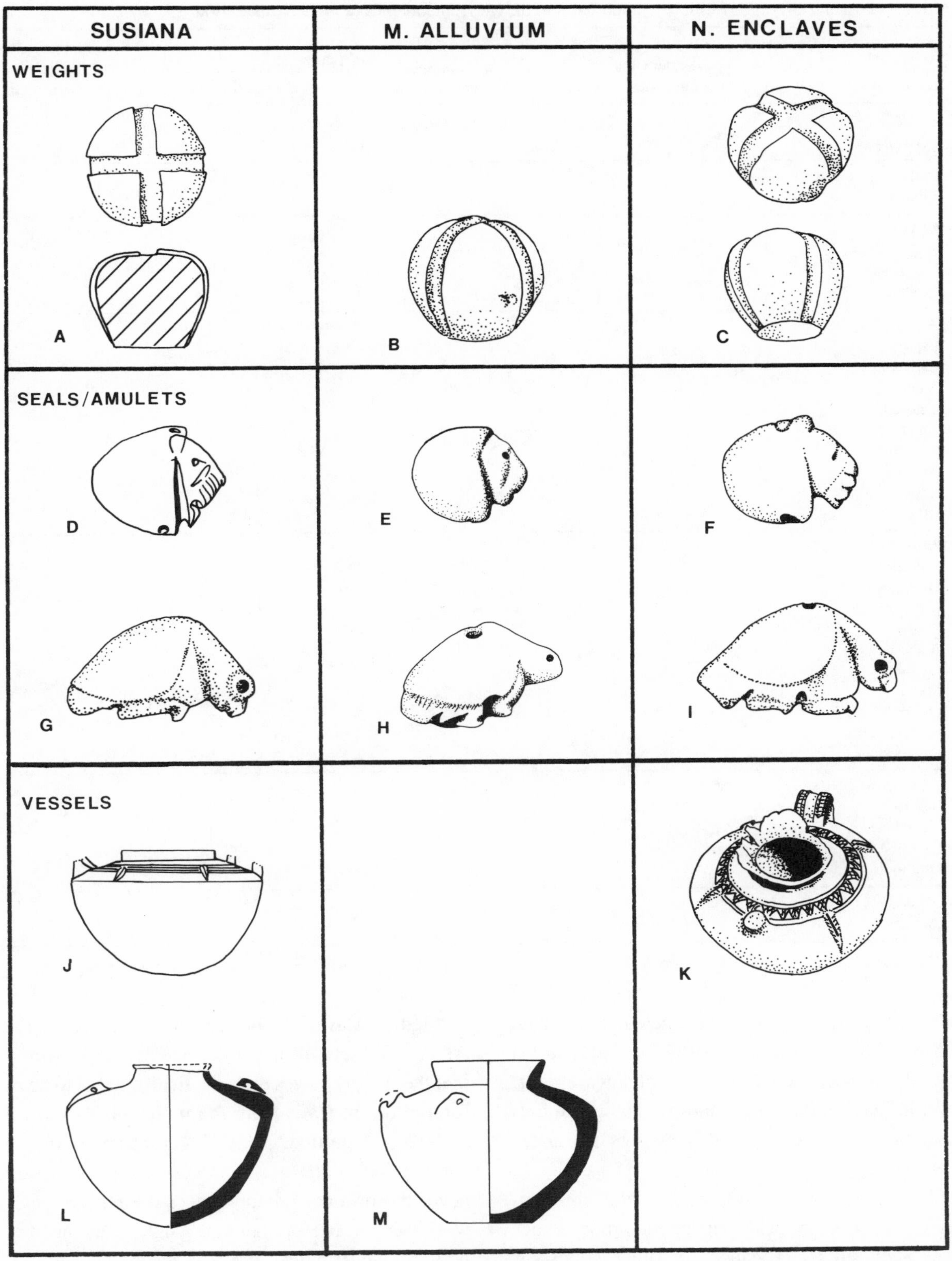

Fig. 38. Selected parallels in stone artifacts between Uruk sites in the Susiana plain, the Mesopotamian alluvium, and Syro-Mesopotamia (not to scale).

TABLE 3.   Possible Origin of Resources Imported into the Mesopotamian Core in the Uruk Period

Resources	Amanus (via Habuba)	Western Taurus (via Euphrates enclaves)	Eastern Taurus		Syro-Mesopotamian Plains (via Northern enclaves)
			(via Euphrates enclaves)	(via Brak/Nineveh)	
LABOR					
POW/slaves					x
WOOD					
Timber	x?		x		
METALS					
Copper			x	x	
Silver/lead		x	x	x	
Gold				x?	
PRECIOUS STONES					
Lapis			x		
Carnelian					
Agate					
Chalcedony					
Amazonite					
Amethist					
Aragonite					
Jasper					
Other					
SEMIPRECIOUS STONES					
Chlorite					
Obsidian		x		x	
Rock crystal					
Quartz					
Alabaster					x
Gypsum				x	x
Marble					
Diorite					
Serpentine					
B. limestone					x
COMMON STONES					
Basalt					x
Limestone					x
Raw flint					x
Flint tools					x
OTHER					
Bitumen					x

Note: * = Afghan origin.

again, for plastic art, such as the celebrated female head from Warka (Moortgat 1969: pl. 26); and (4) variously colored serpentine of unknown origin, used for beads and amulets and for stamp and cylinder seals (Asher-Greve and Stern 1983; Brandes 1979).

A further possible import into the alluvium from the periphery was dependent labor, either slaves acquired in exchange for other goods or, more likely, prisoners of war. The signs for male and female slaves can be recognized already in the Archaic Tablets from Warka, and it is noteworthy that these early slaves are specifically stated to be of foreign origin (i.e., from the mountains) (Vaiman 1976:24). Admittedly, as Weiss (1989) notes on the basis of Gelb's (1976) research, foreign slaves were never the primary component of the public sector work force in Mesopotamia throughout the historic periods. Nevertheless, foreign slaves were indeed occasionally used as dependent workers in the ser-

Iranian Central Plateau			Southeastern Iran (via Susiana)	Southwestern Iran (via Susiana)	Western Desert (direct)	Unknown Provenance
(via Kurdistan, Nineveh)	(via Khorasan Road, direct)	(via Sialk Susiana)				
x?						
x	x	x	x			
		x				
x?*	x?	x?	x?*			
x*	x*	x*	x*			
		x				
		x				
					x	
					x	
					x	
					x	
					x	
					x	
		x				
x						
					x	
					x	
	x	x				
x	x	x	x			
x	x	x				
					x	
					x	
			x			
				x		
			x	x		
			x			

vice of the state, particularly in the case of prisoners of war early after their capture (Gelb 1973).

Available evidence for peripheral resources known to have been imported by Uruk societies and suggestions as to their various sources is summarized in table 3.

Many of the imports ennumerated in the preceding discussions are attested in the archaeological record of sites in southern Mesopotamia for centuries, if not millennia, preceding the Uruk period. What is new in the late fourth millennium, then, is that the variety—and presumably quantity—of imported commodities increased, a result no doubt of the establishment of a network of Uruk enclaves and outposts at strategic locations outside of the Mesopotamian core area. At its peak, this network must have exercised considerable economic power in terms of the overall long-distance trade economy of the Syro-Mesopotamian plains and the immediately surrounding highlands. Uruk states in Khuzestan must have played a similar role in relationship to the eastern Iranian highland periphery. These roles presume that to some degree indigenous communities across the periphery were willing to participate in the wider exchange network established by the intrusive Uruk settlements.

But in addition to their role in interregional exchange, the Uruk enclaves also may have participated in intraregional trade within the periphery. This is suggested by the Uruk bottles in storerooms at Arslan Tepe VIA. Unless one presumes that the jars were imported for their perceived intrinsic value, the vessels furnish evidence for Uruk involvement in the circulation of valuable liquids, most probably wine or oils. But if so, these commodities must have originated in some of the Uruk enclaves across the north, since neither wine nor oils were commonly exported from the alluvium (Pettinato 1972). The most likely candidates for this role are the various enclaves alongside the Euphrates. These installations, it has been argued, must have had access to grain from inland Syria to ensure their survival, and wine and oils from the Gaziantep-Aleppo region, a traditional producer,

could well have formed part of the commodities brought in. These prized liquids could then have been shipped downstream to the alluvium and repackaged for export across the north—as indicated by the Arslan Tepe evidence. Later textual documentation from Mari provides a possible parallel: in the early second millennium, Mari served as an indigenous riverine entrepôt and had a role as a collection, repackaging, and transshipment point for agricultural products from the Aleppo area to the west (Finet 1969: 44).

Details of the relationship between the intruding settlements and the preexisting Late Chalcolithic communities must remain hazy, however, in light of limitations inherent in the interpretation of the purely archaeological evidence at our disposal. Nevertheless, it is possible to speculate on that relationship by contrasting the evidence just discussed for the nature, strategic rationale, and function of the Uruk enclaves in the north with what evidence is available for the nature of indigenous Late Chalcolithic communities in the midst of which they were established. That evidence will now be reviewed.

5

The Late Chalcolithic Period in Syro-Mesopotamia

Compared to the information available about southern Mesopotamian settlements in the north, relatively little is known of indigenous communities that were already in place at the time of the Uruk intrusion. Excavations in Late Chalcolithic sites in Syro-Mesopotamia have been limited, and as a rule only restricted exposures have been obtained, except at a few sites such as Tepe Gawra, Qalinj Agha, and Grai Resh. More informative, although not always entirely comparable, are data on regional settlement patterns derived from a variety of surveys in some portions of the Syro-Mesopotamian plains. However, before the evidence for the nature of local communities in the north can be considered, it is necessary to review the chronological relationship between the indigenous and intrusive settlements, since only then will it be possible to explore the impact of the Mesopotamian intrusion on local communities.

CHRONOLOGY

Until recently, all that was known on the chronological relationship between the Uruk intrusion and the preexisting Late Chalcolithic cultures was derived from excavations at a few far-flung sites across the Syro-Mesopotamian plains. The key sequence was that of Kuyunjik, the larger mound of Nineveh, near Mosul, explored by British archaeologists during the late 1920s and early 1930s (Campbell Thompson and Hutchinson 1931; Campbell Thompson and Hamilton 1932; Campbell Thompson and Mallowan 1933).[1] Excavations in the Ishtar Temple area and a nearby deep sounding revealed at least 14 meters of deposits spanning the Late Chalcolithic (Ninevite III) and Uruk (Ninevite IV) periods and the transition to the Early Bronze Age (Ninevite V). Within this sounding, the relationship between the indigenous Late Chalcolithic assemblage, with its chaff-tempered pottery and stamp seal–based glyptic tradition, and the Uruk-period assemblage, with its unmistakable grit-tempered, mass-produced ceramics and cylinder seal–derived glyptic, appeared to be disjunctive: the preexisting materials were replaced by the intrusive southern Mesopotamian assemblage.

Juxtaposed to the Late Chalcolithic sequence of Nineveh, stood the sequence from the nearby and presumably contemporaneous, but much smaller, site of Tepe Gawra, excavated by an American expedition only a few years after excavations at Nineveh had been completed (Speiser 1935; Tobler 1950; Rothman 1988). In great measure, Tepe Gawra's importance stems from the fact that it was (for its time) carefully excavated, recorded, and published. It provides a broad exposure of Late Chalcolithic levels, much broader in fact than that attained in comparable levels at Nineveh. But in contrast to the latter site, where extensive connections with Uruk-period Mesopotamia could be traced, Tepe Gawra exhibited a local assemblage that was seemingly unrelated to the southern Mesopotamian materials documented at Nineveh.

The antithesis revealed by sites such as Nineveh and Gawra was repeated at other sites and regions of the Syro-Mesopotamian plains. The strong Uruk connections that could be observed at Nineveh appeared to be similar to those uncovered at Tell Brak only a few years after the end of excavations in the Tigris area.[2] But in apparent contrast to the evidence from Brak stood archaeological sequences from several sites with Late Chalcolithic deposits in the Syrian Saddle excavated at about the same time, principally Tabara el-Akrad (Hood 1951), Tell Atçana (Woolley 1955b), Tell es-Sheikh (Woolley 1953), Tell Judeidah, and Tell Dhabab (Braidwood and Braidwood 1960), all in the Antioch region, and Coba Höyük east of Gaziantep (Du Plat Taylor, Seton Williams, and Waechter 1950). The most informative of these sequences was that derived from Oriental Institute soundings at Tell Judeidah (Braidwood and Braidwood 1960). Exposures into pertinent levels at this site yielded a local chaff-tempered assemblage similar, in fact, to that of Late Chalcolithic levels of Nineveh (Ninevite III) and Gawra (XI–VIII). However, as noted in the preceding chapter, a few isolated Uruk types were also identified in the assemblage.

In short, the various strands of evidence just enumerated presented a seemingly confused picture of the chronological relationship between Late Chalcolithic and Uruk sites in the Syro-Mesopotamian plains: did the two assemblages mark contemporaneous but mutually exclusive phenomena as the contrast between Nineveh and Gawra appeared to signify, did they represent two contemporaneous and interacting traditions as the evidence from the Antioch area seemed to indicate, or did they mark different stages along a single continuum of cultural evolution, as the Nineveh sequence appeared to suggest? This confusion is exemplified in Speiser's attempt (1935:153) to correlate the Late Chalcolithic sequence of his own site, Tepe Gawra, with that of the neighboring site of Nineveh, which he correctly observed did not match. Speiser's correlation problem was not archaeological but conceptual, and it disappears once the entirely different nature of the two sites being compared is realized. However, that realization had to wait until a significant amount of new research had been undertaken.

The chronological relationship between indigenous Late Chalcolithic sites in the north and sites with an overwhelming southern Mesopotamian component was clarified only recently by new research in the Atatürk Dam area of the Euphrates in southeastern Turkey, where the two assemblages were found for the first time in clear association in carefully controlled excavations. Particularly important are excavations at Hassek Höyük and Kurban Höyük, both by the river, but some 60 kilometers apart. Of the two sites, Hassek Höyük, a small Uruk station alongside a river ford, has yielded a broader exposure, but no sequence. As noted in chapter 3, the single Uruk phase at Hassek was founded directly over natural soil. That phase, however, is of considerable importance for chronology because in it elements of Uruk material culture appear side by side with a local Late Chalcolithic assemblage, making it clear that the assemblages are at least partially contemporaneous. The ceramics, for example, include a number of typical Uruk types (fig. 39),[3] but these represent only a portion of the total ceramic assemblage at the site, which contains in addition a substantial component of indigenous Late Chalcolithic chaff-tempered forms.[4] The glyptic evidence from Hassek is similarly mixed: a few stamp seals of local style are found together with provincial cylinder seals of Mesopotamian type.[5] Other artifacts at the site, however, are of unmistakable Uruk derivation. As will be recalled, the central structure of the settlement is of Uruk type and finds precise parallels at Habuba Kabira-süd (fig. 23A–B above). This was decorated by means of terra cotta wall cones and plaques imitating cones (Behm-Blancke 1989)—types of architectural decoration frequently found in Uruk public structures.[6] Similarly, a cylinder seal impression depicting a griffin does so in a style typical only for Uruk-period glyptic and without doubt was impressed by an actual Mesopotamian seal (Behm-Blancke et al. 1984: pl. 12:5). Other typical Mesopotamian small artifacts at the site include an eye idol (Behm-Blancke et al. 1981: pl. 12:5).

The key sequence for the Late Chalcolithic period in the Atatürk Dam area, however, is that provided by recent Oriental Institute excavations at Kurban Höyük, an indigenous site in the vicinity of Samsat, where five superimposed phases of the Late Chalcolithic period were delineated. The site thus offers what no other Syro-Mesopotamian site along either the Euphrates or Khabur has yet produced: a stratified sequence that not only correlates

with the onset of Uruk influence in the area, but predates it as well.[7] Since the site has been described in greater detail elsewhere (Algaze et al. 1990), only a brief summary of the pertinent evidence for the Late Chalcolithic period is necessary here.

Kurban Höyük is a double-coned multiperiod site with a maximum extent of about 6 hectares. It is located some 7 kilometers away and on the opposite bank of the river from Samsat. The principal occupation of the site dates to the second half of the third millennium B.C. and there is a considerable depth of deposits directly over Late Chalcolithic levels. Thus, only relatively small exposures of the latter period were practicable. Pertinent strata were recovered in all three of the widely spaced vertical

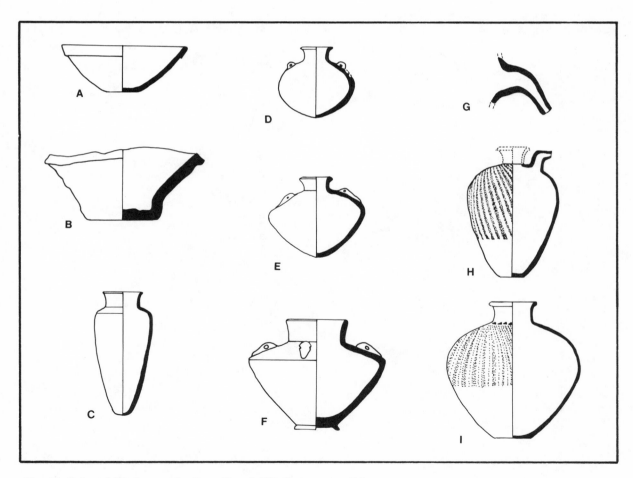

Fig. 39. Selected Uruk ceramics from Hassek Höyük (not to scale).

operations opened—Area A, a 3.5 × 60 meter step trench on the northern flank of the higher south mound; Area C01, a 3 × 9 meter sounding in the center of the lower north mound; and Area F, a 4 × 4 meter sounding on the saddle area between the two mounds—but actual occupational deposits were identified only in Areas A and C01 (fig. 40).

Of the three areas mentioned, a sequence for the Late Chalcolithic period was recovered only in Area A, where some 1.9 meters of deposits were cleared over an area of some 30 meters square, for a total approximate excavated volume of 58 cubic meters. Five Late Chalcolithic phases were distinguished. The earliest was difficult to define, since it

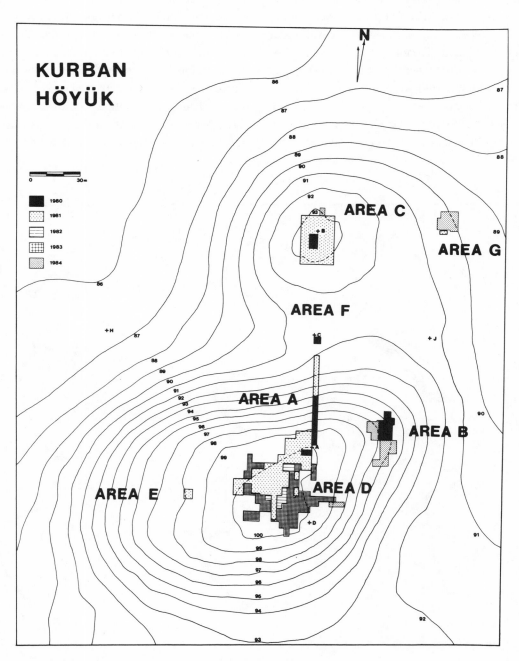

Fig. 40. Plan of Kurban Höyük showing location of excavated areas.

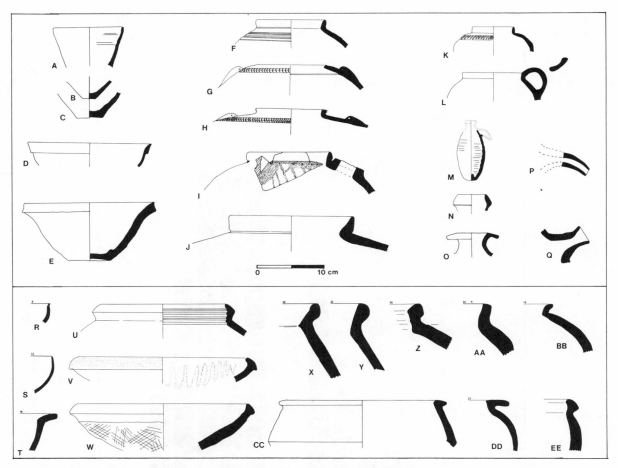

Fig. 41. Selected Uruk (A–Q) and indigenous chaff-tempered (R–EE) ceramics from Late Chalcolithic levels at Kurban Höyük.

consisted of layers of featureless fill associated with an exterior surface on which a hearth was found. The succeeding phases directly above, however, were easier to identify and were characterized by more substantial architecture. Unfortunately, the functional nature of the remains in these latter phases is unclear, since only fragments of the structures were exposed in the narrow trench. However, a clear sequence of superimposed walls and associated interior floors and outdoor surfaces was obtained.

The earliest of the five Late Chalcolithic phases in Area A (Phase 6: Period VIB) was characterized by an indigenous assemblage composed overwhelmingly of chaff-tempered ceramics of the type first defined by Braidwood in the Amuq (fig. 41T–EE) and a very small component of grit-tempered

pottery in a limited repertoire (e.g., fig. 41R, S).[8] Typical Uruk pottery in that phase appears only in statistically insignificant amounts and is presumed to be intrusive.[9] In the succeeding four phases (Phases 7–10: Period VIA), however, a variety of ceramics of unmistakable southern Mesopotamian derivation were introduced and are found in generally increasing proportions, although the indigenous chaff-tempered forms first encountered in the lowest level continue to be produced. Among the characteristic Uruk types in these later phases are many of the same types attested at Hassek Höyük. These include beveled-rim bowls (fig. 41E), four-lugged jars (fig. 41G–H), strap-handled jars (fig. 41F, K–L), drooping and trumpet-shaped spouts (fig. 41P, Q), ovoid spouted jars with diagonally reserved slip decoration (fig. 41I), elongated spouted

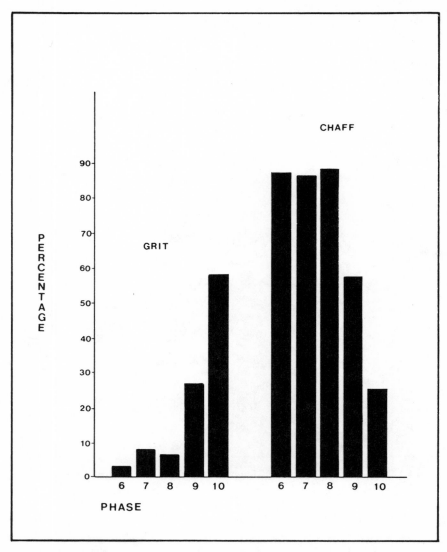

Fig. 42. Relative frequencies (by weight) of indigenous chaff-tempered and plain simple wares in Late Chalcolithic Levels of Area A at Kurban Höyük, Phases 6–10 (Phase 6 = earliest).

bottles with restricted mouths (fig. 41M–O), storage-sized jars with undercut rims (fig. 41J), conical cups with string-cut bases (fig. 41A–C), and band-rimmed bowls (fig. 41D).

A measurable change may be discerned in the ceramic assemblage of the four phases assigned to Period VIA: with each successive phase, the relative proportion of grit-tempered ceramics, many of them of southern affiliation, increases, while that of the indigenous chaff-tempered forms decreases. By the two latest phases, the grit-tempered assemblage

actually becomes more common than the chaff-tempered tradition it replaces. The pertinent data have been summarized in figure 42, which details the relative frequencies by weight of the indigenous chaff-tempered assemblage in relationship to the exogenous grit-tempered tradition for each of the Area A Late Chalcolithic phases at Kurban Höyük (Algaze et al. 1990).

The evidence from Kurban Höyük's Area A expands that from Hassek Höyük insofar as it indicates that an indigenous Late Chalcolithic occupation existed in the Atatürk Dam area prior to the onset of contacts with Uruk polities. Moreover, the Kurban data are in agreement with those from Hassek in showing the partial contemporaneity of Late Chalcolithic sites in the north and the process of Uruk expansion into the area. Had the deep sounding in Nineveh's Ishtar Temple area been excavated with greater care, this conclusion could have been apparent long ago. That the emerging sequence of the Late Chalcolithic period in the Atatürk basin is representative of Syro-Mesopotamia as a whole, and even of the highlands, is shown by recent evidence from the Italian excavations at Arslan Tepe in Malatya, the Yale University excavations at Tell Leilan in the Upper Khabur, and by a reinterpretation of older excavations conducted by the Oriental Institute at Tell Judeidah.

At Arslan Tepe, the earliest Late Chalcolithic level (Period VII) revealed an Amuq F–related assemblage similar in many ways to that from the lowest phase of the Late Chalcolithic period at Kurban Höyük—both assemblages are overwhelmingly chaff-tempered and have only trace amounts of plain simple-ware ceramics, none in typical Uruk styles. By the succeeding excavated level at the site, Period VIA, however, the earlier chaff-tempered assemblage has been replaced by a mixed assemblage in which are found an important regional red/black burnished-ware component as well as a local mass-manufactured plain simple-ware industry with some clear Mesopotamian affinities (Palmieri 1973, 1981; Frangipane and Palmieri 1988). Also found in association were a number of unmistakable Uruk pottery types discussed in chapter 4 (fig. 33). Some of these types, as Sürenhagen (1985) has noted, are surely imported. The nature of the transition between Periods VII and VIA at Arslan Tepe is unclear, since a stratigraphic connection is still lacking. Nevertheless, in its main outlines, the sequence from Arslan Tepe parallels that from Kurban Höyük in that at both sites a chaff-tempered assemblage of the Amuq F type is replaced by a mass-produced ceramic tradition in which some degree of Mesopotamian influence may be discerned.

Recent excavations at Tell Leilan provide a complementary corpus of materials that underscores the long *in situ* development that indigenous Late Chalcolithic sites had prior to the onset of contacts with alluvial Mesopotamia. At Leilan, the Operation 1 step trench has revealed a significantly longer sequence of Late Chalcolithic deposits than that of Kurban Höyük. Seven layers (Period V: Strata 44–51) were characterized by a chaff-tempered assemblage of the Amuq F type with only small traces of grit-tempered ceramics. This assemblage is thus immediately comparable to that of the lower phase of Late Chalcolithic deposits at either Kurban (Period VIB) or Malatya (Period VII). The succeeding three layers at Leilan (Period IV: Strata 41–43) contained a similar assemblage, with the addition of beveled-rim bowls (Schwartz 1988b). Although the increase in the frequency of grit-tempered mass-manufactured ceramics in Kurban's Late Chalcolithic phases, and to a lesser degree in Arslan Tepe VIA, is not yet paralleled at Leilan, the presence of beveled-rim bowls in Leilan IV strata allows us to correlate those layers with the later phases of the Late Chalcolithic period at both Kurban Höyük (Period VIA) and Arslan Tepe (Period VIA).[10]

At Tell Judeidah, the local Late Chalcolithic sequence is also broadly similar to that just described for the Euphrates, Malatya, and Upper Khabur areas, although this was not immediately recognized in the original publication. Like the earliest Late Chalcolithic phase at Kurban Höyük (VIB), the Period VII materials at Malatya, and the Period V assemblage at Leilan, the lowest Late Chalcolithic floor of the JK 3 sounding at Judeidah (22) was characterized by a chaff-tempered assemblage with few traces of grit-tempered pottery. In contrast, the succeeding floor (21) yielded a mixed assemblage that recalls that of the uppermost Late Chalcolithic phases in the Kurban Höyük sequence: predominantly chaff-tempered but with a significant component of grit-tempered ceramics (13–18%) (Braidwood and Braidwood 1960:228, 264, table III). This mixed assemblage continues to characterize the following three floors in the sequence (20–18) all assigned in the publication to the beginnings of the Early Bronze Age (Amuq G). I believe, however, that Floors 20–18 of the JK 3 sounding mark instead the end of the Late Chalcolithic period. This is suggested by several factors.[11] One is that, as already stated, a significant proportion of chaff-tempered Amuq F ceramics (17–23% of the total) continue into the earliest Amuq G floor (20). Another is that, like the uppermost Late Chalcolithic phases at Kurban and Period VIA levels at Arslan Tepe, Floors 20–18 of the Judeidah sounding yielded a number of typical ceramic indicators of the Uruk period, including beveled-rim bowls, drooping spouts, diagonal reversed slip, and elongated noselike lugs (fig. 36A–C above).

In sum, the evidence from Kurban Höyük, Arslan Tepe, Tell Leilan, and Judeidah helps clarify the chronological relationship between indigenous Late Chalcolithic sites in the north and the Uruk enclaves. The intrusion of southern Mesopotamian elements in the northern plains took place only after a long *in situ* evolution of local Late Chalcolithic cultures. Uruk and Late Chalcolithic sites in the north are therefore only partially contemporaneous.

LATE CHALCOLITHIC CULTURE AND SOCIAL INTEGRATION

Since comparatively more is known about the nature of the intrusive Uruk enclaves in the north than about the culture in the midst of which they were established, what can be said about the nature of preexisting communities is for the most part only in contrast and reference to the better-known enclaves. Those enclaves, I would contend, appear to have been significantly larger and presumably more complex socially, politically, and economically than even the largest of the indigenous sites in their vicinity. This inference is borne out by excavations and surveys across the Syro-Mesopotamian plains.

Evidence bearing on the nature of Late Chalcolithic culture and social integration in the north is at best ambiguous. From a variety of surveys and excavations across Syro-Mesopotamia, it is clear that a surprising degree of material culture homo-geneity existed over an exceedingly broad area. This is indicated by the distribution of the distinctive chaff-tempered (Amuq F) ceramic assemblage of the period, which is found along an east-west arc ranging from coastal and northern Syria to northern Mesopotamia and the Transtigridian Plains. To the north, this assemblage extended minimally into the southern flank of the Anatolian highlands. Within this broad geographical horizon, fairly close parallels may be drawn between the ceramic assemblages of, for example, Tell Judeidah in the plain of Antioch (Amuq F), Nineveh on the Tigris (Ninevite III), and Arslan Tepe (VII) in the Malatya region of the Anatolian highlands—to mention only some of the best known and most widely separated sites. But whole areas remain virtually unknown, and comparatively few mounds have been excavated, so that a single coherent corpus of evidence that can be considered conclusive is lacking. Nevertheless, there are some indications that, at least along the Euphrates and the Syrian plains to the west of it, Late Chalcolithic sites were relatively small and dispersed.

A recent survey of the Qoueiq River basin in the environs of Aleppo conducted by Matthers and his associates, for example, shows that the area was relatively densely settled in the Late Chalcolithic period, with a total of thirty-two mounds recognized within the survey limits (Mellaart 1981: 152–53).[12] However, whether or not a settlement hierarchy is discernible within the surveyed area is unclear, since overall sizes are only indicated for fourteen out of eighty sites recorded, and no attempt was made to trace spatial patterns in the distribution of ceramics on the surface of the surveyed sites. Insofar as can be judged on the basis of the few locations with Late Chalcolithic remains for which topographic maps are made available in the publication, most mounds of the period appear to have been no larger than village-sized, even if all of the particular mound's surface would have been occupied at the time—an unlikely proposition at best.[13] Only one of the sites with a Late Chalcolithic occupation in the Qoueiq survey area is substantial: Tell Berne, a 12-hectare multiperiod settlement composed of at least three separate mounds located near the point where the Qoueiq River is lost in salt marshes (Matthers 1981: fig. 42).

Late Chalcolithic materials have also been reported from a small number of other sites in the Aleppo region outside the limits of the Qoueiq survey. The typical chaff-tempered ceramics of the period have been recognized at the base of the important mound of Tell Mardikh/Ebla (Matthiae 1980:52), but pertinent *in situ* materials have not yet been excavated at Mardikh, and the size of the settlement at the time is unknown. Perhaps representative of conditions in the Aleppo region is the small site of Tell Abu Danné, midway on the road between Aleppo and the Euphrates River, some 25 kilometers away from the Tabqa area. Although Late Chalcolithic strata (Abu Danné VII) have only been sounded over a limited area, it is clear that the site represents an indigenous settlement which, surprisingly, appears to have been fortified (Tefnin 1979). No Uruk ceramics have been recognized in the Aleppo region, although as already noted, isolated seals carved in provincial versions of the Uruk style have been recovered from sometimes substantial sites with Late Chalcolithic remains across the border in Turkey (Tell Basher) and scattered ceramics of the period were also found in the plain of Antioch.

Conditions in the Antioch region during the Late Chalcolithic period are also not clearly discerned from available survey evidence. By all accounts, the area was densely settled at the time, since ceramics of the period were identified in at least 26 sites, ranging from smaller settlements to larger multiperiod mounds. However, it is difficult to generalize on the nature of the sites in the area, since overall site measurements are only provided for those sites that were eventually excavated, 4 out of 173 sites surveyed. For those sites, some approximation of the extent of Late Chalcolithic occupation is possible, although this may hardly be representative for the area as a whole. Some, such as Tell Judeidah, may have been fairly sizable, since Late Chalcolithic ceramics are found in cuts at opposite ends of the 9-hectare mound.[14] Other excavated

mounds where a Late Chalcolithic occupation was recognized, however, were much smaller, for instance, Tell Dhahab (Braidwood and Braidwood 1960:13–14).

The situation in the Atatürk basin area of the Turkish Lower Euphrates is clearer than that of either the Aleppo or Antioch regions, since detailed site measurements are available. Özdoğan's (1977) survey revealed a total of twelve sites with Late Chalcolithic remains. Nine of those twelve sites yielded evidence of both chaff-tempered Late Chalcolithic and grit-tempered Uruk ceramics. These sites thus date to the later part of the Late Chalcolithic period in the Atatürk area as revealed by excavations at Kurban and Hassek Höyük (fig. 15 above).[15] The remaining three sites, however, produced only chaff-tempered ceramics and no traces of Uruk types. These sites thus appear to correlate with the earliest phase of the Late Chalcolithic period in the area, once again on the basis of excavations at Kurban Höyük.[16] Save for Samsat, the surveyed sites with traces of a Late Chalcolithic occupation are small—even if the maximum extent of each site had been occupied at the time, as unlikely a proposition in the Atatürk area as it was elsewhere.[17] Of the excavated sites, Kurban Höyük was probably the largest, but it is difficult to estimate the size of the Late Chalcolithic occupation at the site with precision. Occupational deposits of the Late Chalcolithic period were reached in the two principal vertical operations at opposite ends of the mound (Areas A and C01), but were absent in the saddle area in between (Area F), making it likely that the settled area at the time was smaller than the 6 hectares maximum size of the site (fig. 40).

South of the Atatürk region along the Euphrates in Turkey, a similar situation obtained. Only a handful of Late Chalcolithic sites were identified in the Carchemish-Birecik survey area (ca. 80 sq km) and all are uniformly small. The largest and most important was Hacınebi Tepe, slightly over 3 hectares in extent. It is situated on an easily defensible limestone bluff overlooking the river just north of Birecik. Surface ceramics are overwhelmingly Amuq F in type, although a fair number of beveled-rim bowls and a handful of grit-tempered Uruk sherds indicate connections with some of the intrusive Uruk sites in the Birecik-Carchemish area. (Algaze et al. 1991).

A broadly analogous situation is found in the Keban/Altınova region of the Anatolian highlands. There, however, the reliability of the data is enhanced by the availability of detailed site measurements, controlled surface collections, and the fact that a significant number of the pertinent sites were excavated to some degree. These various factors allow for more precise estimates of occupation in the Late Chalcolithic period than are possible in some of the other surveyed areas previously discussed. The pattern of occupation of the Keban/Altınova regions in the Late Chalcolithic period was not particularly intensive, with fourteen sites identified within a surveyed area encompassing some 323 square kilometers. The largest occupations were Norşuntepe and Tepecik, both of which were excavated to some degree. Neither appears to have been much larger than two hectares at the time (Whallon 1979:264, 266–68, table 11), although the extent of the early occupation at Norşuntepe was perhaps obscured by extensive later deposits at the mound.

Compared to the more coherent evidence available for the areas just discussed, little detail is known of conditions in the plains of northern Mesopotamia east of the Euphrates. Other than for Meijer's recently published survey of the Upper Khabur basin east of the Jaghjagh in northeastern Syria, surveys of the Balikh basin and of the Iraqi and Turkish sections of the Khabur and Tigris basins are either unavailable, still in progress, or only preliminarily published. It is thus unclear whether the pattern of small dispersed sites prevalent in the Aleppo region, the Atatürk Dam area, the Birecik-Carchemish areas, and the Keban/Altınova plains holds true in the northern Mesopotamian plains as well, although some evidence suggests a divergent pattern with more sharply delineated settlement hierarchies.

In great measure, the ambiguity stems from the fact that although Late Chalcolithic materials have been excavated at a number of sites and recognized by survey in many others, there has usually been no indication in the published reports of the extent of occupation in the period at those sites. Along the Balikh, for example, Dutch excavations at Tell Hammam et-Turkman have uncovered portions of an important Late Chalcolithic monumental building capping a long sequence of earlier, apparently domestic, installations of the period, which will be discussed in greater detail in chapter 6. However, although Hammam et-Turkman was a mound of considerable importance at the time, the extent of Late Chalcolithic occupation within the 25-hectare site is unknown (van Loon 1988). Similarly unknown is the extent of the Late Chalcolithic occupation of major excavated sites along the Upper Khabur; although in those cases for which there is evidence, it appears certain that the occupations were significantly smaller than the maximum size of the sites in question. At Tell Leilan, an impressive 75-hectare site along the Wadi Jarrah, for example, Late Chalcolithic materials have only been recovered in the step trench against the acropolis of the mound. As those materials are absent from the much broader lower terrace, it is clear that the Late Chalcolithic occupation of the site could not have exceeded the size of the acropolis itself, about 15 hectares (Schwartz 1988b).

Late Chalcolithic materials have also been excavated at Grai Resh (Levels II–IV), one of the already noted sites along the southernmost flank of the Jebel Sinjar. Early British excavations at this site uncovered a small indigenous settlement with a tripartite plan house with a long cruciform central room (Level II). While the house is built in a style that resembles the central *cella* of the Eye Temple at Brak and finds general parallels at Habuba Kabira-süd,[18] the associated assemblage is similar to that of Leilan IV, in that beveled-rim bowls were recovered in the context of an otherwise local chaff-tempered ceramic repertoire (Lloyd 1938, 1940). Six hectares in maximum extent, Grai Resh could not have represented a sizable settlement in the Late Chalcolithic period. Yet, like Tell Abu Danné in the plains west of the Euphrates, it too was fortified (Lloyd 1940:13). Further to the east in the direction of the Tigris is found the group of mounds known as Telul eth-Thalathat. Late Chalcolithic pottery, apparently early (Dunham 1983), was uncovered only in Tell II, the smallest of the mounds and less than 1 hectare in maximum extent (Egami 1958).

Excavated sites in the Transtigridian Plains with Late Chalcolithic levels also appear on the whole to have been relatively small, save for Nineveh, which was surely a mound of considerable size even before the Uruk intrusion. Pertinent materials were found at Tepe Gawra (Levels XI–VIII), Qalinj Agha (Levels III–IV), and Nuzi (L4 pit; Levels X–VII). The size range for each of the sites just mentioned appears clear. Tepe Gawra has already been discussed in some detail and seems to have represented but a small village-sized site, about 1–2 hectares in extent. Qalinj Agha, where a fairly broad exposure of the Late Chalcolithic period was obtained, is not much larger than Gawra, at most 3.3 hectares (Abu al-Soof 1985:82). Nuzi may have been slightly larger at some 4 hectares (Weiss 1983:49, fig. 11), but that presumes that most of the site was occupied at the time.

When the results of regional surveys and excavations are considered in tandem, however, a more sharply marked settlement hierarchy becomes evident. Pertinent published evidence exists only for the plains east of the Wadi Jaghjagh and north of the Jebel Sinjar, where the results of surveys in northeastern Syria (Meijer 1986) can be combined with those from new excavations and surveys centering at Tell al-Hawa across the border in northern Iraq (Ball, Tucker, and Wilkinson 1989; Wilkinson 1990b). The greater majority of sites with traces of Late Chalcolithic occupation in northeastern Syria are relatively small, less than 2 hectares in maximum extent. However, some sites are larger: at least 6 sites fall in the 6–12 hectare range, one site now under excavation by an Italian team, Tell Barri, has a maximum size of 20 hectares, while another Tell Farfara, is considerably larger still (106 hectares).[19] Although in the absence of controlled surface collections the extent in the Late Chalcolithic period of many of these larger sites cannot be ascertained, the possibility exists that some occupations may have been substantial. This is suggested by new evidence from al-Hawa, where a combination of intensive surface surveys and excavations are starting to reveal what appears to have been a sizable indigenous occupation that is at least partially contemporaneous with some of the Uruk enclaves (Wilkinson 1990b).

The evidence just outlined, though fragmentary and of variable reliability, is sufficient to indicate that the northern plains into which societies of alluvial Mesopotamia of the Uruk period intruded were occupied by broadly distributed Late Chalcolithic cultures, which had already had a long prior development. On the whole, preexisting Late Chalcolithic sites appear to have been relatively small, in many cases not much larger than village-sized. This is particularly clear where the corpus of available evidence is most coherent, specifically along the Euphrates in southeastern Anatolia and northern Syria and in the inland plains of northern Syria. However, despite the absence of comprehensively published surveys, there are significant indications of a divergent pattern in the northern Mesopotamian plains east of the Euphrates, where more sizable sites and more complex settlement hierarchies seem to have existed.

Fragmentary as it may be, the evidence outlined above for the size ranges of indigenous Late Chalcolithic sites across Syro-Mesopotamia has brought the dichotomy between them and the sites with an overwhelming southern Mesopotamian component into focus. The two represent functionally very distinct types. The level of community planning exhibited by a settlement such as Habuba/Qannas, the vast resources required for its apparently rapid development, and its underlying strategic rationale show that it and the other, presumably similar, enclaves in the north represent in effect a case of urban implantation: they were appendages of communities at a state level of sociopolitical organization and themselves must have been organized at a similar level. In spite of the evidence furnished by Tepe Gawra for the existence of a significant degree of social differentiation, even within presumably small local communities, it seems that the Uruk enclaves were introduced into a cultural milieu of indigenous polities at a less developed social and, above all, political stage. This may be inferred from the sizes of the Late Chalcolithic sites. While evidence exists for some sizable Late Chalcolithic communities in the north that are *contemporary* with the Mesopotamian enclaves, even the most impressive of those sites, Tell Hammam et-Turkman on the Balikh and Tell al-Hawa on the Upper Khabur, for example, pale in comparison to the larger Uruk enclaves. More important, however, there simply is no Syro-Mesopotamian or highland site *predating* the Uruk intrusion that comes close to matching the size, complexity, and levels of internal differentiation documented for the Mesopotamian enclaves.

To judge on the basis of the significant site-size differentials between the urban-sized southern enclaves in the north and even the largest indigenous Late Chalcolithic sites in their vicinity, it appears reasonably certain that the complexity of the social and administrative structures of those enclaves represented a quantum leap over those of the smaller and more numerous indigenous communities among which they were located. Additionally, the carefully chosen strategic locations of the southern enclaves imply a much more complex economic system than that of the surrounding Late Chalcolithic communities, whose smaller size and more dispersed settlement pattern betray a simpler economic structure and a primarily agricultural orientation. These various strands of evidence suggest that the local communities may have represented examples of that intermediate stage in the evolution of sociopolitical complexity traditionally referred to by sociologists as "patrimonial societies" and by anthropologists as "complex chiefdoms" —an assumption that agrees well with the indications for possible Late Chalcolithic regional settlement hierarchies in northern Mesopotamia and that helps explain existing evidence for social stratification, spatial differentiation, and mortuary segregation at small indigenous sites such as Tepe Gawra.[20]

RELATIONS BETWEEN URUK ENCLAVES AND INDIGENOUS COMMUNITIES

On the basis of the preceding discussions, it is possible to speculate on the nature of relationships between the intrusive Uruk settlements and local communities. A variety of evidence suggests that the enclaves must have exercised considerable power in their respective locations and in some cases may have caused a considerable disruption of preexisting sociopolitical structures. Initially at least, their establishment may have involve some measure of coercion. How else to interpret the location of Mesopotamian enclaves at major previously occupied settlements such as Samsat, Carchemish, Brak, and Nineveh? Moreover, as will be recalled, a number of known Late Chalcolithic sites in the Syro-Mesopotamian plains were fortified. If, indeed, coercion was a significant element in the establishment of at least some of the southern enclaves in the north, an unintended but important consequence of that process may have been the flow of prisoners of war for use as dependent labor in the industrial establishments of the emerging alluvial states. That the signs for male or female slaves of foreign origin can be recognized in the earliest Archaic Tablets from Warka has already been noted.

Admittedly, the role of coercion as a factor in the formation of the network of Uruk enclaves in the Syro-Mesopotamian plains cannot be fully gauged, since we lack both conclusive proof that fortifications in smaller local sites were erected in direct response to the Uruk intrusion and information on the extent of indigenous Late Chalcolithic settlement at any of the previously inhabited regional centers where Uruk enclaves were established. However, on the basis of the later historical development of those centers (Samsat, Carchemish, Brak, and Nineveh), it stands to reason that they must have already occupied a preeminent position at the head of regional hierarchies in prehistoric times. The results of Özdoğan's survey at Samsat (1977: 133) indicate that the mound was already sizable in the Halaf and Ubaid periods; and at Brak the presence of substantial layers dating to the Ubaid period indicates that the mound was also important well before the Late Chalcolithic period (D. Oates 1982:196), although pertinent strata have not yet been excavated. Similarly, the Ishtar Temple sounding at Nineveh indicates the existence of several meters of Late Chalcolithic deposits (Ninevite III) predating the Uruk intrusion (Campbell Thompson and Mallowan 1933), and the excavations at Carchemish also have revealed the existence of Late Chalcolithic levels, unfortunately of an indeterminable depth, nature, and extent (Woolley 1952). In contrast, Uruk settlement in the Tabqa Dam area and in the portions of the river immediately north of Carchemish seems to have taken place at locations devoid of significant Late Chalcolithic settlement.

The divergent patterns represented by the enclaves in the Tabqa and Carchemish areas and by enclaves at previously inhabited sites such as Samsat, Brak, and Nineveh suggest that southern Mesopotamian contacts with the northern plains were adapted to and determined by preexisting differences. In areas where a local settlement hierarchy was already in place, Mesopotamian penetration involved the taking over of the indigenous settlements at the apex of the hierarchy. However, in areas where no such occupation had to be reckoned with, Uruk penetration became a process of urban implantation. While a significant proportion of the inhabitants at newly founded communities such as the Tabqa cluster may have been of southern origin, other enclaves such as Nineveh may have been inhabited by a more limited contingent of settlers ruling over a local population. In neither case does there appear to have been an attempt to control the hinterlands away from the strategic locations where settlements were established. Those hinterlands were controlled, as I have argued already, by local communities willing to trade. When smaller Uruk settlements are found away from the main enclaves, they clearly appear to represent stations along trade routes rather than outposts designed for territorial control.

In short, the Mesopotamian expansion into the northern periphery in the Uruk period was not a process of colonization such as took place in the Susiana plain of Khuzestan. Rather, it involved the taking over of a few selected locations that allowed societies in the alluvium to tap into preexisting lowland-highland trade networks controlled by indigenous communities such as Gawra. The Uruk enclaves were in this way able to funnel that trade into a new (or rather, more extensive and better organized) long-distance trade network oriented toward the alluvium and controlled by alluvial polities. It is thus possible to see the Uruk enclaves in the north as a phenomenon that falls well within the broad parameters of the informal empire model alluded to in the Introduction. The strategically located enclaves certainly dominated long-distance trade and may even have exercised some measure of political control over their immediate surroundings, as indicated by the numerous village-sized Uruk sites surrounding larger enclaves in the Tabqa and Carchemish-Birecik areas, but Syro-Mesopotamia as a whole was not under their political control. By and large, the hinterlands were not interfered with, though they were certainly not unaffected. Although some measure of political dependency may be presumed to have existed between particular enclaves in the north and specific alluvial states, on the whole, the links that tied together the northern periphery and the alluvium in the Uruk period were economic and not political.

For reasons that can only be speculated about, the expansion phase of early Mesopotamian societies came to an abrupt halt at the end of the Uruk period, sometime in the last quarter of the fourth millennium B.C. Nevertheless, the Uruk intrusion was to have important repercussions in the further development of polities in the Mesopotamian periphery for centuries after Uruk enclaves in the northern plains and outposts in the surrounding highlands were abandoned. Those repercussions and the possible causes of the Uruk collapse are explored in the next chapter.

6

Social Change in the Northern Periphery and the Collapse of the Uruk Expansion

THE IMPACT ON INDIGENOUS SOCIETIES

Implanted at the apex of preexisting regional settlement hierarchies, the strategically located Uruk enclaves must have effectively, if indirectly, controlled the long-distance trade economy of the Syro-Mesopotamian plains and the immediately surrounding highlands. The Uruk intrusion, therefore must have had a profound, immediate, and enduring impact on the sociopolitical and economic evolution of neighboring indigenous societies. That impact may be discerned at a number of recently excavated sites across the northern periphery.

Historical and ethnographic studies noted in the introductory chapter indicate that when societies at significantly different levels of sociopolitical and economic integration come into close contact, a certain amount of institutional restructuring may be expected in the social texture of the communities involved. Invariably, however, the impact of contacts is far greater in the communities at the lower end of the complexity spectrum. In those communities, it will be recalled, such contacts are likely to represent a powerful destabilizing force as local elites take advantage of their natural role as mediators in order to further their own standing within their own communities and vis-à-vis their local rivals. Moreover, the effect is magnified if the less differentiated society itself is on the verge of a social evolutionary process fueled by internal pressures (Paynter 1981:124–25). The story of western penetration of Asia and Africa from the sixteenth to the nineteenth centuries, for example, is filled with instances of collaboration as indigenous rulers allied themselves with one or another of the European colonial powers in a Faustian bargain to maintain or improve their standing in the traditional order. By exploiting local rivalries in politically fragmented lands of vast geographic extent and cultural diversity, Europeans were able to achieve a control of native polities not entirely commensurate with their own economic or even military capabilities (Robinson 1976; Scammell 1980).

The transformation of Southeast Asian communities in the earlier centuries of the first millennium A.D. as a result of the incorporation of the area into the wider trading sphere of merchants from the Indian subcontinent can serve as a model to help us better understand the nature of the processes at work in the northern periphery of Mesopotamia in the Late Chalcolithic period. This transformation is thought to have been so pervasive that it is commonly described as the "indianization" of Southeast Asia. Changes in Southeast Asian societies arising from contacts with Indian merchants whose ultimate goal was trade with China have been documented in some detail by scholars using a variety of archaeological, historical, and literary evidence. One important study is that of Wheatley (1975), who combines historical evidence from Chinese sources and native literary traditions to show the adoption of explicitly Indian conceptions of the social order within local communities not long after the establishment of contacts. More specifically, Wheatley is able to trace the growth of complex political systems centered around the figure of a king, where previously simpler, more egalitarian social relationships had prevailed. He documents the development of increasingly sophisticated economic structures based on centralized mobilization and redistribution of resources, where less complex reciprocal economic mechanisms had formerly been the rule.

A case in point is that of the earliest historically attested Southeast Asian state, Funan, on the southern coast of Indochina. Excavations in one of Funan's cities, the large site of Oc Eo, now in present-day Vietnam, have revealed evidence for extensive maritime trade connections, including Roman, Sasanian, Chinese, and Indian artifacts (Higham 1989:249–54). Chinese records indicate that Funan played an important role as an intermediary in exchange between the Indian subcontinent and China—a result of its strategic position opposite the Malay Peninsula and the Straits of Malacca, where sea routes from India and China converge. A variety of evidence attests to the simultaneous processes of political and economic integration in local Southeast Asian communities as a result of participation in this exchange network. Chinese sources dated to the second century A.D., for example, show that hereditary kingship was well established in Funan barely a century after Indian traders first reached Indochina. That this represented a revolutionary development may be inferred from the mythological origins of Funan's kings as recorded in the same sources: kingship is traced back to an original figure of Indian descent who married into the lineage of local chieftains (Hall 1985). Whether or not the myth is taken literally, it is clear that in the context of Southeast Asian societies, the concept of kingship itself is explicitly of Indian origin.

The political transformation just described had clear economic correlates. Surveys of the Mekong River delta indicate that the rise of the Funan state was accompanied by the construction of a network of extensive canals connecting the principal settlements and the development of an advanced agrarian system based on intensive utilization of the delta for flood rice cultivation (Hall 1985; Higham 1989). Moreover, political ideology was not adopted in isolation, but was part of a wider process of acculturation. Chinese documents reveal the presence of Brahman clerks and Buddhist monks in the Funan court. At least from the third century onward, Sanskrit had become the written (but presumably not the spoken) language of Funan. Similarly, the adoption of Indian religious rituals in an otherwise local context is evinced in Funan's art and architecture: statues of Buddha were produced locally, and local temples imitate Indian rock sanctuaries even in areas far away from cliffs. By the sixth century, Buddhism was not only widespread in Southeast Asia but had already made significant inroads into China as well (Hall 1985).

The temporal coincidence of these political, economic, and cultural changes in early Southeast Asian societies is not accidental. Rather, this convergence is indicative of the profound impact that participation in a supraregional exchange network may have on the socioeconomic structure of communities at a pre-state level of sociopolitical organization (Kipp and Schortman 1989). Keeping this in mind as a model of possibilities, we now turn to an examination of the available archaeological evidence for the impact of the Uruk intrusion on indigenous societies across the Mesopotamian periphery.

In the preceding chapter, the argument was advanced that from the observed site-size differentials between the Uruk enclaves and Late Chalcolithic communities in Syro-Mesopotamia and from the strategic rationale underlying the location of the enclaves, it could be concluded (1) that the enclaves were offshoots of communities at a state level of sociopolitical organization and themselves must have been organized in a similar manner, and (2) that they were introduced into a cultural milieu characterized by native polities at a less developed stage, possibly complex chiefdoms. If this was indeed so, we should expect to find archaeologically recognizable evidence within local societies of institutional changes caused by the powerful internal social pressures that the onset of contacts with the more complex southern enclaves must have unleashed. One problem in recognizing such changes, however, is that it is difficult to correlate precisely specific Uruk and Late Chalcolithic sites in the north, since in many cases the two types of sites are mutually exclusive, as we have seen at Tepe Gawra and Nineveh. Nevertheless, there is enough evidence of contacts that some correlations can be made. The clearest evidence comes from Tell Hammam et-Turkman on the Balikh, Kurban Höyük in the Turkish Lower Euphrates, and Arslan Tepe in the Malatya plain of the Anatolian highlands.

Hammam et-Turkman

Recent Dutch excavations at Tell Hammam et-Turkman have uncovered portions of an elaborately niched monumental building (fig. 43) that caps a long uninterrupted sequence of continually rebuilt much smaller domestic structures of the Late Chalcolithic period. Insofar as it has been preserved, the Hammam structure finds close parallels with Mesopotamian architectural styles of the Ubaid and Uruk periods,[1] but the stratigraphic position of the structure, the associated chaff-tempered Amuq F–type ceramics, and a cluster of radiocarbon dates (ca. 3400–3200 B.C.) indicate contemporaneity only with the latter period (Meijer 1988). In fact, precise parallels may be drawn between the Hammam building and monumental tripartite structures in contemporary levels at various Uruk sites in the Mesopotamian alluvium and the nearby Uruk enclave in the Tabqa Dam area to the west.[2] Analysis of the assemblage associated with the Hammam structure (Hammam VB) shows that the Mesopota-

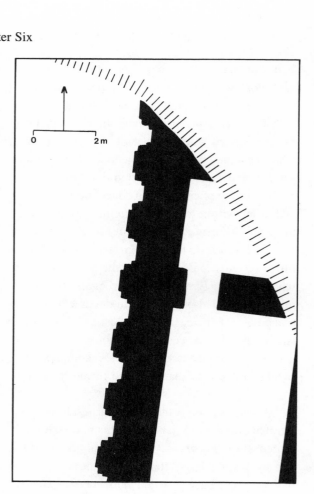

Fig. 43. Plan of Late Chalcolithic tripartite public building from Hammam et-Turkman.

mian architectural scheme appears in the context of an otherwise local site. Typical Uruk pottery was not recorded in association, nor has it been found elsewhere at the mound (Akkermans 1988b:318), although as noted earlier, Uruk ceramics have been reported in one small site in the immediate vicinity of Hammam et-Turkman. Nonetheless, evidence for contacts between the Hammam et-Turkman elites and nearby Uruk enclaves, possibly along the Euphrates or the Khabur, is provided by a jar-neck sealing impressed with a seal cut in a provincial version of the Uruk style found on the surface of the site just downslope from the Hammam VB structure (van Loon 1983:3, fig. 5).

I would suggest that the Hammam evidence may be interpreted to signify the adoption by a local social group, not only of an architectural style that is typically southern in origin, but possibly of parts of the ideology which in the context of Uruk societies was associated with that distinctive structure—much in the same way that in early Southeast Asia elements of Indian culture were taken over by indigenous communities and adapted to serve local needs. In this light, the break in the functional nature of the excavated area at Hammam at the time of the Uruk intrusion from a domestic to a public nature is far from accidental: it represents a case of social and ideological change in a less complex social group suddenly in a situation of intense contact with a more advanced social system. More specifically, I see the Hammam niched structure as suggesting the adoption by local elites of the more complex ideas of rulership, modes of social integration, and concomitant ritual displays introduced into the north by the Mesopotamian enclaves. This adoption was expressed concretely by the use of the precise architectural form that in Mesopotamian society constituted the focal node of whatever administrative and religious activities were being emulated. Such a phenomenon makes sense only if the increased power of those native elites derived from their role as mediators of contacts with the southern enclaves and mobilizers of local and imported resources, presumably for trade, but conceivably for tribute as well.

From the perspective of the Mesopotamian periphery as a whole, the Hammam case and its implications are surely not unique. They represent one facet—ideological—of what must have been a wider range of interactions between indigenous polities and the Mesopotamian enclaves in their midst. Another complementary facet of that interaction may be discerned when we analyze data from other Late Chalcolithic sites in the north, in particular Kurban Höyük and Arslan Tepe. Those sites offer evidence for the sorts of economic changes in preexisting communities that must have accompanied the ideological changes documented at Hammam.

Kurban Höyük

Situated in the immediate vicinity of Samsat, Kurban Höyük yielded a stratified sequence within which it is possible to document economic changes brought about by the onset of contacts with that southern Mesopotamian enclave. As noted in chapter 5, the main Late Chalcolithic sequence at the site consists of five superimposed phases: the lowest predates the intrusion of Uruk elements into the area, while the succeeding four phases are contemporary with it. Within this sequence, it is possible to observe a gradual change from a local ceramic industry to one of exogenous origin, the former producing chaff-tempered vessels by hand or on a slow wheel, and the latter producing mass-manufactured, grit-tempered vessels on a fast wheel, most of clear Uruk derivation (figs. 41–42 above). Further insights into the nature of changes in the production and distribution of ceramics in the Atatürk region at the time of the Uruk intrusion are sure to be provided by a neutron activation analysis project focusing on pottery from the area now underway (Evins 1989; Hopke et al. 1987). In terms of the overall economy of the region, the changes documented thus far in the production of ceramics are relatively unimportant. They are significant because they betray broader changes precipitated by the Uruk intrusion into the area. Presumably, the shift toward mass-produced ceramics is symptomatic of the development of full-scale specialization as an important factor in the economic structure of indigenous societies.

Arslan Tepe

The much broader contemporary exposures at Arslan Tepe provide a greater range of evidence for the impact that contacts with Uruk-period southern Mesopotamia—surely mediated by the network of enclaves across the northern plains—had on local communities in the north, even those in the highlands. As noted in earlier chapters, an internal dichotomy can be discerned within the pottery and glyptic assemblages of the Period VIA monumental structures at Arslan Tepe. In terms of its ceramics, this assemblage is characterized by two distinct and to some degree juxtaposed traditions: a handmade red/black burnished ware that is at home in the eastern Anatolian highlands, and a plain ware made on a fast wheel that has no precedents in the area and, although locally made, is more at home in the Mesopotamian world (Frangipane and Palmieri 1988). The latter represents the local highland version of the mass-manufactured pottery of Uruk sites in the south and their northern enclaves and constitutes an important shift in the technology of pottery manufacture in the highlands. As had been the case in the Atatürk basin area, this shift indicates broader underlying changes leading to full-time craft specialization.

A similar but more revealing dichotomy may also be observed in the contemporary glyptic assemblage recovered at Arslan Tepe.[3] Particularly important are several caches of discarded bullae and sealings recovered in the Period VIA complex (fig. 45), principally by the entrance gateway (Room A206), in a storeroom flanking the gateway (Room A340), and in a nearby structure interpreted as a "temple" (Room A77) (Frangipane and Palmieri 1988, 1988/89). The majority of the sealings bear the impression of stamp seals with schematized animal figures, often arranged antithetically, in a style common to Late Chalcolithic sites in the northern plains and in the Zagros-Taurus highlands (e.g., fig. 44E–H).[4] A small number, however, were impressed by means of cylinder seals (e.g., fig. 44A–D).[5] The latter reveal not only the influence of Mesopotamian sealing practices, but also a knowledge of Mesopotamian iconography. Of special interest is an impression bearing an unmistakable Mesopotamian motif: a presumably royal figure on a sled surrounded by attending personnel (fig. 44A) that, as Sürenhagen (1985) has noted, finds close parallels in Uruk iconography. Other typical Uruk motifs reported on Arslan Tepe cylinder sealings include pairs of rampant lions with entwined tails (fig. 44B), animal files within ladderlike motifs (fig. 44D), and files of horned animals (Frangipane and Palmieri 1988: fig. 67:5).

It is possible that some of these distinctive cylinder seal impressions may have actually originated in southern Mesopotamian enclaves and reached Arslan Tepe as a result of exchange, since some impressed jar stoppers were actually found discarded near Uruk jars in storerooms (chap. 4). Nonetheless, to judge from the technical details of some of the iconography, a local origin must be presumed for most of the cylinder seal impressions at Arslan Tepe. This can be surmised from the fact that in some of the sealings we may discern the transfer into the larger medium provided by cylinder seals of motifs that are far more common in the indigenous stamp seal tradition of the highlands (e.g., tête-bêche animals: fig. 44C). Moreover, functional analyses of impressions at Arslan Tepe show that door locks were occasionally impressed by cylinder seals, thus proving that the seals themselves were in use at the site (Ferioli and Fiandra 1988:508, table V).

The partial adoption of Mesopotamian (cylinder) sealing practices in a highland context side by side with a continuing stamp seal tradition indicates that important economic and administrative changes were taking place. Whether directly or not, it is likely that the partial change toward cylinder seals (capable of conveying more information than stamp seals) was tied to the increasingly complex requirements of a local economy that was expanding—almost certainly as a result of economic contacts with Uruk enclaves in the Syro-Mesopotamian plains. But the glyptic evidence from Arslan Tepe indicates that the Uruk impact on communities in the Anatolian highlands was more profound than the mere adoption of specific glyptic practices and iconography. Detailed analyses show that many of the sealings discarded in upper layers of the closet-like room (A206) by the gateway had been affixed to movable containers and were impressed with a wide variety of seals, the majority being stamp seals in local styles (Frangipane and Palmieri 1988/89). The location and type of these sealings suggests that the building complex in which they were found served as a collection point for resources and tribute drawn from the surrounding region (fig. 45), presumably for later redistribution to palace-controlled labor. The excavators of Arslan Tepe may have identified some such redistributive activity in one of the storerooms flanking the gateway (Room A340). Here were discovered numerous sealings and clay

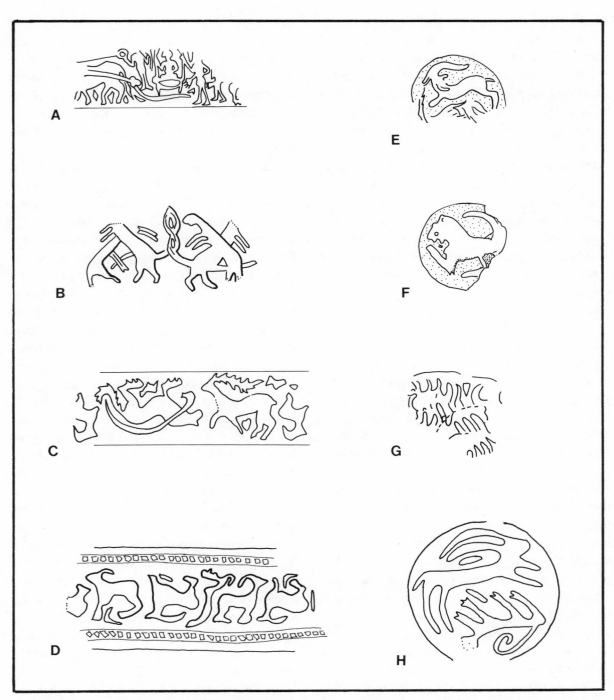

Fig. 44. Cylinder (A–D) and stamp seal (E–H) impressions from Arslan Tepe VIA. (scale 1:1; except A and C, 3:4).

lumps ready to be sealed in association with storage jars and agricultural commodities such as grain and cultivated grapes. The room also contained a high density of mass-produced conical bowls, which the excavators suggest may have been used to measure rations (Frangipane and Palmieri 1988/89). In much the same way as I saw the use of a typically Uruk architectural style at Tell Hammam et-Turkman as evidence for the adoption in an indigenous context of explicitly Mesopotamian ideas of social integration and rulership, Frangipane and Palmieri (1988/89) see the apparent role of the site as a regional redistributive center in Period VIA as reflecting the adoption of modes of social organization that are ultimately also of Mesopotamian origin.[6]

THE COLLAPSE OF THE URUK ENCLAVE NETWORK

The broad geographical distribution of the affected local communities from the northern plains to the highlands is indicative of the degree to which the Mesopotamian enclaves had gained control of the long-distance trade of the region, a control which was no less effective for being indirect. Extrapolating into the fourth millennium B.C. evidence from later third and second millennium documents, it is possible to infer that such control could have only meant an exchange system based on the flow of raw materials from highland sources to a resource-starved alluvial core in return for labor-intensive processed and semiprocessed goods (Leemans 1960:116–34; Yoffee 1981). Some possibilities on the actual materials exchanged have already been suggested in the preceding discussions.

Under such conditions, it will be remembered, we would expect that the onset of exchange would result in an initially vigorous phase of growth in the peripheral regions and the emergence of more complex sociopolitical structures as native elites controlling the resources being exploited took advantage of their natural role as organizers and mediators of the exchange to extend their power. In the long run, however, this initial growth phase would have given way to a second phase of stagnation and regression, since the economic spinoffs of

change would have been relatively negligible, and eventually, overspecialization in the procurement of only a limited variety of specific resources for export would have weakened the economic base of peripheral societies—the logical outcome of unequal terms of trade between societies at significantly different stages of social, political, and economic development.

In contrast, in the alluvium the onset of contacts would have resulted in a long-term strengthening of the communities involved in the exchange. First, the exchange would have had direct effects on the growth of economic complexity and social differentiation in the emerging Mesopotamian city-states, since imports consisted largely of products that required processing before they could be used, and exports consisted mostly of goods that required considerable investments in (dependent) manpower for their production as well as a bureaucratic superstructure to administer, store, and redistribute that production. Second, the organizational requirements needed to mount trade expeditions or military raids and, further, to found and maintain faraway colonies would also have been an important factor in the development of sociopolitical complexity in the alluvium as preexisting elites consolidated the considerable political and economic power inherent in their role as organizers of communal resources for trade or conquest. Another likely outcome would have been the promotion of sharper settlement hierarchies within the alluvium, since the nature of Mesopotamian exports demanded that an adequate flow of local resources for exchange be marshaled at all costs. Thus, the larger centers capable of conducting the exchange would have taken steps to attract, by whatever means necessary, the agricultural and pastoral production of nearby rural communities in their immediate hinterland (Adams 1981:80–81). Last, given the labor-intensive nature of the production of exportable surpluses, a final effect of cross-cultural trade on Uruk societies would have been the creation of larger and more complex urban agglomerations to take advantage of economies of scale (Jacobs 1969).

However, the expected regression in the periph-

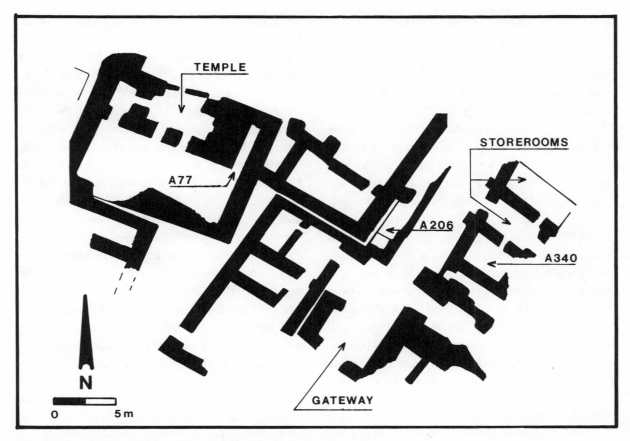

Fig. 45. Plan of Period VIA architectural complex at Arslan Tepe.

ery resulting from Mesopotamian control of the structures of long-distance trade did not materialize. The process was interrupted, I would argue, by the collapse of the expansion of Mesopotamian society at the very end of the Uruk period. Having taken place at the dawn of history, the no doubt complex series of events leading to that breakdown is not yet well understood. Nevertheless, on the basis of later historical parallels, it is possible to hypothesize that in the Mesopotamian case the collapse was the likely result of the conjunction of two independent and diametrically opposed social and environmental processes.

In the alluvium, the very success of Uruk communities in maintaining control of the critical lines of communication, without which centralized urban life could not flourish, also contributed to the eventual disruption of the resulting supraregional interaction system. Effective control of significant portions of the northern exchange network by any

alluvial state would have considerably buttressed its position vis-à-vis its regional rivals. Some archaeological correlates of this process are perhaps discernible: surveys show that while the transition from the earlier to the later part of the Uruk period was marked by a substantial population shift from the northern (i.e., Babylonia) to the southern (i.e., Sumer) portions of the Mesopotamian alluvium, total settled area did not differ markedly between the two periods. Other than the actual location of settlements, what did differ was the relative proportions of the population that lived in urban-sized agglomerations. Whereas in the earlier part of the Uruk period more than half the total estimated population lived in centers deemed urban in size, in the later part of the period that figure had diminished significantly and the proportion of population in smaller dependent settlements increased concomitantly. However, while the overall number of centers considered to be of urban size decreased, the average size of the remaining centers increased considerably. The city of Warka in the Late Uruk period, for example, is estimated by Adams (1981) to have been in the 100 hectare range and recent, more intensive, surveys of its surface suggest that a size of 200 hectares is more likely (Finkbeiner 1987:142). These enlarged centers appear to have been capable of inhibiting the growth of similar agglomerations in their vicinity and were surrounded instead by a dense scatter of smaller satellite settlements engaged, no doubt, in dependent agricultural production (Adams 1981:75).

In the inherently fragile alluvial environment of southern Iraq, the trend toward politico-economic centralization that may be expected to have followed the establishment of the enclave network in the north would have represented a powerful destabilizing force, ultimately leading to a partial collapse of the socioenvironmental system. This inference is in line with arguments presented by Gibson (1974), who has persuasively shown the existence of a close correlation between the onset of political centralization in the alluvium and the intensification and regularization of economic demands on that unstable environment. In the southern Mesopotamian alluvium, this could only have meant progressively shorter fallow periods and increased use of irrigation agriculture as ever more marginal lands were brought into cultivation (Boserup 1965:23–40). The consequences of such a shift are predictable: an inevitable decline in the agricultural productivity of any tract of land brought under regular irrigation as a result of the increase in salinization. Effective agricultural intensification could thus not be maintained over the long run (Jacobsen and Adams 1958; Adams 1978).

The hypothesized weakening of the socioenvironmental system in the alluvium must have taken place at the very end of the Late Uruk period, during the transition to the so-called Jemdet Nasr period. A recent reinterpretation of agricultural texts among the Archaic Texts from Warka appears to show relative proportions of barley to wheat in the order of 3 to 1—suggesting, however tentatively, the onset of salinization problems in the environs of

large urban centers by the last centuries of the fourth millennium B.C. (Powell 1985:14–15). Additionally, there are a number of indications that denote the existence of important settlement discontinuities at this time. A reanalysis of available survey data by Postgate (1986) shows that while the principal urban sites continued from the earlier to the later phase, a significant proportion of surrounding villages were abandoned at the end of the Late Uruk period, and a roughly similar number were established in the succeeding Jemdet Nasr time range. Whatever the actual reasons for this pattern, regional survey data do seem to indicate a certain degree of social disruption in the alluvium that may be correlated broadly with the collapse of the network of Uruk enclaves in the north and the retrenchment from Khuzestan, even though the total occupied area barely differs between the two temporal phases (Adams 1981:82). Moreover, while the disruption affected the rural hinterlands more dramatically than the cities, it is also reflected in discontinuities in the archaeological record of some of the principal urban centers. This is most clearly evidenced in the major reorganization of the Eanna and Anu precincts of Warka immediately following the last Late Uruk phase, Eanna IVa. With the redating of the White Temple from the Jemdet Nasr to the Late Uruk period (Schmidt 1978a), it now seems reasonably certain that none of the principal Late Uruk public structures at the site survived the transition to the Jemdet Nasr period. The relatively meager remains assignable at Warka to the Eanna III phase (Finkbeiner 1986) contrast strikingly with the much more coherent and monumental architectural complexes that had characterized the immediately preceding phases (Eanna VI–IV) in the same area.

Meanwhile, a diametrically opposed process was taking place in the periphery. At the very same time that the economic viability of alluvial communities was being undermined by the degradation of their environment and subsistence base, peripheral societies were becoming stronger as a result of internal development unleashed by contacts with the Mesopotamian enclaves. It is possible, thus, to visualize a scenario whereby the initial strengthening of the sociopolitical structures of the peripheral groups could and probably did result in local communities that became rapidly expansive in their own right, particularly, those communities that may have already been in the throes of internal pressures toward higher levels of integration, a process accelerated and magnified by the Uruk intrusion. If so, such communities could have threatened southern domination of the critical trade routes just as internal rivalries and environmental pressures were weakening the capabilities of alluvial communities to respond effectively, and long before the impact of unequal exchange could take root in the periphery. This scenario, admittedly hypothetical, helps us to understand the otherwise unexplained sudden collapse of the northern network, an event most clearly discerned along the Euphrates, where Uruk stations such as Hassek Höyük were destroyed (Behm-Blancke et al. 1984) and Uruk enclaves in the environs of Carchemish and in the Tabqa area were simply abandoned.

EARLY BRONZE AGE SOCIOPOLITICAL DEVELOPMENT IN THE PERIPHERY

If anything, by removing the eventually suffocating effects of long-term unequal exchange, the collapse of the expansion phase of the Uruk period may have allowed the growth of some indigenous communities in the Mesopotamian periphery to continue unchecked. Modern studies of economic underdevelopment suggest that, historically, socioeconomic development in peripheries is sometimes greatly accelerated in circumstances in which ties to their cores become weakened or disappear altogether. Discussed in detail by Andre Gunder Frank (1967) in terms of the relationship between Latin America and Europe during times of crisis in the eighteenth and nineteenth centuries, this phenomenon is perhaps also relevant to our understanding of Early Bronze Age sociopolitical development in areas surrounding the Mesopotamian alluvium following the Uruk retrenchment from those areas.

More specifically, because of its relatively short duration and ultimate fragility, the Uruk expansion

is likely to have acted as a catalytic factor in the growth of complex, differentiated, and independent sociopolitical systems across some portions of the periphery. Differences in the long-term effects of the asymmetrical contacts would, of course, depend on the nature of preexisting peripheral societies at the time of initial contact, the duration of contacts, and the intensity of the interaction. For instance, as noted by Schwartz (1989) and Weiss (1989), among others, northern Mesopotamia reverted to simpler sociopolitical formations (such as had presumably existed prior to contacts) in the Ninevite V period (Schwartz 1987), immediately following the Uruk intrusion. In contrast, other areas developed further in their own right, commonly by assuming control of regional exchange networks previously held by the intruding core groups. An unambiguous example of the latter outcome is the emergence of the Proto-Elamite state centered at Tal-i Malyan (Anshan) in the Kur River basin of Fars. This successor state replaced Uruk polities in southwestern Iran and not only expanded the trans-Iranian routes toward the east (Alden 1982; Lamberg-Karlovsky 1985), but even appears to have taken control of trade routes feeding in and out of the Mesopotamian alluvium via the Diyala basin (Collon 1987:20). In fact, the emergent Proto-Elamite polity expanded in its own turn in ways that closely paralleled the phases of expansion of the Uruk societies that preceded it. This is noted by Lamberg-Karlovsky (1982), who interprets Sialk (IV.2) and Tepe Yahya (IVC) as faraway Proto-Elamite outposts similar in nature and function to earlier Uruk outposts at Sialk itself and elsewhere.

The rise of various local powers astride portions of the international trade routes explains why exchange between the now shrunken Mesopotamian core (after the abandonment of Khuzestan) and its periphery continued unabated after the collapse of the network of Uruk enclaves and outposts and the transition into the third millennium (Zagarell 1986:420). In fact, to judge from evidence for a generally increasing range of imported materials into the alluvium in the archaeological record of Early Dynastic sites, trade may even have expanded at this time, although one must presume that the terms of the trade would not have been as favorable to the alluvium as before.

In any event, Sumerian royal inscriptions attest, however indirectly, to the existence of a number of local kingdoms across portions of the Mesopotamian periphery by the later half of the Early Dynastic period (Cooper 1986). The prevailing political "balkanization" revealed by these texts mirrors that of the Mesopotamian alluvium itself. The chronic intercity warfare and political fractionation so characteristic of Early Dynastic Mesopotamia can be understood, in part, as being due to increased competition as each city-state attempted to position itself on (and exclude its rivals from) the critical lines of communication and transportation feeding in and out of the alluvium, which were no longer necessarily under Mesopotamian control. Independent city-states were thus forced to deal individually with a kaleidoscope of increasingly powerful peripheral polities, a situation which must have represented a powerful stimulus toward conflict, both inside and outside of the alluvium. A reflection of this situation in the Early Dynastic period from the perspective of the city-state of Uruk, one of the competing centers, has survived in the series of epic poems centering around the figures of Enmerkar and Lugalbanda, which are concerned with trade and warfare between Uruk and the city-state of Aratta, the latter somewhere in the Iranian highlands.

It was not until the very end of the Early Dynastic period and the onset of the Akkadian dynasty, some six to seven hundred years after the collapse of the Uruk enclave network, that societies of the Mesopotamian alluvium once again undertook a coherent process of expansion matching in intensity that of the earlier period. Its rationale was one and the same: the need of alluvial elites to secure and regularize access to the commodities that sustained the export-driven economies on which their social control was predicated. However, the radical alteration of the sociopolitical landscape of the Mesopotamian periphery in the third millennium from that prevalent a millennium earlier meant that the resource-procurement strategies of the Akkadians had to be substantially different from those of Uruk societies. This is explained in part by the enduring impact of the Uruk intrusion. The periphery that the Akkadians attempted to penetrate bore no relationship to that previously controlled, however indirectly, by the Uruk enclaves. Coming after centuries of autochthonous development, the Akkadian empire had to deal with a variety of locally powerful native polities that had developed, in great measure, by explicitly adopting (southern) Mesopotamian cultural norms and politico-economic modes of social organization. Because of the chance discovery of palace archives, the best documented of these rival states is ancient Ebla/Tell Mardikh (56 ha), on the fertile Syrian plains southeast of Aleppo (Matthiae 1980; Pettinato 1991). Surely no less powerful, although until now devoid of historical records, were a number of contemporary kingdoms across central and northern Syria and northern Iraq (Weiss 1983). Among the excavated and therefore better-known examples are (from west to east) Qatna (100 ha) on the Orontes basin (du Mesnil du Buisson 1935), Tell Chuera (100 ha) between the Balikh and the western Khabur (Orthmann 1986), Tell Mozan (ca. 70 ha; Buccellati and Kelly-Buccellati 1988), Tell Brak (minimally 43 ha; D. Oates 1982) and Tell Leilan (75 ha; Weiss 1986) on parallel branches of the Upper Khabur drainage, and Tell Taya (70–160ha) on the plains north of the Jebel Sinjar (Reade 1968).

The dramatic differences in the nature of native communities encountered by the southern Mesopotamian intruders from the Uruk to the Akkadian periods help explain why, when contrasted to the evidence from the earlier period, the Akkadian phenomenon seems geographically more restricted. Granted, portions of the Upper Tigris basin in northern Iraq and of the Upper Khabur catchment in northeastern Syria appear to have been under Akkadian political control, but there is no evidence such as is available in the Uruk period for a permanent Mesopotamian presence along either the Euphrates bend or the Iranian highlands. Those areas, in fact, appear to have been wholly outside the sphere of Mesopotamian control, and Akkadian royal inscriptions detail a litany of military campaigns directed against recalcitrant local polities which, time and again, proved capable of challenging Akkadian power (chap. 1).[7] In the Akkadian period, then, indigenous collaboration across large portions of the periphery could no longer be taken for granted, as had surely been the case in Uruk times (at least initially), and resources could often only be secured by modes of imperial domination that were more formal than those employed by the Uruk intruders. To judge from the periodicity of Akkadian raids against northern Syria, northern Mesopotamia, southeastern Anatolia, and against Zagros piedmont groups, those more formal modes must have been considerably more expensive in the short run and significantly less effective in the long term than the earlier efforts.

7

Conclusions

If the ancient Mesopotamian historian is to give any meaningful account of his materials at all he must of necessity relax the stringent claim of "what the evidence obliges us to believe" and substitute for it a modest "what the evidence makes it reasonable for us to believe," for it is only by taking account of evidence that is suggestive, when the suggestion is in itself reasonable, rather than restricting himself to wholly compelling evidence, that he will be able to integrate his data into a consistent and meaningful presentation. —Thorkild Jacobsen, "Early Political Development in Mesopotamia"

THE VIEW FROM THE PERIPHERY: INFORMAL EMPIRE IN THE URUK PERIOD

I have argued that by the second half of the fourth millennium the highly integrated but resource-deficient societies of the Mesopotamian alluvium had succeeded in the institutionalization of a system of interaction with the resource-rich, but demonstrably less developed, highland communities. This was accomplished by the colonization of the neighboring plains of southwestern Iran and by establishment of enclaves, stations, and outposts at carefully selected locations across the northern periphery. This intrusion was in some ways comparable to the historically documented expansion of the Akkadian empire into some of the same areas some six to seven hundred years after the end of the Uruk period, and was equally short-lived. Nevertheless, the Uruk intrusion was to have important repercussions in the further development of indigenous cultures with which it came into contact, and this partially explains why the resulting supraregional interaction system was doomed to collapse.

In broad terms, a number of stages may be proposed in the processes of expansion of Mesopotamian societies of the Uruk period, although important chronological problems still remain and significant overlaps must be presumed to have existed

between stages. The first stage (fig. 46A) saw the colonization of the plains of southwestern Iran, an essentially *ad hoc* process that transformed those plains into part of the Mesopotamian core and allowed Uruk polities in Susiana unrestricted access to trade routes into the Iranian plateau and points further east via the southern Zagros. Possibly overlapping in part is the second stage (fig. 46B), which entailed the establishment of small settlements in selected areas devoid of significant preexisting occupation (e.g., Sheikh Hassan in the Tabqa area) and, more important, the taking over of a number of previously inhabited Late Chalcolithic sites at the apex of local settlement hierarchies across the Syro-Mesopotamian plains (Nineveh, Brak, Carchemish, Samsat), all situated at the intersection of the most important waterways and overland routes. The third stage (fig. 46C) represents the climax of the northern enclave network. Previously established settlements continued, and the Uruk presence along the Upper Euphrates was rapidly expanded with substantial urban enclaves in the Tabqa (Habuba/Qannas/Aruda) and Carchemish areas (Kum Ocağı/Şadi Tepe/Tiladir Tepe). These enclaves must have effectively controlled both waterborne traffic along the Tigris and Euphrates and the overland route along the rivers between Syro-Mesopotamia and the southern Iraqi alluvium.

Depending on how the Uruk-period sequence in Susiana is correlated with that of the Mesopotamian alluvium, the final stage (fig. 46D) may be conceived either as a further expansion of the preceding pattern or as an altogether different pattern following its collapse. In either case, it appears to have taken place at the very end of the Uruk-period as presently understood and was characterized by the placement of small isolated outposts (Godin, Sialk) at locations of strategic importance along highland routes feeding into Uruk enclaves in the north (e.g., Nineveh) or into Uruk states in the Iraqi alluvium (via the Diyala basin and the Khorasan Road) or southwestern Iran (via southern Zagros passes).

The principal Uruk enclaves across the northern Mesopotamian plains formed a network of surprising geographic breadth and appear to have been exponentially larger and more complex—socially, politically, and economically—than preexisting communities. Although no direct corroborating evidence exists, I presume that these enclaves must have exercised an overwhelming influence, if not outright control, over the long-distance exchange economy of the areas in which they were established. This presumption is based on circumstantial but persuasive evidence: (1) the noticeable differences in scale between the enclaves and surrounding indigenous communities, (2) the strategic rationale underlying the location of the enclaves, and finally, (3) the discernible impact that the intrusion had on nearby indigenous societies.

However, none of this is to argue that individual sites in the network were established as part of a single comprehensive "master plan." Far from it. The growth of the network was surely organic, and a significant temporal dimension must be presumed to have existed, although our understanding of pertinent chronological data from sites such as Nineveh, Brak, Samsat, and Carchemish is not yet sufficient to disentangle its details. What is clear is that at its apogee the Uruk expansion may be conceived as part of the cyclical "momentum toward empire" that characterized Mesopotamian civilization throughout millennia. Made necessary by societal responses to the chronic lack of resources in the Mesopotamian alluvium and facilitated by differences in the sociopolitical and economic structures of communities in the alluvium and its periphery, that recurrent impulse outward took a variety of forms throughout the history of Mesopotamian civilization—from more informal (sporadic trade contacts, institutionalized trade networks, and occasional military expeditions and raids) to more formal modes of interaction (territorial annexation, provincial systems). The specifics for each period and area were to be determined by a combination of factors and conditions that had as much to do with conditions in the periphery as it did with developments in the alluvial core.

In the Uruk period, for example, it is possible to understand the observed differences in the locational pattern of Uruk sites in the Syro-Mesopotamian plains, where far-flung outposts were the preferred contact strategy, and the Susiana area, where a process of wholescale colonization is likely, in reference to a number of factors. An important consideration must have been that Susiana was seven to ten days distant from southern Iraq, either by foot or by donkey caravan (H. T. Wright 1981b:264). By contrast, the northern enclaves could only be reached after one or more months of travel, as shown by surviving accounts of the itinerary of Old Babylonian merchants (early second millennium B.C.) traveling from the Mesopotamian alluvium to the city-state of Emar in the Tabqa Dam area.[1] This meant that the enclaves must have been expensive to found, support, and defend—which may partially explain why Uruk societies were unable (or unwilling) to maintain them in the long run.

However, another factor that surely accounts for some of the observed differences in the strategies of contacts of alluvial societies of the Uruk period toward their northern and eastern peripheries is that in moving eastward into the Susiana plain, the Uruk settlers were drawn by a relative settlement vacuum into which they could step unmolested or with only minimal resistance. It will be recalled that indigenous settlement in southwestern Iran had been in decline for centuries prior to the Uruk

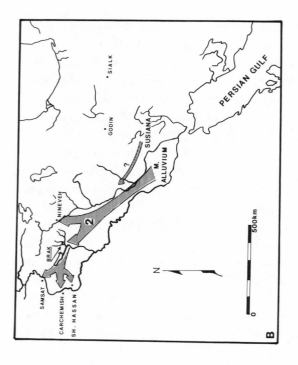

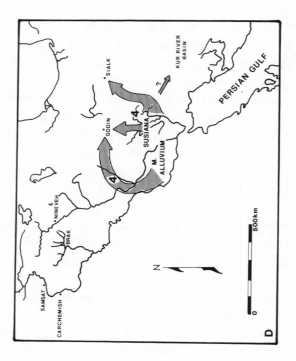

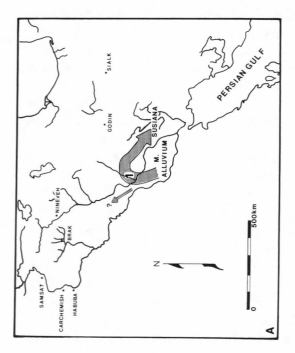

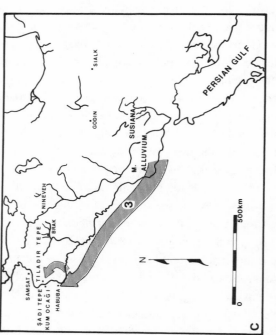

Fig. 46. The Expansion of Mesopotamian polities in the Uruk period.

penetration. In moving northward into the Syro-Mesopotamian plains, however, Uruk settlers intruded into an area where well-developed trade relationships with the surrounding highlands already existed (as evidenced at Gawra) and came into contact with cultures that although less powerful and less complex than the intruders were nevertheless flourishing.

These logistical and cultural differences help explain why the settlement patterns of Uruk sites in the southwestern Iranian plains and the high plains of Syro-Mesopotamia diverged as much as they did. Whereas culturally by the Late Uruk period Susiana had become, in effect, an eastward extension of the Mesopotamian alluvium with at least two independent Uruk polities vying for supremacy, the plains of Syro-Mesopotamia remained a distant alien environment that was best approached by means of specialized settlements at strategic locations (gateway communities).

A profitable way to tackle the question of how the strategies of contact between Mesopotamian societies and peripheral communities were shaped by preexisting conditions in the periphery, and to corroborate whether or not the conclusions already reached as to the nature of peripheral communities are warranted, is to use comparative material from similar or related phenomena for which adequate historical documentation is available. A useful and provocative study is that of Philip Curtin (1984), a historian, who explores the forms cross-cultural exchange has taken through history, the ways in which it has been organized, and the considerable impact such contacts have had on the societies exposed to it. He argues that after a certain point in social evolution, the general outlines of the institutions of cross-cultural trade become remarkably similar across otherwise very different civilizations and historical circumstances, even though the specifics of the institutions and of the trade itself varied considerably. According to Curtin, the most common institutional form of cross-cultural exchange after the emergence of cities was the "trade diaspora," a term that is applicable to the Uruk enclaves, stations, and outposts insofar as it is defined broadly as any community or communities set up for the specific purpose of mediating contacts between areas with different but complementary resource endowments.

Historically, asserts Curtin, trade diasporas have taken a number of diverse forms. These range from commercial specialists removing themselves from their own society and settling as aliens in a foreign community to the diametrically opposed case of posts established as political entities from the beginning, with the founding power or powers retaining some sort of control over the trading settlements. Between these extremes are myriad possibilities in terms of the relationship between the trade diaspora settlements and their host communities, the relationship between the diaspora settlements themselves, their relationship, if any, with their metropolis, and finally in terms of the possible impact of preexisting conditions in shaping the nature of contacts.

This last point is of particular significance for understanding the Uruk expansion, since it is clear from the case studies explored by Curtin that the strategies of contact do vary considerably according to the sociopolitical and economic structures of indigenous societies in the midst of which diaspora settlements are established. In areas of considerable economic potential but relatively undeveloped intraregional trade networks, Curtin finds that trading settlements are more likely to be spread widely into the local hinterland and to be directly involved in the exploitation of resources—a settlement pattern at variance with that observed for Uruk settlements in the north and northwest. However, in areas where local polities already hold control of a developed trade network, trading settlements are more likely to be established only at selected locations, usually at the juncture of interregional and intraregional transportation networks.

In light of the foregoing, what the Uruk enclaves in Syro-Mesopotamia did was to superimpose a new (longer-distance) orientation on preexisting exchange networks uniting the northern plains and the highlands to the north and east. The strategically positioned enclaves controlled the long-distance trade routes in and out of the alluvium and across the Syro-Mesopotamian plains. However, the hinterlands of Syro-Mesopotamia, the highlands, and the highland trade routes feeding into the northern plains were controlled by a kaleidoscope of indigenous polities that must have been amenable to trade. This contact strategy is explained, in part, by what the economic historian Paul Bairoch (1988:11–12) has termed the "tyranny of distance." Simply put, the primitive transportational technologies common to premodern societies meant that direct exploitation of distant resources was prohibitively expensive and time consuming.[2] Under such conditions, the highland resources coveted by Uruk states were much more easily and cheaply obtained by allowing indigenous communities already exploiting them to continue, provided they could be persuaded or coerced (by means of the intrusive settlements in the nearby plains) into trade at terms favorable to the alluvium.

In spite of different historical circumstances, a particularly illuminating parallel for the sort of relationship I presume to have existed between native societies of the Syro-Mesopotamian plains and surrounding highlands and the Uruk settlements in their midst is that of the Portuguese intrusion into Senegambia (West Africa) in the sixteenth and seventeenth centuries A.D. European sources show that by the time Portuguese colonists first arrived on the Senegambian coast in search of slaves, gold, ivory, and spices, the area was occupied by a number of independent chiefdoms and a lively trade in fish, salt, iron, textiles, and agricultural products had long existed between local polities. Moreover, for several centuries prior to the arrival of the Portuguese, overland long-distance trade connections (via the Sahara Desert) also existed between Senegambia and Muslim states in the Mediterranean (Curtin 1975).

Given these conditions, the Portuguese were content with establishing only a limited number of settlements at strategic locations. In the Senegambian case, this did not involve the taking over of important preexisting settlements since those were aligned with the trans-Saharan routes and were located far inland in the self-supporting savannah areas separating the northern desert and the southern rain forests. Rather, Portuguese settlements were established (in almost all cases, it seems, with the consent of local populations) only along the coast and the delta of the Gambia River. At those locations, Portuguese settlements had easy access to both the maritime routes toward western Europe that their navy controlled and the waterways and overland routes leading inland. In this way, the Portuguese were able to bypass the trans-Saharan routes and establish themselves as an important mediator of the long-distance trade economy of the area. Control of inland routes now partially rerouted in order to feed into the Portuguese coastal enclaves, however, was left in the hands of local chieftains willing to trade—the same chieftains who had control of the bulk of long-distance and intraregional trade prior to the arrival of the Europeans. After the intruders set themselves up along the coast, they were supplied with required resources and trading items by a growing class of African middlemen (Curtin 1975; Daaku 1970).

If indeed, as I contend, it is possible to see the expansion of Uruk societies as an early example of the cyclical "momentum toward empire" that characterized Mesopotamian civilization from its inception, then it becomes necessary to define what sort of "empire" is documented by the evidence discussed in the preceding chapters. In all likelihood, associated cluster villages were controlled by the enclaves they surrounded. Moreover, it is probable that the enclaves themselves may have been dependent on specific Uruk city-states. However, neither the northern plains as a whole nor the surrounding highlands were under the direct control of the emerging urban centers of southern Iraq and southwestern Iran. Effective Mesopotamian control of those vast areas would have required a settlement pattern sharply at variance from that observed in the Uruk period: a whole network of administrative posts, garrisons, and way stations in the hinterlands away from the rivers.

In short, available archaeological evidence suggests that the links that tied the northern Mesopotamian periphery and the alluvial lowlands of southern Iraq and Khuzestan in the Uruk period were primarily economic in nature. Nonetheless, those links were deeply influential in the development of peripheral societies. Observable effects vary from the adoption of explicitly Mesopotamian architectural styles, such as may be detected at Tell Hammam et-Turkman, to the increasing convergence in indigenous and Mesopotamian ceramic manufacturing industries and glyptic practices revealed at Arslan Tepe. More important than these easily identifiable transformations, however, were the underlying modifications in social and economic organization, ideology, and concepts of leadership that may be inferred from the archaeological remains.

In terms of the Gallagher and Robinson paradigm of relationships of imperial dependency discussed in the introductory chapter, the network of Uruk enclaves in northern Mesopotamia may be characterized as an informal empire: the boundaries of Mesopotamian economic hegemony far outreached those of its political control. The informal empire of the Uruk period was from the perspective of the periphery not unlike that of the "trading post empires" of Carthage in the Western Mediterranean prior to the third century B.C., or even those of Britain and Portugal in Asia and Africa prior to the twentieth century. At the center of these empires were highly integrated polities possessing little in the way of territory that nonetheless managed to exert a preeminent influence in the economic life of vast regions by means of strategically located enclaves and a network of alliances with otherwise independent local rulers (Curtin 1975, 1984; Gallagher and Robinson 1961). In the absence of historical documentation, the existence of alliances between specific Uruk enclaves and nearby indigenous rulers controlling access to highland resources cannot be demonstrated directly. Nevertheless, whether formalized or not, such alliances must have existed, for in the long run the position of the Uruk enclaves across the north and northwest would have been untenable in the face of active local opposi-

tion. Though coercion is certainly likely to have been part of the expansionary process of the Uruk period, the process as a whole is unintelligible unless a significant measure of indigenous collaboration is presumed.

THE VIEW FROM THE CORE: A WORLD SYSTEM OF THE URUK PERIOD

Though instructive from the point of view of the periphery, the informal empire model fails us in that it presupposes the existence of a single political center. This may have been the case in the Akkadian and later periods, but it was not the case in Uruk times. The survey evidence from southern Iraq and Khuzestan indicates that the political environment of the Uruk world was characterized by a small number of centralized cores, almost certainly in fierce competition. This may be inferred from the already reviewed evidence for changes in Uruk settlement patterns in the Susiana plain culminating in the emergence of an uninhabited buffer zone separating what appear to have been two rival states. Significantly, armed conflict is often portrayed in contemporary representations in both the Iraqi alluvium and Susiana: a common scene in Uruk cylinder seal impressions depicts various military activities and the taking of prisoners.[3]

Within a framework of conflict and strife in the Mesopotamian core, then, the establishment of individual Uruk settlements in the periphery is best conceived as part of an organic process of action and counteraction, with individual Uruk city-states scrambling to found specific enclaves or outposts in order to control the critical lines of communication through which resources were obtainable and, equally important, to deny their local rivals such exclusive control. Specific states would have been oriented toward particular portions of the periphery by virtue of their location and past history of contacts, as represented in figure 47. An important factor in this organic process must have been the colonization of the Susiana plain and the emergence there of independent Uruk polities. This may have acted as a powerful stimulus for independent pro-

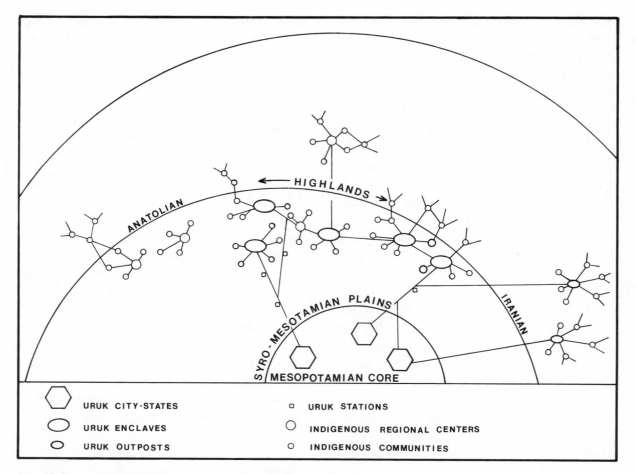

Fig. 47. The supraregional interaction system of the Uruk period.

cesses of expansion northward by competing states in the Mesopotamian alluvium in an attempt to off-set the advantages enjoyed by southwestern Iranian centers, which were ideally situated to tap into trade routes across the Iranian plateau and the east.

A later historical parallel from Mesopotamia is available for the situation envisioned here for the Uruk period. Late in the Isin-Larsa period (first quarter of the second millennium B.C.), after the collapse of the empire of the Third Dynasty of Ur and before the unification of the alluvium under the emerging power of Hammurabi of Babylon, documents indicate that specific states controlled partic-ular segments of the trade routes—whether over-land alongside the Tigris or Euphrates or maritime toward the Gulf. The city of Ur in the southern edge of the alluvium, for example, seems to have been

intimately connected with Persian Gulf trade, whereas Larsa, its neighbor to the northeast, was more closely associated with land routes eastward into southwestern Iran via the Diyala region. Simi-larly, Sippar, in the northeastern edge of the allu-vium, appears more closely tied with trade routes alongside the Tigris toward Assur and the north, while Babylon, on one of the main branches of the Euphrates in the central alluvium, was oriented mainly toward routes in the direction of northern Syria and the northwest (Larsen 1987; Leemans 1960).

From the perspective of the Mesopotamian core in the Uruk period, then, a more useful construct than "informal empire" is a modified "world sys-tem," as discussed in the introductory chapter. What makes this model of historical change pertinent to the study of the expansion of early Mesopotamian civilization is that, like the informal empire paradigm, it presumes that the primary linkages between complementary regions and cultures are economic; but unlike the informal empire model, the world system scheme takes into account the dynamics of competing polities at the center. Initially, at least, the supraregional interaction system of the modern world described by Wallerstein emerges from the independent efforts of a few fiercely competitive cores which, more often than not, were simply reacting to earlier moves and perceived threats from regional rivals. In general, I presume that this was also the historical context for the Uruk expansion.

THE CONTEXT OF EXPANSION

The mass of new and reinterpreted data from the north and northwestern Mesopotamian periphery, summarized in the preceding chapters, bears not only on our understanding of transformations in those peripheral areas but also on our comprehension of developments in the alluvial lowlands of southern Iraq and southwestern Iran in the second half of the fourth millennium B.C. Indeed, in many ways it is possible to gauge better the transformation of Sumerian civilization in the later part of the Uruk period on the basis of peripheral data. The level of centralized community planning perceived in settlements such as the Habuba/Qannas complex, for example, is indicative of the complexity of administrative developments in the urban centers of the Mesopotamian core, for which we have little direct evidence from either southern Iraq or southwestern Iran, where Uruk levels are often buried under meters of later deposition.

Moreover, what peripheral evidence exists concerning the organization of the exchange in the Uruk period also provides clues as to the social structure of early Mesopotamian communities for which, again, the only pertinent evidence from the Mesopotamian core itself is that provided by not always clearly understood glyptic and epigraphic materials.[4] At one end of the spectrum of organizational possibilities stands the hilltop fort at Godin

Tepe (Godin V), where, I have argued, following the excavators, that a group of commercial specialists removed themselves from their own society and settled as aliens with their host's approval in a foreign community (Godin VI). The observed pattern thus recalls the well-documented case of Old Assyrian merchants in Anatolia, although it is not known whether the few occupants of the Godin fort were acting in the interests of their kin group or on behalf of an Uruk state. Little can be said of the situation in sites such as Nineveh, Brak, Samsat, and Carchemish because of limited exposures. It is possible that the Uruk occupation of those previously inhabited centers may have resembled the pattern found at Godin, but on a much larger scale. It is more likely, however, that those sites resembled the diametrically opposed organizational pattern observable in the Habuba/Qannas/Aruda complex in the Tabqa Dam area, where comparatively broad exposures were achieved.

The Uruk sites in the Tabqa region simply cannot be explained as anything other than specialized appendages of an Uruk city-state that must themselves have been organized in a similar manner. Although we do not know whether or not those settlements remained formally dependent on their founding metropolis for long, the level of centralized planning they evince indicates that they represent a case of urban implantation, a cluster of related settlements founded as a political entity to serve a particular function (e.g., mediators of exchange). Unless our preconceptions of the nature of ancient Mesopotamian society are seriously flawed, it must be presumed that the Tabqa enclave represented a conscious and expensive act of policy that simply cannot be ascribed to any kin-based family firm in the Old Assyrian trade model. Rather, the founding of such enclaves would have required levels of planning and resources, expenditures, and access to labor supplies beyond those traditionally thought possible for kin-related organizations, such as existed throughout Mesopotamian history (Diakonoff 1975, 1982; Gelb 1979).

In short, if I am correct in assuming from the carefully chosen locations of the major Uruk enclaves across northern Mesopotamia that control over exchange networks in and out of the alluvium was the strategic rationale that underlay their foundation, then it must be concluded that in the Uruk period it was for the most part the state (which is here equated with the public sector including both palace and temple) that took an active role in ensuring the procurement of resources. From this it may be inferred that, by and large, at the very beginnings of Mesopotamian civilization the state already exercised a preponderant economic role, since it must have held control over the substantial labor and security forces that historically in the Mesopotamian case were necessary for the production of exportable surpluses. (Nissen 1976; Zagarell 1986).

This early role seems supported by available textual and representational evidence from the Mesopotamian core, namely, the still little understood Archaic Texts from Levels IV and III of the Eanna sequence at Warka and cylinder seal impressions in Uruk style from Warka and various other sites. A case in point is the production of textiles, which, as will be recalled, was traditionally a crucial state-controlled export-oriented industry. Although we do not yet have unequivocal evidence for the manufacture of textiles for export in the Uruk period such as exists later in the third millennium, what evidence is available reveals that all the necessary conditions for such an activity were already in place by the floruit of the enclave network (Nissen 1985b). The existence of the required technology is demonstrated by a cylinder seal impression from Susa clearly depicting a horizontal loom and weavers (Amiet 1972: no. 673). State control over necessary raw materials (wool) seems assured in light of a recently published group of Archaic Texts dealing with animal husbandry, which attests to the existence of state-managed flocks (Green 1980). Similarly, control over required labor is implicit in the specific term used for female slaves in the Archaic Texts (SAL + KUR), which means not only slave of foreign origin in the strict sense, but also dependent woman or serf (Gelb 1982:91–93). Such laborers figure prominently in the later documenta-

tion on the production of textiles for export. Significantly, the sealing from Susa showing a weaving scene depicts the attendant personnel as wearing long pigtails, an indication that the labor was performed by women (Amiet 1972:105, no. 673). A final precondition is a state role in the storage and redistribution of raw materials and finished products. This too is indicated in the Archaic Tablets: even the earliest ones, which record but a single transaction, represent the work of central administrators recording inflows or outflows of specific commodities. According to Nissen (1986a:330), a substantial number of the difficult-to-interpret tablets deal with the distribution and storage of textiles.

While the public sector was surely the preeminent economic force behind long-distance trade in Uruk times, there is no need to presume that Uruk elites possessed total command over all facets of the economy. Recent studies on the economy of Sumerian city-states in the third millennium (Foster 1977, 1981; Gelb 1971, 1979; Powell 1977; Westenholz 1984) point, in fact, to considerable evidence for economic forces within Mesopotamian society not under the direct control of central bureaucracies, even in periods of considerable political centralization, such as I presume to have been the case in Uruk times. These studies indicate that a lively measure of internal trade controlled by either private entrepreneurs or by state functionaries taking advantage of their position for private gain can be documented even in times when long-distance exchange was primarily the responsibility of the public sector. More important, the same studies also raise the possibility that a certain measure of private entrepreneurship in the procurement of some resources from outside the alluvium may have existed throughout (Adams 1974). This point is underscored by Foster's (1977) analysis of Akkadian-period trade based on records from the city-state of Umma. He finds whole categories of imports (including such crucial commodities as copper) that are absent altogether from the surviving documentation. Since that documentation was prepared by central bureaucracies, it is possible that at least a portion of the needed imports may have reached the alluvium by more episodic, less formal mechanisms outside of the purview of the great institutions.

These studies of third millennium trade are relevant to our understanding of conditions in the Uruk period because they raise the possibility that by concentrating our attention on the major Uruk enclaves thus far identified, which represent the "official" procurement mechanism of central bureaucracies, we may be missing the complementary "unofficial" procurement efforts of private entrepreneurs that bypassed the enclaves altogether and extended the Mesopotamian presence into areas well beyond their immediate reach. Whether or not Uruk outposts in the highlands such as Godin and Sialk represent the culmination of the expansion phase of the Uruk period or its partial collapse, a tantalizing hypothesis is that those outposts attest to complementary modes of procurement outside the purview of the state in the Uruk period.

OUTSTANDING PROBLEMS AND SUGGESTIONS FOR FURTHER RESEARCH

The Roots of Expansion

Societies in the Mesopotamian alluvium during the Uruk period expanded rapidly, both internally and externally. Internally, this expansion took a variety of forms: (1) new forms of spatial distribution with the growth of cities and their dependencies; (2) new forms of sociopolitical organization with the explosive growth of social differentiation, the emergence of encumbered labor, and the crystallization of the state; (3) new forms of economic arrangements and of record keeping with state control of a substantial portion of the means of production and of its surplus, craft, and occupational specialization on an industrial scale, and the effective origins of writing; and finally, (4) new forms of symbolic representation needed to validate the changes taking place in the realm of social and political relationships, leading to the creation of an artistic tradition and iconographic repertoire that was to set the framework for pictorial representation in Meso-

potamia for millennia to come. Externally, this expansion manifested itself in an actual migration of population and in the formalization (by means of the strategically positioned enclaves, stations, and outposts) of the long-distance trade networks that were necessary to supply the increasingly urbanized and stratified societies in the alluvium. These various phenomena of internal and external expansion were interdependent, and the processes leading to civilization in the alluvium cannot be fully understood unless we treat them as such. However, we have not yet addressed the precise relationship between these parallel sets of processes.

This problem of interpretation has proved particularly obtuse because, while we possess just enough evidence to describe the outlines of Uruk settlement in the Syro-Mesopotamian plains in the Late Uruk period, little is known of how those settlements evolved. There can be little doubt that the bulk of the Uruk expansion must have taken place in the context of societies in which complex political and administrative structures were already in place. However, a crucial question is whether strong centralized states crystallized at precisely those locations through which long-distance exchange was being funneled in earlier times, or whether long-distance contacts developed out of settlements that had evolved into strong centralized states for endogenous reasons not related to cross-cultural interaction.

In an early attempt to answer this question with archaeological data from the Mesopotamian world, Henry Wright (1972) carefully analyzed evidence for imports and exports from Uruk and Jemdet Nasr levels at Farukhabad, a small regional center in the Deh Luran plain of southwestern Iran. Wright concluded that while some evidence for interregional exchange could be found throughout the two periods, large-scale movements of commodities only occurred after the establishment of the state. While representative of conditions in the somewhat peripheral Deh Luran plain, Wright's results need not be applicable to the Mesopotamian alluvium. In the Sumerian core, the issue of the relationship between state formation and long-distance exchange is still clouded by the rather disjointed and non-quantifiable data available for the most important urban centers of the Uruk period—large exposures of pertinent levels exist only for a single site, Warka itself. Moreover, only portions of the administrative quarter of that site were sampled, and as noted by Nissen (1986b:317–19) and Strommenger (1980b), the results from early excavations there are marred by ambiguous stratigraphic information and inadequate record keeping. Making matters more complicated is the fact that we have yet to come to grips with the nature of developments in the surprisingly urbanized Early Uruk period, dating roughly to the first half of the fourth millennium.

Nevertheless, available evidence pertaining to the immediately preceding Late Ubaid period points the way toward an eventual solution. Unless we are prepared to telescope the origins of the state in southern Mesopotamia back into the Ubaid period, of the two alternatives outlined above, it is more likely that long-distance exchange preceded state formation. Resource procurement mechanisms in southern Mesopotamia prior to the Uruk period are still obscure, since with few exceptions we still lack representative exposures of pertinent levels in the principal sites in the south. Nevertheless, many of the imports from the periphery listed in chapter 4 for the Uruk period are already attested in the archaeological record of excavated Ubaid sites, although commonly in limited quantities. Timber for roofing, copper for tools, utensils, and ornaments, flint and obsidian for blades and sickles, common stones for tools and utensils, semiprecious stones for ornaments, seals, and vessels, precious stones and metals for jewelry, mineral ores for paints, and bitumen for architectural waterproofing and hafting tools, to mention only a few of the most obvious examples, are attested in Ubaid and, occasionally, earlier contexts.[5]

More telling are data from northern Mesopotamia indicating that intense cross-cultural contacts with societies in the southern alluvium were already commonplace centuries before the Uruk expansion (Marfoe 1987; Sürenhagen 1986a). Developments along the Upper Khabur and Upper Euphrates ba-

sins remain ill defined,[6] but unequivocal proof of such early contacts exists for the Upper Tigris area. Especially compelling is evidence provided by the Ubaid levels of Tepe Gawra, particularly the impressive Level XIII complex of tripartite structures uncovered more than fifty years ago in the acropolis of the site (Tobler 1950). Whatever the function of these buildings (not all need be interpreted as temples), in them we observe the adoption by an indigenous northern culture of cultural traits and associated institutional forms that are of unmistakable southern origin—a process of acculturation not unlike that evinced later at Hammam et-Turkman and Arslan Tepe. This adoption prefigures patterns of interaction that were to become considerably more intense, widespread, and sharply delineated in the Uruk period.

A number of other clues from the alluvium itself add support to the suggestion that the origins of socioeconomic changes fueling the expansion of Uruk societies were already present in embryonic form by Late Ubaid times. First, some elements of the increasingly complex economy of alluvial societies of the Uruk period can be traced back to Ubaid times. A case in point is the development of relatively sophisticated reckoning systems. While the typical numerical notation tablets of the final phase of the Uruk period evolved directly from the slightly earlier balls with counters (Schmandt-Besserat 1977), functional equivalents such as tabletlike objects and tallying slabs, sometimes with notches or incisions, are attested in the earlier period.[7] Similarly, the emergence of full-time craft specialization which characterized Uruk societies also appears to have Ubaid roots. Archaeological evidence for this is provided by changes in the technology of ceramic production. By the final phase of the Ubaid period, a trend toward simpler painted motifs may be discerned in the pottery repertoire and a generally increasing proportion of the assemblage shows traces of slow wheel manufacture (Nissen 1983:340).

Regional settlement data also point to the Ubaid origins of the Uruk phenomenon. While overall population densities in the alluvium during

Ubaid times were low, a surprising proportion of the total settled area by the Late Ubaid period was represented by settlements that can be categorized as small urban centers on the basis of their size (Adams 1981:58–60).[8] Eridu, for example, was about 12 hectares in extent at this time, and Ur, nearby, was of similar size (H. T. Wright 1981b:325). Tell el'Oueili, near Larsa, was at least 10 hectares in extent, while Uqair further to the north was larger still (Adams 1981:58–59). These sites may be thought of as the direct forerunners of the much larger urban agglomerations of the Uruk period. A final clue is found in the development of public architecture in those early centers. In many cases, the massive structures of the Late Ubaid period give way without interruption to larger versions in the Uruk period. This succession is most clearly seen in the context of what appear to have been temples at Eridu (Safar, Lloyd, and Mustafa 1981) and Warka (Heinrich 1982). Also revealing are equally impressive Late Ubaid buildings of different function found elsewhere. A partially exposed structure at Tell Uqair, for example, is best characterized as a fortified storehouse on account of its massive walls and narrow corridors (Aurenche 1981: pl. 190). A similar function may be posited for the massive Ubaid 4 "annex" at Tell el'Oueili, which has been interpreted as a granary by the excavators. It was attached to a nearby structure of tripartite type that, unlike the buildings at Eridu and Warka, was surely not a temple, since it lacked both a podium and an altar (Forest 1983: pls. 5–6). Larger still, but of more enigmatic purpose, is the Late Ubaid building with *in situ* clay cones at Tell Mismar, near Warka (Schmidt 1978b). Whether secular or religious, these various early structures are no doubt indicative of the growing power of urban elites to command regional resources and of the emerging role of Ubaid towns in the organization of production and in the storage and redistribution of agricultural and other surpluses (H. T. Wright 1986:326)—a precondition in the Mesopotamian case for cross-cultural exchange.

From the above, it may be inferred that the expansionary processes of Mesopotamian societies of the Uruk period were firmly rooted in earlier developments. However, the details of that relationship still elude us. It is not known whether the Late Uruk expansion evolved gradually and without interruption from patterns of interaction that were well established earlier or whether it represented a quantum leap over what had gone on before. Obviously, much information can be gained from an examination of the earliest Uruk-period levels in areas of the northern periphery where the possibility of long-term interaction appears stronger, namely, the Upper Khabur and Upper Tigris areas. And if it can be shown that the floruit of the network of Uruk enclaves did indeed represent some sort of a quantum leap; then an interesting question is what role the domestication of pack animals played in providing the framework within which such an exponential advance could take place.[9]

Apart from more exposures of pertinent northern sites and more representative exposures of the major regional centers, what is needed in order to clarify the nature of contacts between societies in the Mesopotamian alluvium and communities across its northern periphery prior to the Uruk period is the application to the northern Ubaid phenomenon of the sort of systematic regional assemblage and settlement analyses that have only recently been made for the Halaf culture over much of the same area (Davidson 1977; Watson and Leblanc 1971). Only then will it be possible to define issues of regional variation within the conglomerate of cultures that are now subsumed under the term "Ubaid" in northern Mesopotamia, northern Syria, and southern Anatolia. This, in turn, will allow us to differentiate which of the northern Ubaid traditions may have been directly influenced by external contacts with the alluvium and which constitute subsequent indigenous developments only indirectly related to the culture of alluvial Mesopotamia in the Ubaid period.

Moreover, if the nature of the relationship between state formation in the Mesopotamian alluvium and cross-cultural contacts prior to the Uruk period is to be tackled directly, then the quantitative approach based on systematic screening of representative samples that Wright introduced for the analysis of interregional exchange data at Farukhabad must be applied to the archaeological record of a much broader cross-section of pertinent Late Ubaid and Early Uruk sites in the south. Finally, careful collection of relevant faunal data from Late Ubaid and Uruk sites in the alluvium and contemporary sites in the periphery is needed in order to address the question of the possible role that the domestication of pack animals may have had in facilitating the Uruk expansion.

The Initial Impetus for Expansion

I have argued in the preceding discussions that the Uruk expansion into the Syro-Mesopotamian plains may be conceived as a concatenation of autonomous actions and counteractions by a number of rival polities in the Iraqi alluvium responding, perhaps, to the colonization of Susiana and subsequent events there. Additionally, I have suggested that three strands of evidence combine to indicate that the need to secure access to required resources was a critical factor fueling the movement northward: (1) the strategic location of the Uruk enclaves, (2) the apparent (albeit not yet quantifiable) increase in the amount and variety of imports in Uruk sites, and (3) the very specific distribution of indigenous highland sites in which isolated Uruk artifacts are found. However, although surely crucial, the economic imperative just proposed is not sufficient in itself to explain the complex web of motivations and events that originally set in motion and sustained the Uruk expansion. Historically, in fact, expansion and colonization are also closely interwoven with the self-aggrandizing ideologies of ruling elites (Conrad and Demarest 1984). While motivations are not often easily elucidated with the data available to prehistorians, archaeologists who fail to heed the substantivist message of Karl Polanyi (1957) to the effect that in precapitalist societies economic behavior is always embedded in broader sociopolitical and ideologic systems do so at their peril.

In the context of Uruk-period Mesopotamia, this point is raised by Robert McC. Adams (pers. comm., 1987) and Carl Lamberg-Karlovsky (1989),

who see the politico-religious ideologies of emergent, self-conscious urban elites as a pivotal factor in the Uruk expansion. This observation hints at the narrow focus of the foregoing analyses of the Uruk phenomenon—a limitation that can only be partially redressed by the judicious application of models derived from pertinent historic and ethnographic situations. In the final analysis, however, the lack of coherent written records at the very onset of Mesopotamian civilization means that we simply cannot yet properly assess the role of, for example, the desire to spread Sumerian religion as an incentive for emigration. Nor can we evaluate the degree to which expansion was implemented as a conscious state policy by a specific ruler or rulers bent on self-aggrandizement or by a particular interest group which perceived it as advantageous. One possible example of the latter is considered by Rita Wright (1989), who suggests that the requirements of textile production for export may have been an element in the movement into areas of the Syro-Mesopotamian plains propitious for extensive sheep and goat husbandry. Also unknown, but in all likelihood significant, is the role that increasingly onerous urban demands on the population of a newly dependent countryside may have had in spurring emigration as both an escape from oppression (Johnson 1988/89) and as an opportunity for advancement—motivations that were critical in the case of the European colonization of the New World (Scammell 1989) and which also could have been relevant to the Uruk case.

Finally, a number of scholars see population pressure in the southern Mesopotamian core and the need for agricultural land elsewhere as important forces in the Uruk expansion (Areshian 1990; Lamberg-Karlovsky 1989; Schwartz 1988a). Based on the apparently substantial growth in population in the Mesopotamian alluvium throughout the eight hundred years or so between the Late Ubaid and the Late Uruk periods, this view finds some support in newly recovered evidence for additional Uruk enclaves and associated villages in the Birecik-Jerablus area of the Euphrates, suggesting that previous estimates for the number of emigrants from the alluvium in Uruk times must be increased.

However, the relationship, if any, between population growth in the alluvium throughout the late fifth and fourth millennia and the Uruk expansion still eludes us. This is partially owing to problems in estimating population densities for the prehistoric periods in the alluvium, since pertinent Ubaid sites are all too often deeply buried under later alluviation and are seldom recorded in surveys, particularly in the northern portions of the alluvial plain (Adams 1981). In any event, however, overall population density in southern Mesopotamia can only be thought of as a contributory factor: although high, population levels in the second half of the fourth millennium were only a portion of those attained in the earlier half of the third millennium, when no comparable processes of emigration are attested. Moreover, estimates for total occupied hectares (and population) in the Late Uruk period barely differ from those of the preceding Early Uruk time range (Adams 1984:98, table 1), so that population pressure alone can hardly be postulated to explain the Late Uruk expansionary burst.

Potentially more important than total population density as a causal factor in the Uruk expansion is population dislocation as a consequence of environmental catastrophe or political crises resulting in relatively sudden and unmanageable social or environmental stresses in specific portions of the southern lowlands. Much could be gained from exploring the possibility that the Uruk-period population shifts from the northern to the southern and western sectors of the alluvium caused by the natural drying up of a major channel of either the ancient Tigris or the Euphrates (above, chap. 2) may have had a role not only in precipitating the colonization of Susiana—as has already been suggested—but also in initiating the scramble northward into Syro-Mesopotamia.

The Mechanics of Cross-cultural Exchange

In an influential article published over fifteen years ago, Paul Wheatley (1975:230) criticized current archaeological reconstructions of ancient exchange:

So far as ancient commerce is concerned such studies as exist have been undertaken with the limited aims of identifying within a more or less static framework the commodities traded, and charting the routes over which they moved. Only nominal attention has been devoted to exchange values, and none at all to the fundamental and exigent question of the precise modes of exchange involved and the manner in which they articulated with political, administrative, social, religious, and other institutions.

Wheatley's critique, alas, remains all too applicable today. In the Uruk case, for instance, we know little about the ways in which the intrusive enclaves, stations, and outposts may have interacted with indigenous communities in the periphery. To be sure, I have speculated on the general impact of that interaction on the social texture of native communities, and moreover, I have also argued that it may be concluded from the settlement pattern of the enclaves that well-developed local trade networks were already in place prior to the Uruk intrusion and that a measure of indigenous collaboration must be presumed. But the forms such collaboration may have taken are still obscure and the nature of preexisting intraregional trade networks through which highland resources reached the northern plains also remain largely undocumented.

Were resources from the highlands brought first to strategically situated indigenous communities in the northern plains—to Gawra, for example—and through them to the enclaves, or did commodities bypass such sites altogether and reach the enclaves directly? If the former was the case for some commodities, was exchange between indigenous communities in the highlands and the northern plains of the reciprocal (down-the-line) type, or was it more directional (Renfrew 1975)? Or if other commodities were funneled directly into the enclaves, what role did Uruk outposts in the highlands such as those uncovered at Godin and Sialk play in the procurement process? Moreover, which commodities reached the alluvium through the northern enclaves, which enclaves specialized in the procurement of which commodities, which commodities were obtained directly without mediation (via the Diyala), and which were acquired via Uruk states in southwestern Iran? Finally, how was the exchange organized? How was required information on supply and demand obtained, for example, and further, how were values fixed for the commodities traded and transport arranged, who mediated contacts, and on behalf of whom were intermediaries acting?

In view of the inherent limits of the purely archaeological evidence at our disposal, many of the questions just posed must remain unanswered, particularly those dealing with details of the organization of the exchange. It is unlikely that we will ever be able to reconstruct the ever-changing range of interactions and negotiations leading to the successful conclusion of regular transactions in the Uruk period.[10] And while it would be tempting to try to answer some of these questions by extrapolating into the fourth millennium evidence from third millennium myths (such as the cycle dealing with interaction between Uruk and Aratta), it should be remembered that those myths presume the existence of peripheral polities whose power rivaled that of alluvial states. It was argued in the preceding chapter that the stunning success of the Mesopotamian penetration of its periphery in the Uruk period (as compared to later episodes of expansion such as that of the Akkadians) is predicated precisely on the absence of powerful potential rivals in the periphery. Equally unsuitable for the same reasons would be explanatory models based wholly on the later well-documented case of Old Assyrian trade networks.

Present-day political circumstances permitting, however, specific regional studies could be undertaken in order to clarify the broad outlines of the interaction between the Uruk outposts and indigenous communities over particular portions of the Mesopotamian periphery in the late fourth millennium. One important problem of interpretation is the role played by small sites with a broad complement of Uruk ceramics situated in the immediate vicinity of much larger Late Chalcolithic regional centers in areas away from the principal Uruk enclaves. At least three such sites, it will be remembered, have been identified by the Balikh River, and surely other such sites must have existed elsewhere. Whether or not these sites served as "stations"

along a trade route, operating with the implicit permission of nearby local rulers, as was suggested, or whether they played a more complex role could be ascertained by excavation. With broad enough exposures and the proper recovery techniques, it should be possible to draw inferences as to their nature and function, particularly as comparisons could be drawn with the one Uruk station for which a broad exposure already exists, Hassek Höyük.

More difficult given today's political climate would be to clarify the nature of interaction between Uruk outposts and indigenous communities in the highlands and, further, the organization of exchange between highland areas and the northern plains. Most promising (but certainly impossible at this time) would be further examination and trial excavations of strategically located sites with evidence of an apparently broad range of Uruk ceramics in the central and southern Zagros, of which, it will be recalled, a number have been identified. This would go a long way toward clarifying the locational pattern and possible existence of other Uruk outposts in the highlands apart from Godin and Sialk, and the modes of exchange by which commodities were acquired.[11] In turn, this would allow inferences to be made as to the interplay between indigenous and Mesopotamian elements in the procurement of resources.

An immediate and practical way to begin to delineate the interlocking supply and demand systems feeding the growth of Uruk states would be to apply the sort of chemical characterization analyses already devoted to specific imported materials like obsidian (G. A. Wright 1969; Renfrew and Dixon 1976), steatite/chlorite (Kohl, Harbottle, and Sayre 1979), asphalt (Marschner and Wright 1978), and silver and lead alloys (Yener 1983, 1986; Yener et al. 1991) to a broader range of commodities imported into the alluvium during the Uruk period. Much information of potential value could come from the inclusion of fourth millennium copper objects from the northern enclaves and from sites in the alluvium and Khuzestan in the Mesopotamian Metals Project at MASCA (Stech and Piggot 1986). Other ideal candidates for further study are gold and semiexotic stones. A systematic effort to trace the sources for imported timber found in pertinent architectural contexts in the alluvium would also be very useful.

In the absence of associated regional survey and test excavation programs, the sort of characterization studies just suggested would reveal little about the nature of the exchange itself. But they would at least make it possible to trace, however dimly, the outlines of some of the overlapping regional interaction subsystems by which various commodities reached the Mesopotamian lowlands in the fourth millennium. Moreover, coupled with a review of existing evidence from known enclaves and relevant southern sites and (one hopes) with data from new excavations, such an approach would also make it possible to address the associated questions of regional and enclave specialization in the importation of specific resources during the Uruk period.

Undiscovered Uruk Settlements in the Periphery

If the strategic rationale underlying the location of the Uruk enclaves proposed in chapter 3 is correct, then other Uruk enclaves and stations may still remain to be found in the northern plains between the Euphrates and the Tigris. A number of suggestions as to the locations of these hypothesized settlements can be put forward for further testing. One possibility is that landlocked enclaves and stations could exist along the principal east-west routes crisscrossing northern Mesopotamia, away from the rivers. Whether or not this was so cannot yet be ascertained, but recent surveys and excavations in the Jezira region of northwestern Iraq and the Sinjar plains of northeastern Syria promise eventually to help clarify this question. It is also possible that further Uruk enclaves are still to be identified in portions of the principal waterways not yet intensively surveyed. In view of their importance throughout the historical periods, it is possible that the environs of Nuseybin and Ras el'Ain along parallel branches of the Upper Khabur will yet yield traces of Uruk outposts. Similarly, along the Upper Tigris we should expect to find another Mesopotamian enclave well north of the Nineveh/ Mosul area, possibly somewhere along the Tigris in northern Iraq near Faishabur, the traditional terminus of routes from the Euphrates skirting the southern flank of the Tur Abdin massif. Last, it is also likely that further stations linking enclaves still remain to be found. Given the historical importance of the Balikh as a conduit between the Samsat area and the lower elbow of the Euphrates bend, it would not be surprising to find more stations along its course in southeastern Turkey, possibly somewhere along the way to Harran. Another largely unexplored area in which further stations could be expected is the Tigris basin south of Mosul.

THEORETICAL REPRISE AND CROSS-CULTURAL PARALLELS

A critical question must still be examined before closing. Is the conceptual framework adopted in the introduction applicable to developments taking place as early as the fourth millennium B.C.? This question is important, since concepts such as "informal empire" and "world system" represent models developed specifically for the explanation of phenomena connected with the expansion of Europe and the growth of capitalism in the modern world and were never intended for use outside of that historical juncture.

The use of modern eurocentric models in an ancient Near Eastern context is justified, I believe, on two accounts. The first is that the world system/informal empire conceptual framework is not put forth as a prescription of conditions that must have occurred. Rather, it is intended as a model of possibilities, hypotheses to be tested against available archaeological data, which all too often are fragmentary and difficult to interpret. More important, however, the use of the framework is justified because changes resulting from the emergence of modern capitalism may have greatly intensified and brought into sharp focus relationships of asymmetrical exchange and economic dependency leading to unequal development, but by no means created those relationships (Ekholm and Friedman 1979; Gills and Frank 1991). This is clearly understood by Stanley Diamond, who argues that "imperialism and colonialism are as old as the State; they define the political process" (1974:5). Early antiquity is, in fact, full of clear examples of such asymmetrical interactions. A well-documented case is that of the Roman presence in the Maghrib following the final defeat of Carthage in the second century B.C. A. Demans (1975), a historian, has presented a compelling case for understanding the consequences of Roman occupation of North Africa under the Republic within the framework of modern studies of development and underdevelopment. Using a variety of literary and historical evidence, he documents in detail the economic, social, and political consequences of Roman policies that systematically transformed what had for centuries been a flourishing area under the leadership of Carthage into little more than a specialized producer of agricultural products for an expanding Rome—a role complementing that of Spain as supplier of minerals. The thorough character of this transformation in the Maghrib, argues Demans, helps explain both the eventual collapse of Roman authority in the area and the relative lack of further development well into the Islamic era.

Prehistory, too, abounds in examples that can be suitably interpreted in terms of the conceptual models underpinning our discussions. Indeed, some authors contend that the development of asymmetrical core-periphery relationships is at the very root of pristine state formation. Kajsa Ekholm, for instance, asserts that cross-culturally "the characteristic condition for the development of civilisations is access by a local society to a resource base wider than that contained within its own boundaries" (1981:249). While it is too early to assess whether or not Ekholm's insight is universally applicable to the development of pristine states, it appears certain that the Uruk phenomenon, with its complementary processes of physical expansion into nearby areas and the placing of core outposts at key junctions of the outlying periphery was by no means unique. In fact, I am inclined to believe that such complementary exploitative strategies may

well represent the normal form of cross-cultural contact for pristine civilizations. The use of isolated outposts as a contact strategy is well documented through history in situations of initial colonial contact between areas with varying resource endowments and societies at markedly different levels of sociopolitical evolution (Curtin 1984; Smith 1976), and by definition, all cases of pristine state formation mut involve interaction between societies at significantly different levels of complexity.

Four examples will suffice to illustrate the applicability of the world system/informal empire paradigm to prehistory in general and the expansion of early states in particular. As in the Uruk case, following closely on the heels of initial state formation, each confronts us with parallel processes of expansion into immediately contiguous areas and the placing of outposts at considerable distances away from the center, commonly at isolated positions astride trade routes, near resource concentrations, or in the midst of centrally positioned and locally powerful native communities. These are (1) the Predynastic Upper Egyptian intrusion into the Nile Delta (Hassan 1988; Wenke 1989) and the subsequent establishment of Egyptian outposts along the northern rim of the Sinai Peninsula and portions of southern Palestine (Oren 1989; Stager 1992) at the very end of the fourth millennium B.C.; (2) the spread of Mature Harappan polities from their Indus valley core throughout the Kutch-Guharat areas of western India (Possehl 1980) and the subsequent establishment of Harrapan outposts along the Oxus basin in Afghanistan (Francfort and Pottier 1978), the Makran coast of Pakistan (Dales 1962), coastal Oman (Cleuziou, Reade, and Tosi 1990), and, possibly, southern Mesopotamia (Parpola, Parpola, and Brunswig 1977) in the second half of the third millennium B.C.; (3) the consolidation of the Tiwanaco state throughout the Altiplano area of the south central Andes (Browman 1978) and the foundation of Classic and Late Tiwanaco outposts in coastal valleys of southern Peru (Goldstein 1989) and, possibly, northern Chile (Mujica 1985) throughout the Middle Horizon period (ca.

A.D. 600–1000); and (4) the expansion of the Teotihuacán state from the valley of Mexico into immediately surrounding highland valleys (Millon 1981) and the ensuing foundation of Teotihuacán outposts outside of the central Mexican highlands, such as at Matacapan (Santley 1989) in the Tuxlas Mountains of Veracruz and at Kaminaljuyú (Sanders 1977) in the valley of Guatemala during the Middle Classic period (ca. A.D. 300–600).

To be sure, it would be foolhardy to extrapolate indiscriminately into the past modes of social relationships and organization that only emerged as a result of specific, nonreplicable historical circumstances. Whatever the actual processes that culminated in the expansion of Mesopotamian societies of the Uruk period, there is no need to postulate, for instance, the existence of either an "Uruk East India Company" or an "Uruk Encomienda" system. Moreover, Kohl (1987a) is no doubt correct when he observes that there were no major technological gaps in the ancient world such as commonly existed in the modern case between core and periphery groups and that communication and transportation are now facilitated by technologies that are exponentially more efficient than those available to early Old and New World civilizations. Nevertheless, this does not mean that early systems of asymmetrical core-periphery relations, such as the Uruk, were of an inherently different nature than later ex-

amples, but only that they were less integrated and therefore less efficient and more fragile. This, in turn, may help explain both the variety of peripheral responses to the intrusion of core outposts and why early systems commonly collapsed within a relatively short span of time and often well before the pernicious realities of long-term unequal exchange asserted themselves in the affected peripheries. Nonetheless, it stands to reason that differences in the sophistication of sociopolitical and economic organization and administrative procedures between the Uruk city-states and the peripheral communities with which they came into contact may have been of almost as much import in the ancient world as differences in manufacturing and transportation technologies proved to be in modern times. Moreover, while ancient exchange never matched the intensity of the transoceanic trade of modern colonial times in absolute terms, it must have been as powerful a force for change in the context of less-developed indigenous societies in the periphery of the early expansionary states as modern commerce in staples and bullion would prove to be much later.

The Uruk expansion was thus no aberration. It merely represents an example—possibly the earliest—of a mode of cross-cultural interaction repeated many times in history, albeit at sharply varying scales and rates of complexity.

The Uruk Expansion: New Interpretations and New Data

WHAT'S NEW?

Although Iraq and southwestern Iran have largely been closed to new archaeological research since the Iran-Iraq and Gulf wars, new surveys and excavations have continued across parts of Syro-Mesopotamia, the area now located within the borders of northern Syria and southeastern Turkey. Moreover, some earlier work in northern Iraq has also now been published. Much of this work is pertinent to the elucidation of various aspects of the phenomena that have come to be collectively referred to as the "Uruk Expansion." In particular, in the decade since this book was originally published, new details have become available about previously known or suspected intrusive Uruk settlements across Syro-Mesopotamia, and new types of such settlements not previously attested have started to be documented. As importantly, this new work now sheds light on the nature of the indigenous societies that the Uruk intruders encountered there and the social transformations that took place in the northern periphery of Mesopotamia as a consequence of those encounters.

Additionally, new interpretations about developments in the core areas of southern Iraq and southwestern Iran during the Uruk period have appeared in the last decade (e.g., Algaze 2001a, 2002; Boehmer 1999; Collins 2000; de Miroschedji 2003; Englund 1998; Forest 1996, 1999; Hole 1994; Kouchoukos 1998; Kouchoukos and Hole 2003, Liverani 1998; McCorriston 1997; Moorey 1993; Nissen 2002; Pollock 1999, 2001; Potts 1999; Wilkinson 2003; and Wright 1998). At the same time, various aspects of the Uruk Expansion have been profitably reexamined (e.g., Algaze 2001b; Butterlin 2003; Emberling 2002; Frangipane 1996, 2001, 2002; Lupton 1996; Nissen 2001; J. Oates 1993; Rothman 1993, 2001; Rothman et al. 1998; Stein 1999a–b, 2001; Stein [ed.] 1999; and Vallet 1997, 1998). Most important among the latter are the proceedings of two conferences held in 1998, one taking place at the School of American Research in Santa Fe, New Mexico (Rothman 2001), and the other taking place at Manchester University, England (Postgate 2002).

Some of the new data from recent work in southeastern Turkey, northern Syria, and northern Iraq, and some of the ideas that have appeared only recently about the Uruk Expansion challenge parts of my initial interpretations of that phenomenon, presented in chapters 1–7. In the pages that follow, I review aspects of those interpretations that either need to be expanded, clarified, modified, or reconsidered altogether in light of this challenge.

THE CHRONOLOGY OF THE URUK EXPANSION

Earlier, I argued that Uruk settlement in the Mesopotamian periphery was the result of a complex and decentralized competitive process, and that this process was divisible into at least three distinct phases of expansion, which are datable to the Middle and Late Uruk periods (above, fig. 46B–D and pp. 110–11). Furthermore, I argued that this process must have evolved over a substantial amount of time, as shown most clearly by the substantial depth of deposition in sites such as Tell Sheikh Hassan, Nineveh, Brak, and, to a lesser extent, Carchemish (above, pp. 56–57).

This last supposition is now fully supported by a thorough analysis of all available ^{14}C data prepared by Henry Wright and Eric Rupley (2001), and published as part of the aforementioned Santa Fe conference volume. Wright and Rupley laboriously collected all available radiocarbon dates from Uruk sites in southern Mesopotamia, intrusive Uruk sites in the periphery, and indigenous peripheral Late Chalcolithic sites in contact with the Uruk world. More importantly, they recalibrated all the pertinent dates using a single sophisticated ^{14}C calibration software package (OxCal, versions 3 and 3.5). The evidence Wright and Rupley have amassed constitutes the most comprehensive body of data available for determining the absolute chronology of the Uruk expansion.[1] In the aggregate, the radiocarbon data now indicate that the various phases of that expansion, spanning both the Middle and Late Uruk periods in the south, lasted for at least 700 years, and occurred between ca. 3800 and 3100 B.C.

However, it is clear from the discussions that follow that there were important variations in the chronology of Uruk contact with different portions of Syro-Mesopotamia, and that the nature of those contacts varied through time, even within a single area. It is also clear that substantial geographical variation existed in the impact that those contacts had on indigenous societies.

THE IDENTIFICATION OF INTRUSIVE URUK SETTLEMENTS

In chapter 3, the typology of intrusive Uruk settlements in the Mesopotamian periphery was discussed in some detail and therefore only a brief summary of pertinent new data and interpretations is offered here. Before reviewing this data, it is necessary to again outline the difficulties inherent to the identification of intrusive Uruk sites across the periphery of Mesopotamia. This is not always simple because some elements of Uruk material culture are commonly found in many otherwise indigenous sites in the area. As a rule, however, intrusive settlements, irrespective of type, are characterized by a wide variety of cultural traits of southern origin, generally including architectural plans and building techniques of southern type, Uruk ceramics, iconographic motifs, and the use of typically southern reckoning and administrative procedures. Nonetheless, varying proportions of indigenous materials are also commonly found in all of the intrusive Uruk settlements, as are, occasionally, Uruk-style artifacts manufactured using local techniques (Helwing 1999).

Presumably, differences in the assemblages found in Uruk settlements across the Mesopotamian periphery are related to a variety of factors: (1) the distance from the alluvium or from other Uruk settlements, which affects the nature and frequency of relations between the intrusive settlements and the Uruk world; (2) the type, intensity, and frequency of trade between the intrusive Uruk settlements and local societies; (3) the use of local labor for productive activities by the intruding groups; (4) the number and gender ratio of Uruk settlers at any one outpost; and (5) the degree of intermarriage between Uruk colonists and local populations.

Given sufficient archaeological data, indigenous sites should be easily distinguished from intruding settlements. As opposed to the wide vari-

ety of Uruk materials characteristic for the intruding sites, indigenous settlements exhibit only isolated Uruk imports within local assemblages, or locally made imitations of Uruk artifacts resulting
from the emulation of specific aspects of Uruk culture by local elites (Wattenmaker 1990; Pollock
1994). In reality, however, the often meager and often incompatibly recorded archaeological data at
our disposal—determining which sites are intrusive and which are indigenous occupations in contact with, and affected by, intrusive Uruk sites—
are much less straightforward than researchers
would like. Thus, differentiating between the two
types of settlements is possible only in some cases,
and remains one of the most important tasks at
hand for scholars interested in the nature of the
Uruk expansion.

Even when indigenous and intrusive settlements can be distinguished, a further typological
problem must still be tackled—there was substantial variability within sites that can be safely recognized as intrusive, and this variability is not always
neatly encompassed within the initial categories of
enclaves, stations, and outposts offered in chapter 3.

What is clear is the following: in areas where a
local settlement hierarchy was already in place, intrusive Uruk settlements were installed in the
midst of preexisting indigenous centers situated at
focal nodes of transportation networks, often—
but not always—at or near natural river fords
where east-west overland routes and north-to-
south water-borne routes come together. Under
these conditions, intrusive Uruk settlements took
three distinct forms. Some of these forms potentially represent an evolutionary sequence in some
areas, whereas, in others, they constitute distinct
forms of interaction with differently structured societies: (1) small Old Assyrian, Karum-like quarters established in the midst of preexisting indigenous societies, clearly with their consent and
cooperation; (2) small Uruk settlements that are
separate from, but located near, large preexisting
centers, again clearly with their consent and cooperation; and (3) larger Uruk enclaves established
on top of (and replacing) strategically situated pre-

existing centers (a process presumably involving
some coercion).

In areas where no significant preexisting occupation had to be reckoned with, however, intrusive
Uruk settlements took a different form altogether.
In those areas, Uruk penetration became a process
of urban implantation. Initially, this also took
place at focal nodes of transportation networks,
such as river fords, but eventually the areas immediately surrounding the implanted centers appear
to have been colonized as well, as Schwartz (2001)
has correctly noted in connection with some of the
Euphrates data discussed below. We now turn to
an examination of new data bearing on these varying configurations of intrusive settlements.

Karum-like Outposts

Earlier I had argued that Karum-like outposts
situated within preexisting indigenous societies in
control of routes through which coveted resources
flowed existed only deep in the Taurus-Zagros
highlands surrounding Mesopotamia. This needs
to be modified, since such outposts have now also
been documented within the Syro-Mesopotamian
plains. The clearest evidence for this is provided by
Hacınebi Tepe, a small Late Chalcolithic site some
3.3 hectares in extent, situated along the Euphrates River in Turkey just north of the historical
ford at Birecik. Hacınebi has been the locus of six
seasons of excavations during the 1990s under the
direction of Gil Stein (1998, 1999a–b; [ed.] 1999; et
al. 1996a, 1996b, 1997, 1998; Pittman 2001).

The new work at Hacınebi is noteworthy for
two reasons. First, unlike the somewhat comparable and already discussed outpost at Godin
(above, pp. 53–56), which dates to the very final
phase of the Uruk expansion, the Uruk settlement
at Hacınebi dates to the initial (Middle Uruk)
phase of the expansionary process. Second, the
careful excavation and analysis techniques used at
the site by Stein and his coworkers allow us to dis-
tinguish differences in dietary practices, craft production, and accounting procedures between the
preexisting indigenous populations at the site and
the intrusive Uruk elements.

Excavations across the Hacınebi site reveal that the Uruk settlement at this location consisted of a community of southern Mesopotamians living in a segregated area at the edge of a larger and thriving preexisting indigenous settlement. Stein uses the term "trade diaspora" to refer to this community, which presumably was attracted to Hacınebi because the local inhabitants of the site had long been engaged in copper acquisition and production (below). Stratigraphic and radiocarbon evidence suggest that this foreign group survived at Hacınebi for several centuries. Unfortunately, the southeastern edge of the site where the Uruk community was physically located had been badly damaged by modern soil pits and by the encroachment of the nearby village, and accordingly only partial architectural plans of the Uruk occupation were recoverable. Nonetheless, the individuals living in the Uruk quarter of Hacınebi, unlike those living in the rest of the settlement, used a full repertoire of Uruk ceramics (largely of Middle Uruk date) that is quite distinct from the Amuq F assemblage used contemporaneously over the rest of the site (Pollock and Coursey 1995; Pearce 1999). These differences reveal that the Uruk inhabitants of Hacınebi had significantly different food-preparation routines from those of the contemporary indigenous groups at the site (Pearce 1999). This is corroborated by faunal analyses from both sectors of the site, which document that substantial differences existed in the dietary preferences of the inhabitants of the Uruk quarter and those of the indigenous population, with Uruk populations showing an overwhelming preference for sheep and goat and little use of cattle and pig, while the locals consumed all four species more or less evenly (Bigelow 1999; Stein 1998).

More importantly, the Uruk inhabitants at the Hacınebi Karum also used a full repertoire of Mesopotamian accounting devices (including at least one sealed ball and one sealed numerical notation tablet) and recording technology (cylinder seals). This repertoire stands in sharp contrast with the sealing and accounting practices based on stamp-seal technology used by the more numerous indigenous occupants of the site (Pittman 1999, 2001).

Small Settlements near Local Centers

Earlier, I had noted a pattern of small isolated Uruk sites (which I termed "stations"), principally but not only along the Euphrates, established along the main lines of communication crisscrossing Syro-Mesopotamia (above, pp. 48–53 and figs. 22, 24). These sites were largely interpreted as serving to maintain communications between the Uruk world and the larger Uruk emplacements at focal nodes of the lines of communication. This role is still a very likely possibility for most of the sites in question, which unfortunately, save for the small site of Qraya in Syria (above, p. 48), remain largely unexcavated.

Other possible "stations" may have existed along important east-west overland routes. This possibility is raised by the results of surveys of the Upper Jezira region of northern Iraq, north of the Jebel Sinjar, where Wilkinson and Tucker (1995:45, fig. 35) found that sites with southern-type Uruk ceramics on their surfaces were clustered only along east-west hollow-way routes crisscrossing the area. However, because the pertinent sites have not been excavated, the presence of Uruk stations along east-west overland routes must remain conjectural.

Be that as it may, a further possibility must also be raised. This is that some of the small Uruk settlements earlier subsumed under the category of "stations" may have existed instead to mediate contacts between the larger Uruk enclaves and indigenous centers across Syro-Mesopotamia in a way similar to, but less physically immediate than, the Karum-like outposts just discussed. This could well be the explanation for sites with exclusively Uruk ceramics on their surface earlier identified near Samsat (above, p. 50 and fig. 22), which I now believe is most parsimoniously categorized as an indigenous center rather than as an Uruk enclave as previously interpreted (below). A similar case obtains along the Balikh in Syria, where Akkermans's (1988b) surveys documented three small sites with exclusively Uruk materials on their surface, each situated within a short distance of a larger indigenous Late Chalcolithic settlement (fig. 22).

Enclaves Replacing Preexisting Centers

Earlier, I argued that substantial Uruk emplacements comparable to those uncovered in the Carchemish to Meskene portion of the Upper Euphrates (below) had been implanted, almost certainly by force, at a small number of other historical fords across northern Mesopotamia where important indigenous regional centers already existed, such as (1) Samsat along the northern portion of the Euphrates in Turkey, (2) Tell Brak on the Jagh Jagh branch of the Upper Khabur, and (3) Nineveh on the Tigris (above, chapter 3). The existence of such implanted settlements is now supported by new data from these and other pertinent sites, but some details of the original view need to be modified.

Taken together, the evidence from Godin Tepe and Hacınebi Tepe (above) shows that small diaspora communities of Uruk origin could exist within larger preexisting centers with the consent of local populations in widely varying areas of the Mesopotamian periphery. This raises the possibility that Uruk interaction with preexisting Late Chalcolithic settlements in command of known river fords or routes across Upper Mesopotamia would have been closer to the Godin/Hacınebi model than it was to the Habuba model (large population movements) that I had previously espoused, a point already noted by Wattenmaker (1990).

Nonetheless, a precise understanding of the nature of the Uruk emplacements at some of the regional centers commanding river fords across northern Mesopotamia continues to elude us. Since my original views first appeared, much hitherto unknown material from earlier excavations at Nineveh (Gut 1995, 2002) and some of the Uruk and indigenous Late Chalcolithic materials from recent excavations at Samsat (Özgüç 1992; Abay 1997) have been published. These new data leave

no doubt that both indigenous and intrusive Uruk assemblages existed at each of the two sites, but available evidence from either site continues to be insufficient to clarify the cultural context of the materials, their spatial relationships, or their relative frequency. Because of these caveats, I now think that Wattenmaker's (1990) suggestion that Samsat may represent an indigenous settlement in contact with the Uruk world, where a narrow range of typical Uruk artifacts were consumed and emulated by local elites, is more likely to be correct than my earlier suggestion.

I still think that some sort of an Uruk emplacement existed at Nineveh. The reason for this is that Nineveh, unlike Samsat, has yielded a wide variety of categories of characteristic Uruk material culture. This includes a full range of typical Uruk ceramics found in widely separated squares at the very center of the Kuyunjik, the high mound of Nineveh. In fact, Renata Gut's (1995) thorough reassessment and republication of the stratigraphic and artifactual evidence from Kuyunjik show that typical Uruk ceramics were common across Squares MM (the deep sounding), BB, H, G, F, and E of the Ishtar Temple excavation area. Although the context and associations of these finds are no longer reconstructable, these squares spanned a linear area of 50 × 350 feet (ca. 15.4 × 107.7 m) (Gut 1995:277, 282, fig. 5). More importantly, unlike the case at Samsat, these excavations also yielded true Uruk glyptic practices and iconographical representations, as well as characteristic Uruk numerical notation tablets, all used at the site in a typical southern Mesopotamian fashion (Collon and Reade 1983). These finds are strong evidence for an actual Uruk presence at Nineveh. The reason for this is that while Uruk iconography and sealing practices were widely imitated in indigenous sites across the northern periphery of Mesopotamia, such emulations were always used at those sites in the context of recording systems that were substantially simpler than those employed by Uruk societies.

What is left to ascertain is whether the Uruk occupation at Nineveh represents an isolated enclave of foreigners living in the midst or at the edge of a thriving and much larger indigenous settlement, as was the case at Godin and Hacınebi, or whether the Uruk intruders simply took over full control of a site that until then had been a thriving indigenous center. Only future research will allow us to discern which of these scenarios was closer to reality. However, of the two possibilities I believe the latter (full control, possibly involving population replacement) is more likely in view of the fact that the layers with intrusive Uruk materials at Kuyunjik were located at the very center of the mound.

New research at Brak is similarly inconclusive about the nature of the Uruk presence at that site, which certainly was one of the most important Late Chalcolithic centers in Syro-Mesopotamia prior to the Uruk intrusion (below). However, the new evidence from Brak now leaves no doubt that Uruk contacts with polities in the Upper Khabur area started already in the later part of the Middle Uruk period and that southern Mesopotamian populations intruded into the area only later, during the Late Uruk period, when some sort of an Uruk colony was established at the site.

These facts have become clear as a result of recent excavations in Area TW at Brak, a large sounding some 350 meters northeast of Mallowan's Eye Temple area, where a clear sequence of *in situ* deposits spanning the fourth millennium has been recovered (Oates and Oates 1993, 1994, 1997; J. Oates 2002; Emberling et al. 1999, 2001). Levels 20–14 in the sounding document the indigenous Late Chalcolithic sequence at the site and will be discussed in some detail below in terms of what they tell us about the nature of that occupation. Of immediate interest in terms of the nature of the Uruk presence at the site are Levels 13 and 11–12. Level 13 had no clear architectural associations, but a sherd pavement yielded a largely indigenous assemblage in which some isolated Middle Uruk seal impressions and ceramics were found. This level is superimposed on a long sequence of Late Chalcolithic deposits, which lack any evidence of contacts with the Uruk world. Accordingly, Level

13 reflects the onset of contacts between the indigenous inhabitants of Brak and southern Uruk societies.

Levels 11–12, however, reflect a different pattern altogether. They mark a cultural discontinuity in the excavated area and are characterized by an assemblage, which is entirely southern Mesopotamian in style and appears wholly intrusive. This includes portions of a large Habuba-süd-like tripartite-style house with an accompanying array of typically Uruk material and ideological culture, including ceramics, glyptic, and complex tokens (J. Oates 2002). This same assemblage is also found in Areas TX and UA, some 30 meters north and 300 meters south of TW, respectively, where it is again associated with Uruk-style architecture built with riemchen bricks (Wright 2002).

The new evidence from Brak appearing in the last decade means that it is no longer possible to argue whether or not an actual Uruk presence existed at the site (e.g., Frangipane 2002:126). It did. What remains to be ascertained is the extent and nature of that presence. These are exactly the questions that Geoff Emberling (2002), a recent director of excavations at Brak, tackles in an up-to-date reassessment of the Uruk presence at the site. He notes that *in situ* Late Chalcolithic levels are widespread across the main mound at Brak and that such materials are also found at a corona of small sites surrounding the mound (below). In contrast, *in situ* layers characterized *only* by typically southern Late Uruk materials have a more restricted distribution at the site and are only found within the main mound (i.e., in Mallowan's Eye Temple area and in Areas TW, TU, and TX, some 400 meters away). From this Emberling concludes that the Late Chalcolithic settlement at Brak contracted in the Late Uruk period, a phenomenon he tentatively attributes to the colonization of the earlier and larger center by Uruk settlers.

Two reasons led Emberling to this attribution. The first is the fact, previously noted, that materials in Area TW (Levels 11–12) are entirely of southern Late Uruk type and were introduced at the end of a long indigenous sequence. The second is Emberling's realization that a comparable discontinuity can in fact also be observed in the Eye Temple architectural sequence excavated at the site more than 50 years ago. The three partially preserved and partially exposed earlier temple structures, Emberling argues, are clearly characterized by an assemblage that is entirely northern in type, whereas the fourth and last structure was built and decorated according to southern standards of the Late Uruk period, as Mallowan (1947) had already noted. Absent new work in the Eye Temple area, Emberling is unable to decide whether this fourth temple is the creation of powerful local rulers at Brak consciously emulating the temple building practices, decorations, and beliefs of contemporary Uruk polities of the south or whether this last structure was instead built by the intruders themselves—in which case, in Emberling's opinion (2002:88), it would represent "evidence of an extraordinary ideological coercion of the local inhabitants by representatives of the Uruk Expansion."

In the former case, the Uruk presence documented in Areas TW and TX at Brak would be best explained as evidence for a Hacınebi/Godin type mode of interaction. In the latter case, however, Tell Brak would provide evidence for the taking over of a preexisting indigenous center by Uruk intruders from the south. Of the two possibilities, the latter is the more likely one, both in Emberling's (2002:88) opinion and in mine, because the excavations in Areas TW, TU, and TX leave no doubt that, at least over a sizable portion of the site, Uruk elements thoroughly replaced the local material culture and architectural traditions that had had a long history of prior development at Brak.

Replacement rather than just coexistence is also the most logical explanation for the new data that is now emerging from Tell Hamoukar, another important indigenous Late Chalcolithic site in northeastern Syria, where earlier I had suggested that an Uruk enclave would eventually be identified (Algaze 1989:579, note 4). Hamoukar is located astride one of the historical east-west routes across Syro-Mesopotamia that allows passage between the Upper Tigris area in the vicinity of Nineveh and the Upper Khabur area in the vicinity of Nisibin (above, chapter 3, fig. 21).

Here, in a narrow (3 meter wide) Step Trench (Area A), McGuire Gibson and his team have exposed small portions of an Uruk occupation characterized by 3 levels of well-preserved, but incompletely uncovered, structures built using riemchen-style bricks (Gibson et al. 2002). Associated ceramics are reported to be uniformly of Late Uruk type. Elsewhere at the site, numerous pits brimming with Late Uruk–style ceramics and glyptic are also reported. Excavated from now eroded levels, these pits cut into earlier remains characterized either by an entirely local Amuq F–type assemblage of Late Chalcolithic date or, at least in one case (Area B), by an indigenous assemblage in which some influence from Uruk glyptic traditions and practices can be observed (Reichel 2002), a situation paralleling the one attested in Level 13 in Area TW at Tell Brak (below).

The nature of the indigenous Late Chalcolithic levels at Hamoukar will be discussed in greater detail below. For the purposes of our present discussion, what is noteworthy about the Late Uruk phase at the site is that in every case where it has been encountered, it is stratigraphically superimposed on the earlier Amuq F–related occupation. Gibson and his coworkers interpret this superposition as evidence that Uruk colonists replaced the indigenous inhabitants at Hamoukar by the Late Uruk period (Gibson et al. 2002) and suggest that at this point Hamoukar was about 15 hectares in extent (Ur 2002:64). Detailed surveys around Hamoukar show that the intrusive Late Uruk occupation at the site was surrounded by a corona of contemporary and similarly intrusive but smaller Uruk sites (Ur 2002:64–67), a situation immediately comparable to that of the larger intrusive Uruk enclaves on the Euphrates (above, chapter 3; and below). If Gibson's interpretation of the Late Uruk data from Hamoukar holds, as I believe it will, the Hamoukar cluster then represents the clearest case of an important Uruk enclave not associated with an important river-fording area, but rather one situated inland along important east-west transportation routes.

Stages in the Colonization of the Birecik to Meskene Portion of the Upper Euphrates

Earlier, I had interpreted intrusive Uruk settlements along the Upper Euphrates as consisting of a small number of widely separated urban-sized enclaves, each with an immediately associated cluster of supporting agricultural villages, implanted on and near the few natural river-fording places where historical east-west overland routes across the Syro-Mesopotamian plains intersected the river. Specifically, I had argued that three widely separated Uruk clusters existed along the Upper Euphrates: one centered at Samsat, another just north of Carchemish, and a third cluster in the Tabqa Dam area (above, chapter 3). This view now demands considerable modification.

The first thing in need of rethinking is whether an actual Uruk enclave existed at Samsat, as noted earlier. A second problem is that new archaeological work done during the last decade demonstrates that the modalities of Uruk settlement along the Upper Euphrates south of the Samsat ford evolved over time and were more complicated than initially thought. Excavations at the already noted site of Hacınebi Tepe, for instance, have now documented a pattern of interaction that is significantly different from my earlier characterization for the nature of Uruk settlement in the Birecik to Meskene portion of the Euphrates, which I thought typical only for distant highland peripheries.

Also needing modification is the view that two distinct Uruk settlement clusters existed in the Upper Euphrates south of Birecik, one in the Carchemish area and another in the Meskene area. When this view was first elaborated, much of the intervening zone between these two areas along the river had not been explored. Now, new surveys and excavations in the Tishreen Dam of Syria (del Olmo Lete and Montero Fenollós 1999) have doc-

umented a number of small sites with Uruk occupations between the two larger clusters previously identified. When these sites are factored in, Uruk settlement in the Carchemish to Meskene portion of the Euphrates no longer looks like two isolated settlement clusters but rather like a coherent settlement corridor along the river, with population clustering in large sites near the fording areas. In fact, the number of excavated or surveyed sites yielding varying collections of typical Uruk material culture between Birecik and Meskene (a linear distance of some 110 km) is now up to 29.[2]

No doubt, some of the sites in question will turn out to not represent intrusive sites at all but rather indigenous occupations in contact with Uruk settlements nearby. Nonetheless, the number of both certain and possible Uruk sites now attested between Birecik and Meskene is such that an actual colonization (in the classical sense) of this portion of the Upper Euphrates by southern settlers has to be considered a distinct possibility, as Johnson (1988–89) originally argued and as an increasing number of scholars now have come to believe (e.g., Wright 2001 and Schwartz 2001:256–61).

Initially, I had rejected Johnson's colonization hypothesis arguing that the Meskene area, where the greatest concentration of Uruk populations was located (Habuba-süd / Jebel Aruda), was simply too marginal for reliable agriculture (above, p. 62). However, as Schwartz (2001:258) has noted, my earlier position is no longer tenable because new survey work in this area by Wilkinson (1994) clearly shows that the Meskene area *did* support substantial urban populations in the mid to late third millennium, when climatic conditions affecting the area, if anything, were somewhat drier than those prevalent in the second half of the fourth millennium.

However, the view of the Carchemish to Meskene portion of the Euphrates as a colonized southern corridor resulting from substantial movements of Uruk populations into the area is only conceivable for the final (Late Uruk) phase of the Uruk expansion, as shown by the considerable ex-

tent of some of the intrusive Uruk sites on the Upper Euphrates dated to that phase, most notably
the Habuba-süd / Jebel Aruda and Kum Ocaği /
Şadı Tepe site pairings, discussed earlier (above,
pp. 25–33).

Even then, however, it appears that the colonization process took place gradually over a number of generations. This has become clear as a result of recent reassessments of pertinent data from
Habuba-süd and Jebel Aruda by Regis Vallet
(1997, 1998) and Govert van Driel (2002). Though
both settlements are entirely of Late Uruk date,
each can now be shown to have grown in distinct
stages. This is clearest at Habuba Kabira-süd,
where Vallet distinguishes three stages of development. The fortified town discussed earlier (chapter
3)—with carefully laid-out streets and well-differentiated residential, industrial, and administrative
quarters—represents, in fact, a second stage in the
growth of the city, and maximal size with extra-
mural occupations was achieved even later still.
Vallet surmises that in its initial phase, the Uruk
settlement at Habuba extended over an area of
only 6 hectares or so and was unfortified. The ability to differentiate phases of growth in the Habuba
settlement throughout the Late Uruk phase is important because almost certainly the process in operation at the site mirrors the expansion of Late
Uruk settlers across the Upper Euphrates corridor
as a whole.

Nonetheless, my initial characterization of
Uruk settlement along the Upper Euphrates as
isolated emplacements situated on or near fording
locations and established primarily to serve as
trading outposts remains a good characterization
for the initial phase of Uruk intrusion into the Upper Euphrates area, dated to the Middle Uruk period. All the evidence we do have for that initial
phase points to the Middle Uruk as a time when
only a small number of widely separated intrusive
outposts/enclaves existed along the Birecik to
Meskene portion of the river. Minimally, these included (1) Hacınebi Tepe near Birecik, (2) Tiladir
Tepe opposite Carchemish, (3) Tell Abr in the

Tishreen Dam area south of the Turkish Border,
and (4) Tell Sheikh Hassan near Meskene.

The nature of the small, embedded Middle
Uruk–period colony at Hacınebi becomes under-
standable in the context of this earlier phase of the
Uruk expansion into the Upper Euphrates. Located at what then was the northernmost extent of
the Uruk intrusion along the river, that colony
made sense as a way of mediating relationships between groups that were mutually communicative
but still not contiguous. Accordingly, the colony
was abandoned once Uruk populations swelled in
the Upper Euphrates area during the second (Late
Uruk) phase of the Uruk expansion, creating a
populated corridor out of what had started as isolated outposts at strategic locations near the river.
At that stage, there was no further need for specialized mediation between groups that were now
able to engage in face-to-face contact.

At this point, the best and most concise
summary of Uruk expansionary processes on the
Upper Euphrates is that of Glenn Schwartz
(2001:261), who argues that "small earlier colonial
emplacements like Hacınebi and Sheik Hassan . . .
were established for trading purposes, whereas
later large scale colonies like Habuba served
broader needs." More specifically, he draws a parallel between the expansionary dynamics of Uruk
societies along the Upper Euphrates and those of
the much later Greek societies in the first millennium B.C. In both cases, Schwartz notes that "voyages to acquire exotic raw materials for emerging
elites preceded and facilitated the subsequent
large-scale colonial ventures."

VARIATION IN URUK SETTLEMENT ACROSS SYRO-MESOPOTAMIA

What accounts for the differences between the
strategies of Uruk settlement along the Euphrates
as opposed to those attested in other areas? The
evidence indicates that contact strategies of expanding Uruk societies varied depending on the
level of complexity of the indigenous societies encountered. In areas of Syro-Mesopotamia where

preexisting settlement was less dense, or where nomadic elements were more numerous, such as in the lower half of the Great Euphrates Bend, the Uruk intrusion started earlier, lasted longer, and eventually metamorphosed into a colonial situation resembling the mode of contact most typical for the "formal" empires discussed earlier (chapter 1). On the other hand, in areas where substantial indigenous settlement already existed, such as the Upper Khabur and Upper Tigris basins, Uruk penetration appears to have been shorter lived and resembled instead the types of contact earlier discussed as most characteristic for "informal" or "trading post" empires (chapter 1). This took the form of isolated enclaves established at centers that already served as nodes for preexisting trade networks. Almost certainly this involved some amount of coercion, but we cannot discount the possibility that more peaceful Karum-like modes of contact may have also existed in the initial stages of Uruk penetration of the Upper Khabur and Upper Tigris drainages, or in the more remote portions of those drainages.

Be that as it may, there is no evidence that the establishment of Uruk colonies across the Mesopotamian periphery, whatever their type, was part of a centrally controlled and organized process. Rather, as discussed earlier (pp. 115–17), the Uruk colonial process is best conceived as part of an organic process of action and counteraction, wherein individual Uruk city-states scrambled to found specific enclaves or outposts in order to secure access to the critical lines of communication through which resources were obtainable and, equally important, to deny their local southern rivals such access.

Whatever their origin, from the perspective of the Syro-Mesopotamian plains as a whole there is no doubt that the intrusive Uruk settlements, whether isolated or part of the colonized Euphrates corridor, were embedded at the edges of much vaster alien hinterlands. This conclusion follows from the available surveys of the region (e.g., Algaze et al. 1991, 1994; Danti 1997; Eidem and

Warburton 1996; Hole 1997; Kouchoukos 1998; Lyonnet 1997; Meijer 1986; Mellaart 1981; Özdoğan 1977; Schwartz et al. 2000; Stein and Wattenmaker 1990; Ur 2002; Wilkinson 1990a, 1994, 1998, 2000a–b, 2003; Wilkinson and Tucker 1995; Yardımcı 1993), which clearly show that preexisting indigenous societies continued to exist away from the few locations or areas where intrusive settlements are found.

The locational circumstances of the larger intrusive Uruk settlements, and the nature of the communities in the surrounding hinterlands, meant that Uruk sites were at the head of dendritically arranged settlement networks within the intruded areas. This reflects the primary rationale for the intrusion itself, as this settlement configuration is ideally suited only for tapping into preexisting trade networks and not for the exercise of political control over vast hinterlands. Additionally, Rita Wright (1989) and Nicholas Kouchoukos (1998) have correctly noted that the location of many of the intruding Uruk settlements at the watered edges of wide steppe lands in Syro-Mesopotamia is also ideal to ensure access to the considerable pastoral resources of the area. This observation is potentially significant since those resources would have been of considerable strategic value to the growing textile industries of the then burgeoning Uruk cities (McCorriston 1997; above, pp. 4–5, 118). Their argument further buttresses the importance of trade and the acquisition of resources as factors in the Uruk Expansion, and has the advantage of explaining the otherwise puzzling presence of Uruk artifacts in the context of what must have been ephemeral pastoral encampments in the Syrian Jezira (e.g., in the Wadi Agig area of the Middle Khabur Basin; cf. Pfälzner 1984).

In light of the above, there can be little question that one of the most important functions of Uruk settlements across Syro-Mesopotamia was to engage in exchange with the variously configured peripheral societies in the area, which already controlled the resources Uruk societies coveted. Depending on variables of geography, climate, and history, those preexisting societies ranged from pastoral nomads to fully settled polities, themselves already well on their way to complexity. It is to these latter that we now turn.

LATE CHALCOLITHIC SOCIAL COMPLEXITY

A consistent theme of many scholars reviewing the evidence for the nature of Late Chalcolithic societies that existed in the Mesopotamian periphery prior to the Uruk Expansion has been that my earlier assessment (above, chapter 4) substantially underestimated the scale and degree of social complexity of those societies (e.g., Emberling et al. 1999; Frangipane 1997a–b, 2001, 2002; Oates 2001; Stein 1999a–b, 2001; Schwartz 2001; Wilkinson 2001). Much of this criticism is well taken. New work at indigenous sites across the Syro-Mesopotamian plains now leaves little doubt that societies of substantial complexity existed across large portions of the Mesopotamian periphery prior to the Uruk Expansion and, to a lesser extent, during it.

The clearest case in point is the already discussed site of Tell Brak. Late Chalcolithic remains have been excavated over a variety of areas in the last decade, but the most reliable sequence of *in situ* remains of the period is that uncovered in Area TW. This sequence was sealed by levels dated to the Uruk intrusion (TW, 11–12), noted earlier, and consisted of a substantial depth of habitation and public structures (Levels 13–20), some of which were of considerable scale. Associated with these structures was evidence for far-flung contacts in the form of imports, including gold and ivory artifacts, and evidence for substantial economic activity within the site in the form of simple tokens, stamp seals, and sealings. Particularly noteworthy are portions of a niched tripartite building with a large oven in an enclosed court found in Level 18. Clearly public in nature, this structure is not yet fully uncovered, but the portions thus far exposed measure over 10 × 15 meters. Also noteworthy is a massive two-meter-wide wall and associated threshold cleared in Levels 19–20, which Joan and David Oates (1997) suggest

may form part of a fortification wall protecting the site (Oates 2002; Emberling et al. 1999:2–8; Emberling and MacDonald 2001:21–31).

More significant still for the interpretation of the nature of the Late Chalcolithic occupation at Brak is new data for the extent of the site prior to the period of Uruk contact. This has become clear only recently as a result of new detailed surveys of the mound and immediately surrounding areas. These surveys show that Brak achieved its maximum size during the fourth millennium in the so-called "Northern Middle Uruk period," equivalent to TW, Levels 13–20, and datable to the second quarter of the fourth millennium (Matthews 2000:67; Wright and Rupley 2001). At this time, the full extent of the Brak high mound was occupied and contemporary occupations also existed in a small number of immediately surrounding low mounds that appear to have represented both suburbs and specialized production areas.

Joan Oates (2002:118–19) argues that the extent of Brak at this point was somewhere between 110 and 160 hectares, depending on how the size of the smaller surrounding settlements is calculated. This figure is problematic because it presumes that the totality of the intervening area between the main mound and the ring of satellites surrounding it was occupied. However, recent work in this area found no evidence for such an occupation (Emberling et al. 1999:16–17, 25) and shows instead that a large portion of the intervening area consisted of large clay pits excavated in support of building activities at the main site (Wilkinson 2000b:127). Be that as it may, Oates's point is still correct: in the period immediately predating the Uruk expansion into the Upper Khabur area, Brak was indeed a very substantial Late Chalcolithic settlement. Even if the area intervening between the main mound and the outer ring of contemporary smaller settlements is left out of the calculations, the site would still have had the very substantial extent of more than 65 hectares at the time.

Other contemporary sites of considerable extent also existed elsewhere in the Syro-Mesopotamian plains, albeit in widely separated areas. Work conducted by David Stronach (1994:89–90) and his team at Nineveh just before the first Gulf War suggests that Late Chalcolithic Kuyunjik may have been in the 40 hectare range. Similarly, detailed surface surveys now show that Tell el-Hawa in the plains north of the Jebel Sinjar in northern Iraq was somewhere in the 30–50 hectare range during parts of the Late Chalcolithic period (Wilkinson and Tucker 1995:44).

Other relatively well understood Late Chalcolithic settlements in the area include Hamoukar and Hacınebi, both already noted as the locus of later Uruk occupations. Recent excavations give us insights into the nature of the indigenous components of each site prior to the time of Uruk contact. Detailed surveys show that Late Chalcolithic Hamoukar was about 15 hectares in extent (Ur 2002). Exposures to date reveal that the site was fortified at the time. Portions of a large public building with numerous associated ovens, which may have served some sort of institutional use, have been cleared. As was the case in the lower levels of TW at Brak, associated artifacts are entirely of the indigenous Amuq F–related tradition. Near this structure, but stratified above it, was found a burnt house, tripartite in plan. Because of the burning, numerous seals and sealings were found *in situ* within storerooms at the house, including basket, jar, and door sealings. These artifacts document the existence of a complex regional redistributive economy centered at Hamoukar (Gibson et al. 2002), comparable to the one more extensively documented by excavations at Arslan Tepe (below).

The remains within the Hamoukar burnt house have been the subject of an exemplary preliminary study by Clemens Reichel (2002). He documents a situation immediately comparable to that of Brak, TW 13 (above), in that a small number of Uruk-style cylinder-seal impressions are found within a wider ceramic and glyptic assemblage of indigenous (Amuq F) type. Because of its clear architectural association, the Burnt House assemblage at Hamoukar provides us with a glimpse of the onset of contacts (of as yet undeter-

mined nature) between what was then a complex indigenous Late Chalcolithic polity and representatives of the Uruk world.

Preliminary results are already tantalizing. Reichel's study shows that at least some door seals found within storerooms in the Burnt House were sealed with both stamp and cylinder seals, the former local in style and the latter bearing clear Uruk iconography. This sealing practice clearly indicates the existence of two levels of responsibility over the stored materials. It is yet unclear whether this reflects the interaction of two separate populations at the site, as was the case of Hacınebi, or the workings of two separate local institutions, one of which consciously imitated the sealing practices and iconography of Uruk Mesopotamia, as appears to have been the case at Arslan Tepe. In either case, however, the evidence is clear in that contacts between Hamoukar and the Uruk world took place just before Hamoukar was taken over by intrusive Uruk populations (above)—a situation that exactly mirrors what happened at Brak.

Substantial sociopolitical complexity prior to the onset of contacts with the Uruk world is also attested at Hacınebi Tepe, where the earliest attested Uruk outpost was established in the Syro-Mesopotamian plains. More specifically, the precontact phases (A–B1) at the site have yielded evidence for a long sequence of *in situ* development that predates the onset of Uruk contacts along the Euphrates by as much as 400 years. Exposures show that in its precontact phase, Hacınebi was already surrounded by a massive fortification wall. Excavated architecture of this period is noteworthy for its scale and sophistication, and includes a series of storage structures, portions of a large building with a niched façade, and two monumental stone platforms of uncertain function (Stein 1999a–b).

Associated with these remains were the usual assemblage of Amuq F–type ceramics and an indigenous accounting tradition based on stamp seals similar to that of Hamoukar (above) and Arslan Tepe (below). Also found in these early levels is clear evidence for the import and *in situ* processing and smelting of copper ores in specialized workshop areas, as well as for the export of the refined metals in the form of ingots (Özbal, Adriaens, and Earl 1999). These metallurgical activities appear central to the economy of the local inhabitants of Hacınebi, since they are attested both in the precontact phases of the site and, later, in the indigenous areas of the settlement at the time of contact. Stein and his coworkers hypothesize, correctly no doubt, that these metallurgical activities almost certainly had a role in attracting Uruk traders to the site in the first place (Özbal, Adriaens, and Earl 1999; Stein et al. 1996a–b, 1997, 1998; Stein 1999a–b, 2001).

A final case in point is Arslan Tepe, a very important Late Chalcolithic site in the Malatya area of the Taurus Mountains. As will be remembered (above, pp. 101–4, figs. 44–45), impressive remains were found here dating to Period VIA, which Marcela Frangipane and her coworkers interpret as an indigenous "palace" complex serving both administrative and religious functions and dating to the final phase of the Late Chalcolithic period in the periphery (ca. 3350–3000 B.C.). Associated with these remains were a number of arsenical copper swords, which were almost certainly imported into the site from the Caucasus (Hauptmann et al. 2002), as well as thousands of discarded sealings that were once attached to commodities brought into the palace or disbursed from palace storerooms. These sealings leave little doubt that Arslan Tepe VIA functioned as the primate regional redistributive center of its time in the Malatya area (Frangipane 1994).

Earlier, I had suggested that the emergence of Arslan Tepe VIA as such a center could be understood as a local response to the onset of commercial contacts with the more advanced urban and state polities of Late Uruk–period Mesopotamia. Work at the site during the last decade, however, has now revealed substantial remains of the phases underlying the VIA palace. These remains suggest that my earlier interpretation as to the roots of social complexity at Arslan Tepe was wrong. Rather,

it would appear that the specialized elite institutions in control of the regional economy of the Malatya area in Period VIA represent the culmination of local developments that were underway before the onset of contacts between the Malatya area and the Uruk world, as Frangipane now argues (1997a–b, 2001, 2002).

A number of lines of evidence suggest that Frangipane is correct. One is the scale of the newly uncovered Late Chalcolithic (Period VII) architecture at the site, which now includes a massive tripartite ceremonial structure built on a promontory near the preserved top of the mound (Building XXIX). Though not yet completely uncovered, this structure has a massive central hall ca. 18×7 meters in extent (Frangipane 2002:127, figs. 4–6). Another is provided by the contents of Building XXIX, which included numerous string-cut mass-produced bowls in the main hall of the building and many discarded (stamp) sealings in an adjoining room. A further concentration of mass-produced bowls and nearby discarded sealings was also found within one of three Period VII storerooms cleared just a few meters to the northeast of Building XXIX (Frangipane 2001b:328–29). Similar associations of sealings, sealing clay, and bowls were a common feature of the Period VIA remains at the site, where they were correctly interpreted as evidence for the disbursement of rations out of palace storerooms (Frangipane 1994). It stands to reason that the comparable recurring association in the underlying Period VII levels should be similarly seen as evidence for the existence of centralized economic redistributive activities at the site in that earlier level.

URUK SOCIAL COMPLEXITY

The evidence outlined in the preceding sections suggests that Uruk intruders naturally gravitated toward important preexisting indigenous regional centers. No doubt, this was facilitated by earlier histories of contact/knowledge between individual Uruk societies and specific peripheral regions. Further, it appears clear that the intruders approached preexisting centers as either traders or colonists, or as both in succession, depending on the nature of the centers themselves and distance away from the Uruk world at the time of contact. Thus, preexisting centers clearly helped shape the strategies of contact and direction of the Uruk intrusion(s). It does not follow from this, however, that indigenous Late Chalcolithic societies in the Mesopotamian periphery were comparable in scale to the Uruk polities that emerged in southern Mesopotamia by the second half of the fourth millennium or that they possessed an equivalent level of organizational complexity (Algaze 2001a–b). This becomes clear when we compare available survey data for patterns of settlement in the southern Mesopotamian alluvium against pertinent data for regions at its periphery, and particularly for Syro-Mesopotamia, throughout the fourth millennium B.C.

For the south, available survey data (Adams 1981; Adams and Nissen 1972; and Wright 1981b; for a reworking of the data, see Kouchoukos 1998:230–49; and Pollock 2001) reveal that both absolute population levels and relative agglomeration rates were significantly higher throughout the various phases of the Uruk period than anything that existed in any one coherent area of the Mesopotamian periphery (Kouchoukos 1998: tables 5.4–5.6, fig. 5.9).[3] In fact, Adams's surveys documented multiple interacting urban sites (more than 40 ha in extent) within the surveyed portions of the alluvium throughout *every* phase of the Uruk period, all situated alongside canals and within relatively short distances of each other, and each positioned at the apex of a variegated settlement structure. Development in the area reaches its peak by the final phase of the Uruk period, when the site of Warka grew to the extraordinary size of 250 hectares (Finkbeiner 1991) and was surrounded by numerous dependent villages and towns, totaling a minimum of 280 hectares of further occupation (Adams 1981; Adams and Nissen 1972).

The sites just discussed are likely to be only the tip, so to speak, of the Uruk-period settlement iceberg in southern Mesopotamia because a number of sites exist outside of the surveyed areas that were occupied during one or more phases of the Uruk period. These sites are not considered in recent reviews of the nature of Uruk-period settlement in southern Mesopotamia (e.g., Algaze 2001a; Pollock 2001; Wilkinson 2000a), but several are likely to have been quite substantial at the time. Foremost among these are Umma and the nearby site of Umm al-Aqarib.[4] Numerous Archaic Tablets recently plundered from either (or both) of those sites appear immediately comparable to the earliest (Uruk IV script) examples from Warka (R. Englund, pers. comm., 2001). At the least, these tablets attest to the economic importance of the Umma area in the Late Uruk period. However, since these tablets are part of a wider urban assemblage of great extent and complexity, their presence in the Umma area argues for the existence of a similar context.

Though circumstantial, this evidence suggests that Umma and its satellites may have been second only to Warka itself in terms of urban and social development in the Late Uruk period. Buttressing this possibility is a glaring anomaly in the settlement data for Late Uruk southern Mesopotamia: the largest site (Warka) is four times as large (i.e, populous) as second-tier settlements (e.g., Site WS 1306). This is anomalous because analyses of modern urban systems show that urban populations arrange themselves in rank order by size in predictable ways ("Zipf's Law"), with each tier of settlement being anchored by a site roughly double the size of the largest settlement of the preceding tier (Krugman 1996). If comparable rank-size behavior characterized the ancient Mesopotamian urban world, as I would expect to be the case, then 60-hectare range sites such as WS 1306 should not represent a second Uruk-period settlement tier, but rather a third. The missing (second) tier should be anchored by a site roughly half the extent (population) of Warka. I expect that the missing tier will eventually be identified in the Umma/Aqarib environs, and that this will take the form of a Late Uruk site in the 120-hectare size range at this location.

DEVELOPMENTAL TRAJECTORIES: CORE VS. PERIPHERY

The long sequence of urban growth in southern Mesopotamia throughout the various phases of the Uruk period contrasts starkly with the overall developmental trajectory of contemporary polities across the northern Mesopotamian periphery. To be sure, as Henry Wright (2001:145) presciently noted, both sequences similarly start the fourth millennium with an initial burst of settlement growth and expansion of social complexity. Across the Syro-Mesopotamian plains, this is reflected in the growth of a small number of relatively large indigenous centers, such as (possibly) Samsat on the Euphrates, Brak on the Khabur, Nineveh on the Tigris, and Hawa and Hamoukar in the intervening plains, to name only excavated sites.

Although, individually, the largest of these sites (e.g., Brak and Hawa) are comparable in absolute scale with the average extent of contemporary (Middle Uruk) urban sites in the south, there are some key differences. One difference has to do with the density and level of differentiation of the settlement systems of both areas through the fourth millennium. Even at their peak, the Late Chalcolithic societies of the north hardly equaled their southern counterparts in organizational complexity. This is reflected in the available survey data. Existing coverage of the Brak and Nineveh areas is not reliable,[5] but systematic surveys for the Hawa and Samsat environs by Wilkinson show that during the first half of the fourth millennium both sites were surrounded by a corona of uniformly small village- or hamlet-sized sites (Wilkinson 1990; Algaze 1999; Wilkinson and Tucker 1995: fig. 35, top). This compares unfavorably with the more complex settlement grids of variously sized and hierarchically organized dependent settlements that surrounded contemporary urban centers in the south (Adams 1981; Pollock 2001). Further, surveys of the Hawa and Samsat environs

show that a more complex three-tiered settlement-pattern structure appears in their vicinity only *after* the onset of contacts with the Uruk world, not before (Algaze 1999; Wilkinson and Tucker 1995: fig. 35, bottom).

More important still is a further difference between southern Mesopotamia and areas at its periphery. Large Late Chalcolithic settlements in the Syro-Mesopotamian plains were situated in different drainages and were separated from each other by hundreds of kilometers. Thus, they were isolated from one another in terms of day-to-day contacts. This was not the case in the south where multiple competing settlements connected by waterways existed within short distances of each other. This, in addition to easy communication (via water), had important developmental consequences. As Colin Renfrew and his colleagues have repeatedly argued (Renfrew and Cherry 1986), the long-term presence of multiple polities within relatively short distances of each other invariably engenders important processes of competition, exchange, emulation, and technological innovation. The social evolutionary impact of these mutually reinforcing processes has been explained by Robert Wright (2000:165–68), who notes that in situations where antagonistic but mutually communicative polities exist, social and economic innovations that prove maladaptive in any one society are likely to be weeded out more quickly than in less competitive settings. Conversely, innovations that prove advantageous are more likely to spread quickly across the various polities in competition, thus accelerating the overall pace of change of the system as a whole.

In light of this, it should not be surprising to find sharp differences in the overall developmental trajectories of both areas through the fourth millennium. Most salient among these is that in the north, unlike the south, the initial burst of growth and development was not sustained for long. Data from Nineveh, Hawa, and Samsat are unreliable on this point, but, as noted earlier, new detailed surveys of Tell Brak show that it contracted just as the expansion of southern sites such as Warka reached their Late Uruk peak. This contraction meant that by the Late Uruk period, Warka and the multiple other urban centers of the alluvium were much larger than even the most impressive Late Chalcolithic centers in the Mesopotamian periphery. The fact that this differential developed at precisely the time of the maximum expansion of the Uruk colonial network is unlikely to be a mere coincidence.

Survey evidence from various areas across northern Mesopotamia (summarized in Algaze 1999: table 3; Wilkinson 2000a) shows that the area was effectively ruralized by the end of the fourth millennium and the transition to the third. The indigenous centers that had existed in the region through much of the Late Chalcolithic period had essentially disappeared by this time, and indigenous centers of comparable size did not reappear in the area for centuries—until the final phases of the Ninevite V period, sometime in the second quarter of the third millennium (Algaze 1999: table 4; Schwartz 1994; Weiss 1990; Wilkinson 1994; Ur 2002). In contrast, urbanism in the southern alluvial plains continued to flourish and expand not only through the Late Uruk period but throughout the fourth/third-millennium transition (Jemdet Nasr) as well (Adams 1981; Postgate 1986). The urban spiral of the south continued unabated well into the third millennium (Early Dynastic I): older sites such as Ur, Kish Nippur, Abu Salabikh, Warka, and, possibly, Umma grew further, and new cities were founded across the alluvium, including, most notably, Lagash (Al-Hiba) and Shuruppak (Fara) (Adams 1981; Wright 1981b; Gibson 1973). Warka reached 600 hectares in extent at this point (Finkbeiner 1991) but this was no longer exceptional; Al-Hiba situated at the edge of the easternmost marshes in the alluvium was almost as large (Carter 1985).

In sum, no unequivocal regional survey from the north has yet appeared that requires us to interpret the precontact societies in the area as anything other than complex chiefdoms (but, for a contrary argument, see Frangipane 1997a–b, 2001; and Oates 2001), although this view may well change once additional data become available for the indigenous levels of the Late Chalcolithic settlement at Brak (Emberling, pers. comm., 2000). Be that as it may, it is clear that the Uruk enclaves in Syro-Mesopotamia were appendages of state-level societies and must themselves have been organized at a similar level. More to the point, although individual Late Chalcolithic sites in the north could have been larger than even the largest of the Uruk outposts established in their midst (Habuba/Qannas/Aruda), Late Chalcolithic polities as a group were no match for contemporary Uruk societies in the Mesopotamian alluvium. There is nothing in the Mesopotamian periphery that comes even close to matching the extent of the urban agglomeration at Warka in the Late Uruk period or the scale and monumentality of its central administrative district at the time. Equally unparalleled is the density of interacting urban agglomerations that existed in the southern Mesopotamian alluvium throughout the various phases of the Uruk period.

THE URUK IMPACT ON PREEXISTING SOCIETIES

As noted in the introductory chapter, when societies at different levels of social, political, and economic integration come into intense contacts, important institutional changes are often the result. Historic and ethnographic studies of comparable situations (chapter 6) show that elites in the less complex communities involved in the interaction commonly emulate some institutions and ideologies of their more complex partners in order to further their own standing within their own communities and acquire a competitive edge vis-à-vis local rivals. Accordingly, in view of the disparities in scale and complexity noted earlier between Uruk societies and contemporary polities at their periphery, we should expect to find evidence for the impact that the intrusion of Uruk societies had on the social fabric of the Late Chalcolithic communities with which they came into contact.

Until wider exposures of the latest indigenous Late Chalcolithic levels at sites such as Brak and

Hamoukar are achieved, our clearest data for this impact comes from Arslan Tepe, a site that was never taken over by the Uruk intruders, but which was nonetheless clearly affected by its interaction with Uruk societies. To be sure, Arslan Tepe was well on its way to achieving a substantial measure of complexity on its own prior to the Uruk intrusion. However, it is still fair to ask whether the site would have developed the way it did in Period VIA if contacts with the Uruk world had not existed. While this question is ultimately unanswerable given the nature of both archaeological evidence and the dynamics of history, clues as to the potential impact that contacts with Uruk polities had on the development of Arslan Tepe VIA do exist.

One set of clues is provided by the ceramic repertoire found within the Period VIA complex. Elites at the site were consuming a large proportion of locally made vessels in wares and styles that imitated what must have been more prestigious Uruk prototypes (Frangipane 1997b:70). The meaning of this emulation cannot be untangled without knowing what commodities were contained within those vessels. However, it is possible to monitor the ideological consequences that contacts with the Uruk world had on elite behavior at Arslan Tepe VIA by looking at the glyptic tradition in use at the site at the same time. It is clear that the VIA elites adopted some glyptic practices that are unmistakably of southern Mesopotamian origin. These include the use of cylinder seals, which are capable of conveying more information than the stamp seals typical of the local glyptic tradition, and the use of selected Uruk iconographic themes (Ferioli and Fiandra 1983 [1988]; Frangipane 1997b:67–69).

Of the Uruk themes that they chose to emulate, one stands out as particularly important because it was reproduced at Arslan Tepe not only in glyptic media (Frangipane 1997b: fig 16:1) but in much larger wall frescoes (Frangipane 1997b: fig 15) as well. This was a depiction of a presumably royal or chiefly figure on a cattle-driven sledge surrounded by attending personnel. Particularly in its glyptic rendition, this theme finds very close parallels in the iconography of the Uruk world where the figure at issue is commonly depicted in a variety of media (Sürenhagen 1985), and is unquestionably that of a city ruler (Schmandt-Besserat 1993). The prominent use of this Uruk-derived iconography at Arslan Tepe VIA can be interpreted as evidence for the partial adoption at that local site of explicitly Mesopotamian ideas of the social order.

No doubt, as Frangipane (2001, 2002) correctly surmises, this adoption neither gave rise to trends toward social complexity in the Malatya area nor did it change the general direction of those trends. However, it stands to reason that the southern ideologies being emulated by Arslan Tepe rulers in their quest for legitimation and power must have had an important impact on the tempo and intensity of those ongoing processes.

CONCLUSIONS

While some limited areas of the Syro-Mesopotamian plains, such as the Euphrates corridor, were eventually colonized in the classical sense, most of the northern periphery of Mesopotamia was not taken over, and Uruk settlement in those areas was limited to strategically situated but isolated enclaves floating in an alien sea. It is impossible to characterize the nature of the system as a whole without knowing the details of the political relationships that may have existed between individual enclaves or colonized areas and specific Uruk city-states in the south. One possibility is to argue for a Greek colony model—as Schwartz (1988a, 2001) and others (Johnson 1988/89; Wright 2001) have repeatedly done—in which enclaves and colonized areas were politically independent and were only related to the Sumerian motherland by ties of commerce and culture. This is a plausible model that, to my knowledge, is not contradicted by any available data.

However, equally plausible at this point, and, in my view, certainly more consistent with the known history of ancient Mesopotamian states, is to presume that in addition to ties of commerce and culture, particular enclaves or colonized areas were also politically dependent on specific southern polities. In this scenario, the Uruk Expansion presents itself as a mixture of formal and informal modes of imperial domination, with different strategies of contact being applied in different areas depending on prior history of contacts, distance and ease of transport, and, most importantly, the nature of the preexisting societies in the intruded areas. If this scenario is ultimately proved correct by further research, the Uruk Expansion will then have to be seen as Mesopotamia's—and the world's—first imperial venture.

Whether or not the Uruk phenomenon was Mesopotamia's first empire, it certainly was the world's earliest "world system." As will be argued in some detail below, this was so in the sense of constituting a hierarchically organized transregional system of asymmetrical economic interactions between differentially structured societies with varying divisions of labor and productive capabilities, as well as varying access to technologies of social control and economic administration. The inherent asymmetry of the system is inferable from two facts, both already noted in the preceding discussions. First, developmental trends for Uruk and Late Chalcolithic societies through the second half of the fourth millennium are inversely correlated. Uruk cities and their dependencies become increasingly large and differentiated, and their ability to expand into surrounding peripheries increases, at the very same time that previously thriving centers in those very same peripheries start to contract.

Second, and equally telling, are the locational circumstances of intrusive Uruk settlements across the Mesopotamian periphery. The fact that both the earliest and the largest of such sites were invariably located at focal nodes of historically attested land and riverine routes leaves little doubt that those sites served as strategic "gateways" channeling contacts between core and peripheral groups. This strategic placement meant that the gateways must have been able to tap into preexisting exchange networks in the areas they intruded

into and funnel a portion of the resources flowing through those networks to southern markets.

In so doing, the variously configured Uruk gateways created a system of cross-cultural interactions that differentially favored the economic, social, and political development of southern societies. The reasons for this have already been discussed (above, pp. 3–5) and have to do with the fact that trade between the two regions consisted largely of raw or semiprocessed commodities from the periphery being exchanged for fully processed commodities from the core. This pattern of trade was necessarily asymmetrical in its impact, since southern societies needed to process both the imports and the exports into usable products, thereby creating a dynamic and self-amplifying process of economic and social differentiation and urban growth (Jacobs 2000). This could not be matched in contemporary peripheral societies, where neither the imports nor the exports, save for the metals, required substantial processing.

Accordingly, throughout this book, my review of the Uruk Expansion presumes that, when considered in the aggregate, interactions between individual southern Mesopotamian polities and societies at their periphery would favor southern societies over the long term. To be sure, this cannot be proven without access to the sort of detailed economic data that is seldom, if ever, available to archaeologists. Perhaps for this reason it is not surprising that my world-systems-derived approach to the study of the Uruk expansion has been criticized by many scholars (e.g., Frangipane 2001, 2002; Lamberg-Karlovsky 1996; Rothman 1993, 2001; Schwartz 2001; Stein 1999a–b, 2001; Wright 2001).

Critics generally contend that the sorts of exploitative asymmetrical relationships that I presume to be characteristic between all early state societies and communities at their periphery (Algaze 1993b), and typical for the Uruk case in particular, could not have existed in prehistoric times. Whether explicitly or not, these critics start from the premise that such asymmetries can only be the result of substantial differences in material technologies between societies, and that such differences only came to exist in the modern era as a result of capital imperialism and the industrial revolution. Only then, it is argued, did exponentially more efficient modes of transportation come into being, allowing for raw materials and finished commodities to be moved in bulk between regions and for the efficient and sustained projection of coercive power to be conducted (Wallerstein 1995). Accordingly, these scholars question the applicability of the world-systems model to the early Mesopotamian data, noting that there were no essential differences in either the extractive, productive, or transportation technologies available to Uruk and Late Chalcolithic groups throughout the fourth millennium (Kohl 1987b; Lamberg-Karlovsky 1996:92; Stein 1999a–b).

Perhaps the most cogent expositions of these critical views are those of Marcela Frangipane (2001, 2002) and Gil Stein (1999a–b), the excavators of the sites of Arslan Tepe and Hacınebi, respectively. Stein, in particular, tackles the question directly, and structured his research design at Hacınebi as a test of the applicability of world-systems approaches to the study of the Uruk Expansion. As noted earlier, Stein and his coworkers show that an Uruk group subsisted for many generations at the edge of a larger indigenous polity at Hacınebi, and that both groups at the site were equally complex, socially distinct, and economically self-sufficient. From this, Stein concludes that Hacınebi failed to produce evidence for the sorts of economic and power asymmetries presupposed by world-systems models. He argues that asymmetric relationships are just one possibility in a potential spectrum of possible relationships between differentially structured societies and proposes an alternative explanatory model that he believes is more consistent with the Hacınebi evidence, which he terms the "distance-parity model." This model presumes that under premodern conditions distance and increasing transport costs impair the ability of cores to exercise economic and political dominance in far-away peripheries and that, accordingly, relationships in such peripheries will be largely symmetrical, as he finds to have been the case at Hacınebi.

It does not follow from this, however, that world-systems approaches are not pertinent to pre- and protohistoric situations, as Wallerstein has explicitly claimed (1995). Stein's findings at Hacınebi in fact show the need to adopt a *modified* world-systems approach that acknowledges the effects of "the tyranny of distance" in shaping core strategies of contact with peripheral polities, as well as the differences in the nature of trade goods, and the scale of trade flows in prehistoric and modern times (e.g., above, pp. 6–9, 114, and 125–27). Most archaeologists who use a world-systems-derived approach do so without expecting a one-to-one correspondence between their data and the theory as originally formulated. Rather, they employ the approach only as a way to generate hypotheses that can be tested against the often fragmentary and always ambiguous archaeological record at their disposal (e.g., Peregrine and Feinman 1996; Smith and Berdan 2003).

In the final analysis, we must not forget that while the emergence of modern capitalism greatly intensified relationships of asymmetrical exchange leading to unequal development, those relationships well antedate the modern era, as Ekholm and Friedman (1979) suggested more than 20 years ago (see now Frank 1993 and associated comments). Indeed, inversely correlated regional developmental trajectories have been with us ever since the first states arose across the world and quickly expanded into peripheries that, by definition, were occupied by less-developed communities (Algaze 1993b). Analytical frameworks premised on the existence of asymmetries in power and economic productivity between regions, and on the willingness of rulers, institutions, and entrepreneurs to take advantage of those asymmetries, are therefore always broadly applicable to all cases of cross-cultural interaction between states (pristine or otherwise) and their peripheries.

In terms of the Uruk Expansion, this means that the condition of parity in relationships between Uruk and preexisting populations that Stein and Frangipane found to exist at their respective research locales cannot be extrapolated to the whole of the periphery. That parity is a local condition, not a general one. The fact that power decays with distance, as Stein properly emphasizes, does not mean that the system of interaction between the Uruk world and peripheral societies was not inherently asymmetrical *in the aggregate*. Rather, it only means that degrees of asymmetry lessened in direct proportion to distance between the interacting groups, with contacts towards the edges of the system of interaction becoming increasingly symmetrical. In this light, the results from Hacınebi and Arslan Tepe are neither surprising nor unexpected. The former was located at the very northern edge of the Uruk interaction system in the Middle Uruk period, while the latter appears to have been situated just outside that edge by the Late Uruk period.

Stein and Frangipane provide a valuable service in refocusing our attention to the fact that peripheries are not passive participants in broader cross-cultural interaction systems. Their work leaves no doubt whatsoever that attempts to explain the dynamics of interregional interaction systems solely from the perspective of developments in core areas are necessarily flawed. However, as Roger Matthews (2003:122) and Philip Kohl (2001:231) have recently noted, they have moved too far in the opposite direction and have adopted an equally flawed perspective, one that unduly privileges developments in peripheral areas while neglecting those in Uruk southern Mesopotamia. I agree.

However complex Hacınebi and Arslan Tepe may be, both Stein and Frangipane ultimately overestimate the level of social complexity of Late Chalcolithic societies *as a group*. Moreover, they underestimate the impact that the emergence of highly differentiated urban societies in southern Mesopotamia had on peripheral areas. If indeed the intruding and preexisting groups dealt with each other as equals across the periphery, why then are Uruk ideologies and Uruk artifacts the ones being emulated in peripheral groups and not the

reverse? More to the point, why is it that Uruk societies maintained variously structured colonies in peripheral areas for hundreds of years, while the opposite was not the case? Finally, and most tellingly, why do developmental trends for Uruk and Late Chalcolithic societies through the second half of the fourth millennium appear to be inversely correlated, with growth in the south taking place seemingly at the expense of northern groups?

Stein and Frangipane do not address these questions. Perhaps this is because their disproportionate focus on developments in the periphery leads them to pay insufficient attention to the crucial role of trade in the formation of long-term regional developmental asymmetries favoring southern polities, which, once set, became increasingly compounded through the centuries-long expansionary process of Uruk societies. More specifically, they fail to realize that even if transactions between Uruk and Late Chalcolithic populations would have been perceived as symmetrical by the participants, the ultimate impact of these transactions on their respective societies would still have been asymmetrical. As noted earlier, the nature of the commodities being traded, in and of itself, ensured that social-multiplier effects of the trade would accrue differentially, and this difference favored core societies where *both* imports and exports required substantial processing before they could be incorporated into the economy.

Scholars who minimize the existence of significant developmental asymmetries between southern Mesopotamian and peripheral polities in the Middle and Late Uruk periods also miss the mark in other key respects. First, they fail to take into account the environmental advantages in productivity of the southern alluvium over neighboring areas, including a more varied concentration of exploitable subsistence resources and higher and more reliable agricultural yields (from irrigation agriculture). These advantages provided opportunities for elite groups exploiting the alluvium's rich and diverse ecological niches to amass larger and more reliable surpluses than their competitors could acquire in less resilient peripheral environments. This in turn allowed southern elites to maximize the amount of labor at their disposal and, in so doing, set in motion the export-driven economies that differentially strengthened the economic and social growth of southern cities at the expense of their trading partners.

Second, they fail to take note of the fact that southern Mesopotamian societies had a substantial advantage over peripheral polities in that capital and labor were more easily mobilized, redistributed, and deployed in the south than elsewhere because of the inherent superiority of southern water-borne transport systems. Stein is entirely correct in demanding that we consider transport costs as a factor in structuring the ability of southern societies to extract resources from peripheral areas. However, if one considers the issue from a perspective broader than that of the periphery alone, then it is hard not to conclude that overall transport costs for Uruk societies must have been significantly lower than those of their peripheral contemporaries. The cities of the alluvium were, in effect, at the head of an enormous dendritic transportation system created by the north-to-south-flowing rivers. This allowed them to procure information, labor, and commodities from areas within the vast Tigris-Euphrates watershed more efficiently and at lower cost than any potential upstream competitors or rivals away from the rivers (Bairoch 1988:11, 14). Of equal importance, the network of canals surrounding Mesopotamian cities and connecting them with the main courses of the rivers allowed them to move bulky agricultural commodities across their immediate dependent hinterlands with great efficiency (Weiss 1986:94). In contrast, societies in the Mesopotamian periphery had to rely wholly on less efficient modes of overland communication, such as donkeys or carts, both for their long-distance exchange needs and for the movement of subsistence resources across their immediate hinterlands.

Third, and most important, they fail to acknowledge that differences in ideologies of social organization are as capable of creating significant

developmental asymmetries between different societies as imbalances in material technology. More specifically, I am suggesting that by the Middle and Late Uruk periods southern societies possessed a variety of organizational advantages in economic administration and modes of social control that were unparalleled in the periphery, and which conferred on them important competitive advantages over their peripheral rivals. These advantages fall in the realm of what Jack Goody (2000) has recently termed "technologies of the intellect." A case in point is provided by the greater ability of southern Mesopotamian societies to process socially useful information.

Bluntly put: no contemporary peripheral site has yet provided any evidence for the existence of formal reckoning and writing systems comparable in their complexity to those that emerged in southern Mesopotamia during the Middle and Late Uruk periods. While thousands of sealings have been found at indigenous Late Chalcolithic sites such as Arslan Tepe (Periods VII–VIA: Ferioli and Fiandra 1983 [1988]) and Tepe Gawra (Levels XI–VIII: Tobler 1950; Rothman 1994, 2002), those sealings commonly bear the impression(s) of but a single seal. Impressions of more than one seal on a single sealing surface, while known, remain exceptional (Fiandra 1994:168; M. Rothman, pers. comm., 1999). In contrast, contemporary procedures in Uruk cities in the south and in Uruk outposts in the north regularly exhibit the imprints of multiple seals. This is relevant because the number of impressions of different seals superimposed on a single sealing gives us a glimpse of both the number of agents and the hierarchical levels of institutional responsibility involved in the transaction being recorded (Nissen 1977). Multiple impressions of different superimposed seals in Uruk centers and colonies can thus be taken as a proxy for the greater number of levels of bureaucratic control and accountability that existed within those centers, compared to the simpler recording systems in use at contemporary northern sites (Pittman 1993).

Moreover, there is nothing in the periphery

that compares with the more elaborate reckoning systems that southern societies started to create already by the end of the Middle Uruk period, which initially relied on complex combinations of numbers and images (seal-impressed balls and early numerical notation tablets), and which eventually evolved into the pictographic tablets of the final phase of the Uruk period (Uruk IV script). The latter gave southern administrators a way to record inflows and outflows of commodities in a form transmissible through space and time and allowed them to express nuances of time, location, persons involved, and action effected. They also allowed southern scribes to abstract and summarize detailed data about collections and disbursements of goods and labor in a form usable by themselves at a later time, by higher-level supervisory officials at any time, and by later generations of similarly trained bureaucrats. And finally, although rare, the new lexical lists that also appear at this time (Uruk IV script) gave southern Mesopotamian scribes the ability to organize, categorize, and transmit information about their material, social, and ideological world across both space and time (Nissen, Damerow, and Englund 1993; Englund 1998).

There is no evidence whatsoever that contemporary northern societies had comparable capabilities at their disposal. At most, their much simpler glyptic practices allowed them to record information that was solely of economic import, and this was done in a form that could not be communicated beyond the immediate temporal and spatial context of the individual institutions collecting the sealings.

In short, by the end of the Uruk period, cumulative innovations in the ways knowledge was gathered, processed, and transmitted through time and space provided southern Mesopotamian decision makers and the urban institutions they worked for with a flow of varied and reliable economic data of the sort that is necessary for the formation, maintenance, and effective expansion of large-scale sociopolitical hierarchies. This furnished Uruk societies with important competitive advantages over contemporary neighboring polities, in which similar breakthroughs in accounting, accountability, and classification appear to have been absent (Algaze 2001a).

Taking place in the context of the already discussed advantages that southern societies had in surplus formation and ease of transport, the ideational innovations just discussed explain why it was Uruk societies that expanded northwards in the second half of the fourth millennium rather than the reverse. They also help us understand why so many aspects of Uruk culture were seen as worthy of emulation by societies in the areas into which they intruded.

Notes to Chapter 8

1. A few pertinent Late Uruk dates from Tell Hamoukar (Gibson et al. 2002:33, samples 006–009) and Tell Kuran (Hole 2001:76), both in Syria, have appeared since the publication of Wright and Rupley's seminal article, but these dates do not alter their conclusions in any way.

2. Excavations and surveys allow us to identify at least 9 nine sites of various sizes with Uruk materials in the Tabqa Reservoir area. Details and references for these sites are provided above in pages 25–29 and in Boese 1995–96. At least 4 sites with Uruk materials, all apparently small village-sized sites, are known from ongoing excavations in the Tishreen Dam area. The Tishreen data are still largely unpublished but the following references are now available: Tell 'Abr (Hammade and Yamazaki 1993; Yamazaki 1999), Tell Kosak Shamali (Nishiaki 1999), Tell Jerablus Tahtani (Peltenburg 2000; Peltenburg et al. 1995, 1996, 1997; Stephen and Peltenburg 2002), and Tell Siyuh Fauqani (Dr. D. M. Bonacossi, pers. comm. 1998). In addition, the site of Tell Siyuh Tahtani has produced evidence for beveled rim bowls, but the context of those finds is still unclear (Falsone 1999). Of these sites, Tell Abr is noteworthy because it has produced excavated evidence for both Middle and Late Uruk period levels, the latter associated with riemchen bricks. A further Uruk occupation, thus far attested only by pottery, existed at Nizal Hussain, a small hilltop site on the western bank of the Euphrates just north of its confluence with the Sajur River (www.aushariye.hum.ku.dk). Finally, 16 sites of various sizes with surface Uruk materials were recorded in the Carchemish and Birecik Dam areas of the Euphrates in southeastern Turkey (Algaze et al. 1994: 10–12, fig. 15 B). Two of these sites, Yarim Tepe and Zeytin Bahçe Höyük have now been excavated (Rothman et al. 1998; Frangipane and Bucak 2001; Frangipane et al.

2002) and have produced ceramic assemblages that are overwhelmingly southern in type. Regretfully, coherent architectural remains of the Uruk period were not recovered at Yarim Tepe, but portions of a storage building divided into numerous small cells similar to an example from Middle Uruk layers at Tell Sheik Hassan are reported from Zeytin Bahçe Höyük.

3. Note, however, that Wilkinson's detailed surveys of the Upper Jezira plains west of the Tigris in northern Iraq show what appear to be higher overall regional population densities in that area than in the south (Wilkinson 2000a: fig. 5). I believe this to be a spurious pattern resulting from the more intensive and systematic nature of the Jezira surveys and from the fact that erosional forces maximize site recognition in the north while sedimentation and aeolian deposition depress site

counts in the southern alluvial lowlands (Wilkinson 1990c, 2000a:244). In any event, it is certain that the south still had a much greater proportion of its overall population living in agglomerated settlements and that these settlements were situated at much shorter distances from each other than such northern centers as existed across Syro-Mesopotamia.

4. Both Umma (WS 197) and Aqarib (WS 198) were at the edge of Adams's 1968 survey area, but could not be properly surveyed at that time because of extensive sand dunes covering the area (Adams and Nissen 1972:227–28). The dunes have since cleared the area.

5. See Eidem and Warburton (1996) for the immediate environs of Brak. A new more intensive survey of the area around Brak is now underway under the direction of Henry Wright, but results have not yet appeared.

References for Chapter 8

Abay, E.
    1997   *Die Keramik der Frübronzezeit in Anatolien.*
            Münster: Ugarit Verlag.
Algaze, G.
    1993a   *The Uruk World System: The Dynamics of
            Expansion of Early Mesopotamian Civilization.*
            Chicago: University of Chicago Press.
    1993b   "Expansionary Dynamics of Some Early
            Pristine States." *American Anthropologist* 95:304–
            33.
    1999.   "Trends in the Archaeological Development
            of the Upper Euphrates Basin of Southeastern
            Anatolia during the Late Chalcolithic and Early
            Bronze Ages." In G. del Olmo Lete and J.-L. Montero Fenollós, eds., *Archaeology of the Upper Syrian Euphrates: The Tishrin Dam Area,* pp. 535–72.
            Barcelona: Editorial Ausa.
    2001a   "Initial Social Complexity in Southwestern
            Asia: The Mesopotamian Advantage." *Current
            Anthropology* 42:199–233.
    2001b   "The Prehistory of Imperialism: The Case of
            Uruk Period Mesopotamia." In M. Rothmann, ed.,
            *Uruk Mesopotamia and Its Neighbors: Cross-cultural Interactions and Their Consequences in the
            Era of State Formation,* pp. 27–85. Santa Fe:
            School of American Research.
    2002   "The Uruk Period: A Research Agenda for
            the Future." In S. Kerner, A. Hausleiter, and B.
            Müller-Neuhof, eds., *Material Culture and Mental
            Spheres: Rezeption archäologisher Denkrichtungen
            in der Vorderasiatischen Altertumskunde,* pp. 205–
            13. Münster: Ugarit Verlag.
Algaze, G., R. Breuninger, C. Lightfoot, and M. Rosenberg
    1991   "The Tigris-Euphrates Archaeological Re-

connaissance Project, 1989–90." *Anatolica* 17:175–
            240.
Algaze, G., R. Breuninger, and J. Knudstad
    1994   "The Tigris-Euphrates Archaeological Reconnaissance Project: Final Report of the Birecik and
            Carchemish Dam Survey Areas. *Anatolica* 20:1–96.
Bigelow, L.
    1999   "Zooarchaeological Investigations of Economic Organization and Ethnicity at Late Chalcolithic Hacınebi: A Preliminary Report." *Paléorient*
            25:83–90.
Boehmer, R. M.
    1999   *Uruk: Früheste Siegelabrollungen.* Ausgrabungen in Uruk-Warka Endberichte 24. Mainz
            am Rhein: Phillip von Zabern.
Boese, J.
    1995/96 "Tell Sheikh Hassan in Nordsyrien: Eine
            Stadt des 4 Jahrtausends v. Chr. am Euphrat."
            Nürnberger Blätter zur Archäologie 12:157–72.
Butterlin, P.
    2003   *Le Temps proto-urbaines de Mèsopotamie.*
            Paris: CNRS éditions.
Carter, E.
    1985   "Lagash (Tell Al-Hiba)." *Iraq* 47:222.
Collins, P.
    2000   *The Uruk Phenomenon: The Role of Social
            Ideology in the Expansion of Uruk Culture during
            the Fourth Millennium BC.* BAR International Series 900. Oxford: Archeopress.
Danti, M. D.
    1997   "Regional Surveys and Excavations." In R.
            Zettler, ed., *Subsistence and Settlement in a Marginal Environment: Tell es-Sweyhat, 1989–1995
            Preliminary Report,* pp. 85–94. Philadelphia:
            MASCA.

del Olmo Lete, G., and J.-L. Montero Fenollós, eds.
  1999   *Archaeology of the Upper Syrian Euphrates:
         The Tishrin Dam Area.* Barcelona: Editorial Ausa.
de Miroschedji, P.
  2003   "Susa and the Highlands." In N. Miller and K.
         Abdi, eds., *Yeki Bud, Yeki Nabud: Essays on the
         Archaeology of Iran in Honor of William M. Sum-
         ner,* pp. 17–38. Los Angeles: Cotsen Institute of
         Archaeology.
Eidem, J., and D. Warburton.
  1996   "In the Land of Nagar: A Survey Around Tell
         Brak." *Iraq* 58:51–64.
Emberling, G.
  2002   "Political Control in an Early State: The Eye
         Temple and the Uruk Expansion in Northern
         Mesopotamia." In L. Al-Gailani Werr, J. Curtis, H.
         Martin, A. McMahon, J. Oates, and J. Reade, eds.,
         *Of Pots and Plans: Papers on the Archaeology and
         History of Mesopotamia and Syria Presented to
         David Oates in Honor of His 75th Birthday,* pp. 82–
         90. London: Nabu Publications.
Emberling, G., J. Cheng, T. Larsen, H. Pittman, T.
         Skuldboel, J. Weber, and H. T. Wright
  1999   "Excavations at Tell Brak 1998: Preliminary
         Report." *Iraq* 61:1–41.
Emberling, G., and H. MacDonald
  2001   "Excavations at Tell Brak 1998: Preliminary
         Report." *Iraq* 63:21–54.
Englund, R. K.
  1998   "Texts from the Late Uruk Period." In P. At-
         tinger and M. Wafler, eds., *Mesopotamien: Spätu-
         ruk-Zeit und Frühdynastische Zeit.* Gottingen:
         Vandenhoeck and Ruprecht.
Falsone, G.
  1999   "Tell Shiyukh Tahtani on the Euphrates: The
         University of Palermo Salvage Excavations in North
         Syria (1993–1994)." *Akkadica* 109/110:22–64.
Fiandra, E.
  1994   "Discussion." In P. Ferioli, E. Fiandra, G. G.
         Fissore, and M. Frangipane, eds., *Archives before
         Writing,* p. 168. Rome: Centro Internazionale di
         Recerche Archaeologiche Anthropologiche e
         Storiche.
Finkbeiner, U.
  1991   *Uruk Kampagne 35–37, 1982–1984: Die
         archäologische Oberflächenuntersuchung (Survey).*
         Ausgrabungen in Uruk-Warka Endberichte 4.
         Mainz: Philipp von Zabern.
Forest, J.-D.
  1996   *Mésopotamie: L'apparition de l'Etat, VIIe–
         IIIe Millénaires.* Paris: Paris-Mediterranée.
  1999   *Les premieres temples de Mésopotamie.*
         British Archaeological Reports, 765. Oxford:
         Archeopress.
Frangipane, M.
  1994   "The Record of Clay Sealings in Early Ad-

ministrative Systems as Seen from Arslantepe-
         Malatya." In P. Ferioli, E. Fiandra, G. G. Fissori,
         and M. Frangipane, eds., *Archives before Writing,*
         pp. 125–36.
  1996   *La nascita dello Stato nell Vicino Orientale.*
         Rome: Laterza.
  1997a "Arslantepe-Malatya: External Factors and
         Local Components in the Development of an
         Early State Society." In L. Manzanilla, ed., *Emer-
         gence and Change in Early Urban Societies,* pp. 43–
         58. New York: Plenum Press.
  1997b "A Fourth Millennium Temple/Palace
         Complex at Arslantepe-Malatya: North-South Re-
         lations and the Formation of Early State Societies
         in the Northern Regions of Southern
         Mesopotamia." *Paléorient* 23:45–73.
  2001   "Centralization Processes in Greater
         Mesopotamia: Uruk 'Expansion' as the Climax of
         Systemic Interactions among Areas of the Greater
         Mesopotamian Region." In M. Rothmann, ed.,
         *Uruk Mesopotamia and Its Neighbors: Cross-cul-
         tural Interactions and Their Consequences in the
         Era of State Formation,* pp. 307–48. Santa Fe:
         School of American Research.
  2002   "Non-Uruk" Developments and Uruk-linked
         Features on the Northern Borders of Greater
         Mesopotamia." In J. N. Postgate, ed., *Artefacts of
         Complexity: Tracking the Uruk in the Near East,*
         pp. 123–48. Warminster: Aris and Phillips, Ltd.
Frangipane, M. and E. Bucak
  2001   "Excavations and Research at Zeytinbahçe
         Höyük, 1999." In N. Tuna, J. Öztürk, and J. Velibe-
         yoğlu, eds., *Salvage Project of the Archaeological
         Heritage of the Ilısu and Carchemish Dam Reser-
         voirs, 1999 Activities,* pp. 65–132. Ankara: METU.
Frangipane, M., C. Alvaro, F. Balossi, and G. Siracu-
         sano
  2002   "The 2000 Campaign at Zeytinbahçe
         Höyük." In N. Tuna and J. Velibeyoğlu, eds., *Sal-
         vage Project of the Archaeological Heritage of the
         Ilısu and Carchemish Dam Reservoirs, 2000 Activi-
         ties,* pp. 57–99. Ankara: METU.
Frank, A. G.
  1993   "The Bronze Age World System and its
         Cycles." *Current Anthropology* 34:383–429.
Gibson, McG., A. al-Azm, C. Reichel, S. Quntar, J. A.
         Franke, L. Khalidi, C. Fritz, M. Altaweel, C. Coyle,
         C. Colantoni, J. Tenney, G. Abdul Aziz, and T.
         Hartnell
  2002   "Hamoukar: A Summary of Three Seasons of
         Excavations." *Akkadica* 123:11–34.
Goody, J.
  2000   *The Power of the Written Tradition.* Washing-
         ton, DC: Smithsonian Institution Press.
Gut, R.
  1995   *Das prähistorische Ninive: zur relativen

*Chronologie der fruhen Perioden Nordme-
sopotamiens.* Mainz am Rhein: Phillip von Zabern.

2002   "The Significance of the Uruk Sequence at
Nineveh." In J. N. Postgate, ed., *Artefacts of Complexity: Tracking the Uruk in the Near East,* pp. 17–
48. Warminster: Aris and Phillips.

Hammade, H., and Y. Yamazaki
1993   "Some Remarks on the Uruk Levels at Tell
al-'Abr on the Euphrates." *Akkadica* 84/85:53–62.

Hauptmann, A., S. Schmitt-Strecker, F. Begemann, and
A. Palmieri
2002   "Chemical Composition and Lead Isotopy of
Metal Objects from the 'Royal' Tomb and Other
Related Finds at Arslantepe, Eastern Anatolia."
Paléorient 28:43–69.

Helwing, B.
1999   "Cultural Interaction at Hassek Höyük,
Turkey: New Evidence from Pottery Analysis."
Paléorient 25:91–99.

Hole, F.
1994   "Environmental Instabilities and Urban Origins." In G. Stein and M. S. Rothman, eds., *Chiefdoms and Early States in the Near East,* pp. 121–52.
Madison: Prehistory Press.
1997   "Evidence for Mid-Holocene Environmental
Change in the Western Khabur Drainage, Northeastern Syria." In H. Nüzhet Dalfes, G. Kukla, and
H. Weiss, eds., *Third Millennium B.C. Climate
Change and Old World Collapse,* pp. 39–66.
Berlin: Springer Verlag.
2001   "A Radiocarbon Chronology for the Middle
Khabur, Syria." *Iraq* 63:67–98.

Jacobs, J.
2000   *The Nature of Economies.* New York: Modern Library.

Kohl, P.
2001   "Review of Gil Stein's Rethinking World-Systems: Diasporas, Colonies, and Interaction in Uruk
Mesopotamia." *American Anthropologist*
103:230–31.

Kouchoukos, N.
1998   "Landscape and Social Change in Late Prehistoric Mesopotamia." Ph.D. dissertation, Department of Anthropology, Yale University.

Kouchoukos, N. and F. Hole
2003   "Changing Estimates of Susiana's Prehistoric
Settlement." In N. Miller and K. Abdi, eds., *Yeki
Bud, Yeki Nabud: Essays on the Archaeology of
Iran in Honor of William M. Sumner,* pp. 53–60.
Los Angeles: Cotsen Institute of Archaeology.

Krugman, P.
1996   "Confronting the Mystery of Urban Hierarchy." *Journal of the Japanese and International
Economies* 10:399–418.

Lamberg-Karlovsky, C. C.
1996   *Beyond the Tigris and Euphrates: Bronze Age*

Civilizations. Jerusalem: Ben Gurion University of
the Negev Press.

Liverani, M.
1998   *Uruk: la prima città.* Rome: Laterza.

Lupton, Alan
1996   *Stability and Change: Socio-political Development in North Mesopotamia and South-East Anatolia 4000–2700 BC.* BAR International Series
627. Oxford: Archeopress.

Lyonnet, B.
1997   "Questions sur l'origine des porteurs de pots
en Haute-Mésopotamie du VIe au milieu du IIe
Millénaire." *Florilegium marianum* III:133–44.

Matthews, R.
2000   "Fourth and Third Millennium Chronologies:
The View from Tell Brak." In C. Marro and H.
Hauptmann, eds., *Chronologies des pays du Cau-
case et de l'Euphrate aux IVe–IIIe millenaires,*
pp. 65–72. Istanbul: French Archaeological Institute.
2003   *The Archaeology of Mesopotamia, Theories
and Approaches.* London: Routledge.

McCorriston, J.
1997   "The Fiber Revolution: Textile Extensifica-
tion, Alienation, and Social Stratification in Ancient Mesopotamia." *Current Anthropology*
38:517–49.

Moorey, P. R. S.
1993   "Iran: A Sumerian El Dorado?" In J. Curtis,
ed., *Early Mesopotamia and Iran: Contact and
Conflict 3500–1600 B.C.,* pp. 31–76. London:
British Museum Press.

Nishiaki, Y.
1999   "Tell Kosak Shamali: Preliminary Report of
the Excavations." In G. del Olmo Lete and J.-L.
Montero Fenollós, eds., *Archaeology of the Upper
Syrian Euphrates: The Tishreen Dam Area,* pp. 71–
82. Barcelona: Editorial Ausa.

Nissen, H.-J.
2001   "Cultural and Political Networks in the Ancient Near East during the Fourth and Third Millennia B.C." In M. Rothman, ed., *Uruk Mesopotamia and its Neighbors,* pp. 149–80. Santa Fe:
SAR Press.
2002   "Uruk Key Site of the Period and Key Site of
the Problem." In J. N. Postgate, ed., *Artefacts of
Complexity: Tracking the Uruk in the Near East,*
pp. 1–16. Warminster: Aris and Phillips.

Nissen, H-J., P. Damerow, and R. K. Englund
1993   *Archaic Bookkeeping.* Chicago: University of
Chicago Press.

Oates, Joan
1993   "Trade and Power in the Fifth and Fourth
Millennia BC: New Evidence from Northern
Mesopotamia." *World Archaeology* 24 (3): 403–22.
2001   "Comment." *Current Anthropology* 42:223–24.

2002 "Tell Brak: The 4th Millennium Sequence and Its Implications." In J. N. Postgate, ed., *Artefacts of Complexity: Tracking the Uruk in the Near East,* pp. 111–22. Warminster: Aris and Phillips.

Oates, J., and D. Oates
1993 "Excavations at Tell Brak 1992–93." *Iraq* 55:155–99.
1994 "Tell Brak: A Stratigraphic Summary." *Iraq* 56:167–76.
1997 "An Open Gate: Cities of the 4th Millennium B.C. (Tell Brak 1997)." *Cambridge Archaeological Journal* 7:287–307.

Özbal, H., A. Adriaens, and B. Earl
1999 "Hacınebi Metal Production and Exchange." *Paléorient* 25:57–66.

Özgüç, N.
1992 "The Uruk Culture at Samsat." In B. Hrouda, S. Kroll, and P. Spanos, eds., *Von Uruk nach Tuttul: Eine Festschrift für Eva Strommenger,* pp. 151–65. Munich: Profil Verlag.

Pearce, J.
1999 "Investigating Ethnicity at Hacınebi: Ceramic Perspectives on Style and Behavior in 4th Millennium Mesopotamian-Anatolian Interaction." *Paléorient* 25:35–42.

Peltenburg, E.
2000 "Jerablus Tahtani, 1999." http://www.arcl.ed.ac.uk/arch/jerablus/JT99/

Peltenburg, E., S. Campbell, P. Croft, D. Lunt, M. Murray, and M. Watt
1995 "Jerablus-Tahtani, Syria, 1992–4: Preliminary Report." *Levant* 27:1–28.

Peltenburg E., D. Bolger, S. Campbell, M. Murray, and R. Tipping
1996 "Jerablus Tahtani, Syria 1995: Preliminary Report." *Levant* 28:1–25.

Peltenburg, E., S. Campbell, S. Carter, F. M. K. Stephen, and R. Tipping
1997 "Jerablus Tahtani, Syria 1996: Preliminary Report." *Levant* 29:1–18.

Peregrine, Peter N., and Gary M. Feinman, eds.
1996 *Pre-Columbian World System*s. Madison, WI: Prehistory Press.

Pittman, H.
1993 "Pictures of an Administration: The Late Uruk Scribe at Work." In M. Frangipane, H. Hauptmann, M. Liverani, P. Matthiae, and M. Mellink, eds., *Between the Rivers and Over the Mountains: Archaeologica Anatolica et Mesopotamica Alba Palmieri Dedicata,* pp. 235–46. Rome: Universita di Roma "La Sapienza."
1999 "Administrative Evidence from Hacınebi: An Essay on the Local and the Colonial." *Paléorient* 25:43–50.
2001 "Mesopotamian Intraregional Relations Reflected through Glyptic Evidence in the Late Chalcolithic 1–5 Periods." In M. Rothman, ed., *Uruk Mesopotamia and Its Neighbors,* pp. 233–64. Santa Fe: SAR Press.

Pollock, S.
1994 "Review of G. Algaze's *The Uruk World System—The Dynamics of Expansion of Early Mesopotamian Civilization.*" *Science* 264:1481–82.
1999 *Ancient Mesopotamia: The Eden That Never Was.* Cambridge: Cambridge University Press.
2001 "The Uruk Period in Southern Mesopotamia." In M. Rothman, ed. *Uruk Mesopotamia and Its Neighbors,* pp. 191–232. Santa Fe: SAR Press.

Pollock, S., and C. Coursey
1995 "Ceramics from Hacınebi Tepe: Chronology and Connections." *Anatolica* 21:101–41.

Postgate, J. N., ed.
2002 *Artefacts of Complexity: Tracking the Uruk in the Near East.* Warminster: Aris and Phillips.

Potts, D. T.
1999 *The Archaeology of Elam: Formation and Transformation of an Ancient Iranian State.* Cambridge: Cambridge University Press.

Reichel, C.
2002 "Administrative Complexity in Syria During the 4th Millennium B.C.—The Seals and Sealings from Tell Hamoukar." *Akkadica* 123:35–56.

Renfrew, C., and J. F. Cherry, eds.
1986 *Peer Polity Interaction and Socio-political Change.* Cambridge: Cambridge University Press.

Rothman, M.
1993 "Another Look at the 'Uruk Expansion' from the Tigris Piedmont." In M. Frangipane, H. Hauptmann, M. Liverani, P. Matthiae, and M. Mellink, eds., *Between the Rivers and Over the Mountains: Anatolia, Transcaucasia and Syro-Mesopotamian Regions in Prehistory,* pp. 163–77. Rome: Universita di Roma.
1994 "Sealings as a Control Mechanism in Prehistory." In G. Stein and M. Rothman, eds., *Chiefdoms and Early States in the Near East: The Organizational Dynamics of Complexity,* pp. 103–20. Madison, WI: Prehistory Press.
2002 *Tepe Gawra: The Evolution of a Small Prehistoric Center in Northern Iraq.* Philadelphia: University of Pennsylvania Museum.

Rothman, M., R. Ergeç, M. Miller, J. Weber, and G. Kozbe
1998 "Yarim Höyük and the Uruk Expansion." *Anatolica* 24:65–99.

Rothman, M., ed.
2001 *Uruk Mesopotamia and Its Neighbors.* Santa Fe: SAR Press.

Schmandt-Besserat, D.
1993 "Images of Ensiship." In M. Frangipane,

H. Hauptmann, M. Liverani, P. Matthiae, and
M. Mellink, eds., *Between the Rivers and Over the
Mountains: Archaeologica Anatolica et Meso-
potamica Alba Palmieri Dedicata,* pp. 201–20.
Rome: Universita di Roma "La Sapienza."

Schwartz, G.M.
1994   "Before Ebla: Models of Pre-State Political
Organization in Syria and Northern Mesopotamia." In G. Stein and M. Rothman, eds., *Chiefdoms and Early States in the Near East: The Organizational Dynamics of Complexity,* pp. 153–74.
Madison, WI: Prehistory Press.
2001   "Syria and the Uruk Expansion." In M. Rothman, ed., *Uruk Mesopotamia and Its Neighbors,*
pp. 233–64. Santa Fe: SAR Press.

Schwartz, G., H. Curvers, F. Gerritsen, J. MacCormack,
N. Miller, and J. Weber
2000   "Excavation and Regional Analysis in the
Jabbul Plain, Western Syria: The Umm el-Marra
Project, 1996–97." *American Journal of Archaeol-
ogy* 104:419–62.

Smith, Michael E., and Frances F. Berdan, eds.
2003   *The Postclassic Mesoamerican World.* Salt
Lake City: University of Utah Press.

Stein, G.
1998   "World Systems Theory and Alternative
Modes of Interaction in the Archaeology of Culture Contact." In J. Cusick, ed., *Studies in Culture
Contact: Interaction, Culture Change, and Archae-
ology,* pp. 220–55. Carbondale: Southern Illinois
University Press.
1999a   *Rethinking World-Systems: Diasporas,
Colonies, and Interaction in Uruk Mesopotamia.*
Tucson: University of Arizona Press.
1999b   "Material Culture and Social Identity: The
Evidence for a 4th Millennium bc Mesopotamian
Uruk Colony at Hacınebi, Turkey." *Paléorient*
25:11–22.
2001   "Indigenous Social Complexity at Hacınebi
(Turkey) and the Organization of Uruk Colonial
Contact." M. Rothman, ed., *Uruk Mesopotamia and
Its Neighbors,* pp. 265–306. Santa Fe: SAR Press.

Stein, G., ed.
1999   "The Uruk Expansion: Northern Perspectives from Hacınebi, Hassek Höyük and Gawra."
Paléorient 25:5–172.

Stein, G., R. Bernbeck, C. Coursey, A. McMahon, N.
Miller, A. Mısır, J. Nicola, H. Pittman, S. Pollock,
and H. Wright
1996a   "Uruk Colonies and Anatolian Communities: An Interim Report on the 1992–1993 Excavations at Hacınebi, Turkey." *American Journal of
Archaeology* 100:205–60.

Stein, G., C. Edens, N. Miller, H. Özbal, J. Pierce, and
H. Pittman
1996b   "Hacınebi, Turkey: Preliminary Report on
the 1995 Excavations." *Anatolica* 22:85–128.

Stein, G., K, Boden, C. Edens, J. Pierce Edens,
K. Keith, A. McMahon, and H. Özbal
1997   "Excavations at Hacınebi, Turkey—1996 Preliminary Report." *Anatolica* 23:111–71.

Stein, G., C. Edens, J. Pierce Edens, K, Boden,
N. Laneri, H. Özbal, B. Earl, M. Adriaens, and
H. Pittman
1998   "Southeast Anatolia Before the Uruk Expansion: Preliminary Report on the 1997 Excavations
at Hacınebi, Turkey." *Anatolica* 24:143–94.

Stein, G., and P. Wattenmaker
1990   "The 1987 Tell Leylan Regional Survey: A
Preliminary Report." In N. Miller, ed., *Economy
and Settlement in the Near East: Analyses of Ancient Sites and Materials,* pp. 8–18. Philadelphia:
MASCA.

Stephen, F. M. K., and E. Peltenburg
2002   " Scientific Analyses of Uruk Ceramics from
Jerablus Tahtani and Other Middle-Upper Euphrates sites." In J. N. Postgate, ed., *Artefacts of
Complexity: Tracking the Uruk in the Near East,*
pp. 173–91. Warminster: Aris and Phillips.

Stronach, D.
1994   "Village to Metropolis: Nineveh and the Be-
ginnings of Urbanism in Northern Mesopotamia."
In S. Mazzoni, ed., *Nuove Fondazioni nel Vicino
Oriente Antico: Realtà e Ideologia,* pp. 85–114.
Pisa: Giardini Editori.

Ur, J.
2002   "Settlement and Landscape in Northern
Mesopotamia: The Tell Hamoukar Survey 2000–
2001." *Akkadica* 123:57–88.

Vallet, R.
1997   "Habuba Kabire ou la naissance de l'Urbanisme." *Paléorient* 22:45–76.
1998   "L'urbanisme colonial urukien, l'example de
Djebel Aruda." *Subartu* 4:53–87.

Van Driel, G.
2002   "Jebel Aruda: Variations on a Late Uruk Domestic Theme." In J. N. Postgate, ed., *Artefacts of
Complexity: Tracking the Uruk in the Near East,*
pp. 191–206. Warminster: Aris and Phillips.

Wallerstein, I.
1995   "Hold the Tiller Firm: On Method and the
Unit of Analysis." In S. K. Sanderson, ed., *Civilizations and World Systems,* pp. 239–47. Walnut
Creek, CA: Altamira Press.

Weiss, H.
1990   "Tell Leilan 1989: New Data for Mid Third
Millennium Urbanization and State Formation.
Mitteilungen der Deutschen Orient-Gesselschaft
122:193–218.

Wilkinson, T. J.
1990c   "Early Channels and Landscape Development around Abu Salabikh: A Preliminary Report." *Iraq* 52:75–84.
1994   "The Structure and Dynamics of Dry-Farm-

ing States in Upper Mesopotamia." *Current An-thropology* 35:483–520.

1998   "Tell Beydar Survey." *The Oriental Institute: 1997–1998 Annual Report,* pp. 19–28. Chicago: Oriental Institute.

2000a   "Regional Approaches to Archaeology: The Contribution of Archaeological Surveys." *Journal of Archaeological Research* 8:219–67.

2000b   "Remote Sensing and Geographical Infor-mation Systems." *The Oriental Institute: 1997–1998 Annual Report,* pp. 123–30. Chicago: Oriental In-stitute.

2001   "Comment." *Current Anthropology* 42:224–25.

2003   "Archaeological Survey and Long-Term Pop-ulation Trends in Upper Mesopotamia and Iran." In N. Miller and K. Abdi, eds., *Yeki Bud, Yeki Nabud: Essays on the Archaeology of Iran in Honor of William M. Sumner,* pp. 39–52. Los An-geles: Cotsen Institute of Archaeology.

Wilkinson, T. J., and D. J. Tucker.

1995   *Settlement Development in the North Jazira, Iraq: A Study of the Archaeological Landscape.* London: British School of Archaeology in Iraq.

Wright, H.

1998   "Uruk States in Southwestern Iran." In G. M. Feinman and J. Marcus, eds., *Archaic States,* pp. 173–98. Santa Fe: SAR Press.

2001   "Cultural Action in the Uruk World." In M. Rothman, ed., *Uruk Mesopotamia and Its Neighbors,* pp. 123–48. Santa Fe: SAR Press.

2002   "Arrows and Arrowheads in the Uruk World." In L. al-Gailani Werr, J. Curtis, H. Martin, A. McMahon, J. Oates, and J. Reade, eds., *Of Pots and Plans: Papers on the Archaeology and History of Mesopotamia and Syria Presented to David Oates in Honor of His 75th Birthday,* pp. 373–78. London: Nabu Publications.

Wright, H., and E. Rupley

2001   "Calibrated Radiocarbon Age Determina-tion of Uruk Related Assemblages." In M. Roth-man, ed., *Uruk Mesopotamia and Its Neighbors,* pp. 85–122. Santa Fe: SAR Press.

Wright, R.

2000   *Nonzero: The Logic of Human Destiny.* New York: Pantheon Books.

Yamazaki, Y.

1999   "Excavations at Tell al-'Abr." In G. del Olmo Lete and J.-L. Montero Fenollós, eds., *Archaeol-ogy of the Upper Syrian Euphrates: The Tishreen Dam Area,* pp. 83–96. Barcelona: Editorial Ausa.

Yardımcı, N.

1993   "Excavations, Survey, and Restoration Works at Harran. In M. Frangipane, H. Hauptmann, M. Liverani, P. Matthiae, and M. Mellink, eds., *Be-tween the Rivers and Over the Mountains: Archaeo-logica Anatolica et Mesopotamica Alba Palmieri Dedicata,* pp. 437–49. Rome: Universita di Roma "La Sapienza."

Notes

CHAPTER 1

1. The terms "trade" and "exchange" are used here interchangeably and in their broadest sense to refer simply to the transfer of goods between two or more parties by barter or sale, whether directly (face-to-face) or indirectly (through middlemen).

2. The term "market" is used here in a generic sense and no implication is made as to the existence of market trading (Polanyi 1975:150) as a mode of exchange in the fourth millennium B.C.

CHAPTER 2

1. The problem lies in ascertaining whether the 16 hectare Apadana mound was abandoned after the Middle Uruk period as is often claimed (Johnson 1973:70–71; Amiet 1986:63). The recent exposure of an Uruk kiln area in the Apadana indicates that this was not the case. The materials recovered have precise parallels up to Level 18 of the Acropolis I sounding (de Miroschedji 1976:22–23), a level assigned by Johnson (1973:45) to the Late Uruk period. Additionally, as noted by Dittmann (1986:183), a variety of evidence from earlier French excavations also suggests that the Apadana may have been at least partially occupied in the Late Uruk period.

2. The absence of artifacts characteristic only for Level 17 of the Acropolis I sounding at Susa from Chogha Mish suggests that the hypothesized collapse took place at the time of Susa, Acropolis I, Level 18. This inference is based on the following evidence:

    a. While impressed balls are common at Chogha Mish, where they occur in houses, numerical notation tablets are rare and what few examples do exist were recovered principally in pits cutting into the houses in which most of the balls were found (H. J. Kantor, pers. comm., 1985).

    b. The preponderance of balls over tablets as accounting devices recalls the pattern of Level 18 at Susa and contrasts with that of Level 17, when tablets become far more common than balls (Dittmann 1986a:336).

    c. The apparent absence at Chogha Mish of numerical notation tablets of the convex cushion-shaped type, sometimes with a single pictographic sign (e.g., fig. 27I), which at Susa do not appear prior to Level 17 (see chap. 3, n. 29).

    d. A number of characteristic pottery types with later Proto-Elamite connections restricted to Level 17 at Susa appear absent at Chogha Mish, in spite of extensive exposures. These types include: tall beveled-rim bowls (Le Brun 1978a: fig. 20:9); rimless, bag-shaped jars with long through spouts (Le Brun 1978a: fig. 24:9–10); and four-lugged jars with alternating black and white bands (Le Brun 1978a: fig. 53:4).

3. Particularly important for these correlations is the first use of cylinder seals. It is difficult to ascertain exactly when they were introduced at Warka, as much of the pertinent evidence remains unpublished (Nissen 1986b). Moreover, many of the impressions that are published come from levels of the Anu Ziggurat sequence that cannot be precisely correlated with specific levels of the better-understood Eanna sequence. Recent reassessments of the glyptic evidence from that latter sequence, however, suggest that cylinder seal impressions and impressed artifacts are common in the various Level IV subphases. Whether or not they started earlier is unclear, although a small number of impressions, unfortunately without clear architectural association, are assigned to Level V (Brandes 1979; Dittmann 1986c). A conservative assessment, therefore, would associate the first ap-

pearance of cylinder seals at Warka with Levels VI to IV of the Eanna sequence, which exhibit significant continuity on both ceramic and architectural grounds (Nissen 1986b). At Nippur, the earliest seals (of the so-called Jemdet Nasr type depicting pig-tailed women) appear in Level XVI of the Inanna Temple sequence and the earliest cylinder seal impressions in Level XV. It is not entirely certain, however, how representative the Nippur evidence is since the exposed area was minimal (Wilson 1986). At Susa the situation is clearer, although the exposed area is also relatively restricted: the earliest cylinder seal impressions are reported in Level 20 of the Acropolis I sounding (Le Brun, cited in Dittmann 1986:333, n. 5), the earliest impressed tablets in Level 19, and the earliest impressed balls in Level 18, although the related tokens were also found in Level 19 (Dittmann 1986c: table 50).

4. While well-preserved monumental structures of the Uruk period have not been identified in the Susiana plain, glyptic representations indicate that such structures must have been of the well-known tripartite plan with elaborate exterior niches and buttresses that is typical for Uruk architecture. One structure depicted in a sealing from Susa (fig. 3Y) illustrates what without doubt is a temple (marked by horns) on top of a buttressed platform in a style identical to actual Uruk-period buildings exposed in the alluvium (e.g., at Warka [fig. 3AA], Tell Uqair [Heinrich 1982: fig. 105], and Eridu [Safar, Lloyd, and Mustafa 1981:78–82]) and in some of the northern Uruk enclaves (e.g., Tell Qannas [fig. 17W], Jebel Aruda [fig. 6], and Tell Brak [fig. 18A]).

5. Compare, for example, Amiet 1972: nos. 695, 700 (Susa); Amiet 1986: fig. 22:1 (Chogha Mish); and Amiet 1980: nos. 636ff. (various and unknown provenances, principally from Warka).

6. For detailed comparisons of similarities and differences between Uruk glyptic motifs in Susiana and the alluvium, see Amiet 1972, 1986. Amiet's observation (1979a) that secular scenes in Uruk glyptic seem more common at Susa in particular and Khuzestan in general than in the Mesopotamian alluvium, where religious scenes predominate, should not be interpreted to mean that the two traditions are substantially different, particularly as the evidence from Susa has been dealt with thoroughly and the evidence from Warka remains only incompletely published (Nissen 1986b). Rather, the iconographic differences that Amiet draws attention to are more likely to reflect the varying nature of the contexts in which the glyptic material was found. Most of the evidence from southern Mesopotamia comes from the Eanna and Anu precincts, arguably the religious/administrative center of Uruk. In contrast, insofar as can be ascertained, sealings from Susiana appear to come from contexts that are largely secular and private in nature. This is clear in the case of sealings recovered in new excavations at Susa and Chogha Mish (Le Brun 1971, 1978a; Delougaz and Kantor, n.d.), although the nature

of the original context for much of the Uruk glyptic from Susa excavated earlier in the century can no longer be ascertained.

7. The types in question include a variety of forms bearing simple painted motifs and a distinctive small pointed bottle with an open mouth (Nissen 1972:100–101, fig. 30d-e; von Haller 1932: pls. 17D:r, s–u [Eanna XIII]; 18A:k′–n′ [Eanna XII]; 18B:a–d [Eanna XII], z, a′–c′ [Eanna XI-X]; and 18C:k, q′–t′ [Eanna IX–VIII]). See Sürenhagen 1986b for a clarification of the context of the Warka parallels.

8. For a discussion of the pertinent evidence, see below chapter 3, note 29.

9. Of a total of sixteen types assigned to the Early Uruk period in Susiana, eleven are not reported at Warka (Johnson 1973: 54–55, Types 1, 3–10, 13, and 15).

10. Johnson 1973:54–55. The types in question are Type 2 (to Johnson's discussion add the following occurrences of this type in the Eanna sequence: von Haller 1932: pls. 18C:e′ [Eanna IX-VIII], 19C:1 [Eanna VI]); Type 11; Type 12 (add von Haller 1932: pls. 18C:b′ [Eanna IX-VIII], 18D:i [Eanna VII], and 19B:e′, h′ [Eanna VI]); Type 14 (add von Haller 1932: pls. 18 C:u [Eanna VIII], 19B:k″ [Eanna VI], and 19D:a [Eanna VI]); and Type 16. For a clarification of the context of the Warka parallels, see now Sürenhagen 1986b.

CHAPTER 3

1. Although the 200–250 millimeter of average precipitation per year is usually taken as the minimum necessary to ensure reliable crops, this figure may be too low (Fischer 1978:375–76 n. 1). A case in point is provided by a study of variation in annual rainfall patterns from 1928 to 1946 within portions of the Syro-Mesopotamian plains within modern-day southeastern Turkey. Interannual variability was found to be so high that for at least eleven out of the nineteen years for which data are available, most of Urfa, Adiyaman, and Gaziantep provinces, all well within the 300–400 millimeter average range, had to be classified as semiarid (Erinç 1950:223, fig. 9). Similarly, to the south in Syria, during a recent dry spell lasting three years (1958 to 1960) large portions of the country that usually fall well within the 300–400 millimeter annual precipitation average became marginal. The areas affected included the otherwise usually well-watered environs of Aleppo and even substantial portions of the Upper Khabur region (Wirth 1971:91–92, maps 3–4).

2. In his *Geography,* Strabo, for example, distinguishes clearly between the territory of *Coele Syria,* namely, the Levantine coastal strip, the Bekaa valley, and the Lebanon/Anti-Lebanon range, from Syria proper, which he defined as follows: "Syria is bounded in the north by Cilicia and Mt. Amanus. . . . on the east by the Euphrates and *Arabia Scenitae* east of the Euphrates, and on the south by *Arabia Felix*" (1966:16.II.1–2).

3. Sites in which van Loon (1967:3 n. 3) reports

unspecified Uruk materials are Tell Zreyjiye-south, near Sheikh Hassan on the east bank of the river, Mureybit Ferry, also on the east bank but just south of Mureybit, and Tell Kreyn on the west bank of the river but on the southern end of the area flooded by the dam. Van Loon also reported Uruk pottery at Tell Abu Hureyra. However, no such materials were identified during excavations at the site (A. Moore, pers. comm., 1990).

4. Save for Carchemish, the Uruk sites in southeastern Turkey illustrated in figure 8 were identified in a recent survey under my direction (Algaze 1989a; Algaze et al. 1991). The presence of Uruk pottery at Jerablus Tahtani in Syria is reported by Gil Stein (pers. comm., 1989), who visited the site in 1988 as part of the Chicago Euphrates Project's survey of areas affected by the Tishreen Dam reservoir. Uruk levels at Jerablus, also in Syria, are reported by Strommenger (1980a:62).

5. The seal in question was found at an undetermined depth under the second millennium wall surrounding the Carchemish acropolis (Woolley 1921: pl. 25B:2; compare fig. 19L [Nineveh] and Amiet 1980: no. 348 [Warka, out of context]).

6. A rough impression of the depth of Uruk occupation in the acropolis mound at Carchemish may be obtained from the fact that a typical four-lugged jar with characteristic shoulder incisions and plum-red burnished wash is said to have been recovered at an elevation between 22 and 23 meters above the level of the Euphrates floodplain (Woolley 1952:228, pl. 66A), while beveled-rim bowls continue to be common three to four meters above this level, at the 26-meter contour (ibid). Similarly, another Uruk jar with a characteristic spout attached to the rim (fig. 10F; compare Le Breton 1957:96, fig. 10:16 [Susa B]) was found inside a room at an elevation of 26–27 meters above the same datum (cf. the schematic section in Woolley 1952:209, fig. 84).

7. A second cylinder seal from Samsat, a surface find, is also engraved in a similar style—in this case a row of erect stylized animals (goats?), once again under ladderlike motifs (Özgüç 1987:431, fig. 9). This seal is of interest because the version of the animal-file motif it depicts can be readily paralleled in the glyptic repertoire of Uruk sites elsewhere, including Jebel Aruda (van Driel 1983:38–40, nos. 5 and 9), Susa (Amiet 1972: nos. 525 [Late Uruk] and 911 [Proto-Elamite]) and Warka (Schott 1933: pl. 28E [Eanna III]; Amiet 1980: no. 379 [from the Sammelfund, Eanna III]. Similar seals are known from Syrian sites, unfortunately all of uncertain context and chronology (e.g., Amiet 1963:66–67, fig. 12 [illustrated here as fig. 36D, said to be from Ras Shamra, context unknown] and Buchanan 1966: no. 716a).

8. The small site near Bozova is Söğüt Tarlası, some 25 kilometers away from Samsat (Benedict 1980:178, pl. 18). Sites in the vicinity of Samsat were identified in Özdoğan's survey (1977). In 1983, with Dr. Özdoğan's kind permission, I was able to examine the

collection which is now stored at the Prehistory Laboratory of the University of Istanbul. The remarks that follow are based largely on observations made at that time. Sites yielding grit-tempered ceramics and beveled-rim bowls of Uruk type in addition to indigenous chaff-tempered pottery are Kurban Höyük (U50:7), situated some 7 kilometers downstream from Samsat but on the opposite bank (see now Algaze et al. 1990); Hayaz Höyük (U50:4) some 15 kilometers southwest and on the same bank (see now Thissen 1985); Grik (T52:20) about 4 kilometers due north away from the river; Karadut Mevkii (T51:33) some 12 kilometers upstream from Samsat (see now Schwartz 1988a), Lidar Höyük (T51:40) some 9 kilometers from Samsat but on the opposite bank, and Torçik Mevkii (T51:49) about 1 kilometer upstream of Lidar.

9. The sites in question are Toprak Kale (S52:19) and Hassek Höyük (S52:18) on the east bank of the river and Tille (S52:11) on the opposite bank almost directly across from Hassek (Özdoğan 1977).

10. The full extent of the site is 10.6 hectares. Uruk ceramics, however, were only observed eroding out of the lower 10 meters or so of the much smaller high mound, which is about 125 meters in diameter.

11. Since the date of the Eye Temple sequence at Brak is crucial to my argument, it is necessary to review the evidence marshaled by Mallowan (1947:31) to assign all the structures save for the earliest (Red) to the Jemdet Nasr period. That dating is said to rest on the similarity of "seals, amulets, pot forms, architecture, and applied decoration" at Brak with comparable materials from Jemdet Nasr levels elsewhere. Although largely accurate at the time Mallowan wrote (save for the pottery), a variety of evidence now indicates that this assessment can no longer be sustained.

A reconsideration of the evidence from Uruk-period levels at Tello (Buchanan 1967:535) and recent evidence from sites such as Habuba Kabira-süd and Jebel Aruda in northern Syria and Chogha Mish and Susa in southwestern Iran leaves no doubt that much of so-called Jemdet Nasr style glyptic (characterized by schematic and carelessly drilled designs) appears already in the Uruk period (Nissen 1986b:327–28). Similarly, many of the amulets that Mallowan assigns to the Jemdet Nasr period can now be shown to be *in situ* in Uruk levels as well (for references, see below chap. 4, no. 14). The eye amulets which figure prominently in Mallowan's argument, for instance, appear not only in Jemdet Nasr levels at Khafajah (Sin IV), as correctly noted by Mallowan, but are now also found in Uruk-period contexts in a variety of sites in Khuzestan, for example at Chogha Mish (Delougaz and Kantor, n.d.) and at KS 54 (G. Johnson, pers. comm., 1988).

But the main argument used by Mallowan to assign the Eye Temple to the Jemdet Nasr period was the similarity of its plan, platform, and wall decoration to corresponding features of the White Temple at Warka and the

Painted Temple at Tell Uqair, both also considered to be of Jemdet Nasr date by Mallowan (1947:32, 58, 61–62). This argument, too, can no longer be supported. Recent reconsiderations of the evidence from Warka now indicate that the White Temple must be redated to the Uruk period (Schmidt 1978a; Strommenger 1980b:486–87). The situation at Uqair is similar. Although the "Chapel" by the side of the temple platform is certainly of Jemdet Nasr date, the Painted Temple itself and associated platform, which form the core of Mallowan's parallels, are stratigraphically earlier and unquestionably Uruk in date, as correctly noted by the original excavators (Lloyd and Safar 1943:148–49).

12. For other out-of-context Uruk seals and seal impressions from Brak, see Mallowan 1947: pl. XXI:11, 15, 17; Buchanan 1966: nos. 708, 709, 711, 714, 716, 726; and D. Oates 1985: pl. XXXa. For other out-of-context Uruk ceramic types from Brak, see J. Oates 1986: fig. 3, pls. 4–5.

13. Compare, for example, Amiet 1972: no. 493 (Susa); Schott 1933: pl. 24A; and Lenzen 1960: pl. 19A (Warka).

14. For the hunting scene, compare Amiet 1972: no. 604 (Susa). For the animals with crossed necks, compare Amiet 1972: nos. 479, 588 (Susa), and Amiet 1980: no. 195 (Warka).

15. For further references to this seal type and design, see Le Brun 1971: fig. 43:10 (Susa, Level 21[!]), and Amiet 1980: nos. 352 (Tello), 348 (Warka, out of context).

16. Pertinent evidence on routes and communications during the classical age may be gleaned from a variety of archaeological, literary, and historical sources. Among the most useful archaeological sources are a series of wide-ranging overland and aerial surveys conducted during the 1930s and 1940s (Poidebard 1934; Poidebard and Mouterde 1945; Gregory and Kennedy 1985). These surveys provide data on the actual layout of routes across Western Asia in the Roman period and complement surviving written sources. Of particular importance among the latter are Herodotus' *History,* Pliny's *Natural History,* and Strabo's *Geography.* Also useful are a number of traveler's accounts, such as the detailed itinerary of Isodore of Charax, the *Parthian Stations.*

But without question the single most important historical source is the *Tabula Peutingeriana,* a map dating from the fourth century A.D. that purports to show the trade routes of the Roman world from England to India. Although the *Tabula* has been shown to contain a number of inaccuracies and omissions, it still represents the best framework available for the layout of routes across Western Asia in the Late Roman period (Miller 1962).

17. The location of Bezabde has been the subject of considerable debate (summarized in Lightfoot 1983). The problem now appears solved by the finding of a large Late Roman occupation with substantial standing architecture spanning both sides of the Tigris River some 13 kilometers north of Cizre, which almost certainly can be equated with the Bezabde/Phaenicia of Ammianus' chronicle. For details on the site, see now Algaze 1989a; Soylemez and Lightfoot 1991.

18. The overland route alongside the Tigris seems to have been preferred by the Seleucids, at least if one is to judge from the orientation of their colonies and new foundations across northern Mesopotamia, and from the fact that Seleucus Nicator replaced the Euphrates-bound Babylon with a new Tigris-based capital, Ctesiphon (Stark 1966:102). Moreover, the Tigris route was also important throughout the Late Roman period: Trajan used the overland route alongside the Tigris in his descent toward Ctesiphon early in the second century A.D. (Stark 1966:210), and that route was the one known to the anonymous author of the *Tabula Peutingeriana,* although, admittedly, his map reflects conditions at a time when most of northern Mesopotamia was under undisputed Roman control (Miller 1962: map X).

19. Additionally, Uruk pottery of undetermined type is also reported at the important site of Tell Zaidan, in the immediate environs of Raqqa (Sürenhagen 1986a:15). In the absence of excavations or more precise site surveys, however, the nature and extent of Uruk occupation at Zaidan, if any, must remain a matter for future investigation.

20. On the west bank: Site 1 (Mulla Matar), Site 7 (Ziyade), and possibly Site 26 (Fleti-north). On the east bank: Site 40 (Umm Qseir-west) and Site 58 (Masnaqa) (Monchambert 1984:2, 5–7, n. 8).

21. Presumably, one of these sites is Tepe Deshawar, 7 kilometers from Kermanshah, where Braidwood (pers. comm., 1988) and his colleagues excavated a variety of Uruk pottery types.

22. With few exceptions (e.g., Dyson 1965:227), Period IV at Sialk has traditionally been thought to postdate the Uruk period (e.g., Alden 1982:615; Lamberg-Karlovsky 1985:60). This was so principally on the strength of typical Proto-Elamite ceramics (e.g., Ghirshman 1938: pl. XXVI:4) and fully developed Proto-Elamite administrative tablets (e.g., Ghirshman 1938: pls. XXXI:1 and XCII:S28) found in Period IV levels at the site. Recently, however, Pierre Amiet used unpublished excavation records to differentiate more precisely the provenance of most of the published Sialk IV materials. This reanalysis allowed Amiet (1985, 1986:66–70) to demonstrate that early third millennium materials in Sialk IV were found only in the latest level assigned to that occupation (IV.2) and that the materials from the much better preserved Sialk IV.1 phase appear to be largely Late Uruk in type.

23. For other examples, see Ghirshman 1938: pl. XCIV:S1609-S1614, S1633, S1634. For clarification of context, see Amiet 1985:306.

24. Compare, for example, the corpus of sealings and accounting devices from Uruk levels of the Acropolis I sounding at Susa (Le Brun and Vallat 1978; Le

Brun 1978b) and those from Jebel Aruda (van Driel 1982, 1983) and Habuba Kabira-süd (Töpperwein 1973: Strommenger 1980a: figs. 55–57). For an iconographic study of the sealings from the various regions, see Teissier 1987.

25. This dating contradicts that of Sürenhagen (1986a:32), who assigns the Habuba/Qannas/Aruda complex to the Eanna VII–VI time range, principally on the basis of ceramic parallels.

26. Nevertheless, it should be noted that according to Le Brun (the excavator of the Acropolis I sequence at Susa) the el-Kowm 2 Caracol ceramics belong to a "developed but not final phase of Uruk culture" (Cauvin and Stordeur 1985:195).

27. See also Ghirshman 1938: pls. XXXI:2, 5, 7; XCII:1617–1619, 1621; XCIII:1620, 1622, 1625, 1627, 1632.

28. The tablets in question are Ghirshman 1938: pls. XXXI:3, 4, 6; XCII:1626; XCIII:1624.

29. Characteristic for this largely hypothetical subphase would be a group of tablets from the older excavations at Susa bearing typical Uruk sealings in conjunction with an isolated pictogram (Le Brun and Vallat 1978:31–32 n. 94). Published examples include: Amiet 1972: nos. 474 [square] and 604 [cushion-shaped]; Amiet 1979a: fig. 7 [cushion-shaped]; Dittmann 1986a: fig. 9:6 [cushion-shaped]).

CHAPTER 4

1. It cannot yet be ascertained conclusively whether or not conditions in the Syro-Mesopotamian plains at the time of the Uruk intrusion differed markedly from modern ones. Available pollen cores are of little help, as they derive mostly from highland lakes and their distribution is uneven (van Zeist and Bottema 1982, with references). Similarly, deep sea sediment cores from the Persian Gulf principally reflect conditions in the river headwaters in Anatolia and Iran rather than conditions in the plains to the south and southwest. To be sure, there appears to be some evidence from the cores suggesting an increase in river run-off (and therefore in precipitation) in the Tigris-Euphrates-Karun drainage system between circa 5000 and 3500 B.C. (Nützel 1976, with references), but this evidence is based solely on scattered radiocarbon dates and cannot be correlated with any degree of precision with thus far available archaeological data.

2. A cautionary note, however, is sounded by Henry Wright (pers. comm., 1992) who plausibly suggests that if grain-storage facilities existed at Habuba-süd, more likely than not they would have been located along the river front, an area not adequately sampled by the excavators.

3. Although no Uruk ceramics were recovered at Qalinj Agha, the tripartite plan of the houses is paralleled at Uruk sites elsewhere (e.g., Ludwig 1979: fig. 2A–B) and the association of the houses with a nearby buttressed platform is also matched in Uruk contexts, more specifically in the West Area exposure at Chogha Mish (H. J. Kantor, pers. comm., 1988).

4. Specifically, compare Mallowan 1947: pls. XII:3, 4; XVII:12–13; XX:7–8.

5. As used here the term "Early Banesh" predates the consolidation of Tal-i Malyan into a major regional center and encompasses the Initial and Early Banesh phases of Alden's (1979) periodization.

6. More precisely, in the Duzd-i-Gabri Pass in Bavanat district, near Mung (Stein 1936:209–10, map). The deposit is said to have contained at least fourteen intact vessels, but photos are only published for four out of that total (Stein 1936: pl. XIX:9, 12; XX:21–22). Two of the four are well known Uruk forms, a spouted jar (fig. 31D) and a ladle (fig. 31C).

7. The jars in question were attributed to Level III.6 in the original publication (Ghirshman 1938:47), but are now reassigned to III.7 in Amiet's (1986:66) reconsideration of the stratigraphy and finds at Sialk.

8. It should be noted, however, that these beveledrim bowl sherds appear to have been dismissed as intrusive by the excavators and are not mentioned in the final report (Lamberg-Karlovsky and Beale 1986).

9. For example: Tunca 1979: nos. 103; Amiet 1963: nos. 7–11; Buchanan 1966: nos. 1, 18, 703–6, 712–13, 716a, and 725; and Hogarth 1920: fig. 60. Uruk-style seals from the Marcopoli collection (Teissier 1984: nos. 1–13, 15–16, 53) are presumably largely of Syrian origin, but this is not demonstrable in all cases. Two seals from this group (Teissier 1984: nos. 2–3), however, have loop-bored perforations that betray a northern Syrian origin (Hogarth 1920:54; Braidwood and Braidwood 1960:488 n. 15).

10. Two of the four are from Judeidah JK 3, Levels 18–19, and appear in situ (Braidwood and Braidwood 1960:332, fig. 254:2–3), while the other two were found out of context in later levels (Braidwood and Braidwood 1960: figs. 297:5 and 381:7.

11. For example, at Tepe Gawra (e.g., Tobler 1950: pls. CLXV:104, CLXVI:107), Arpachiyah (Buchanan 1967: figs. 5, 6, 9, 13), and Arslan Tepe (Frangipane and Palmieri 1988: figs. 70:18, 74:50).

12. Fig. 37A (Anu Ziggurat, between Layers C and D, under the White Temple: compare Tobler 1950: pl. CLXV:109 (Gawra XII); Speiser 1935: pl LVI:9, 12 (Gawra VIII); Frangipane and Palmieri 1988: fig. 74:50 (Arslan Tepe VIA); and Buchanan 1967: fig. 12 (Arpachiyah). Fig. 37B (below ramp of Anu Ziggurat, Level X [for location, see Heinrich 1937:28]): compare Frangipane and Palmieri 1988: fig. 74:41 (Arslan Tepe VIA). Fig. 37C (Anu Ziggurat, between Layers C and D under the White Temple): compare fig. 44H and Frangipane and Palmieri 1988: fig. 71:22 (Arslan Tepe VIA). Fig. 37D (Eanna XII): compare fig. 44G (Arslan Tepe VIA).

For other seals that are also of possible northern origin and from the White Temple/Anu Ziggurat area, but of uncertain stratification, see Jakob-Rost 1975: nos. 15 and 27.

13. Much new information on the range of imported resources in Uruk sites in the Mesopotamian alluvium will undoubtly emerge as the long-awaited publication of the final reports of the Warka excavations gets underway. For publication schedules and plans, see now Boehmer 1991.

14. These are not limited to the birds of prey and lion heads illustrated in figure 38. Other widely distributed types include, for instance, couchant bovids (compare Susa [Le Breton 1957: fig. 31:1–2; for clarification of context, see Amiet 1986:57 n. 3] and Warka, Sammelfund hoard [Behm-Blancke 1979: pl. 2:11, 13]) and couchant animals with heads turned sideways (compare Susa [Amiet 1972: nos. 418, 423], Tello [de Genouillac 1934: pl. 36:6i], and Brak [Mallowan 1947: pl. XV:18, 22]).

15. In addition to examples illustrated in figure 38, compare pear-shaped jars with everted necks from Susa (Le Breton 1957: fig. 28:43; Le Brun 1978a: fig. 37:1, 3, 4), Tello (de Genouillac 1934: pls. 6:3a–c and 7:3) and Tell Qannas (Weiss 1985:112, no. 31) and theriomorphic vessels from Susa (Le Breton 1957: fig. 30:1) and Warka (Jordan 1932: pl. 18A).

16. Compare, for example, Alden 1979: fig. 58:1–3, and de Genouillac 1934: pl. X:4858, 5297 (Tello), and Heinrich 1937: pl. 60 (Warka).

CHAPTER 5

1. Even though Late Chalcolithic and Uruk materials had been recovered together at Carchemish (Woolley 1952:214–26) significantly earlier than at Nineveh, delays in the publication of results meant that Nineveh and **not** Carchemish provided our first real suggestion that substantial contacts between the southern Mesopotamian alluvium and the Syro-Mesopotamian plains had taken place in the Uruk period.

2. However, Brak has yet to produce evidence of the chronological relationship between the indigenous Late Chalcolithic assemblage (Fielden 1981a) and the intrusive Uruk tradition (J. Oates 1985, 1986).

3. I am grateful to Messrs. M. R. Behm-Blancke, M. R. Hoh, and Alwo von Wickede, who, over a series of visits to Hassek Höyük, allowed me and other members of the Kurban Höyük excavation team to follow the progress of their excavations and see some of the pertinent material.

4. Exact proportions must await the final publication of data from the site, but it is clear from the preliminary reports that indigenous chaff-tempered ceramics are numerically the more significant component (Behm-Blancke et al. 1981:42–45).

5. Compare Behm-Blancke et al. 1981: pl. 12:3, 4; Behm-Blancke et al. 1984: pl. 12:1; and Behm-Blancke 1985:101, fig. 9.

6. Compare Behm-Blancke 1986:146, fig. 2 (Has-

sek); Mallowan 1947: pl. XXX:12 (Brak); and Jordan 1931:32, fig. 19 (Warka).

7. Ironically, a site such as Nineveh with its long sequence could have provided the key to understanding the development of the Late Chalcolithic period in the north, in particular the relationship between the indigenous assemblage of Ninevite III, paralleled at Gawra and elsewhere, and the Mesopotamian-derived evidence of Ninevite IV. Unfortunately, as even the excavator himself recognized, the critical deep sounding where the transition from one assemblage to the other was first detected was not dug with the necessary precision to allow the nature of the process to be elucidated (Campbell Thompson and Mallowan 1933:29).

8. An even earlier Late Chalcolithic assemblage can be identified at Kurban Höyük. A pit (Locus C01–203), unfortunately of somewhat uncertain stratification, was exposed in another excavation area at the site, Area C01. The ceramics inside the pit were exclusively chaff-tempered and appear to represent a coarser version of the assemblage typical for the lowest Late Chalcolithic phase in Area A: some of the same types are attested, but they were generally more crudely made and lacked any evidence of wheel manufacture such as may be detected in the Area A assemblage. This typologically earlier phase would predate the introduction of the fast wheel into the Atatürk Dam area and is distinguished by the complete absence of grit-tempered ceramics, although otherwise it is similar to the earliest Late Chalcolithic phase in Area A (Algaze et al. 1990: pls. 17–18, table 18).

9. Of a total of 2,159 sherds from the lowest Late Chalcolithic phase in Area A, Phase 6, only two represent Uruk types (a beveled-rim bowl rim and a conical cup sherd). In relative proportions these two sherds represent less than 1/10 of 1% of the total count (Algaze et al. 1990: table 11).

10. I thank Dr. Harvey Weiss for his kind permission to study some of the Leilan materials at New Haven in November 1983.

11. This view is also held by Maria Trentin of the Institute of Archaeology of the University of London. Her advice and insights are gratefully acknowledged.

12. Note, however, that the shallow platters with club or beveled-ledge rims (Mellaart 1981: figs. 164–67) that are common in excavated Late Chalcolithic contexts at numerous sites were incorrectly assigned by Mellaart in the Qoueiq area to the "EB III" period. Nevertheless, this does not significantly affect the estimates for the total number of Late Chalcolithic sites in the area, since most of the sites in which the misassigned platters were found were still assigned to the Late Chalcolithic period on the basis of other diagnostics.

13. The sites in question are Hailane, Mouslimiye, Fafine, Maled, Dabiq, Bahourte, Archaq, Kadrich, and Chair (for plans and measurements see, Matthers 1981: figs. 46, 50, 45, 49, 44, 41, 39, 48, and 43, respectively).

14. Late Chalcolithic levels were exposed at Tell Judeidah in the JK 3 sounding on the western edge of the mound (Braidwood and Braidwood 1960:5–11, fig. 4). Additionally, Late Chalcolithic pottery can also be recognized on the opposite (northeastern) side of the site, where recent soil cuts have been made by local villagers (personal observation, 1988).

15. For details, see above, chapter 3, notes 8–9.

16. The three sites are situated near Samsat: Biricik (U50:01) and Almalık (U50:13), on the same bank of the river but downstream, and Incırlı (T51:42) some 4 kilometers upstream and on the opposite bank.

17. In addition to Samsat, Kurban Höyük, and Hassek Höyük, all of which are discussed at greater length elsewhere, the sites in question are Biricik, Almalık, Hayaz, Grik, Lidar, Incırlı, Torçik Mevkii, Tille, and Toprakale. With the exception of Lidar Höyük, these sites are all relatively small (Özdoğan 1977:142, 184, 144, 94, 174, 176, 170, 92, and 158, respectively). Lidar is much larger than the preceding, about 15 hectares in maximum extent. However, the size of the mound in the Late Chalcolithic period is likely to have been smaller, since a series of vertical operations on the outer and middle slopes of the mound failed to reveal in situ materials of the period.

I am grateful to Dr. Harold Hauptmann who allowed me to follow the progress of the excavations at Lidar and see some of the pertinent material over a series of visits during 1981–84.

18. Compare Lloyd 1940: fig. 2 (Grai Resh); chap. 3 above, fig. 18A (Brak); and Ludwig 1979: fig. 3a-b (Habuba).

19. For a listing of sites with Late Chalcolithic materials in the survey area, see Meijer 1986:51. The six sites in the 6–12 hectare range noted are Sites 53, 94, 96, 146, 163, and 231 (Meijer 1986:48–49).

20. For the nature of patrimonial societies, see Doyle 1986:198–208. On the nature of chiefdoms in general, see Service 1962 and Flannery 1972. For a review of complex chiefdoms in the context of ancient Near Eastern data, see H. T. Wright 1984a.

CHAPTER 6

1. Compare, for example, northern Mesopotamian Ubaid structures at Tepe Gawra, Level XIII (Tobler 1950: pl. 12) and southern Mesopotamian Ubaid buildings at Warka (Heinrich 1982: fig. 74). For Uruk-period comparisons, see below, note 2.

2. More specifically, compare Uruk-period buildings in the Mesopotamian alluvium such as the White Temple at Warka (Heinrich 1982: fig. 90) and the Painted Temple at Tell Uqair (ibid.: fig. 105) and similar structures in Uruk enclaves on the Upper Euphrates, such as Habuba-süd/Qannas (ibid.: fig. 129) and Jebel Aruda (van Driel and van Driel-Murray 1983: map 1).

3. I wish to thank the Arslan Tepe excavation team for their hospitality when I and other members of the Oriental Institute's Kurban Höyük expedition came to visit in Malatya during the 1983 season. I am particularly grateful to Drs. Palmieri, Frangipane, Ferioli, and Liverani for showing us at that time some of the pertinent materials from the site.

4. Compare, for example, Tobler 1950:182–192, pls. CLXV–CLXX (Gawra); Amiet 1973:217–224, figs. 2–4; and Frangipane and Palmieri 1988: figs. 69–78 (Arslan Tepe). For references to related glyptic in highland sites, see Buchanan 1967 and D. H. Caldwell 1976.

5. Frangipane and Palmieri 1988: figs. 67–68, 78:2; Frangipane and Palmieri 1988/89: fig. 8. Among the 1,600 or so sealings recovered as a single cache in Room A206, some 76 different stamp seals and 10 cylinder seals are said to be represented (Collon 1987:14).

6. However, plausible as this suggestion is in light of the unmistakable evidence from Arslan Tepe for close contacts with Uruk societies, it should still be noted that coherent exposures of Period VII levels directly underlying the Period VIA structures and elsewhere across the site are not yet sufficient to demonstrate conclusively that the role of the site as a regional redistributive center emerged only after the onset of contacts and not before.

7. If anything, the expansion northward of early Akkadian kings only accelerated preexisting processes in the northern periphery leading to the creation of ever larger political units, thus ensuring that later successors would encounter even greater resistance. The emergence late in the Akkadian period of the Hurrian kingdom of Urkish and Nawar, against which Mesopotamian rulers of the Ur III period were to launch repeated and largely unsuccessful campaigns (Hallo 1978), appears to be a reflection of this process.

CHAPTER 7

1. According to one version of the Old Babylonian Itinerary, it took eighty-seven days to travel from Larsa to Emar (in the lower corner of the Euphrates bend in Syria some 15 kilometers south of the Habuba/Qannas enclave) via the overland route alongside the Tigris. This includes, however, a lengthy delay at three alluvial cities along the way, which took almost one month. Thus, it is possible that a direct trip with no layovers would have taken something on the order of two months. It is difficult to estimate the length of time required to reach some of the other enclaves, such as Nineveh, for example, since the route northward given in the itinerary followed the Tigris only up to Assur and then veered northwestward across the Lower Jezira in the direction of Shubat Enlil (Tell Leilan). However, it took fifty-six days to reach Zalipa, a station along the way, somewhere north of Ashur and south of Nineveh on the Tigris. By inference, then, after deducting the month lost in layovers, the trip to Nineveh would have taken about a month (Hallo 1964).

We have no records of the length of time that would have been required if the more direct route to Emar alongside the Euphrates (which was shorter by about a third in terms of total distance) had been used. However, it is clear that even for that route time must still be reckoned in terms of more than one month. If, as has been argued, from Larsa to Nineveh with no layovers (a distance by air of some 700 kilometers) would have taken about a month, then from Larsa to Emar would have taken at least forty days (a distance of some 1,000 kilometers by air).

2. Bulk commodities such as timber from Anatolia, northern Syria, and northern Iraq could be floated with relative ease down the Tigris and Euphrates rivers using simple rafts or boats. However, movement northward from the southern Mesopotamian core was still tied to slow-moving donkey caravans (see above, note 1 and below note 9), as was movement eastward across the Iranian plateau.

3. Compare, for example, sealings from Susa (Amiet 1972: nos. 682–683, 688–689, 691, 695) and Warka (Brandes 1979: pls. 1–13).

4. For an intriguing attempt to reconstruct fairly precise administrative divisions and hierarchies in the later part of the Uruk period using glyptic data from Khuzestan, see Dittmann 1986a. For a summary of pertinent epigraphic evidence from the Warka Archaic Texts (Eanna IV/III), see Nissen 1976 and 1986a.

5. Although rare in Ubaid-period sites thus far excavated in the alluvium, copper appears to be common in contemporary levels in the Susiana plain, where numerous copper implements were recovered in the Late Susiana Necropolis at Susa (de Morgan 1912). For a review of copper and copper utensils in prehistoric contexts in Mesopotamia, see Moorey 1985. Also rare but attested in Ubaid contexts are other precious metals such as gold. Gold wire was recovered in a Late Ubaid level (Pit F, 3.25 m) at Ur (Woolley 1955a:14, 185:U16981). Stone vessels made from semi-exotic imported stones are more common in Ubaid sites. At Eridu and Ur, for instance, they were frequently recovered in association with burials (Safar, Lloyd, and Mustafa 1981:232–33, figs. 112–13; Woolley 1955a:87), while at Tell Abada they are found in houses. Also found in Ubaid-period levels at Abada are precious stones such as carnelian, which were found in some burials (Jasim 1985:202). Bitumen and mineral ore-based paints are documented in Ubaid levels at Tell el cOuelli (Hout 1989). Finally, for the distribution of obsidian in early sites in the alluvium, see G. A. Wright 1969.

6. A significant Ubaid occupation appears to have existed at both Tell Brak (J. Oates 1986:253) and Samsat (Özdoğan 1977:133, pls. 84–85). However, Ubaid levels have not yet been excavated at Brak, and Samsat has now been submerged by the reservoir of the Atatürk Dam.

7. Compare, for example, Jasim and Oates 1986: 356, fig. 3, bottom (Tell Abada), and Tobler 1950: pl. CLVII:71 (Gawra).

8. It should be noted, however, that the pattern of relatively substantial Ubaid centers largely without associated rural settlements documented by Adams for the Uruk and Nippur survey areas does not hold in the southernmost edge of the alluvium, in the environs of Ur and Eridu surveyed by H. T. Wright (1981b). There, a greater range of site sizes was discerned, with clusters of smaller dependent sites in the immediate surroundings of the major centers. It is unclear whether the relative paucity of smaller Ubaid sites outside the Ur/Eridu region represents an actual archaeological pattern or is the result of differential recovery caused by later alluviation obscuring the majority of small sites over significant portions of the surveyed area further north. The case of Ras el Amiya, a small Ubaid site near Kish accidentlly found under the modern alluvial surface while an irrigation trench was being dug, indicates how much we may be missing.

9. While incontrovertible osteological evidence for domestic asses and half asses is not yet recorded in Mesopotamia and its immediate periphery before the first quarter of the third millennium B.C. (Clutton-Brock 1986:210–13; Zeder 1986:407), actual remains of asses have been identified in mid fourth millennium levels at Maadi, in Egypt just south of the Nile Delta region (Bökönyi 1985). Further confirmation is provided by pictorial and representational evidence from Egypt and Palestine. Clearly recognizable asses are depicted in the so-called Libyan Booty Palette found at Abydos (Kantor 1974:237, pl. 214b), which is assigned on stylistic grounds to the late fourth millennium or Late Gerzean period (Dynasty 0) (H. J. Kantor, pers. comm., 1988). Earlier by a few centuries is a clay figurine brought to my attention by Roger Moorey (pers. comm., 1988). The figurine is clearly recognizable as a donkey carrying two baskets and was found in a Ghassulian-period burial in a cave at Giv²atayim, near Tel Aviv (Kaplan 1969:31, 39, pl. VII).

10. But for useful surveys as to the range of possibilities we should be looking for in available archaeological data, see Cohen 1971, Curtin 1984, and Polanyi 1975.

11. For a cogent discussion of possible modes of exchange and concomitant archaeologically identifiable spatial correlates, see Renfrew 1975. Note, however, recent criticism to the effect that Renfrew's model fails to consider factors other than the institutional form of the trade that would possibly account or at least affect the observed fall-off curves. These factors are (1) the effect of increasing distance and cost on decreasing demand, and (2) the possibility that improvements in transportational technologies increase costs and thereby increase demand (Earle 1985).

Sources for Illustrations

FIG. 1.   Algaze 1989b: fig. 4. redrawn after Carter and Stolper 1984: fig. 4.

FIG. 2.   Redrawn after Johnson 1987: fig. 23.

FIG. 3.   Algaze 1989b: fig. 1. Redrawn after (A) Le Breton 1957: fig. 13a; (B) Le Brun 1978a: fig. 30:14; (C) Steve and Gasche 1971: pl. 32:14; (D) Le Brun 1978a: fig. 24:4; (E) Sürenhagen 1986b:69, no. 39; (F) de Genouillac 1934: pl. IV:5434; (G) Sürenhagen 1986b:32, no. 100; (H) von Haller 1932: pl. 19D:b; (I) Amiet 1972: no. 474; (J) Amiet 1972: no. 475; (K) Schott 1933: pl. 26B; (L) Schott 1933: pl. 26C; (M) Amiet 1972: no. 695; (N) Amiet 1980: no. 330; (O) Le Brun and Vallat 1978: fig. 7:8; (P) Amiet 1980: no. 611; (Q) Amiet 1980: no. 337; (R) Lenzen 1961: pl. 25N; (S) Le Brun 1978b: fig. 8:6; (T) Vallat 1986: fig. 1; (U) Amiet 1986: figs. 24:2, 8, and 25:4; (V) Lenzen 1964: pl. 26G; (W) Lenzen 1960: pl. 31E; (X) Lenzen 1965: pl. 19c; (Y) Amiet 1972: no. 695; (Z) Le Brun and Vallat 1978: fig. 7:7; (AA) Heinrich 1982: fig. 94; (BB) Schott 1933: pl. 22A.

FIG. 5.   Redrawn after Strommenger 1980a: fig. 12, and back cover, and Sürenhagen 1974/75: map 2.

FIG. 6.   Redrawn after van Driel and van Driel-Murray 1983: map 1.

FIG. 7.   Redrawn after van Loon 1967: fig. 1.

FIG. 10.   Redrawn after (A) Woolley 1952: fig. 94:7; (B) Woolley 1952: fig. 94:13; (C) Woolley 1952: fig. 94:15; (D) Woolley 1952: fig. 89; (E) Woolley 1952: fig. 94:16; (F) Woolley 1952: fig. 95.

FIG. 14.   Photo by and courtesy of Dr. Gil Stein.

FIG. 15.   Redrawn after Özdoğan 1977: pl. 12.

FIG. 16.   Algaze 1986b: fig. 1.

FIG. 17.   Redrawn after (A) Stucky et al. 1974: fig. 7; (B) Sürenhagen 1974/75: pl. 18:124; (C) Sürenhagen 1974/75: pl. 16:92; (D) Sürenhagen 1974/75: pl. 17:102; (E) Sürenhagen 1974/75: pl. 7:64; (F) Hansen 1965: fig. 4; (G) Hansen 1965: fig. 11a; (H) Hansen 1965: fig. 26; (I) LeBrun 1978a: fig. 30:12; (J) LeBreton 1957: fig. 12:9; (K) Strommenger 1980a: fig. 56; (L) Strommenger 1980a: fig. 59; (M) Le Brun 1978b: fig. 9:4; (N) Amiet 1986: fig. 24:8, 14, and Schmandt-Besserat 1977: fig. 9: (O-R) van Driel 1983: figs. 23, 6, 5, and 24; (S-V) Amiet 1972: nos. 712, 525, 511, and 633; (W) Finet 1979: fig. 15; (X) van Driel 1983: fig. 36; (Y) Heinrich 1982: fig. 90; (Z) Le Brun and Vallat 1978: fig. 7:7.

FIG. 18.   Redrawn after (A) Weiss 1985: fig. 13; (B) J. Oates 1986: fig. 3:40; (C) J. Oates 1986: fig. 3:49; (D) J. Oates 1986: fig. 3:48; (E) Mallowan 1947: pl. XXI:2; (F) Amiet 1980: pl. 21E; (G) Mallowan 1947: pl. LI:34; (H) Mallowan 1947: pl. V:1, (I) Finkel 1985: fig. 1; (J) Jasim and Oates 1986: fig. 4.

FIG. 19.   Redrawn after (A-H) Campbell Thompson and Hamilton 1932: pl. LXI:27, 26, 23, 21, 15, 20, 1, and 16; (I) Collon and Reade 1983: fig. 1a; (J) Collon and Reade 1983: fig. 2a, and Campbell Thompson and Hutchinson 1931: pl. XXII:10; (K) Collon and Reade 1983: fig. 1b: (L) Collon 1987: no. 32; (M) Wiseman 1962: pl. 2B.

FIG. 21.   Algaze 1989b: fig. 2.

FIG. 23.   Redrawn after (A) Sürenhagen 1974/75: map 4; (B) Behm-Blancke 1989: fig. 1;

FIG. 25.   Redrawn after Weiss and Young 1975:4.

FIG. 26.   Redrawn after (A) Weiss and Young 1975: fig. 3:3; (B) Weiss and Young 1975: fig. 3:5; (C)

Young 1969: fig. 9:2; (D) Weiss and Young 1975: fig. 3:1b; (E) Weiss and Young 1975: fig. 3:1a; (F) Weiss and Young 1975: fig. 5:5; (G) Weiss and Young 1975: fig. 5:7; (H) Weiss and Young 1975: fig. 4:4; (I) Weiss and Young 1975: fig. 4:2.

FIG. 27.   Redrawn after (A) Amiet 1985: fig. 2:S.49; (B) Ghirshman 1938: pl. LXXXIX; S.43d; (C) Ghirshman 1938: pl. LXIX:S.135; (D) Ghirshman 1938: pl. LXXXVIII:S.115; (E) Ghirshman 1938: pl. LXXXVIII:S.41; (F) Amiet 1985: fig. 4; (G) Ghirshman 1938: pl. LXXXIX:S.80; (H) Ghirshman 1938: pl. LXXXIX:S2; (I) Ghirshman 1938: pl. XCIV:S1609; (J) Amiet 1985: fig. 2:S.42; (K) Amiet 1985: fig. 2:S89; (L) Amiet 1985: fig. 3; (M) Ghirshman 1938: pl. XCIII:S.1627; (N) Ghirshman 1938: pl. XCII:S.1630.

FIG. 28.   Redrawn after Hijara 1973: pl. 1.

FIG. 29.   Redrawn after (A) Starr 1939: pl. 40C; (B) Starr 1939: pl. 40U; (C) Starr 1939: pl. 41F; (D) Starr 1939; pl. 41D; (E) Hijara 1976: pl. 11, top; (F) Hijara 1976: pl. 11, top; (G) Starr 1939: pl. 51L; (H) Hijara 1976: pl. 18, top right; (I) Starr 1939: pl. 41K, (J) Starr 1939: pl. 41L; (K) Abu al-Soof 1964: pl. II:IM 60399; (L) Abu al-Soof 1964: pl. III, center; (M) Abu al-Soof 1964: pl. II:IM 60412; (N) Hijara 1976: pl. 6:2.

FIG. 30.   Algaze 1989b: fig. 3. Redrawn after Levine 1974a: fig. 1.

FIG. 31.   Redrawn after (A) Alden 1979: fig. 35:18; (B) Alden 1979: fig. 57:21; (C) Stein 1936: pl. XX:22; (D) Stein 1936; pl. XX:21; (E) Alden 1979: fig. 48:3; (F) Alden 1979: fig. 50:4; (G) Alden 1979: fig. 47.2; (H) Alden 1979: fig. 47:22; (I) Alden 1979: fig. 50:10; (J) Alden 1979: fig. 49.6.

FIG. 33.   Redrawn after (A) Palmieri 1973: fig. 68:17; (B) Palmieri 1973: fig. 68:18; (C) Palmieri 1981: fig. 2:6; (D) Frangipane and Palmieri 1987: fig. 5:8; (E) Frangipane and Palmieri 1987: fig. 5:6; (F) Palmieri 1973: fig. 64:3; (G) Palmieri 1981: fig. 2:5.

FIG. 34.   Redrawn after (A) Esin 1982: pl. 1:20; (B) Esin 1982: pl. 3a:3; (C) Esin 1982: pl. 3a:4; (D) Esin 1982: pl. 3a:4; (E) Esin 1982: pl. 3a:4; (F) Esin 1982: pl. 3b:7; (G) Esin 1982: pl. 3b:7; (H) Esin 1982: pl. 3b:6.

FIG. 35.   Algaze 1989b: fig. 5. Redrawn after Berthoud et al. 1982:41, and J. R. Caldwell 1967:12.

FIG. 36.   Redrawn after (A) Braidwood and Braidwood 1960: fig. 175:1; (B) Braidwood and Braidwood 1960: fig. 213:2; (C) Braidwood and Braidwood 1960: fig. 219.3; (D) Amiet 1963: no. 11 (presumably from Ras Shamra/Ugarit); (E) Amiet 1980: no. 340 (presumably from northern Syria); (F) Amiet 1980: no. 314 (from Çatal Höyük).

FIG. 37.   (A) Heinrich 1937: pl. 50A; (B) Heinrich 1937: pl. 50D; (C) Heinrich 1938: pl. 29D; (D) Jordan 1932: pl. 19A.

FIG. 38.   Redrawn after (A) Le Brun 1978a: fig. 39:1; (B) de Genouillac 1934: pl. 8; (C) Strommenger 1980a: fig. 47: (D) Le Breton 1957: fig. 18:7; (E) Tell Agrab, Registration no. 35:809, Locus L14:1: Shara Temple, Early Dynastic 2; (F) Mallowan 1947: pl. XIII:8; (G) Amiet 1972: no. 430 bis; (H) de Genouillac 1934: pl. 36:4; (I) Mallowan 1947: pl. XLVII:7; (J) Le Breton 1957:110, fig. 28:27; (K) Sürenhagen 1986a:21, fig. 18; (L) Le Brun 1978a: fig. 37:5; (M) de Genouillac 1934: pl. IX:4880.

FIG. 39.   Redrawn after (A) Behm-Blancke et al. 1984: fig. 11:2; (B) Behm-Blancke et al. 1981: fig. 8:9; (C) Behm-Blancke et al. 1984: fig. 14:5; (D) Behm-Blancke et al. 1981: fig. 23:1; (E) Behm-Blancke et al. 1981: fig. 23:2; (F) Behm-Blancke et al. 1984: fig. 12:4; (G) Behm-Blancke et al. 1981: fig. 24:13; (H) Behm-Blancke et al. 1984: fig. 14:4; (I) Behm-Blancke et al. 1984: fig. 14:8.

FIG. 40.   Algaze 1989b: fig. 6.

FIG. 42.   Algaze et al. 1990: fig. 139.

FIG. 43.   Redrawn after van Loon et al. 1988: pl. 27.

FIG. 44.   Redrawn after (A) Collon 1987: no. 10; (B) Frangipane and Palmieri 1988: fig. 78:2; (C) Collon 1987: no. 11; (D) Frangipane and Palmieri 1988: fig. 67:10; (E) Amiet 1973: fig. 4:4; (F) Amiet 1973: fig. 4:1; (G) Amiet 1973: fig. 4:4; (H) Frangipane and Palmieri 1988: fig. 72:27.

FIG. 45.   Redrawn after Palmieri 1985: fig. 4.

References

Abdul Amir, S. J.
  1988 "Archaeological Surveys of Ancient Settlements and Irrigation Systems in the Middle Euphrates Region of Mesopotamia." Ph.D. dissertation, Department of Near Eastern Languages and Civilizations, University of Chicago.

Abu al-Soof, B.
  1964 "Uruk Pottery from the Dokan and Shahrzur Districts." *Sumer* 20:37–44.
  1969 "Excavations at Tell Qalinj Agha (Erbil)." *Sumer* 25:3–42.
  1970 "Mounds in the Rania Plain and Excavations at Tell Basmusian." *Sumer* 26:65–104.
  1985 *Uruk Pottery.* Baghdad: State Organization of Antiquities and Heritage.

Adams, R. McC.
  1962 "Agriculture and Urban Life in Southwestern Iran." *Science* 136:109–22.
  1966 *The Evolution of Urban Society.* Chicago: Aldine.
  1972 "The Urban Revolution in Lowland Mesopotamia." In B. Spooner, ed., *Population Growth: Anthropological Implications,* pp. 60–62. Cambridge: MIT Press.
  1974 "Anthropological Perspectives on Ancient Trade." *Current Anthropology* 15:239–58.
  1978 "Strategies of Maximization, Stability, and Resilience in Mesopotamian Society, Settlement, and Agriculture." *Proceedings of the American Philosophical Society* 122:329–35.
  1981 *Heartland of Cities.* Chicago: University of Chicago Press.
  1984 "Mesopotamian Social Evolution: Old Outlooks and New Goals." In T. Earle, ed., *On the Evolution of Complex Societies: Essays in Honor*

of Harry Hoijer, 1982, pp. 79–129. Malibu: Undena.

Adams, R. McC., and H.-J. Nissen
  1972 *The Uruk Countryside.* Chicago: University of Chicago Press.

Akkermans, P. P. M. G.
  1984 "Archäologische Geländebegehung im Balih-Tal." *Archiv für Orient-forschung* 31:188–90.
  1988a "The Period IV Pottery of Tell Hammam et Turkman." In M. N. van Loon, ed., *Hammam et Turkman I: Report of the University of Amsterdam's 1981–1984 Excavations in Syria,* pp. 287–349. Leiden: Dutch Archaeological Institute in Istanbul.
  1988b "The Period V Pottery of Tell Hammam et Turkman." In M. N. van Loon, ed., *Hammam et Turkman I: Report of the University of Amsterdam's 1981–1984 Excavations in Syria,* pp. 181–285. Leiden: Dutch Archaeological Institute in Istanbul.
  1989 "Tradition and Social Change in Northern Mesopotamia during the Later Fifth and Fourth Millennium B.C." In E. F. Henrickson and I. Thuesen, eds., *Upon This Foundation—The Ubaid Reconsidered,* pp. 339–68. Copenhagen: Museum Tusculanum Press.

Alagoa, E. J.
  1970 "Long-distance Trade and States in the Niger Delta." *Journal of African History* 11:319–29.

Alden, J.
  1979 "Regional Economic Organization in Banesh Period Iran." Ph.D. dissertation, Department of Anthropology, University of Michigan.
  1982 "Trade and Politics in Proto-Elamite Iran." *Current Anthropology* 23:613–28.

Alden, J.
   1987   "The Susa III Period." In F. Hole, ed., *The Archaeology of Western Iran*, pp. 157–70. Washington, D.C.: Smithsonian Institution Press.
Algaze, G.
   1986a   "Kurban Höyük and the Late Chalcolithic Period in the Northwest Mesopotamian Periphery." In U. Finkbeiner and W. Röllig, eds., *Gamdat Nasr: Period or Regional Style?* pp. 274–315. Beihefte zum Tübinger Atlas des Vorderen Orients, Reihe B, Nr. 62. Weisbaden: Ludwig Reichert.
   1986b   "Habuba on the Tigris: Archaic Nineveh Reconsidered." *Journal of Near Eastern Studies* 45:125–37.
   1989a   "A New Frontier: First Results of the Tigris-Euphrates Archaeological Reconnaissance Project, 1988." *Journal of Near Eastern Studies* 48:241–81.
   1989b   "The Uruk Expansion, Cross-cultural Exchange in Early Mesopotamian Civilization." *Current Anthropology* 30:571–608.
Algaze, G., M. E. Evins, M. L. Ingraham, L. Marfoe, and K. A. Yener
   1990   *Town and Country in Southeastern Anatolia.* Vol. 2: *The Stratigraphic Sequence at Kurban Höyük.* Oriental Institute Publications 110. Chicago: Oriental Institute.
Algaze, G., R. Breuninger, C. Lightfoot, and M. Rosenberg
   1991   "The Tigris-Euphrates Archaeological Reconnaissance Project: A Preliminary Report on the 1989–1990 Seasons." *Anatolica* 17:175–240.
Allchin, B.
   1979   "The Agate and Carnelian Industry of Western India and Pakistan." In J. E. van Lohuizen-De Leeuw, ed., *South Asian Archaeology 1975*, pp. 91–105. Leiden: E. J. Brill.
Amiet, P.
   1963   "La glyptique syrienne archaïque: Notes sur la diffusion de la civilisation mésopotamienne en Syrie du Nord." *Syria* 40:57–83.
   1972   *Glyptique susienne.* Mémoires de la délégation archéologique française en Iran 43. Paris: Geuthner.
   1973   "Aperçu préliminaire sur la glyptique archaïque d'Arslantepe." *Origini* 7:217–24.
   1979a   "Alternance et dualité: Essai d'interprétation de l'histoire Élamite." *Akkadica* 15:2–22.
   1979b   "Archaeological Discontinuity and Ethnic Duality in Elam." *Antiquity* 52:195–204.
   1980   *La glyptique Mésopotamienne archaïque.* Paris: Centre National de la Recherche Scientifique.
   1985   "La période IV de Tépé Sialk reconsidérée." In J.-L. Hout et al., eds., *De L'Indus aux Balkans: Recueil à la mémoire de Jean Deshayes*, pp. 293–

312. Paris: Éditions Recherche sur les Civilisations.
   1986   *L'âge des échanges inter-iraniens.* Paris: Éditions de la Réunion de Musées Nationaux.
Amin, S.
   1976   *Imperialisme et sous-développement en Afrique.* Paris: Éditions Anthropos.
Archi, A., P. E. Pecorella, and M. Salvini
   1971   *Gaziantep e la sua regione.* Rome: Edizioni dell'Ateneo.
Areshian, G. E.
   1990   "Further Thoughts on the Uruk Expansion." *Current Anthropology* 31:396–98.
Aronowitz, S.
   1981   "A Metahistorical Critique of Immanuel Wallerstein's the Modern World System." *Theory and Society* 10:503–20.
Arrian
   1976   *Anabasis of Alexander.* Edited by P. A. Brunt. Cambridge: Harvard University Press.
Asher-Greve, J. M., and W. B. Stern
   1983   "A New Analytical Method and Its Application to Cylinder Seals." *Iraq* 45:157–62.
Aurenche, O.
   1981   *La maison orientale.* Paris: Geuthner.
Bairoch, P.
   1988   *Cities and Economic Development.* Chicago: University of Chicago Press.
Ball, W., D. Tucker, and T. J. Wilkinson
   1989   "The Tell Al-Hawa Project: Archaeological Investigations in the North Jazira, 1986–87." *Iraq* 51:1–66.
Baran, P. A.
   1957   *The Political Economy of Growth.* New York: Monthly Review Press.
Beale, T. W.
   1973   "Early Trade in Highland Iran: A View from a Source Area." *World Archaeology* 5:133–48.
   1978   "Bevelled Rim Bowls and Their Implications for Change and Economic Organization in the Later Fourth Millennium B.C." *Journal of Near Eastern Studies* 37:289–313.
Behm-Blancke, M. R.
   1979   *Das Tierbild in der Altmesopotamischen Rundplastik.* Mainz am Rhein: Phillip von Zabern.
   1985   "Die Ausgrabungen auf dem Hassek Höyük im Jahre 1984." *VII. Kazı Sonuçları Toplantısı*, pp. 87–102. Ankara: Eski Eserler ve Müzeler Genel Müdürlügü.
   1986   "Die Ausgrabungen auf dem Hassek Höyük im Jahre 1985." *VIII. Kazı Sonuçları Toplantısı*, pp. 139–48. Ankara: Eski Eserler ve Müzeler Genel Müdürlügü.
   1989   "Mosaiksifte am oberen Euphrat—Wandschmuck aus Uruk-Zeit." *Istanbuler Mitteilungen* 39:73–83.

Behm-Blancke, M. R., J. Boesneck, A. van der Driesch, M. R. Roh, and G. Wiegand
1981 "Hassek Höyük: Vorläufiger Bericht über die Ausgrabungen den Jahren 1978–1980." *Istanbuler Mitteilungen* 31:11–94.

Behm-Blancke, M. R., M. R. Roh, N. Karg, L. Masch, F. Parsche, K. L. Weiner, A. V. Wickede, and G. Wiedermayer
1984 "Hassek Höyük. Vorläufiger Bericht über die Grabungen in den Jahren 1981–1983." *Istanbuler Mitteilungen* 34:31–150.

Benedict, P.
1980 "Survey Work in Southeastern Anatolia." In H. Çambel and R. J. Braidwood, eds. *Prehistoric Research in Southeastern Anatolia,* pp. 151–206. Istanbul: Edebiyat Fakültesi Basimevi.

Berthoud, T., S. Cleuziou, L. P. Hurtel, M. Menu, and C. Volfovsky
1982 "Cuivres et alliages en Iran, Afghanistan, Oman au cours des IVe und IIIe millénaires." *Paléorient* 8:39–54.

Boehmer, R. M.
1985 "Kalkstein für das Urukzeitliche Uruk." *Baghdader Mitteilungen* 15:141–49.
1991 "Uruk 1980–1990: A Progress Report." *Antiquity* 65:465–78.

Boese, J.
1986/87 "Excavations at Tell Sheikh Hassan, Preliminary Report on the Year 1987 Campaign in the Euphrates Valley." *Annales Archéologiques Arabes Syriennes* 36/37:67–100.

Bökönyi, S.
1985 "The Animal Remains of Maadi, Egypt: A Preliminary Report." In *Studi di Paletnologia in onore di S.M. Puglisi,* pp. 495–99. Rome: Università di Roma "La Sapienza."

Boserup, E.
1965 *The Conditions of Agricultural Growth.* Chicago: Aldine.

Braidwood, R. J.
1937 *Mounds in the Plain of Antioch.* Oriental Institute Publications 48. Chicago: University of Chicago Press.

Braidwood, R. J., and L. S. Braidwood
1960 *Excavations in the Plain of Antioch I.* Oriental Institute Publications 61. Chicago: University of Chicago Press.

Brandes, M.
1979 *Siegelabrollungen aus den archäischen Bauschichten in Uruk-Warka.* Freiburger Altorientalischen Studien 3. Weisbaden: Franz Steiner.

Brandt, R. E.
1978 "The Other Chalcolithic Finds." In M. N. van Loon, ed., *Korucutepe II,* pp. 61–66. Amsterdam: North Holland.

Braudel, F.
1972 "History and the Social Sciences." In P. Burke, ed., *Economy and Society in Early Modern Europe,* pp. 11–42. New York: Harper and Row.

Breniquet, C.
1989 "Les origines de la culture d'Obeid en Mésopotamie du nord." In E. F. Henrickson and I. Thuesen, eds., *Upon This Foundation—The Ubaid Reconsidered,* pp. 325–38. Copenhagen: Museum Tusculanum Press.

British Admiralty, Naval Intelligence
1917 *A Handbook of Mesopotamia,* Vol. 4. London.
1919 *A Handbook of Asia Minor.* London.
1943 *Syria.* London.
1944 *Iraq and the Persian Gulf.* London.

Browman, D. L.
1978 "Toward the Development of the Tiahuanaco State." In D. L. Browman, ed., *Advances in Andean Archaeology,* pp. 327–49. The Hague: Mouton.

Buccellatti, G., and M. Kelly-Buccellatti
1988 *Mozan I: The Soundings of the First Two Seasons.* Malibu: Undena.

Buchanan, B.
1966 *Catalogue of Ancient Near Eastern Seals in the Ashmolean Museum,* vol. 1. Oxford: Clarendon Press.
1967 "The Prehistoric Stamp Seal: A Reconsideration of Some Old Excavations." *Journal of the Ancient Oriental Society* 87:265–79, 525–40.

Buchanan, B., and P. R. S. Moorey
1984 *Catalogue of Ancient Near Eastern Seals in the Ashmolean Museum.* Oxford: Clarendon Press.

Burghardt, A. F.
1971 "A Hypothesis about Gateway Cities." *Annals of the Association of American Geographers* 61:269–87.

Caldwell, D. H.
1976 "The Early Glyptic of Gawra, Giyan, and Susa and the Development of Long-Distance Trade." *Orientalia* 45:227–50.

Caldwell, J. R., ed.
1967 *Investigations at Tal-i-Iblis.* Illinois State Museum Preliminary Reports, no. 9. Springfield: Illinois State Museum.

Campbell Thompson, R., and R. W. Hamilton
1932 "The British Museum Excavations on the Temple of Ishtar at Nineveh, 1930–31." *Liverpool Annals of Archaeology and Anthropology* 19:55–116.

Campbell Thompson, R., and R. W. Hutchinson
1931 "The Site of the Palace of Ashurbanipal at Nineveh Excavated in 1929–30 on Behalf of the British Museum." *Liverpool Annals of Archaeology and Anthropology* 18:79–112.

Campbell Thompson, R., and M. E. L. Mallowan
  1933 "The British Museum Excavations at Nine-
        veh, 1931–32." *Liverpool Annals of Archaeology
        and Anthropology* 20:71–186.
Canal, D.
  1978 "La terrace de l'Acropole de Suse." *Cahiers
        de la Délégation Archéologique Française en Iran*
        9:11–55.
Carter, E., and M. W. Stolper
  1984 *Elam.* Berkeley: University of California
        Press.
Cauvin, J., and D. Stordeur
  1985 "Une occupation d'époche Uruk en Palmy-
        rène: Le niveau supérieur d'El Kowm 2-Caracol."
        Cahiers de l'Euphrate 4:191–206.
Charlesworth, M. P.
  1924 *Trade Routes and Commerce of the Roman
        Empire.* Cambridge: Cambridge University Press.
Chase-Dunn, C., and T. D. Hall
  1991 "Conceptualizing Core/Periphery Hierarchies
        for Comparative Study." In C. Chase-Dunn and
        T. D. Hall, eds., *Core/Periphery Relations in Pre-
        capitalist Worlds,* pp. 5–44. Boulder: Westview
        Press.
Cleuziou, S., J. Reade, and M. Tosi
  1990 "The Joint Hadd Project: Summary Report of
        the Third Season." Manuscript.
Clutton-Brock, J.
  1986 "Osteology of the Equids from Sumer." In
        R. H. Meadow and H.-P. Uerpmann, eds., *Equids
        in the Ancient World,* pp. 207–29. Beihefte zum
        Tübinger Atlas des Vorderen Orients, Reihe A, Nr.
        19/1. Weisbaden: Ludwig Reichert.
Cohen, A.
  1971 "Cultural Strategies in the Organization of
        Trading Diasporas." In C. Meillassoux, ed., *The
        Development of Indigenous Trade and Markets in
        West Africa.* pp. 266–78. Oxford: Oxford Univer-
        sity Press.
Collon, D.
  1987 *First Impressions: Cylinder Seals in the An-
        cient Near East.* Chicago: University of Chicago
        Press.
Collon, D., and J. Reade
  1983 "Archaic Nineveh." *Baghdader Mitteilungen*
        14:33–43.
Conrad, G. W., and A. A. Demarest
  1984 *Religion and Empire: The Dynamics of Aztec
        and Inca Expansionism.* Cambridge: Cambridge
        University Press.
Contenau, G., and R. Ghirshman
  1935 *Fouilles du Tépé Giyan.* Paris: Geuthner.
Cooper, J. S.
  1986 *Presargonic Inscriptions.* New Haven: Amer-
        ican Oriental Society.

Crawford, H. E. W.
  1973 "Mesopotamia's Invisible Exports in the
        Third Millennium." *World Archaeology* 5:232–41.
Curtin, P. D.
  1975 *Economic Change in Precolonial Africa.*
        Madison: University of Wisconsin Press.
  1984 *Cross-cultural Trade in World History.* Cam-
        bridge: Cambridge University Press.
Daaku, K. Y.
  1970 *Trade and Politics on the Gold Coast, 1600–
        1720.* Oxford: Clarendon Press.
Dales, G.
  1962 "Harrapan Outposts on the Makran Coast."
        Antiquity 36:86–92.
Davidson, T. E.
  1977 "Regional Variation within the Halaf Ceramic
        Tradition." Ph.D. dissertation, University of Edin-
        burgh.
de Genouillac, H.
  1934 *Fouilles de Tello I.* Paris: Geuthner.
de Jesus, Prentiss S.
  1980 *The Development of Prehistoric Mining and
        Metallurgy in Anatolia.* British Archaeological Re-
        view, International Series 74. Oxford.
Delougaz, P., and H. J. Kantor
  1969 "New Light on the Emergence of Civilization
        in the Near East." *UNESCO Currier* 22:22–28.
  N.d. *Chogha Mish: Report on the First Five Sea-
        sons of Excavations, 1961–1971.* Oriental Institute
        Publications 101. Chicago: Oriental Institute.
        Forthcoming.
Demans, A.
  1975 "Matériaux et réflexions pour servir à une
        étude du développement et sous-développement
        dans les provinces de l'empire romain." In H.
        Temporini, ed., *Austieg und Niedergang der röm-
        ischen Welt,* vol. 2, pp. 3–97. Berlin: Walter de
        Gruyter.
de Mecquenem, R.
  1943 "Fouilles de Suse, 1933–1939." *Mémoires de
        la Délégation Archéologique Française en Iran*
        29:3–161.
Demirji, M. S., ed.
  1987 *Researches on the Antiquities of the Saddam
        Dam Basin Salvage and Other Researches.* Bagh-
        dad: State Organization of Antiquities and Heritage.
de Miroshedji, P.
  1976 "Un four de poitier du IVe millénaire sur
        le tell de l'Apadana." *Cahiers de la Délégation
        Archéologique Française en Iran* 6:13–46.
de Morgan, J.
  1912 "Observations sur les couches profundes de
        l'Acropole à Suse." *Mémoires de la Délégation de
        Perse* 13:1–25.
Diakonoff, I. M.
  1975 "The Rural Community in the Ancient Near

East." *Journal of the Economic and Social History of the Orient* 18:121–33.

1982 "The Structure of Near Eastern Society before the Middle of the Second Millennium B.C." *Oikumene* 3:7–100.

Diamond, S.
1974 *In Search of the Primitive: A Critique of Civilization.* New Brunswick: Transaction Books.

Dillemann, L.
1962 *Haute Mésopotamie orientale et pays adjacents.* Paris: Geuthner.

Dittmann, R.
1986a "Seals, Sealings, and Tablets: Thoughts on the Changing Pattern of Administrative Control from the Late Uruk to the Proto-Elamite Period at Susa." In U. Finkbeiner and W. Röllig, eds., *Gamdat Nasr: Period or Regional Style?* pp. 332–66. Beihefte zum Tübinger Atlas des Vorderen Orients, Reihe B, Nr. 62. Weisbaden: Ludwig Reichert.

1986b "Susa in the Proto-Elamite Period and Annotations on the Painted Pottery of Proto-Elamite Khuzestan." In U. Finkbeiner and W. Röllig, eds., *Gamdat Nasr: Period or Regional Style?* pp. 171–96. Beihefte zum Tübinger Atlas des Vorderen Orients, Reihe B, Nr. 62. Weisbaden: Ludwig Reichert.

1986c *Betrachtungen zur Frühzeit des Südwest-Iran.* Berlin: Dietrich Reimer.

Dobel, A. G.
1978 "The Location of Wassukanni." Ph.D. dissertation, Department of Near Eastern Civilizations, University of California at Berkeley.

Dornemann, R. H.
1988 "Tell Hadidi: One Bronze Age Site among Many in the Tabqa Dam Salvage Area." *Bulletin of the American Schools of Oriental Research* 270:13–42.

Dorrell, P. G.
1981 "The Qoueiq Valley: The Physical Background." In J. Matthers, ed., *The River Qoueiq, Northern Syria, and Its Catchment,* pp. 75–80. British Archaeological Review, International Series 98. Oxford.

Doyle, W. M.
1986 *Empires.* Ithaca: Cornell University Press.

du Mesnil du Buisson, R.
1935 *Le site archéologique de Mishrife-Qatna.* Paris: E. du Boccard.

Dunham, S.
1983 "Notes on the Relative Chronology of Early Northern Mesopotamia." *Journal of the Ancient Near Eastern Society* 15:13–38.

Du Plat Taylor, J., M. V. Seton Williams, and J. Waechter

1950 "The Excavations at Sakce Gözü." *Iraq* 12:53–138.

Dussaud, R.
1931 *La Syrie antique et médiévale illustrée.* Paris: Geuthner.

Dyson, R. H.
1965 "Problems in the Relative Chronology of Iran, 6000–2000 B.C." In R. W. Ehrich, ed., *Chronologies in Old World Archaeology,* 2d ed., pp. 215–56. Chicago: University of Chicago Press.

Earle, T.
1985 "Prehistoric Economics and the Evolution of Social Complexity: A Commentary." In A. B. Knapp and T. Stech, eds., *Prehistoric Production and Exchange,* pp. 106–11. University of California, Los Angeles: Institute of Archaeology.

Egami, N.
1958 *Telul Eth Thalathat: The Excavation of Tell II,* vol. 1. Tokyo: Institute for Oriental Culture.

Eichmann, R.
1986 "Die Steingeräte aus dem 'Riemchengebäude' in Uruk-Warka." *Baghdader Mitteilungen* 17:97–130.

Eisenstadt, S. N.
1979 "Observations and Queries about Sociological Aspects of Imperialism in the Ancient World." In M. T. Larsen, ed., *Power and Propaganda,* pp. 21–34. Copenhagen: Akademisk Forlag.

Ekholm, K.
1977 "External Exchange and the Transformation of Central African Social Systems." In J. Friedman and M. J. Rowlands, eds., *The Evolution of Social Systems,* pp. 115–36. London: Duckworth.

1981 "On the Structure and Dynamics of Global Systems." In J. S. Kahn and J. P. Llobera, eds., *The Anthropology of Precapitalist Societies,* pp. 241–62. London: Macmillan.

Ekholm, K., and J. Friedman
1979 "'Capital' Imperialism and Exploitation in Ancient World Systems." In M. T. Larsen, ed., *Power and Propaganda,* pp. 41–58. Copenhagen: Akademisk Vorlag.

Emmanuel, A.
1972 *Unequal Exchange: A Study of the Imperialism of Trade.* New York: Monthly Review Press.

Erinç, S.
1950 "Climatic Types and the Variation of Moisture Regimes in Turkey." *Geographical Review* 40:224–35.

1980 "Human Ecology in Southeastern Anatolia." In H. Çambel and R. J. Braidwood, eds., *Prehistoric Research in Southeastern Anatolia,* pp. 73–90. Istanbul: Edebiyat Fakültesi Basimevi.

Esin, U.
1975 "Tepecik, 1974." *Anatolian Studies* 25:46–49.

Esin, U.

1982   "Die kulturellen Beziehungen zwischen Ostanatolien und Mesopotamien sowie Syrien anhand
einiger Grabungs und Oberflachfunde aus dem oberen Euphrattal im 4. Jt.v.Chr." In H. J. Nissen
and J. Renger, eds., *Mesopotamien und Seine
Nachbarn,* pp. 13–22. Berlin: Dietrich Reimer.

Evins, M. A.

1989   "The Late Chalcolithic/Uruk Period in the
Karababa Basin, Southeastern Turkey." In M.
Rothman, ed., "Out of the Heartland: The Evolution of Complexity in Peripheral Mesopotamia during the Uruk Period, Workshop Summary." *Paléorient* 15:270–71.

Fales, F. M., S. Tusa, G. Wilhelm, and C. Zaccagnini

1987   "Preliminary Report on the First Campaign of
Excavations within the Saddam Dam Reservoir Archaeological Rescue Project (1984)." In M. S. Demirji, ed., *Researches on the Antiquities of the
Saddam Dam Basin Salvage and Other Researches,* pp. 99–128. Baghdad: State Organization of Antiquities and Heritage.

Ferioli, P., and E. Fiandra

1988   "Clay Sealings from Arslantepe VIA: Administration and Bureaucracy." In M. Frangipane and
A. Palmieri, eds., "Perspectives on Protourbanization in Eastern Anatolia: Arslantepe (Malatya). An
Interim Report on 1975–1983 Campaigns." *Origini*
12:455–509.

Fielden, K. J.

1981a   "The Chronology of Settlement in Northeastern Syria during the Fourth and Third Millennia B.C. in the Light of Ceramic Evidence from
Tell Brak." D.Phil. dissertation, Faculty of Oriental Studies, Corpus Christi College, Oxford University.

1981b   "A Late Uruk Pottery Group from Tell
Brak." *Iraq* 43:157–66.

Finet, A.

1969   "L'Euphrate, route commerciale de la Meso-
potamie." *Annales Archéologiques Arabes Syriennes* 19:37–48.

1979   "Bilan provisoire des fouilles belges du Tell
Kannas." In D. N. Freedman, ed., *Archaeological
Reports from the Tabqa Dam Project—Euphrates
Valley, Syria. Annual of the American Schools of
Oriental Research* 44:79–96.

Finkbeiner, U.

1985   "Uruk-Warka XXXVII: Survey des Stadge-
bietes vom Uruk. Vorläufiger Bericht über die 3.
Kampagne 1984, I. Durchfurung und ergebnisse
des Survey." *Baghdader Mitteilungen* 15:17–59.

1986   "Uruk-Warka: Evidence of the Gamdat Nasr
Period." In U. Finkbeiner and W. Röllig, eds.,
Gamdat Nasr: Period or Regional Style? pp. 33–
56. Beihefte zum Tübinger Atlas des Vorderen

Orients, Reihe B, Nr. 62. Weisbaden: Ludwig
Reichert.

1987   "Uruk-Warka, 1983–1984." *Archiv für Orientforschung* 34:140–44.

Finkel, I. L.

1985   "Inscriptions from Tell Brak." *Iraq* 47:187–
201

Finley, M. I.

1976   "Colonies—An Attempt at a Typology."
Transactions of the Royal Historical Society, 5th
series 26:167–88.

Fischer, W. B.

1968   "Physical Geography." In W. B. Fischer, ed.,
The Cambridge History of Iran, vol. 1, pp. 3–110.
Cambridge: Cambridge University Press.

1978   *The Middle East.* Cambridge: Cambridge
University Press.

Flannery, K. V.

1972   "The Cultural Evolution of Civilizations."
Annual Review of Ecology and Systematics 3:399–
426.

Forest, J. D.

1983   "Rapport préliminaire sur la 3eme campagne
à Tell el'Oueili." In J. L. Hout, ed., *Larsa et
'Oueili: Travaux de 1978–1981,* pp. 71–80. Paris:
Éditions Recherche sur les Civilisations.

Foster, B.

1977   "Commercial Activity in Sargonic Mesopotamia." *Iraq* 39:31–44.

1981   "A New Look at the Sumerian Temple State."
*Journal of the Economic and Social History of the
Orient* 24:225–41.

Francfort, H. P., and M. H. Pottier

1978   "Sondage preliminaire sur l'etablissement
protohistorique Harappeen et Post-Harappeen de
Shortugai." *Arts Asiatiques* 34:29–69.

Frangipane, M., and A. Palmieri

1987   "Urbanisation in Perimesopotamian Areas:
The Case of Eastern Anatolia." *Studies in the Neo-
lithic and Urban Revolutions,* pp. 295–318. British
Archaeological Review, International Series 349.
Oxford.

1988   "A Protourban Centre of the Late Uruk Period." In M. Frangipane and A. Palmieri, eds.,
"Perspectives on Protourbanization in Eastern Anatolia: Arslantepe (Malatya). An Interim Report on
1975–1983 Campaigns." *Origini* 12:287–454.

1988/89   "Aspects of Centralization in the Late
Uruk Period in the Mesopotamian Periphery. *Origini* 14.

Frank, A. G.

1967   *Capitalism and Underdevelopment in Latin
America.* New York: Monthly Review Press.

Frankenstein, S., and M. J. Rowlands

1978   "The Internal Structure and Regional Context
of Early Iron Age Society in Southwest Germany."

Bulletin of the Institute of Archaeology of London
15:73–112.

Friedman, J., and M. J. Rowlands
1977 "Notes Towards an Epigenetic Model of the Evolution of 'Civilisation'" In J. Friedman and M. J. Rowlands, eds., *The Evolution of Social Systems*, pp. 201–76. London: Duckworth.

Gallagher, J., and R. Robinson
1953 "The Imperialism of Free Trade." *Economic History Review*, 2d series 6:1–15.
1961 *Africa and the Victorians*. London: Macmillan.

Galtung, J.
1971 "A Structural Theory of Imperialism." *Journal of Peace Research* 2:81–117.

Gelb, I. J.
1971 "On the Alleged Temple and State Economies in Ancient Mesopotamia." In *Studi in onore de Edoardo Volterra*, vol. 6, pp. 137–54. Milan: Dott. A. Giuffrè.
1973 "Prisoners of War in Early Mesopotamia." *Journal of Near Eastern Studies* 32:70–98.
1976 "Quantitive Evaluation of Slavery and Serfdom." In B. L. Eichler, ed., *Cuneiform Studies in Honor of Samuel Noah Kramer*, pp. 195–207. Alter Orient und Altes Testament 25. Neukirchener-Vluyn: Neukirchener Verlag.
1979 "Household and Family in Ancient Mesopotamia." In E. Lipinsky, ed., *State and Temple Economy in the Ancient Near East*, pp. 1–98. Leuven: Katholieke Universiteit.
1982 "Terms for Slaves in Ancient Mesopotamia." In *Societies and Languages of the Ancient Near East: Studies in Honor of I. M. Diakonoff*, pp. 81–98. Warminster: Aries and Phillips.

Geyer, B., and J.-Y. Monchambert
1987 "Prospection de la moyenne vallée de l'Euphrate: Rapport préliminaire, 1982–1985." *Mari Annales de Recherches Interdisciplinaires* 5:293–344.

Ghirshman, R.
1938 *Fouilles de Sialk I*. Paris: Geuthner.

Gills, B. K., and A. G. Frank
1991 "Five Thousand Years of World Systems History: The Cumulation of Accumulation." In C. Chase-Dunn and T. D. Hall, eds., *Core/Periphery Relations in Precapitalist Worlds*, pp. 67–112. Boulder: Westview Press.

Gibson, McG.
1973 "Population Shift and the Rise of Mesopotamian Civilization." In C. Renfrew, ed., *The Explanation of Culture Change: Models in Prehistory*, pp. 447–63. London: Duckworth.
1974 "Violation of Fallow and Engineered Disaster in Mesopotamian Civilization." In T. E. Downing and McG. Gibson, eds., *Irrigation's Impact on So-ciety*, pp. 7–20. Tucson: University of Arizona Press.
1976 "By Cycle and Stage to Sumer." In D. Schmandt-Besserat, ed., *The Legacy of Sumer*, pp. 51–58. Bibliotheca Mesopotamica 4. Malibu: Undena.

Goff, C.
1968 "Luristan in the First Millennium B.C." *Iran* 6:105–34.
1971 "Luristan before the Iron Age." *Iran* 9:131–52.

Goldstein, P. S.
1989 "The Tiwanaco Occupation of Moquegua." In D. S. Rice, C. Stanish, and P. R. Scarr, eds., *Ecology, Settlement, and History in the Osmore Drainage, Peru*, pp. 257–68. British Archaeological Review, International Series 545. Oxford.

Grant, C. P.
1937 *The Syrian Desert*. New York: Macmillan.

Green, M. V.
1980 "Animal Husbandry at Uruk in the Archaic Period." *Journal of Near Eastern Studies* 39:1–35.

Gregory, S., and D. Kennedy
1985 *Sir Aurel Stein's Limes Report*. British Archaeological Review, International Series 272. Oxford.

Hall, K. R.
1985 *Maritime Trade and State Development in Early Southeast Asia*. Honolulu: University of Hawaii Press.

Hallo, W.
1964 "The Road to Emar." *Journal of Cuneiform Studies* 18:57–96.
1978 "Simurrum and the Hurrian Frontier." *Revue Hittite et Asianique* 36:71–83.

Hanbury Tenison, J.
1983 "The 1982 Flaked Stone Assemblage at Jebel Aruda, Syria." *Akkadica* 33:27–33.

Hansen, D. P.
1965 "The Relative Chronology of Mesopotamia, Part II: The Pottery Sequence at Nippur from the Middle Uruk to the Old Babylonian Period (3400–1600 B.C.)." In R. W. Ehrich, ed., *Chronologies in Old World Archaeology*, 2d ed., pp. 201–15. Chicago: University of Chicago Press.

Hansman, J.
1972 "Elamites, Achaemenians, and Anshan." *Iran* 10:127–42.

Hauptmann, H.
1975 "Norşuntepe, 1974." *Anatolian Studies* 25:35–38.
1979 "Die Grabungen auf dem Norşuntepe, 1973." *Keban Project 1973 Activities*, pp. 61–78. Middle Eastern Technical University. Keban Project Publications, series 1, no. 6. Ankara: Türk Tarih Kurumu Basimevi.

Hassan, F. A.
  1988   "The Predynastic of Egypt." *Journal of World
          Prehistory* 2:135–85.
Heinrich, E.
  1936   *Kleinfunde aus den archäischen Tempelschi-
          chten in Uruk.* Leipzig: Otto Harrassowits.
  1937   "Die Grabung im Planquadrat K XVII." *Vor-
          läufiger Bericht über die von der Deutschen For-
          schungsgemeinschaft in Uruk-Warka unternomme-
          nen Ausgrabungen* 8:27–55.
  1938   "Grabungen im Gebiet des Anu-Antum-
          Tempels." *Vorläufiger Bericht über die von der
          Deutschen Forschungsgemeinschaft in Uruk-Warka
          unternommenen Ausgrabungen* 9:19–30.
  1982   *Die Tempel und Heiligtümer in Alten Meso-
          potamien.* Berlin: Walter de Gruyter.
Heinrich, E., E. Strommenger, D. R. Frank, W. Lud-
    wig, D. Sürenhagen, E. Töpperwein, H.-J.
    Schmidt, J.-C. Heusch, K. Kohlmeyer, D. Ma-
    chule, M. Wäfler, and T. Rhode
  1973   "Vierter vorläufiger Bericht über die von der
          Deutschen Orient Gesellschaft mit Mitteln der Stif-
          tung Volkswagenwerk in Habuba Kabira und in
          Mumbaqat unternommenen archäologischen Unter-
          suchungen, erstattet von Mitgliedern der Mission."
          Mitteilungen der Deutschen Orient-Gesellschaft
          105:5–58.
Henrickson, R. C.
  1986   "A Regional Perspective on Godin III Cul-
          tural Development in Central Western Iran." *Iran*
          24:1–55.
Hermann, G.
  1968   "Lapis Lazuli: The Early Phases of Its
          Trade." *Iraq* 30:21–57.
Herodotus
  1942   *The Persian Wars.* Edited by G. Rawlinson.
          New York: Modern Library.
Higham, C.
  1989   *The Archaeology of Mainland Southeast Asia.*
          Cambridge: Cambridge University Press.
Hijara, I.
  1973   "Excavations at Tell Qalinj Agha (Erbil),
          Fourth Season." *Sumer* 29:13–35 [Arabic Section].
  1976   "Excavations at Shahrzur Plain, Tell
          Kurdrsh." *Sumer* 32:59–80 [Arabic Section].
Hirsch, H.
  1963   "Die Inschriften der Könige von Agade."
          Archiv für Orientforschung 20:1–82.
Hirth, K.
  1978   "Interregional Trade and the Formation of
          Prehistoric Gateway Communities." *American
          Antiquity* 43:35–45.
Hogarth, D. G.
  1920   *Hittite Seals.* Oxford: Oxford University
          Press.
Hole, F., and G. A. Johnson
  1986/87 "Umm Qseir on the Khabur: Preliminary

Report on the 1986 Excavation." *Annales Archéo-
          logiques Arabes Syriennes* 36/37:172–218.
Holzer, H. F., M. Momenzadeh, and G. Gropp
  1971   Ancient Copper Mines in the Vesnoveh Area,
          Kuhestan-E-Qom, West Central Iran." *Archaeolo-
          gia Austriaca* 49:1–22.
Hood, S.
  1951   "Excavations at Tabara el Akrad." *Anatolian
          Studies* 1:113–47.
Hopke, K., M. A. Evins, and others
  1987   "The Interpretation of Multielemental INAA
          Data Using Pattern Recognition Methods." *Journal
          of Radioanalytical and Nuclear Chemistry*
          112:215–22.
Hout, J.-L.
  1989   "Ubaidian Villages of Lower Mesopotamia."
          In E. F. Henrickson and I. Thuesen, eds., *Upon
          This Foundation—The Ubaid Reconsidered*, pp.
          19–42. Copenhagen: Museum Tusculanum Press.
Hout, J.-L., and C. Maréchal
  1985   "L'emploi du gypse en Mésopotamie du sud à
          l'époque d'Uruk." In J.-L. Hout et al., eds. *De
          L'Indus aux Balkans: Recueil à la mémoire de Jean
          Deshayes*, pp. 261–76. Paris: Éditions Recherche
          sur les Civilisations.
Isodore of Charax
  1914   *Parthian Stations.* Translated by W. H.
          Schoff. Philadelphia: The Commercial Museum.
Jacobs, J.
  1969   *The Economy of Cities.* New York: Vintage.
Jacobsen, T.
  1953   "On the Textile Industry at Ur under Ibbi-
          Sin." Reprinted in W. L. Moran, ed. *Towards the
          Image of Tammuz*, pp. 216–30. Cambridge: Har-
          vard University Press, 1970.
  1957   "Early Political Development in Mesopota-
          mia." *Zeitschrift für Assyriologie* 52:91–140.
Jacobsen, T., and R. McC. Adams
  1958   "Salt and Silt in Ancient Mesopotamian Agri-
          culture." *Science* 128:1251–58.
Jakob-Rost, L.
  1975   *Die Stempelsiegel im Vorderasiatischen Mu-
          seum.* East Berlin: Akademie Verlag.
Jasim, S. A.
  1985   *The Ubaid Period in Iraq.* British Archaeo-
          logical Review, International Series 267. Oxford.
Jasim, S. A., and J. Oates
  1986   "An Archaic Recording System and the Ori-
          gins of Writing." *World Archaeology* 17:348–62.
Johnson, G. A.
  1973   *Local Exchange and Early State Development
          in Southwestern Iran.* Ann Arbor: University of
          Michigan, Museum of Anthropology.
  1976   "Early State Organization in Southwestern
          Iran: Preliminary Field Report." In F. Bagherza-
          deh, ed., *Proceedings of the Fourth Annual Sym-
          posium on Archaeological Research in Iran*, pp.

190–223. Tehran: Iranian Centre for Archaeological Research.

1987   "The Changing Organization of Uruk Administration in the Susiana Plain." In F. Hole, ed., *The Archaeology of Western Iran*, pp. 107–39. Washington, D.C.: Smithsonian Institution Press.

1988/89   "Late Uruk in Greater Mesopotamia: Expansion or Collapse?" *Origini* 14:595–611.

Jones, A. H. M.

1970   "Asian Trade in Antiquity." In D. S. Richards, ed., *Islam and the Trade of Asia*, pp. 1–10. Oxford: Bruno Cassirer.

1971   *Cities of the Eastern Roman Empire*. Oxford: Clarendon Press.

Jordan, J.

1931   "Ausgrabungen in Uruk 1929/30." *Vorläufiger Bericht über die von der Deutschen Forschungsgemeinschaft in Uruk-Warka unternommenen Ausgrabungen* 2:1–55.

1932   "Ausgrabungen in Uruk 1930/31." *Vorläufiger Bericht über die von der Deutschen Forschungsgemeinschaft in Uruk-Warka unternommenen Ausgrabungen* 3:1–37.

Kipp, R. S., and E. M. Schortman

1989   "The Political Impact of Trade in Chiefdoms." *American Anthropologist* 91:370–85.

Kantor, H. J.

1974   "Ägypten." In M. Mellink and J. Filip, eds., *Fruhe Stufen der Kunst*, pp. 227–56. Propyläen Kunst Geschichte, vol. 13. Berlin: Propyläen Verlag.

1992   "The Relative Chronology of Egypt and Its Foreign Correlations before the First Intermediate Period." In R. Ehrich, ed., *Chronologies in Old World Archaeology*, 3d. ed., 1:3–21. Chicago: University of Chicago Press.

Kaplan, J.

1969   "'Ein el Jarba, Chalcolithic Remains in the Plain of Esdraelon." *Bulletin of the American Schools of Oriental Research* 194:2–39.

Killick, R.

1986   "The Eski Mosul Region." In U. Finkbeiner and W. Röllig, eds., *Gamdat Nasr: Period or Regional Style?* pp. 229–43. Beihefte zum Tübinger Atlas des Vorderen Orients, Reihe B, Nr. 62. Weisbaden: Ludwig Reichert.

Kirkby, M. J.

1977   "Land and Water Resources of the Deh Luran and Khuzistan Plains." In F. Hole, *Studies in the Archaeological History of the Deh Luran Plain: The Excavation of Chagha Sefid*, pp. 263–72. Ann Arbor: University of Michigan, Museum of Anthropology.

Kohl, P. L.

1978   "The Balance of Trade in Southwestern Asia in the Third Millenium B.C." *Current Anthropology* 19:463–75.

1979   "The World Economy of West Asia in the Third Millennium B.C." In M. Taddei, ed., *South Asian Archaeology, 1977*, pp. 55–85. Naples: Istituto Universitario Orientale.

1987a   "The Ancient Economy, Transferable Technologies, and the Bronze Age World-System: A View from the Northeastern Frontier of the Ancient Near East." In M. Rowlands et al., eds., *Centre and Periphery in the Ancient World*, pp. 13–24. Cambridge: Cambridge University Press.

1987b   "The Use and Abuse of World Systems Theory: The Case of the Pristine West Asian State." In M. B. Schiffer, ed., *Advances in Archaeological Method and Theory*, vol. 11, pp. 1–36. San Diego: Academic Press.

Kohl, P. L., G. Harbottle, and E. V. Sayre

1979   Physical and Chemical Analyses of Soft Stone Vessels from Southwest Asia." *Archaeometry* 21:131–59.

Kohlmeyer, K.

1985   "Euphrat-Survey: Die mit Mitteln der Gerda Henkel Stiftung durchgeführte archäologische Geländebegehung in syrischen Euphrattal." *Mitteilungen der Deutschen Orient-Gesellschaft* 116:95–118.

Kramer, S. N.

1952   *Enmerkar and the Lord of Aratta*. Philadelphia: The University Museum.

Lamberg-Karlovsky, C. C.

1982   "Sumer, Elam, and the Indus: Three Urban Processes Equal One Structure?" In G. L. Possehl, ed., *Harrapan Civilization: A Contemporary Perspective*, pp. 61–68. New Delhi: Oxford and IBH Publishing.

1985   "The longue dureé of the Ancient Near East." In J.-L. Hout et al., eds., *De L'Indus aux Balkans: Recueil à la mémoire de Jean Deshayes*, pp. 55–72. Paris: Éditions Recherche sur les Civilisations.

1989   "Comments." In G. Algaze, "The Uruk Expansion, Cross-cultural Exchange in Early Mesopotamian Civilization." *Current Anthropology* 30:595–96.

Lamberg-Karlovsky, C. C., and T. W. Beale

1986   *Excavations at Tehpe Yahya, Iran 1967–1975*. Cambridge: Peabody Museum of Archaeology and Ethnology.

Larsen, M. T.

1979   "The Tradition of Empire in Mesopotamia." In M. T. Larsen, ed., *Power and Propaganda*, pp. 75–106. Copenhagen: Akademisk Forlag.

1987   "Commercial Networks in the Ancient Near East." In M. Rowlands, M. T. Larsen, and K. Kristiansen, eds., *Centre and Periphery in the Ancient World*, pp. 47–56. Cambridge: Cambridge University Press.

Le Breton, L.
1957 "The Early Periods at Susa: Mesopotamian Relations." *Iraq* 19:79–124.
Le Brun, A.
1971 "Recherches stratigraphiques à l'Acropole de Suse, 1969–1971." *Cahiers de la Délégation Archéologique Française en Iran* 1:163–216.
1978a "Le niveau 17B de l'Acropole de Suse." *Cahiers de la Délégation Archéologique Française en Iran* 9:57–154.
1978b "La glyptique du Niveau 17B de L'Acropole (campagne de 1972)." *Cahiers de la Délégation Archéologique Française en Iran* 8:61–79.
Le Brun, A., and F. Vallat
1978 "L'origine de l'écriture à Suse." *Cahiers de la Délégation Archéologique Française en Iran* 8:11–60.
Leemans, W. F.
1960 *Foreign Trade in the Old Babylonian Period.* Leiden: E. J. Brill.
Lenzen, H.
1958 "Liste der funde aus dem Riemchengebäude." *Vorläufiger Bericht über die von dem Deutshen Archäologischen Institut und der Deutschen Orient-Gesellschaft aus Mitteln der Deutschen Forschungsgemeinschaft in Uruk-Warka unternommenen Ausgrabungen* 14:30–35.
1959 "Die Grabungen der Westecke von E-anna." *Vorläufiger Bericht über die von dem Deutshen Archäologischen Institut und der Deutschen Orient-Gesellschaft aus Mitteln der Deutschen Forschungsgemeinschaft in Uruk-Warka unternommenen Ausgrabungen* 15:8–19.
1960 "Die Kleinfunde. D. Siegelabrollungen." *Vorläufiger Bericht über die von dem Deutshen Archäologischen Institut und der Deutschen Orient-Gesellschaft aus Mitteln der Deutschen Forschungsgemeinschaft in Uruk-Warka unternommenen Ausgrabungen* 16:48–56.
1961 "Die Kleinfunde. D. Siegelabrollungen auf Tontafeln und Krugverschlüssen." *Vorläufiger Bericht über die von dem Deutshen Archäologischen Institut und der Deutschen Orient-Gesellschaft aus Mitteln der Deutschen Forschungsgemeinschaft in Uruk-Warka unternommenen Ausgrabungen* 17:29–36.
1964 "Die Siegelabrollungen." *Vorläufiger Bericht über die von dem Deutshen Archäologischen Institut und der Deutschen Orient-Gesellschaft aus Mitteln der Deutschen Forschungsgemeinschaft in Uruk-Warka unternommenen Ausgrabungen* 20:22–23.
1965 "Amulette." *Vorläufiger Bericht über die von dem Deutshen Archäologischen Institut und der Deutschen Orient-Gesellschaft aus Mitteln der Deutschen Forschungsgemeinschaft in Uruk-Warka unternommenen Ausgrabungen* 21:32.

Levine, L.
1973 "Geographical Studies in the Neo Assyrian Zagros I." *Iran* 11:1–28.
1974a "Geographical Studies in the Neo Assyrian Zagros II." *Iran* 12:99–124.
1974b "Archaeological Investigations in the Mahidasht, Western Iran—1975." *Paléorient* 2:487–90.
Levine, L., and T. C. Young, Jr.
1987 "A Summary of Ceramic Assemblages of the Central Western Zagros from the Middle Neolithic to the Late Third Millennium B.C." In J.-L. Hout, ed. *Préhistoire de la Mésopotamie,* pp. 15–54. Paris: Centre National de la Recherche Scientifique.
Lightfoot, C. S.
1983 "The Site of Roman Bezabde." In S. Mitchell, ed., *Armies and Frontiers in Roman and Byzantine Anatolia,* pp. 189–204. British Archaeological Review, International Series 156. Oxford.
1986 "Tilli—A Late Roman Equites Fort on the Tigris." In P. Freeman and D. Kennedy, eds., *The Defense of the Roman and Byzantine East,* pp. 509–29. British Archaeological Review, International Series 297. Oxford.
Lloyd, S.
1938 "Some Ancient Sites in the Sinjar District." *Iraq* 5:123–42.
1940 "Iraq Government Soundings at Sinjar." *Iraq* 7:13–21.
Lloyd, S., and F. Safar
1943 "Tell Uqair, Excavations by the Iraq Government Directorate of Antiquities in 1940 and 1941." *Journal of Near Eastern Studies* 2:131–58.
Ludwig, W.
1979 "Mass, Sitte, und Technik des Bauens in Habuba Kabira-süd." In J.-Cl. Margueron, ed., *Le Moyen Euphrate: Zone de contacts et d'échanges,* pp. 63–74. Leiden: E. J. Brill.
McDonald, M.
1986 "The Chipped Stone Sequence." In L. Marfoe et al., "The Chicago Euphrates Archaeological Project 1980–1984: An Interim Report." *Anatolica* 13:60–66
Maeda, T.
1984 "'King of the Four Regions' in the Dynasty of Akkade." *Orient* 20:67–82.
Maekawa, K.
1980 "Female Weavers and Their Children in Lagash—Presargonic and Ur III." *Acta Sumerologica* 2:81–125.
Majidzadeh, Y.
1976a "The Early Prehistoric Cultures of the Central Plateau in Iran: An Archeological History of Its Development during the Fifth and Fourth Millennia B.C." Ph.D. dissertation, Department of Near Eastern Languages and Civilizations, University of Chicago.

1976b "Land of Aratta." *Journal of Near Eastern Studies* 36:105–13.

1979 "An Early Prehistoric Coppersmith Workshop at Tepe Gabrestan." *Archäologische Mitteilungen aus Iran, Ergänzungsband* 6:82–92.

1982 "Lapis Lazuli and the Great Khorasan Road." *Paléorient* 8:59–70.

Malbran-Labat, F.

1982 *L'armee et l'organisation militaire de l'Assyrie: d'apres les letres des Sargonides trouvees a Ninive.* Geneva: Droz.

Mallowan, M. E. L.

1947 "Excavations at Brak and Chagar Bazar." *Iraq* 9:1–87.

Marschner, R. F., and H. T. Wright

1978 "Asphalts from Middle Eastern Archaeological Sites." In G. F. Carter, ed., *Archaeological Chemistry II*. pp. 150–71. Washington, D.C.: American Chemistry Association.

Marfoe, L.

1987 "Cedar Forest to Silver Mountain: Social Change and the Development of Long-Distance Trade in Early Near Eastern Societies. In M. Rowlands et al., eds., *Centre and Periphery in the Ancient World*, pp. 25–35. Cambridge: Cambridge University Press.

Margueron, J.-Cl.

1992 "Le bois dans l'architecture." *Bulletin on Summerian Agriculture* 6:79–96.

Matthers, J., ed.

1981 *The River Qoueiq, Northern Syria, and Its Catchment.* British Archaeological Review, International Series 98. Oxford.

Matthiae, P.

1980 *Ebla: An Empire Rediscovered.* London: Hodder and Stoughton.

Maxwell-Hyslop, K. R.

1977 "Sources of Sumerian Gold." *Iraq* 39:83–86.

Meijer, D. K.

1986 *A Survey of Northeastern Syria.* Leiden: Dutch Archaeological Institute in Istanbul.

1988 "Tell Hammam: Architecture and Stratigraphy." In M. N. van Loon, ed., *Hammam et Turkman I: Report of the University of Amsterdam's 1981–1984 Excavations in Syria*, pp. 69–128. Leiden: Dutch Archaeological Institute in Istanbul.

Mellaart, J.

1981 "The Prehistoric Pottery from the Neolithic to the Beginning of the E.B. IV." In J. Matthers, ed., *The River Qoueiq, Northern Syria, and Its Catchment*, pp. 131–319. British Archaeological Review, International Series 98. Oxford.

Mellink, M.

1988 "Archaeology in Asia Minor, Samsat." *American Journal of Archaeology* 92:110.

1989 "Archaeology in Asia Minor, Samsat." *American Journal of Archaeology* 93:114.

Métral, F.

1987 "Périmetrès irrigués d'État sur l'Euphrate syrien: Modes de gestion et politique agricole." In P. Louis, F. Métral, and J. Métral, eds., *L' homme et l'eau en Méditerranée et au Proche Orient*, pp. 111–45. Paris: Maison de l'Orient.

Meyer, C.

1981 "Stone Artifacts from Tutub, Eshnunna, and Nippur." Ph.D. dissertation, Department of Near Eastern Languages and Civilizations, University of Chicago.

Miller, K.

1962 *Die Peutingersche Tafel.* Suttgart: Brockhaus.

Millon, R.

1981 "Teotihuacán: City, State, and Civilization." In V. R. Bricker and J. A. Sabloff, eds., *Supplement to the Handbook of Middle American Indians*. Vol. 1: *Archaeology*, pp. 198–243. Austin: University of Texas Press.

Mintz, S.

1985 *Sweetness and Power: The Place of Sugar in Modern History.* New York: Viking.

Monchambert, J.-Y.

1984 "Prospection archéologique sur l'emplacement du futur lac du Moyen Khabour." *Akkadica* 39:1–7.

Moorey, P. R. S.

1985 *Materials and Manufacture in Ancient Mesopotamia: The Evidence of Archaeology and Art.* British Archaeological Review, International Series 237. Oxford.

Moortgat, A.

1969 *The Art of Ancient Mesopotamia.* London: Phaidon.

Mortensen, P.

1976 "Chalcolithic Settlements in the Holailan Valley." In F. Bagherzadeh, ed., *Proceedings of the Fourth Annual Symposium on Archaeological Research in Iran*, pp. 42–62. Tehran: Iranian Centre for Archaeological Research.

Mujica, E.

1985 "Altiplano-Coast Relationships in the South-Central Andes: From Indirect to Direct Complementarity." In S. Masuda, I. Shimada, and C. Morris, eds., *Andean Ecology and Civilization*, pp. 103–40. Tokyo: University of Tokyo Press.

Musil, A.

1927 *The Middle Euphrates.* New York: American Geographical Society.

Nissen, H.-J.

1970 "Grabung in den Planquadraten K/L XII in Uruk-Warka." *Baghdader Mitteilungen* 5:101–92.

1972 "Typological Dating Criteria." In R. McC. Adams and H.-J. Nissen. *The Uruk Countryside*, pp. 97–104. Chicago: University of Chicago Press.

1976 "Zur Frage der Arbeitsorganisation in Babylonien während der Spät-uruk-Zeit." In J. Harmatta and G. Komaróczy, eds., *Wirschaft und Gesellschaft in Alten Vorderasien,* pp. 5–14. Budapest: Akadémiai Kiadó.

1977   "Aspects of the Development of Early Cylinder Seals." In McG. Gibson and R. Biggs, eds., *Seals and Sealings in the Ancient Near East,* pp. 15–24. Malibu: Undena.

1983   "Political Organization and Settled Zone." In T. C. Young, Jr., et al., eds., *The Hilly Flanks and Beyond,* pp. 335–46. Studies in Ancient Oriental Civilization 36. Chicago: Oriental Institute.

1985a   "Problems of the Uruk-Period in Susiana, Viewed from Uruk." *Paléorient* 11:39–40.

1985b   "The Emergence of Writing in the Ancient Near East." *Interdisciplinary Science Reviews* 10:349–61.

1986a   "The Archaic Texts from Uruk." *World Archaeology* 17:317–34.

1986b   "The Development of Writing and Glyptic Art." In U. Finkbeiner and W. Röllig, eds., *Gamdat Nasr: Period or Regional Style?* pp. 316–31. Beihefte zum Tübinger Atlas des Vorderen Orients, Reihe B, Nr. 62. Weisbaden: Ludwig Reichert.

Nützel, W.
1976   "The Climate Changes of Mesopotamia and Bordering Areas." *Sumer* 32:11–24.

Oates, D.
1968   *Studies in the Ancient History of Northern Iraq.* London: Oxford University Press.

1977   "The Excavations at Tell Brak, 1976." *Iraq* 39:233–44.

1982   "Recent Excavations in Northern Mesopotamia: Tell el Rimah and Tell Brak." *Bulletin of the Society for Mesopotamian Studies* 4:7–23.

1983   "Excavations at Tell Brak, 1978–81." *Iraq* 44:187–204.

1985   "Excavations at Tell Brak, 1983–84." *Iraq* 47:159–73.

Oates, J.
1983   "Ubaid Mesopotamia Reconsidered." In T. Cuyler Young, Jr., et al., eds., *The Hilly Flanks and Beyond,* pp. 251–82. Studies in Ancient Oriental Civilization 36. Chicago: Oriental Institute.

1985   "Tell Brak: Uruk Pottery from the 1984 Season." *Iraq* 47:175–86.

1986   "Tell Brak: The Uruk/Early Dynastic Sequence." In U. Finkbeiner and W. Röllig, eds., *Gamdat Nasr: Period or Regional Style?* pp. 245–73. Beihefte zum Tübinger Atlas des Vorderen Orients, Reihe B, Nr. 62. Weisbaden: Ludwig Reichert.

Oppenheim, A. L.
1976   "Trade in the Ancient Near East." *International Congress of Economic History V,* pp. 126–47. (Leningrad 1970). Moscow: Nauka.

Oren, E.
1989   "Early Bronze Age Settlement in Northern Sinai: A Model for Egypto-Canaanite Interconnections." In P. de Miroschedji, ed., *L'urbanization de la Palestine à l'âge du Bronze Ancien,* pp. 389–405. British Archaeological Review, International Series 527. Oxford.

Orthmann, W.
1986   "The Origins of Tell Chuera." In H. Weiss, ed., *The Origins of Cities in Dry-Farming Syria and Mesopotamia in the Third Millennium B.C.,* pp. 61–70. Connecticut: Four Quarters Publishing.

Özdoğan, M.
1977   *Lower Euphrates Basin Survey, 1977.* Istanbul: Middle Eastern Technical University.

Özgüç, N.
1987   "Samsat Mühürleri." *Belleten* 200: 429–40.

Özten, A.
1984   "Two Pots Recovered in the Excavations at Samsat Belonging to the Late Chalcolithic Period." *Anadolu* 20 (1976/77): 267–71.

Palmieri, A.
1973   "Scavi nell'area sud-occidentale di Arslantepe." *Origini* 7:55–179.

1981   "Excavations at Arslantepe (Malatya)." *Anatolian Studies* 31:101–19.

1985   "1984 Excavations at Arslantepe." *VII. Kazı Sonuçları Toplantısı,* pp. 29–36. Ankara: Eski Eserler ve Müzeler Genel Müdürlüğü.

1989   "Storage and Distribution at Arslantepe-Malatya in the Late Uruk Period." In K. Emre et al., eds., *Anatolia and the Ancient Near East: Studies in Honor of Tahsin Özgüç,* pp. 419–29. Ankara: Türk Tarih Kurumu.

Parpola S.; A. Parpola, and R. Brunswig,
1977   "The Melluhha Village: Evidence of Acculturation of Harrapan Traders in Late Third Millennium Mesopotamia?" *Journal of the Economic and Social History of the Orient* 20:129–65.

Paynter, R.
1981   "Social Complexity in Peripheries: Problems and Models." In S. E. van der Leeuw, ed., *Archaeological Approaches to the Study of Complexity,* pp. 118–43. Amsterdam: University of Amsterdam.

Pettinato, G.
1972   Il commercio con l'estero della Mesopotamia meridionale nel 3.millennio av.Cr. alla luce delle fonti letterarie e lessicali sumeriche. *Mesopotamia* 7:43–166.

1991   *Ebla: A New Look at History.* Baltimore: Johns Hopkins University Press.

Pfälzner, P.
1984   "Eine archäologische Geländebegehung in Gebiet des Wadi ʿAgig/Ost syrien." *Archiv für Orientforschung* 31:178–84.

Poidebard, A.
1934 *La trace de Rome dans le désert de Syrie.* Paris: Geuthner.

Poidebard, A., and R. Mouterde
1945 *Le Limes de Chalcis.* Paris: Geuthner.

Polanyi, K.
1957 "The Economy as Instituted Process." In K. Polanyi et al., eds. *Trade and Market in the Early Empires,* pp. 243–69. Chicago: Henry Regnery.
1975 "Traders and Trade." In J. A. Sabloff and C. C. Lamberg-Karlovsky, eds., *Ancient Civilization and Trade,* pp. 133–54. Albuquerque: University of New Mexico Press.

Possehl, G. L.
1980 *Indus Civilization in Saurashtra.* New Delhi: B. R. Publishing.
1986 *Kulli: An Exploration of Ancient Civilization in Asia.* Durham: Carolina Academic Press.

Postgate, J. N.
1986 "The Transition from the Uruk to the Early Dynastic: Continuities and Discontinuities in the Record of Settlement." In U. Finkbeiner and W. Röllig, eds., *Gamdat Nasr: Period or Regional Style?* pp. 90–106. Beihefte zum Tübinger Atlas des Vorderen Orients, Reihe B, Nr. 62. Weisbaden: Ludwig Reichert.

Powell, M.
1977 "Sumerian Merchants and the Problem of Profit." *Iraq* 39:23–30.
1985 "Salt, Seed, and Yields in Sumerian Agriculture: A Critique of the Theory of Progressive Salinization." *Zeitschrift für Assyriologie* 75:7–38.

Reade, J.
1968 "Tell Taya 1967: A Summary Report." *Iraq* 30:234–64.

Reimer, S.
1989 "Tell Qraya on the Middle Euphrates." In M. Rothman, ed., "Out of the Heartland: The Evolution of Complexity in Peripheral Mesopotamia during the Uruk Period, Workshop Summary." *Paléorient* 15:273.

Renfrew, C.
1975 "Trade as Action at a Distance: Questions of Integration and Communication." In J. A. Sabloff and C. C. Lamberg-Karlovsky, eds., *Ancient Civilization and Trade,* pp. 3–60. Albuquerque: University of New Mexico Press.

Renfrew, C., and J. Dixon
1976 "Obsidian in Western Asia: A Review." In G. de G. Sieveking, I. H. Longworth, and K. E. Wilson, eds., *Problems in Economic and Social Archaeology,* pp. 137–52. London: Duckworth.

Robinson, R.
1976 "Non-European Foundations of European Imperialism: Sketch for a Theory of Collaboration." Reprinted in Wm. Roger Louis, ed., *Imperialism: The Gallagher and Robinson Controversy,* pp. 128–52. New York: Franklin Watts.

Röllig, W., and H. Kühne
1977/78 "The Lower Habur: A Preliminary Report on a Survey Conducted by the Tübinger Atlas des Vorderen Orients in 1975." *Annales Archéologiques Arabes Syriennes* 27/28:115–40.

Rosen, S.
1983 "Tabular Scrapper Trade: A Model of Material Culture Dispersion." *Bulletin of the American Schools of Oriental Research* 249:79–86.

Rostovseff, M.
1972 *The Social and Economic History of The Hellenistic World.* Oxford: Clarendon Press.

Rothman, M. S.
1988 "Centralization, Administration, and Function at Fourth Millennium B.C. Tepe Gawra, Northern Iraq." Ph.D. dissertation, Department of Anthropology, University of Pennsylvania.

Rowton, R.
1967 "The Woodlands of Ancient Western Asia." *Journal of Near Eastern Studies* 26:261–77.

Safar, F., S. Lloyd, and M. A. Mustafa
1981 *Eridu.* Baghdad: State Organization of Antiquities and Heritage.

Sanders, W. T.
1977 "Ethnographic Analogy and the Teotihuacán Horizon Style." In W. T. Sanders and J. W. Michels, eds., *Teotihuacán and Kaminaljuyú,* pp. 397–410. University Park: Pennsylvania State University Press.

Sanlaville, P., ed.
1985 *Holocene Settlement in Northern Syria.* British Archaeological Review, International Series 238. Oxford.

Santley, R. S.
1989 "Obsidian Working, Long-Distance Exchange, and the Teotihuacán Presence on the South Gulf Coast." In R. A. Diehl and J. C. Berlo, eds., *Mesoamerica after the Decline of Teotihuacán, A.D. 700–900,* pp. 131–52. Washington, D.C.: Dumbarton Oaks.

Scammell, G. V.
1980 "Indigenous Assistance in the Establishment of Portuguese Power in Asia in the Sixteenth Century." *Modern Asian Studies* 14:1–11.
1989 *The First Imperial Age.* London: Unwin Hyman.

Schmidt, J.
1978a "Anu-Zikkurrat." *Vorläufiger Bericht über die von dem Deutschen Archäologischen Institut und der Deutschen Orient-Gesellschaft aus Mitteln der Deutschen Forschungsgemeinschaft in Uruk-Warka unternommenen Ausgrabungen* 28:19–23.
1978b "Tell Mismar: Ein Prähistorischer Fundort in Südiraq." *Baghdader Mitteilungen* 9:10–17.
1979 "Steingebäude." *Vorläufiger Bericht über die von dem Deutschen Archäologischen Institut und der Deutschen Orient-Gesellschaft aus Mitteln der*

Deutschen Forschungsgemeinschaft in Uruk-Warka unternommenen Ausgrabungen 29/30:13–25.

Schmandt-Besserat, D.
1977   "An Archaic Recording System and the Origins of Writing." *Syro-Mesopotamian Studies* 1:2.
1986   "Tokens at Susa." *Oriens Antiquus* 25:93–125.

Schneider, J.
1977   "Was There a Pre-Capitalist World-System?" *Peasant Studies* 6:20–29.

Schott, E.
1933   "Die siegelbilder der Uruk-Schicht IV." *Vorläufiger Bericht über die von den Notgemeinschaft der Deutschen Wissenschaft in Uruk-Warka unternommenen Ausgrabungen* 5:42–54.

Schwartz, G.
1987   "The Ninevite V Period and the Development of Complex Society in Northern Mesopotamia." *Paléorient* 13:93–100.
1988a   "Excavation at Karatut Mevkii and Perspectives on the Uruk/Jemdet Nasr Expansion." *Akkadica* 56:1–42.
1988b   *A Ceramic Chronology from Tell Leilan: Operation 1.* New Haven: Yale University Press.
1989   "Comments." In G. Algaze, "The Uruk Expansion, Cross-cultural Exchange in Early Mesopotamian Civilization." *Current Anthropology* 30:596–97.

Seeliger, T. C., E. Pernicka, G. A. Wagner, F. Begemann, S. Schmitt-Strecker, C. Eibner, Ö. Öztunali, and Istvan Beranyi
1985   "Archäometallurgische Untersuchungen in Nord- und Ostanatolien." *Jahrbuch des Römisch-Germanischen Zentralmuseums Mainz* 32:597–659.

Service, E.
1962   *Primitive Social Organization.* New York: Random House.

Semple, E. C.
1930   *The Geography of the Mediterranean Region.* New York: Henry Holt.

Simpson, K.
1983   "Stability and Change along the Middle Euphrates, Syria." Ph.D. dissertation, Department of Anthropology, University of Arizona.
1988   "Qraya Modular Reports, No. 1: Early Soundings." *Syro-Mesopotamian Studies* 4:4.

Smith, C. A.
1976   "Exchange Systems and the Spatial Distribution of Elites: The Organization of Stratification in Agrarian Societies." In C. A. Smith, ed., *Regional Analysis,* vol. 2, pp. 309–74. New York: Academic Press.

Smith, P. E. L., and T. C. Young, Jr.
1972   "The Evolution of Early Agriculture and Culture in Greater Mesopotamia: A Trial Model." In

B. Spooner, ed., *Population Growth: Anthropological Implications,* pp. 1–59. Cambridge: MIT Press.

Söylemez, M., and C. S. Lightfoot
1991   "The Tigris-Euphrates Archaeological Reconnaissance Project Numismatic Notes." In C. S. Lightfoot, ed., *Recent Turkish Coin Hoards and Numismatic Studies,* pp. 313–31. Oxford: Oxbow Books.

Speiser, E. A.
1935   *Excavations at Tepe Gawra,* vol. 1. Philadelphia: University of Pennsylvania Press.

Spuler, B.
1970   "Trade in the Eastern Islamic Countries." In D. S. Richards, ed., *Islam and the Trade of Asia,* pp. 11–20. Oxford: Bruno Cassirer.

Stager, L.
1992   "The Periodization of Palestine from Neolithic to Early Bronze Times." In R. Ehrich, ed., *Chronologies in Old World Archaeology,* 3d. ed., 1:22–41. Chicago: University of Chicago Press.

Stark, F.
1966   *Rome on the Euphrates.* London: John Murray.

Starr, R. F. S.
1939.   *Nuzi.* Cambridge: Harvard University Press.

Stech, T., and V. C. Piggot
1986   "The Metals Trade in Southwest Asia in the Third Millennium B.C." *Iraq* 48:39–64.

Stein, A.
1936   "An Archaeological Tour in the Ancient Persis." *Iraq* 3:111–225.
1937   *Archaeological Reconnaissances in North-Western India and South-Eastern Iran.* London: Macmillan.
1940   *Old Routes of Western Iran.* London: Macmillan.

Steve, M.-J., and H. Gasche
1971   *L'Acropole de Suse.* Mémoires de la délégation archéologique française en Iran 46. Paris: Geuthner.

Strabo
1966   *Geography.* Edited by H. L. Jones. Cambridge: Harvard University Press.

Strommenger, E.
1962   *Fünf Jahrtausende Mesopotamien.* Munich: Hirmer Verlag.
1980a   *Habuba Kabira: Eine Stadt vor 5000 Jahren.* Mainz am Rhein: Phillip von Zabern.
1980b   "The Chronological Division of the Archaic Levels of Uruk-Eanna VI to III/II: Past to Present." *American Journal of Archaeology* 84:477–87.

Stucky, R., P. Bridel, C. Krause, H.-P. Spycher, P. Suter, and S. Zellweger
1974   *Tell el Hajj: Zweiter Vorläufiger Bericht.* Bern: Universität Bern.

Sumner, W.
   1977   "Early Settlement in Fars Province, Iran." In
          L. D. Levine and T. C. Young, Jr., eds., *Moun-
          tains and Lowlands: Essays in the Archaeology of
          Greater Mesopotamia*, pp. 291–306. Malibu: Un-
          dena.
   1986   "Proto-Elamite Civilization in Fars." In U.
          Finkbeiner and W. Röllig, eds., *Gamdat Nasr: Pe-
          riod or Regional Style?* pp. 199–211. Beihefte
          zum Tübinger Atlas des Vorderen Orients, Reihe
          B, Nr. 62. Weisbaden: Ludwig Reichert.
Sürenhagen, D.
   1974/75 "Untersuchungen zur Keramikproduction
          innerhalb der Spät-Uruklichen siedlung Habuba
          Kabira-süd in Nord Syrien." *Acta Praehistorica et
          Archaeologica* 5/6:43–164.
   1985   "Einige Kulturelle Kontakte zwischen Arslan-
          tepe VI.A und den Frühsumerisch-hochproto-
          elamischen Stadkulturen." In M. Liverani, A. Pal-
          mieri, and R. Peroni, eds., *Studi di Paletnologia in
          onore di Salvatori M. Puglisi*, pp. 229–36. Rome:
          Università di Roma "La Sapienza".
   1986a "The Dry-Farming Belt: The Uruk Period
          and Subsequent Developments." In H. Weiss, ed.,
          *The Origins of Cities in Dry-Farming Syria and
          Mesopotamia in the Third Millennium* B.C., pp.
          7–43. Gulford: Four Quarters Publishing.
   1986b "Archaische Keramik aus Uruk-Warka. Ers-
          ter Teil: Die Keramik der Schichten XVI–VI aus
          den Sondagen 'Tiefschnitt' und 'Sagengraben' in
          Eanna." *Baghdader Mitteilungen* 17:7–96.
Tarn, W. W.
   1938   *The Greeks in Bactria and India.* Cambridge:
          Cambridge University Press.
Tefnin, R.
   1979   "Deux campagnes de fouilles au Tell Abou
          Danné, 1975–76." In J.-Cl. Margueron, ed., *Le
          Moyen Euphrate: Zone de contacts et d'échanges*,
          pp. 179–99. Leiden: E. J. Brill.
Terray, M.
   1974   "Long-Distance Exchange and the Formation
          of the State: The Case of the Abron Kingdom of
          Gyaman." *Economy and Society* 3:315–45.
Teissier, B.
   1984   *Ancient Near Eastern Cylinder Seals from the
          Marcopoli Collection.* Los Angeles: University of
          California Press.
   1987   "Glyptic Evidence for a Connection between
          Iran, Syro-Palestine, and Egypt in the Fourth and
          Third Millennia." *Iran* 25:27–54.
Thissen, L. C.
   1985   "The Late Chalcolithic and Early Bronze Age
          Pottery from Hayaz Höyük." *Anatolica* 12:76–130.
Thuesen, I.
   1988   *Hama, Fouilles, et Recherches, 1931–1938.*
          Vol. 1: *The Pre- and Protohistoric Periods.* Co-
          penhagen: Nationalmuseet.

Tobler, A. J.
   1950   *Excavations at Tepe Gawra*, vol. 2. Philadel-
          phia: The University Museum.
Töpperwein, E.
   1973   "Kleinfunde." In E. Heinrich et al. "Vierter
          Vorläufiger Bericht über die von der Deutschen
          Orient-Gesellschaft mit mitteln ser Stiftung
          Volkswagenwerk in Habuba Kabira und in Mum-
          baqat unternommenen archäologischen Untersu-
          chungen, erstattet von Mitgliedern der Mission."
          Mitteilungen der Deutschen Orient-Gesellschaft
          105:20–32.
Tunca, Ö.
   1979   "Catalogue des sceaux-cylindres du musée re-
          gional d'Adana." *Syro-Mesopotamian Studies* 3:1.
Vaiman, A. A.
   1976   "Über die Protosumerische schrift." In J.
          Harmatta and G. Komaróczy, eds., *Wirschaft und
          Gesellschaft in Alten Vorderasien*, pp. 15–27.
          Budapest: Akadémiai Kiadó.
Vallat, F.
   1986   "The Most Ancient Scripts of Iran: The Cur-
          rent Situation." *World Archaeology* 17:336–47.
van Driel, G.
   1982   "Tablets from Jebel Aruda." In G. van Driel
          et al., eds., *Zikir Sumin: Assyriological Studies
          Presented to F. R. Kraus*, pp. 12–25. Leiden: E. J.
          Brill.
   1983   "Seals and Sealings from Jebel Aruda, 1974–
          1978." *Akkadica* 33:34–62.
van Driel, G., and C. van Driel-Murray
   1979   "Jebel Aruda, 1977–78." *Akkadica* 12:2–8.
   1983   "Jebel Aruda, the 1982 Season of Excava-
          tions." *Akkadica* 33:1–26.
van Liere, W. J., and J. Laufrey
   1954/55 "Nouvelle prospection archéologique dans
          la Haute Jezireh Syrienne." *Annales Archéolo-
          giques Arabes Syriennes* 4/5:128–48.
van Loon, M. N.
   1967   *The Tabqa Reservoir Survey 1964.* Damas-
          cus: Directorate General of Antiquities and Mu-
          seums.
   1968   "The Oriental Institute's Excavations at Mu-
          reybit, Syria: Preliminary Report on the 1965
          Campaign." *Journal of near Eastern Studies*
          27:265–90.
   1978   "Architecture and Stratigraphy." In M. N.
          van Loon, ed., *Korucutepe II*, pp. 3–46. Amster-
          dam: North Holland.
   1983   "Hammam et Turkman on the Balikh: First
          Results of the University of Amsterdam's 1982 Ex-
          cavations." *Akkadica* 35:1–23.
van Loon, M. N., ed.
   1988   *Hammam et Turkman I: Report of the Univer-
          sity of Amsterdam's 1981–1984 Excavations in
          Syria.* Leiden: Dutch Archaeological Institute in
          Istanbul.

van Zeist, W., and S. Bottema
  1982 "Vegetational History of the Eastern Mediter-
         ranean and the Near East during the Last 20,000
         Years." In J. L. Bintliff and W. van Zeist, eds.,
         *Paleoclimates, Paleoenvironments, and Human
         Communities in the Eastern Mediterranean Region
         in Later Prehistory,* pp. 277–321. British Archaeo-
         logical Review, International Series 133. Oxford.
von Haller, A.
  1932 "Die Keramik der archäischen Schichten von
         Uruk." *Vorläufiger Bericht über die von der
         Deutschen Forschungsgemeinschaft in Uruk-Warka
         unternommenen Ausgrabungen* 4:38–42.
Waetzoldt, H.
  1972 *Untersuchungen zur neusumerischen Textil-
         industrie.* Rome: Centro per le Antichità e la Sto-
         ria dell'Arte del Vicino Oriente.
Wagner, J.
  1976 *Seleukeia am Euphrat/Zeugma.* Weisbaden:
         Ludwig Reichert.
Wallerstein, I.
  1974 *The Modern World System,* vol. 1. New
         York: Academic Press.
Watson, P. J., and S. A. Leblanc
  1971 "A Comparative Statistical Analysis of
         Painted Pottery from Seven Halaf Sites." *Paléo-
         rient* 1:117–33.
Wattenmaker, P.
  1990 "On the Uruk Expansion." *Current Anthro-
         pology* 31:67–68.
Wattenmaker, P., and G. Stein
  1989 "Leilan 1987 Survey: Uruk Summary." In M.
         Rothman, ed., "Out of the Heartland: The Evolu-
         tion of Complexity in Peripheral Mesopotamia dur-
         ing the Uruk Period, Workshop Summary." *Paléo-
         rient* 15:272–73.
Weiss, H.
  1977 "Periodization, Population, and Early State
         Formation in Khuzestan." In L. D. Levine and
         T. C. Young, Jr., eds., *Mountains and Lowlands:
         Essays in the Archaeology of Greater Mesopota-
         mia,* pp. 347–70. Malibu: Undena.
  1983 "Excavations at Tell Leilan and the Origins of
         North Mesopotamian Cities in the Third Millen-
         nium B.C." *Paléorient* 9:39–52.
  1986 "The Origins of Tell Leilan and the Conquest
         of Space in Third Millennium North Mesopota-
         mia." In H. Weiss, ed., *The Origins of Cities in
         Dry-Farming Syria and Mesopotamia in the Third
         Millennium B.C.,* pp. 71–108. Connecticut: Four
         Quarters Publishing.
  1989 "Comments." In G. Algaze, "The Uruk Ex-
         pansion: Cross-cultural Exchange in Early Meso-
         potamian Civilization." *Current Anthropology*
         30:597–98.
Weiss, H., ed.
  1985 *Ebla to Damascus: Art and Archaeology of

Ancient Syria.* Washington, D.C.: Smithsonian
         Institution.
Weiss, H., and T. C. Young, Jr.
  1975 "The Merchants of Susa: Godin V and
         Plateau-Lowland Relations in the Late Fourth Mil-
         lennium B.C." *Iran* 13:1–18.
Wertime, T. A.
  1973 "The Beginnings of Metallurgy: A New
         Look." *Science* 182:875–87.
Westenholz, A.
  1979 "The Old Akkadian Empire in Contemporary
         Opinion." In M. T. Larsen, ed., *Power and Propa-
         ganda,* pp. 107–24. Copenhagen: Akademisk
         Forlag.
  1984 "The Sargonic Period." In A. Archi, ed., *Cir-
         culation of Goods in Non-Palatial Context in the
         Ancient Near East,* pp. 17–30. Rome: Edizioni
         Dell'Ateneo.
Wenke, R. J.
  1989 "Egypt, Origins of Complex Societies."
         Annual Review of Anthropology 18:129–55.
Whallon, R.
  1979 *An Archaeological Survey of the Keban Res-
         ervoir Area of East Central Turkey.* Ann Arbor:
         Museum of Anthropology, University of Michigan.
Wheatley, P.
  1975 "Satyanrta in Suvarnadvipa: From Reciproc-
         ity to Redistribution in Ancient Southeast Asia."
         In J. A. Sabloff and C. C. Lamberg-Karlovsky,
         eds., *Ancient Civilization and Trade,* pp.
         227–83. Albuquerque: University of New Mexico
         Press.
Whittaker, C. R.
  1978 "Cartagenian Imperialism in the Fifth and
         Fourth Centuries." In P. D. A. Garnsey and C. R.
         Whittaker, eds., *Imperialism in the Ancient World,*
         pp. 59–90. Cambridge: Cambridge University
         Press.
Whitehouse, D., and R. Williamson
  1973 "Sasanian Maritime Trade." *Iran* 11:29–50.
Wilcke, Cl.
  1969 *Das Lugalband Epos.* Weisbaden: Otto Har-
         rassowits.
Wilkinson, T. J.
  1990a *Town and Country in Early Southeastern
          Anatolia.* Vol. 1: *Settlement and Land Use in the
          Lower Karababa Basin.* Oriental Institute Publica-
          tions 109. Chicago: Oriental Institute.
  1990b "The Development of Settlement in the
          North Jazira Region between the Seventh and First
          Millennia B.C." *Iraq* 52:49–62.
Willcox, G. H.
  1974 "A History of Deforestation as Indicated by
         Charcoal Analysis of Four Sites in Eastern Anato-
         lia." *Anatolian Studies* 24:116–33.
  1992 "Timber and Trees." *Bulletin on Sumerian
         Agriculture* 6:1–31.

Wilson, K. L.
1986 "Nippur: The Definition of a Mesopotamian Gemdat Nasr Assemblage." In U. Finkbeiner and W. Röllig, eds., *Gamdat Nasr: Period or Regional Style?* pp. 57–89. Beihefte zum Tübinger Atlas des Vorderen Orients, Reihe B, Nr. 62. Weisbaden: Ludwig Reichert.

Wirth, E.
1971 *Syrien: Eine Geographische Landeskunde.* Darmstadt: Wissenschaftliche Buchgesellschaft.

Wiseman, D. J.
1962 *Catalogue of the Western Asiatic Seals in the British Museum,* vol. 1. London: British Museum.

Woolley, L.
1921 *Carchemish II: The Town Defenses.* London: British Museum.
1952 *Carchemish III: The Excavations in the Inner Town.* London: British Museum.
1953 *A Forgotten Kingdom.* Baltimore: Penguin.
1955a *Ur Excavations IV: The Early Periods.* Philadelphia: The University Museum.
1955b *Alalakh.* Oxford: Oxford University Press.

Wright, G. A.
1969 *Obsidian Analyses and Prehistoric Near Eastern Trade: 7500–3500 B.C.* Ann Arbor: University of Michigan, Museum of Anthropology.

Wright, H. E.
1955 "Geologic Aspects of the Archaeology of Iraq." *Sumer* 11:83–92.

Wright, H. T.
1972 "A Consideration of Interregional Exchange in Greater Mesopotamia, 4000–3000 B.C." In E. Wilmsen, ed., *Social Exchange and Interaction,* pp. 95–105. Ann Arbor: University of Michigan, Museum of Anthropology.
1981a "Conclusions." In H. T. Wright, ed., *An Early Town on the Deh Luran Plain: Excavations at Tepe Farukhabad,* pp. 262–79. Ann Arbor: University of Michigan, Museum of Anthropology.
1981b "The Southern Margins of Sumer: Archaeological Survey of the Area of Eridu and Ur." Appendix to R. McC. Adams, *Heartland of Cities,* pp. 295–346. Chicago: University of Chicago Press.
1984a "Prestate Political Formations." In T. Earle, ed., *On the Evolution of Complex Societies: Essays in Honor of Harry Hoijer,* pp. 41–78. Malibu: Undena.
1984b "Excavations of Fourth Millennium Levels on the Northern Acropolis of Susa, 1978." *National Geographic Research Reports* 19:725–34.
1986 "The Evolution of Civilizations." In D. J. Meltzer et al., eds., *American Archaeology Past and Future,* pp. 323–68. Washington, D.C.: Smithsonian Institution.
1987 "The Susiana Hinterlands during the Era of Primary State Formation." In F. Hole, ed., *The Archaeology of Western Iran,* pp. 141–56. Washington, D.C.: Smithsonian Institution.

Wright, H. T., ed.
1979 *Archaeological Investigations in Northeastern Xuzestan, 1976.* Ann Arbor: Museum of Anthropology, University of Michigan.

Wright, H. T., and G. A. Johnson
1975 "Population, Exchange, and Early State Formation in Southwestern Iran." *American Anthropologist* 77:267–89.
1985 "Regional Perspectives on Southwest Iranian State Development." *Paleorient* 11:25–30.

Wright, H. T., J. A. Neely, G. A. Johnson, and J. Speth
1975 "Early Fourth Millennium Developments in Southwestern Iran." *Iran* 13:129–48.

Wright, H. T., R. W. Redding, and N. Miller
1980 "Time and Process in an Uruk Rural Center." In Marie-Thérèse Barrelet, ed., *L'Archéologie de l'Iraq du début de l'epoche néolitique à 333 avant notre ère: Perspectives et limites de l'interpretation anthropologique des documents,* pp. 265–84. Paris: Éditions du Centre National de la Recherche Scientifique.

Wright, R.
1989 "Comments." In G. Algaze, "The Uruk Expansion: Cross-cultural Exchange in Early Mesopotamian Civilization." *Current Anthropology* 30:599–600.

Yakar, J., and A. Gürsan-Salzmann
1979 "Archaeological Survey in Malatya and Sivas Provinces—1977." *Tel Aviv* 6:34–53.

Yardımcı, N.
1991 "1989 Yılı Şanlıurfa-Harran Ovası Yüzey Araştırmaları." VIII. *Araştırma Sonuçları Toplantısı,* pp. 401–418. Ankara: Anıtler ve Müzeler Genel Müdürlügü.

Yener, A. K.
1983 "The Production, Exchange, and Utilization of Silver and Lead Metals in Anatolia." *Anatolica* 10:1–15.
1986 "The Archaeometry of Silver in Anatolia: The Bolkardağ Mining District." *American Journal of Archaeology* 90:469–72.

Yener, A. K., H. Özbal, A. Minzoni-Deroche, and B. Aksoy
1989 "Bolkardağ: Archaeo-metallurgy Surveys in the Taurus Mountains, Turkey." *National Geographic Research* 5:477–94.

Yener, A. K., E. V. Sayre, E. C. Joel, H. Özbal, and others
1991 "Stable Lead Isotope Studies of Central Taurus Ore Sources and Related Artifacts from Eastern Mediterranean Chalcolithic and Bronze Age Sites." *Journal of Archaeological Science* 18:541–77.

Yoffee, N.
1981 "Explaining Trade in the Ancient Near East." *Monographs on the Ancient Near East* 2:2.

Young, Jr., T. C.
1966 "Survey in Western Iran, 1961." *Journal of Near Eastern Studies* 25:228–39.
1969 *Excavations at Godin Tepe: First Progress Report.* Toronto: Royal Ontario Museum.
1986 Godin Tepe Period VI/V and Central Western Iran at the End of the Fourth Millennium." In U. Finkbeiner and W. Röllig, eds., *Gamdat Nasr: Period or Regional Style?* pp. 212–28. Beihefte zum Tübinger Atlas des Vorderen Orients, Reihe B, Nr. 62. Weisbaden: Ludwig Reichert.

Zagarell, A.
1978 "The Role of Highland Pastoralism in the Development of Iranian Civilization." Ph.D. dissertation, Free University of Berlin.

1982 *The Prehistory of the Bahtiyari Mountains, Iran.* Beihefte zum Tübinger Atlas des Vorderen Orients, Reihe B, Nr. 42. Weisbaden: Ludwig Reichert.
1986 "Trade, Women, Class, and Society in Ancient Western Asia." *Current Anthropology* 27: 415–30.

Zeder, M. A.
1986 "The Equid Remains from Tal-e Malyan, Southern Iran." In R. H. Meadow and H.-P. Uerpmann, eds., *Equids in the Ancient World,* pp. 366–412. Beihefte zum Tübinger Atlas des Vorderen Orients, Reihe A, Nr. 19/1. Weisbaden: Ludwig Reichert.

Zohary, M.
1973 *Geobotanical Foundations of the Near East.* Stuttgart: Gustav Fischer Verlag.

Index

Italicized page numbers refer to figures in the text.